RENEWALS 458-4574

DATE DUE

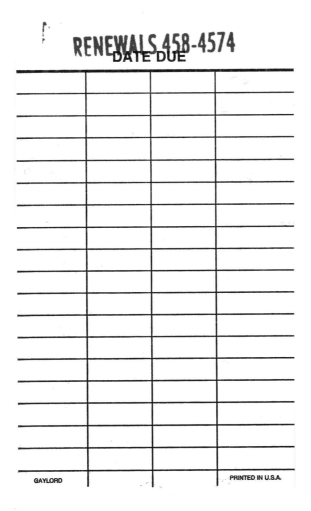

GAYLORD			PRINTED IN U.S.A.

INVESTMENT THINK TANK

Also by Deena B. Katz

Deena Katz's Tools and Templates for Your Practice

Deena Katz on Practice Management

Also available from Bloomberg Press

Hedge Fund of Funds Investing: An Investor's Guide
by Joseph G. Nicholas

The PPLI Solution: Delivering Wealth Accumulation,
Tax Efficiency, and Asset Protection Through
Private-Placement Life Insurance
edited by Kirk Loury

Market-Neutral Investing:
Long/Short Hedge Fund Strategies
by Joseph G. Nicholas

Hedge Funds Risk Fundamentals:
Solving the Risk Management and Transparency Challenge
by Richard Horwitz

Wall Street Secrets for Tax-Efficient Investing:
From Tax Pain to Investment Gain
by Robert N. Gordon with Jan M. Rosen

A complete list of our titles is available at
www.bloomberg.com/books

THE

INVESTMENT THINK TANK

Theory, Strategy, and Practice for Advisers

EDITED BY

Harold Evensky *and* Deena B. Katz

BLOOMBERG PRESS

PRINCETON

The first part of Jean Brunel's chapter, "The Tax-Efficient Portfolio," is heavily inspired by Jean L. P. Brunel, "A Tax-Efficient Portfolio Construction Model," *Journal of Wealth Management* (Fall 2001): 43–50; and Jean L. P. Brunel, *Integrated Wealth Management: The New Direction for Portfolio Managers* (Institutional Investor Books, 2002), chap. 6, pp. 102–111.

Most of the ideas presented in chapter 3, "A Holistic Approach to Asset Allocation," by William W. Jennings and William Reichenstein, are treated in their book *Integrating Investments and the Tax Code* (John Wiley & Sons, 2003).

The ideas in Ross Levin's chapter, "The Why of Wealth Management," are developed from the themes introduced in his book *The Wealth Management Index* (McGraw-Hill, 1997).

David Nawrocki's chapter, "Downside Risk Measures: A Brief History," is based on the article "A Brief History of Downside Risk Measures," which originally appeared in the fall 1999 issue of the *Journal of Investing*. For more information, please visit www.iijoi.com.

Meir Statman's chapter, "Lessons in Behavioral Finance," appears with the permission of the CFA Institute:

First edition published 2004
1 3 5 7 9 10 8 6 4 2

Library of Congress Cataloging-in-Publication Data

The investment think tank : theory, strategy, and practice for advisers / edited by Harold Evensky and Deena B. Katz.
    p. cm.
    Includes bibliographical references and index.
    ISBN 1-57660-165-X (alk. paper)
1. Portfolio management. 2. Risk management. 3. Investments. 4. Hedge funds. I. Evensky, Harold. II. Katz, Deena B.
    HG4529.5.I587 2004
    332.6--dc22   2004017389

For our parents,
Sylvia and Herbert Evensky
and Kenneth and Gladys Boone

CONTENTS

Ben G. Baldwin, CLU, ChFC, CFP, is president and owner of Baldwin Financial Systems, Inc., in Arlington Heights, Illinois, a registered investment-advisory firm serving both individual and corporate clients. He is a consultant and educator for major financial-services firms and broker-dealer organizations on life insurance, particularly variable universal life insurance and annuities, and he has designed and taught insurance courses for the American Institute of CPAs, the Illinois CPA Society, and the American Bankers Association. Baldwin has served on the board of governors for the Certified Financial Planner Board of Standards, on the board of regents for the College for Financial Planning in Denver, and on the board of directors of the Society of Financial Service Professionals. He is a member of the *CCH Financial & Estate Planning* advisory board and the insurance columnist for the *CCH Journal of Retirement Planning*. Baldwin is a nationally known speaker and writer in the areas of insurance and financial planning and the author of the best-selling consumer book on life insurance *The New Life Insurance Investment Advisor* (McGraw-Hill, 2002), as well as *The Complete Book of Insurance* (Irwin Professional Publishing, 1996), and *The Lawyer's Guide to Insurance* (American Bar Association, 1999). His insurance books are sought out by consumers and professionals alike.

Thomas J. Boczar, Esq., CFA, is director of marketing/financial institutions at Twenty-First Securities in New York and is a frequent author, speaker, and instructor on using financial instruments to enhance after-tax returns. Boczar began his career as a tax consultant with Touche Ross and later practiced law with Mudge Rose Guthrie Alexander & Ferdon and Cahill Gordon & Reindel. Boczar serves as vice chairman of the Private Wealth Management Committee of the New York Society of Security

Analysts. He also serves on the Wealth Management Committee of the Investment Management Consultants Association and is an instructor for IMCA's Wealth Management Certificate Program. Boczar is a member of the bar in both New York and Connecticut. He holds a JD, MBA, and master's degree in accounting and is pursuing an LLM in tax law from New York University School of Law.

Jean L. P. Brunel, CFA, is the managing principal of Brunel Associates, a firm in Edina, Minnesota, and Bonita Springs, Florida, offering wealth-management consulting services to ultra-affluent families. Brunel began his career in the investment-management group of J. P. Morgan, where he worked in the United States and abroad from 1976 until his retirement in 1999. In 1990, he assumed the position of chief investment officer of J. P. Morgan's global private bank, where he focused on the issues of special concern to individual investors, such as tax efficiency and downside-risk protection. Before that, Brunel served in New York, Tokyo, Hong Kong, Singapore, and Melbourne in various investment and managerial capacities for the firm. Upon retiring from J. P. Morgan, he began consulting for wealthy individuals and the institutions that serve them. He served as chief investment officer of Private Asset Management at U.S. Bancorp until 2001, when he left to found Brunel Associates. Brunel is the editor of *Journal of Wealth Management,* has participated in various task forces for the CFA Institute, and was elected trustee of the Research Foundation of the CFA Institute in 2003. He authored *Integrated Wealth Management: The New Direction for Portfolio Managers* (Institutional Investors and Euromoney Books, 2002). A graduate of Ecole des Hautes Etudes Commerciales in France, Brunel holds an MBA from the Kellogg Graduate School of Management at Northwestern University and is a chartered financial analyst.

John B. Brynjolfsson, CFA, is managing director, portfolio manager, and head of PIMCO Real Return Products. He is the coauthor of *Inflation-Protection Bonds* (Wiley, 2002) and coeditor of *The Handbook of Inflation-Indexed Bonds* (Fabozzi, 1999). Brynjolfsson joined PIMCO in 1989, having worked with Charles River Associates and J. P. Morgan Securities. He has seventeen years of investment experience and holds a bachelor's degree in physics and mathematics from Columbia College and a MBA in finance and economics from the MIT Sloan School of Management.

Peng Chen, PhD, CFA, is managing director and director of research at Ibbotson Associates in Chicago. Ibbotson Associates is an independent asset-allocation consulting firm that provides data, software, consulting, research, training, and presentation materials to investment professionals, and Chen is responsible for the firm's overall research activities. His research projects focus on asset allocation, portfolio risk measurement, nontraditional assets, and global financial markets, and he has contributed to the development of various Ibbotson products and services, including software, consulting services, educational services, and presentation materials. A recipient of the Articles of Excellence award from the Certified Financial Planner Board in 1996 and the 2003 Graham and Dodd Scroll Award from *Financial Analysts Journal*, Chen has written for numerous publications including *Financial Analysts Journal, Journal of Portfolio Management, Journal of Investing, Journal of Financial Planning, Bank Securities Journal, Journal of the Association of American Individual Investors, Consumer Interest Annual*, and *Journal of Financial Counseling and Planning*. Chen received his bachelor's degree in industrial management engineering from Harbin Institute of Technology and his master's and doctorate in consumer economics from Ohio State University.

Neal E. Cutler, PhD, has held the Boettner/Gregg Chair in Financial Gerontology at Widener University in Chester, Pennsylvania, since 1992. He has a joint appointment as professor in the School of Business Administration and the School of Human Service Professions. Cutler's research and teaching focus on how population aging, individual aging, family aging, and generational aging interact to influence new patterns of wealth span planning. From 1973 to 1989, he held a joint appointment as professor of political science and professor of gerontology at the University of Southern California and was associate director of the USC Andrus Gerontology Center's Institute for Advanced Study in Gerontology and Geriatrics. In 1997–99, he was principal investigator of a three-year SBIR grant from the National Institute on Aging to develop long-term-care decision-making software in association with Quicken Financial Planner. From 1997 to 2003, he was director of survey research for the National Council on the Aging (NCOA). Cutler is former chair of the National Institute of Financial Services for Elders and was a board member and chair of the Research Committee of the American Society on Aging. He is a fellow of both the Gerontological Society of America and the Employee Benefit Research Institute. In 2003, in recognition of his innovative teaching in gerontology, Cutler was elected a fellow of the Association for Gerontology in Higher Education, and he is a member of the Projects Advisory Board of the International Longevity Center/USA. Cutler is associate editor of *Journal of Financial Service Professionals* and serves as a member of the editorial boards of *The Gerontologist* and *American Journal of Alzheimer's Disease and Other Dementias*. He is the coauthor of *Aging, Money, and*

Life Satisfaction: Aspects of Financial Gerontology (Springer, 1992) and of *Can You Afford to Retire?* (Probus, 1992). His newest books are *Advising Mature Clients: The New Science of Wealth Span Planning* (Wiley, 2002), and (as senior coauthor) *American Perceptions of Aging in the 21st Century* (National Council on the Aging, 2003). More than two hundred of his articles have appeared in such journals as *Public Opinion Quarterly, Journal of Gerontology, American Political Science Review, Psychology Today, Journal of Financial Service Professionals, Generations, Journal of Behavioral Economics,* and *The Gerontologist.* His work has been featured in the *Wall Street Journal,* the *New York Times, Philadelphia Inquirer,* and *Kiplinger's Personal Finance* and on CBS News programs and NPR's *All Things Considered.* Cutler won Senior Fulbright Fellowships to Helsinki University in 1972 and to Glasgow University in 1988.

Gobind Daryanani, CFP, PhD, is president of Digiqual Inc., in Chatham, New Jersey. He is a financial-planning consultant specializing in high-end financial-planning tools and technologies. He consults for RegentAtlantic Capital, Merrill Lynch, and other financial-planning firms; his specialization is tax-efficient investing. Daryanani is the inventor of a sensitivity-based simulation method called Beyond Monte Carlo and the author of *Roth IRA Book: An Investor's Guide* (DQI, 1998). He is a certified financial planner and has a PhD in engineering from Michigan State University.

Geoff Davey is one of a handful of practitioners who pioneered financial planning in Australia. Following a post-university period as a systems engineer with IBM, he entered financial services in 1972 as an adviser to new graduates. By 1989, when he retired, Davey & Associates, his financial-planning firm in Sydney, Australia, was a national partnership, with a staff of one hundred, providing comprehensive personal financial-management services, including accounting and practice management to doctors, dentists, and lawyers. After a three-year sabbatical, Davey reentered the industry as a consultant and in 1995 joined forces with Paul Resnik, another industry veteran, to form ProQuest (now FinaMetrica). FinaMetrica focuses on the human intangibles relevant to financial decision making. Its mission is to develop tools that will assess these intangibles in terms that are meaningful to consumers and their advisers. FinaMetrica's first tool, a Web-based, psychometric risk-profiling system, was released in Australia in 1998, in the United States in 2002, and in the United Kingdom in 2004.

Harold Evensky, CFP, is chairman of Evensky, Brown & Katz, a wealth-management firm in Coral Gables, Florida. Before forming his company, he served as a vice president in investments with major brokerage firms. Evensky is a featured speaker at numerous national and international conventions and serves as chair of the TIAA-CREF Institute Financial Advisor Advisory Board. He is a member of the FPA, the Academy of Financial Services, and the CFA Institute and is an associate member of the American Bar Association. He has served on the IAFP Board and as chair of the CFP Board and the International Council. He is an NASD arbitrator and has been a principal in his own broker-dealer firm. Evensky, the author of *Wealth Management* (McGraw-Hill, 1997), has written for and is quoted frequently in the national press and is a contributing writer for *Financial Advisor* and *Asia Financial Planning Journal.* Evensky received his bachelor's and master's degrees from Cornell.

Gary L. Gastineau is managing director of ETF Consultants, LLC, in Summit, New Jersey. Gastineau, a recognized expert in open-end exchange-traded funds, organized ETF Consultants in May 2003 to provide specialized exchange-traded fund consulting services to ETF issuers, exchanges, market makers, research organizations, and investors. Before joining ETF Advisors, LP, a new ETF management firm, as managing director in May 2002, he was managing director for ETF product development at Nuveen Investments. Before that, he directed product development at the American Stock Exchange. As senior vice president in new product development, Gastineau was instrumental in the introduction of many of the popular ETF products that have attracted more than $100 billion in assets since their first appearance in 1993. Gastineau has also held senior positions in research, product development, and portfolio management at major investment banking firms. Gastineau's book *The Exchange-Traded Funds Manual* was published in 2002 by Wiley, and he is also the author of *The Options Manual* (3rd ed., McGraw-Hill, 1988) and coauthor of the *Dictionary of Financial Risk Management* (Fabozzi, 1999) and *Equity Flex Options* (Fabozzi, 1999). The author of numerous journal articles, Gastineau serves on the editorial boards of *Journal of Portfolio Management, Journal of Derivatives, Journal of Indexes,* and *Financial Practice and Education.* He is a member of a number of advisory boards, including the review board for the Research Foundation of the CFA Institute. He is an honors graduate of both Harvard College and Harvard Business School.

Robert Gordon is founder and chief executive officer of Twenty-First Securities Corporation in New York. Before he started the company in 1983, Gordon was partner in charge of arbitrage and tax at Oppenheimer

& Company and was senior vice president at Laidlaw, Adams & Peck. He is the author of *Wall Street Secrets for Tax-Efficient Investing* (Bloomberg Press, 2001) and serves on the editorial boards of *Journal of Taxation and Investments*, *Journal of Wealth Management*, and *Derivative Reports*. Gordon serves on the boards of the Wharton School's Securities Industry Institute, the Adler Planetarium in Chicago, and the Securities Industry Foundation for Financial Education. He is also adjunct professor at New York University's School of Business and served as chairman of the tax policy committee of the Securities Industry Association.

Michael C. Henkel, president of Ibbotson Associates since 1997, joined the firm in 1993 as vice president in charge of the firm's institutional software group. Before joining Ibbotson, Henkel worked for a variety of companies, including Knight Ridder, Lotus Development Corp, NewsEdge Corp, and Data Resources, integrating technology, data, and investments. Henkel's opinions have been widely quoted in various publications including *Pensions & Investments*, *Plan Sponsor*, *Global Finance*, *Journal of Financial Planning*, the *Wall Street Journal*, *Worth*, and *Financial Planning*. Henkel, who was selected as a delegate to the National Summit on Retirement Savings in 2002, frequently speaks at investment conferences in the United States and in Europe on topics including disbursement planning and the role of technology in investment advice. He received his bachelor's degree in mathematics and economics from Rhodes College and his master's in finance and quantitative methods from Vanderbilt University.

Mark Hurley was the founder and chief executive officer of Undiscovered Managers, LLC, a mutual fund and research company in Dallas, that was acquired by J. P. Morgan Investment Management in January 2004. Before forming Undiscovered Managers, Hurley worked for nearly eight years at Goldman, Sachs & Co. and at Merrill Lynch Asset Management, his last position there being managing director. Hurley also served as a Schedule C Presidential Appointee at a unit of the U.S. Department of Treasury during the first Bush administration, working on the cleanup of the savings and loan mess. He is a graduate of the United States Military Academy at West Point and received an MBA from the Stanford Graduate School of Business.

Roger G. Ibbotson, PhD, is a professor in the practice of finance at Yale School of Management. He is also chairman of Ibbotson Associates in Chicago, New York, and Tokyo, which provides investment consulting, software, data, and financial publishing for financial institutions. Ibbotson conducts research on a broad range of financial topics, including investment returns, mutual funds, international markets, portfolio management, and valuation. He serves on numerous boards, including Dimensional Fund Advisors' Funds, and is a partner at Zebra Capital Management, LLC, a manager of equity hedge funds. Ibbotson's book *Stocks, Bonds, Bills, and Inflation,* coauthored with Rex Sinquefield, is updated in the annual yearbooks published by Ibbotson Associates and serves as the standard reference for information on investment market returns. He also coauthored *Investment Markets* (1987) and *Global Investing* (1993) with Gary Brinson (McGraw-Hill) and the textbook *Investments: A Global Perspective* (Prentice Hall, 2002) with Jack C. Francis. He is currently working on *The Equity Risk Premium* and is a regular contributor and editorial board member on both trade and academic journals. A recipient of many awards—including the Graham and Dodd Scrolls in 1979, 1982, 1984, 2001, and 2003 and the CFA Institute's James R. Vertin award in 2001—Ibbotson frequently speaks at universities, conferences, and other professional forums. He received his bachelor's degree in mathematics from Purdue University, his MBA from Indiana University, and his PhD from the University of Chicago, where he taught for more than ten years and served as executive director of the Center for Research in Security Prices.

William W. Jahnke is chairman of Comprehensive Wealth Management, LLC. After graduate school, he joined Wells Fargo in 1969, where he held the positions of director of research, manager of institutional portfolio management, and manager of the trust and investment group. In 1983, Jahnke founded Vestek Systems to provide investment-decision software to investment managers and pension-plan sponsors. In 1996, he joined Financial Design as chairman of Financial Design Education Corporation and began developing financial-planning and investment solutions for individual investors. With Al Coles from Financial Design, Jahnke founded Comprehensive Wealth Management in 1999 to provide open-source investment solutions for financial advisers. He has been recognized for his pioneering work in investing, including his work on stock valuation, indexing, and asset allocation. Jahnke's articles have been published in numerous financial journals, including *Journal of Financial Planning, Journal of Investing,* and *Financial Analysts Journal,* and he received the Graham & Dodd Award for his article "The Growth Stock Mania." He earned his undergraduate degree in economics from Stanford University and an MBA from the University of California at Berkeley.

William W. Jennings, PhD, is deputy head of management education and teaches investment and finance courses at the United States Air Force Academy, where he is responsible for the management curriculum, faculty development, assessment, and accreditation. Jennings's research covers portfolio management and rebalancing strategies for taxable investments. He is coauthor, with William Reichenstein, of *Integrating Investments and the Tax Code* (Wiley, 2003). His applied interests focus on nontaxable and eleemosynary investment management, and he serves the Air Force community and the public as counselor to and member of several investment committees that manage more than ten billion dollars in pension and endowment funds. Jennings is a chartered financial analyst; his doctorate in finance is from the University of Michigan.

Deena B. Katz, CFP, is president of Evensky, Brown & Katz, a wealth-management firm in Coral Gables, Florida, and author of the best-selling *Deena Katz on Practice Management* (Bloomberg Press, 1999). Katz, who was editor-in-chief of *Journal of Retirement Planning* and has been published widely in such magazines as *Financial Planning, Investment Advisor,* and *Financial Advisor,* is an internationally sought-after speaker for national and international legal, accounting, and financial organizations. She has offered financial advice on *Good Morning America* and on *CBS This Morning* and was the authority selected by *Consumer Reports* to evaluate the work of other planners. In *Financial Planning* magazine in 2001, she was named by her peers as one of the five most influential people in the planning profession. Katz is a graduate of Adrian College and received a doctor of humane letters from Adrian in 2001. Her latest book on practice management, *Deena Katz's Tools and Templates for Your Practice* (Bloomberg Press, 2001), is an international best seller.

S. Timothy Kochis, CFP, is president of Kochis Fitz Tracy Fitzhugh & Gott, Inc., a wealth-management firm with offices in San Francisco and Menlo Park, California. Before forming Kochis Fitz in 1991, he was national director of personal financial planning for Deloitte & Touche and, before that, for Bank of America. Kochis is chair-elect of the Financial Planning Standards Board and chair of the Foundation for Financial Planning. He has served as president of the CFP Board of Standards and as chairman of its board of examiners and is a cofounder and former chairman of the advisory board and instructor of the U.C. Berkeley Personal Financial Planning Program. Named financial planner of the year in 1987 by the San Francisco chapter of the then International Association of Financial Planning, Kochis has been included in *Worth* magazine's list of the country's best financial advisers each year since the list was first published in 1994. A member of the advisory board of *CCH Financial and Estate Planning Reporter* and coauthor with his Kochis Fitz colleagues of *Wealth Management: A Concise Guide to Financial Planning and Investment Management for Wealthy Clients* (CCH, 2003), Kochis is frequently quoted in the *Wall Street Journal*, the *New York Times*, and other publications and is a sought-after speaker for financial and investment forums throughout the world. He earned his MBA from the University of Chicago, his JD from the University of Michigan, and his undergraduate degree from Marquette University. Kochis served in the United States Army, which included a tour of duty in Vietnam, where he received a Purple Heart for wounds received in action.

Craig J. Lazzara is managing director of Abacus Analytics, a Connecticut-based quantitative consulting firm serving the brokerage and investment-management communities. Before joining Abacus in early 2004, Lazzara directed marketing and client services for ETF Advisors, for Salomon Smith Barney's Global Equity Index Group, and for Salomon Brothers' Equity Portfolio Analysis group. He was chief investment officer of Centurion Capital Management and Vantage Global Advisors, managing quantitatively disciplined equity, tactical asset allocation, and currency-management strategies. He also served as a managing director of TSA Capital Management, with responsibilities for both applied research and client relations, and as a vice president and portfolio manager for Mellon Bank and T. Rowe Price Associates. A chartered financial analyst, Lazzara is a graduate of Princeton University and Harvard Business School.

Ross Levin, CFP, is president and founding principal of Accredited Investors, Inc., in Edina, Minnesota. A nationally recognized expert in financial planning, Levin has been quoted in numerous publications, including the *Wall Street Journal, Changing Times, Fortune,* the *New York Times, Newsweek,* and *Money,* and has appeared on such national television and radio shows as *NBC Nightly News with Tom Brokaw, The Oprah Winfrey Show, CBS This Morning,* and NPR's *Sound Money.* He was named one of the nation's top financial planners by *Money, Worth,* and *Mutual Funds* magazines and by *Medical Economics* and was a featured adviser in Mary Rowland's *Best Practices for Financial Advisors* (Bloomberg Press, 1997). Levin was named by *Financial Planning* as one of the five most influential people in the industry, and *Investment Advisor* listed him as one of the twenty-five most influential people in the industry. He launched the *CCH Journal of Retirement Planning,* serving as editor for two years, and is a regular columnist for *Journal of Financial Planning.* The author of *The Wealth Management Index* (McGraw-Hill/Irwin, 1997), which provides a framework for advisers to assess and manage their clients' plans and goals, Levin speaks frequently to financial groups on issues such as the delivery of financial-planning services, helping clients reach their objectives, and asset management. He served as chairman of the International Association for

Financial Planning, now the FPA, an organization of more than 28,000 financial-service professionals, and on the board of governors for the CFP Board based in Denver, Colorado. A graduate of the Carlson School at the University of Minnesota, Levin is on the board of trustees for the Minneapolis Foundation.

Moshe A. Milevsky, PhD, is associate professor of finance, teaching PhD, MBA, and BBA courses at the Schulich School of Business at York University in Toronto, and executive director of the Individual Finance and Insurance Decisions (IFID) Centre, in Toronto. Milevsky's teaching, research, and consulting focus on the interplay between financial risk management and personal wealth management. He serves as a consultant to a variety of global companies and agencies in the financial-services sector and lectures widely on pensions, investments, and personal wealth management. Milevsky has published more than thirty scholarly research articles and is the coeditor of *Journal of Pension Economics and Finance*. He is also the author of the Canadian best seller *Money Logic: Financial Strategies for the Smart Investor* (Stoddart, 1999), *The Probability of Fortune: Financial Strategies with the Best Odds* (published in the United States by Stoddart, 2000), *Insurance Logic* (Stoddart, 2002), and *Wealth Logic: Wisdom for Improving Your Personal Finances* (Captus, 2003). His innovative research has been cited in *BusinessWeek*, the *Wall Street Journal*, the *New York Times*, *Barron's*, *Fortune*, and *Money*, and he was a regular columnist for the *National Post Business Magazine*. Milevsky has a PhD in finance, an MA in mathematics and statistics, and a BA in mathematics and physics.

David N. Nawrocki, PhD, is the Katherine M. and Richard J. Salisbury Professor of Finance at Villanova University, which he joined in 1981. He is a registered investment adviser, working through the QInsight Group, and is the director of the Institute for Research in Advanced Financial Technology (IRAFT) at Villanova. Nawrocki's research includes work in financial market theory, downside-risk measures, systems theory, portfolio theory, and business cycles. His research articles appear in such journals as *Journal of Financial and Quantitative Analysis, Financial Review, International Review of Financial Analysis, Journal of Business Finance and Accounting, Applied Economics, Journal of Financial Education,* and *Journal of Financial Planning*. Nawrocki is a member of the editorial advisory board of *Journal of Financial Planning* and an associate editor at *International Review of Financial Analysis*. He holds an MBA and a PhD in finance from Pennsylvania State University.

Don Phillips is a managing director of Morningstar, Inc. He joined the firm in 1986 as its first mutual fund analyst and soon became the editor of its flagship publication, *Morningstar Mutual Funds™*, establishing the editorial voice for which the company is best known. Phillips helped to develop the MorningstarStyle Box™, the Morningstar Rating™, and other distinctive proprietary Morningstar innovations that have become industry standards. As a member of Morningstar's executive team, he is responsible for corporate strategy, research, corporate communications, and the Morningstar indexes. Journalists regularly turn to Phillips for his insight on industry trends, and he frequently speaks about investing at conferences and seminars. In 2003 both *Financial Planning* and *Investment Advisor* magazines named him to their lists of the most influential people in the financial-planning industry. In 2002 *Registered Rep.* named him one of the investment industry's ten key players. He was also selected as a member of the Ultimate Investment Club by *Money* in 2000 and 1999. Phillips holds a bachelor's degree from the University of Texas and a master's degree from the University of Chicago.

William Reichenstein, PhD, CFA, holds the Pat and Thomas R. Powers Chair in Investment Management at Baylor University. He has written more than seventy articles for professional and academic journals and is the coauthor of *Integrating Investments and the Tax Code* (Wiley, 2003). He serves as associate editor for academic and professional journals and is a frequent contributor to *Journal of Financial Planning, Financial Services Review, Journal of Portfolio Management,* and *Journal of Investing* and is frequently quoted in the *Wall Street Journal.* He received his doctorate in 1978 from the University of Notre Dame.

John W. Rogers Jr. is chairman and chief executive officer of Ariel Capital Management, LLC, an institutional money-management firm that he founded in 1983 in Chicago. With more than $17 billion in assets under management, the firm manages separate accounts for institutional clients and also serves individual investors and 401(k) plans through its four no-load mutual funds. As the firm's chief investment officer, Rogers has direct responsibility for the management of Ariel's small- and midcap value portfolios as well as the publicly traded Ariel Fund and Ariel Appreciation Fund. Ariel also offers two subadvised funds: Ariel Premier Growth Fund and Ariel Premier Bond Fund. Before founding Ariel, Rogers worked for the investment-banking firm of William Blair & Company. He serves on the boards of several companies, including Aon Corporation, Exelon Corporation, and McDonald's Corporation. Also dedicated to giving back to the community, Rogers's civic affiliations include his role as chairman of the Chicago Urban League and director of the University of Chicago. He was president of the board of the Chicago Park District for a six-year term. Frequently quoted in business publications, Rogers speaks at many academic institutions and has made guest appearances on television shows ranging from *Wall Street Week with Louis Rukeyser* to *The Oprah Winfrey Show*. In 1995, Rogers was profiled in *The Mutual Fund Masters* along with Peter Lynch and John Templeton, and in 1994, he was named as one of *Time*'s "50 for the Future," a roster of the country's most promising leaders under age forty. In 1988, *Sylvia Porter's Personal Finance* magazine named him Mutual Fund Manager of the Year. He received an AB in economics in 1980 from Princeton University.

Meir Statman, PhD, is Glenn Klimek Professor of Finance at the Leavey School of Business, Santa Clara University. In his research in behavioral finance, he attempts to understand how investors and managers make financial decisions and how these decisions are reflected in financial markets. Statman's work, which has been supported by the National Science Foundation, the Research Foundation of the CFA Institute, and the Dean Witter Foundation, addresses a range of questions, including: What are the cognitive errors and emotions that influence investors? What are investors' aspirations? How can financial advisers and plan sponsors help investors? and What is the nature of risk and regret? He has consulted with many investment companies and presented his work to academics and professionals in many forums in the United States and abroad. Statman's research has been published in *Financial Analysts Journal, Journal of Portfolio Management, Journal of Finance, Journal of Financial Economics,* and *Journal of Financial and Quantitative Analysis.* Statman is on the editorial board of *Financial Analysts Journal,* on the advisory boards of *Journal of Portfolio Management* and *Journal of Investment Consulting,* and associate editor of *Journal of Financial Research, Journal of Behavioral Finance,* and *Journal of Investment Management.* He's a recipient of a Batterymarch Fellowship, a William F. Sharpe Best Paper Award, a Bernstein Fabozzi/Jacobs Levy Outstanding Article Award, and two Graham and Dodd Awards of Excellence. He received his PhD from Columbia University and his BA and MBA from the Hebrew University of Jerusalem.

David M. Stein, PhD, is managing director and chief investment officer at Parametric Portfolio Associates, an investment-management firm in Seattle. Stein's work at Parametric, where he directs the investment, research, and technology activities, is focused on advancing the art and science of investment management in the presence of taxes. Before joining Parametric, Stein held senior research, development, and portfolio-management positions at GTE Investment Management Corp., Vanguard Group, and IBM Retirement Funds. As a research scientist at IBM Research Laboratories, Stein designed computer hardware and software systems. He is on the After-Tax Subcommittee of the AIMR-PPS standards committee and on the advisory board of *Journal of Wealth Management*. His articles have appeared in numerous journals, including *Mathematics of Operations Research, Journal of Wealth Management,* and *Journal of Portfolio Management*. He holds a number of patents, a PhD from Harvard University in applied mathematics, and an MSc from the University of Witwatersrand, South Africa.

Stephen C. Winks is chairman of Portfolio Construction Technologies in Richmond, Virginia, which counsels leading financial-services firms on the processes, technology, and infrastructure necessary to empower financial advisers to address and manage the full range of investment and administrative values required by regulatory mandate. Winks is the founding editor of www.SrConsultant.com, a publication of the investment-management consulting industry, reaching 70,000 readers, and managing director of the High Net Worth Standards Initiative, which has delineated the breadth and depth of professional investment and administrative counsel required for financial advisers to fulfill their fiduciary responsibilities. Winks is the founder of the Society of Senior Consultants, which recognizes outstanding achievement and the pioneering work of leading investment-management consultants. He ran the national retail and institutional investment management initiatives for Prudential Securities; as president of FSC Advisory, he worked with its founder and chairman, John Bell Keeble, widely known as the father of financial planning. Winks also built and managed most of the major product areas of Wheat, First Securities (now Wachovia). He is a graduate of the E. Claiborne Robins School of Business at the University of Richmond and the Securities Industry Institute at the Wharton School at the University of Pennsylvania.

PART ONE

THE PORTFOLIO

If you're the type who can't help wondering about the emperor's clothes, you're in for a treat. Make that several treats, because every one of the authors in this section challenges widely held beliefs about portfolio design and management. If you think of yourself as a sophisticated adviser, be prepared to have some of your most cherished notions challenged. If you're more of a contrarian when it comes to modern investment theory and practice, you'll enjoy learning that even the experts don't have all the answers. Whatever your background and experience, each of the chapters in this section will introduce you to critical investment issues and help you develop your own approach to the effective design and implementation of investors' portfolios.

Jean Brunel

The managing principal of Brunel Associates, Jean Brunel is also the editor of the *Journal of Wealth Management,* published by *Institutional Investor.* He and David Stein (see "Part Two: Strategy") are at the forefront of practitioners addressing the question of investment management in a taxable environment. In this chapter, Brunel argues that the need to keep the total portfolio in mind forces investor and manager alike to reconsider long-practiced approaches.

Brunel's proposal is the implementation of a core-and-satellite strategy. Has this conclusion been generally accepted by the retail financial-services world? No. Although core-and-satellite designs have become standard for many global institutional advisers, unfortunately, retail planning advice—from small, single-practitioner firms to multinational financial-services behemoths—is still based on institutional, tax-insensitive portfolio design. This reality makes Brunel's ideas that much more important to know about. We believe this issue is important, so important that our firm devoted more than a year of effort to redesigning and repositioning 100 percent of our clients' portfolios to a core-and-satellite design.

William Jahnke

We often disagree with Bill Jahnke, but few authors in our profession can—with such passion and intellect—force the reader to seriously reconsider (and perhaps modify) their most cherished investment beliefs. That's why we invited Jahnke to contribute to this book. His response exceeded our expectations.

No one can accuse Jahnke of being wishy-washy in presenting his case. From his provocative title—"Death to the Policy Portfolio"—to his pointed challenges to the work of finance and investment gurus (including Malkiel, Fama, Ibbotson, Brinson, Ellis, and Samuelson), Jahnke marshals his arguments and supports his conclusion that "the policy portfolio is a crutch for those who prefer to operate in a fantasy world. Its proposition is not just obsolete; it was invalid from the start. The policy deserves to be buried."

Every page is a wake-up call for the practitioner. If you're involved in or responsible for advising clients regarding portfolio design, this chapter is for you.

William W. Jennings and William Reichenstein

Perhaps in keeping with their academic credentials, Bill Jennings and Bill Reichenstein don't promise to make your life easier by answering your questions with formulaic truisms. Rather, they warn that the chapter may make your life harder by raising issues and posing questions that you haven't considered. Specifically, they note that many investment tools used by financial advisers were designed for institutional investors. Unfortunately, these tools are often used in the planning process for individual investors without considering the differences between individuals and institutions. (A number of contributors, including Brunel, Stein, and Evensky, approach this theme from other directions).

Although most advisers, including Evensky, Brown & Katz, use some form of asset-allocation analysis in their investment planning, most do so without explicitly incorporating either the impact of taxes or the influence of off-balance-sheet assets (for example, Social Security payments). Jennings and Reichenstein introduce a holistic approach to asset allocation that incorporates both the impact of taxes and a client's extended portfolio. The carrot they hold out to you, as a reward for facing the unpleasant realities of a client's complex financial life, is that tackling these issues will make you a better financial adviser.

Harold Evensky

Bow tie in place, I continue in the vein of Jennings and Reichenstein by contributing a chapter designed to make your life harder—namely, by agreeing with Brunel and arguing that most taxable portfolios are currently imprudently designed. The need to redesign portfolios in light of retail investors' very real expense and tax constraints receives little or no recognition. The reasons for the obscurity are threefold: a lack of awareness of the problem; an uncertainty about how to design portfolios that meet the tax constraints of retail investors; and a reluctance to give up the marketing cachet associated with a portfolio consisting of many "exciting, world-class" managers. Each manager has its own attractive marketing story, requires careful "professional monitoring" (that is, by the client's adviser), and provides opportunity for frequent planner-advised manager changes.

Jennings, Reichenstein, and Brunel provide awareness; in my chapter, the process continues with a specific and practical solution for implementing a core-and-satellite design. (Readers who know I've been an avid student of Brunel's writings won't be surprised to hear the echoes of his conclusions in my own.)

CHAPTER 1

The Tax-Efficient Portfolio

JEAN L. P. BRUNEL

Portfolio managers typically construct a diversified portfolio by following a sequential process in which they seek the best possible strategies in targeted market segments and assemble them in a way that makes for optimal risk/return trade-offs. This approach requires regular rebalancing, and although it may achieve some of the manager's key objectives, tax efficiency is not one of them.[1] The reasons are twofold. First, regular portfolio rebalancing is costly. In an article that appeared in the *Journal of Private Portfolio Management* in 1998,[2] I discussed the costs associated with rebalancing the portfolio to a long-term strategic mix. In fact, the costs associated with the regular rebalancing of the portfolio across these individual building blocks may indeed be higher than the potential loss of value added that arises from entrusting the management of the portfolio to a generalist rather than to a number of specialists.[3] Second, each specialist will tend to operate in a relative vacuum, preventing them from taking maximum advantage of opportunities to raise the overall portfolio's tax-efficiency.

Tax efficiency requires investors to change the way they construct a diversified portfolio. This chapter investigates overall portfolio construction, explores why achieving tax efficiency naturally leads away from the traditional portfolio-construction model, and then proposes a different model—core and satellites—that can achieve greater tax efficiency.

Value Added and Portfolio Activity

Tax efficiency is tied to the relationship between portfolio activity and expected value added. In this context, we'll define "value added" as the return earned over and above the relevant market benchmark as a result of decisions that move the portfolio away from that index. To create a level playing field, assume that we keep manager insight constant: that is, the manager expects to generate that value added in a way that's proportional to the level of activity he or she undertakes. For example, every time the manager executes a transaction, he or she expects to add 0.05 percent to the return on the portfolio. It stands to reason that there would be a linear relationship between the manager's activity level and the portfolio's expected value added. **FIGURE 1.1** represents that relationship as a straight line. Note that we're not talking about the observed, actual value added, which depends on the manager's success. We're depicting only the value added that the manager expects to generate. Note also that we don't need to limit ourselves to a return-based definition of value added. We can adjust it for risk, assuming that the manager also has a tracking-error expectation associated with the value added.

Tax Efficiency and Portfolio Activity

In their 1993 article in the *Journal of Portfolio Management,* Robert D. Arnott and Robert H. Jeffrey[4] eloquently demonstrated that the relationship between tax efficiency and portfolio turnover is nonlinear. Rather

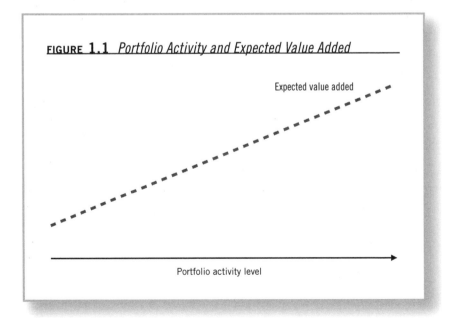

FIGURE 1.1 *Portfolio Activity and Expected Value Added*

Expected value added

Portfolio activity level

than defining portfolio activity in terms of portfolio turnover, one might consider a slight variation on the theme. Indeed, one can argue that portfolio turnover is not a decision variable: in short, there is both good and bad turnover. Good turnover occurs when you execute an "alpha-enabling" transaction, that is, a loss-harvesting trade that enables the execution of another trade that was hitherto precluded by the likelihood of too large an unrealized gain in the position intended to be sold. Although an alpha-enabling transaction raises portfolio turnover, it tends to improve tax efficiency. Consequently, portfolio turnover is not the best measure of portfolio activity as it relates to tax efficiency. Rather, it seems best to think in terms of portfolio activity defined as net capital gain realization rate.

The observed tax efficiency of a portfolio is therefore a function of two distinct factors: first, the degree to which the manager's portfolio activity generates gross capital gains and, second, the degree to which the manager's tax-sensitivity will allow some of these gains to be sheltered by realized capital losses. **FIGURE 1.2** illustrates the basic truism that tax efficiency falls rapidly as portfolio activity rises. A tax-sensitive investment process can defer some of the inevitable, but it cannot eliminate it. This relationship simply reflects the fact that certain strategies require a high level of portfolio activity and do not naturally lend themselves to tax efficiency. Consider an interest rate arbitrage between a Treasury bond and a corporate bond. Assume that you expect the difference in the yields between the two bonds to decrease. You'll typically buy a corporate bond (or a portfolio of such bonds to diversify away the bond-specific risk if the move you are

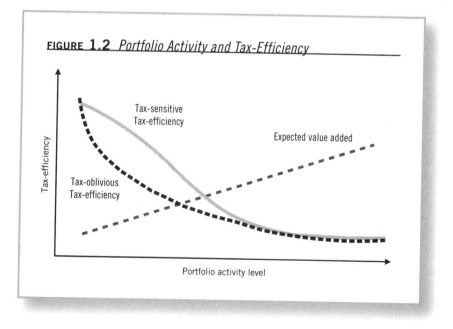

FIGURE 1.2 *Portfolio Activity and Tax-Efficiency*

trying to capture is generic to the corporate bond market rather than to an individual bond) and sell short an equivalent notional amount of same-maturity Treasury obligations. Though you may have some time frame in mind when the transaction is initiated, you will surely close the trade—repurchase the Treasury bond and sell the corporate bond—when you feel that the gap, or spread, between the two yields is back to normal, or even expensive. You may have to realize a short-term gain, but that would be preferable to waiting and not booking any gain, or worse, booking a loss.

The Murky Middle

The typical portfolio manager occupies the murky middle of portfolio activity—a place somewhere between the extremes represented, on the one hand, by the totally passive manager who aims to replicate the index and, on the other, by the very active trader. That the typical manager falls in that slot should not surprise for two simple reasons. First, the average investor likes to strike a balance between no activity and a lot of activity. Second, for the manager—particularly a large organization or one associated with an organization susceptible to reputational risk—targeting a middle-of-the-pack value added and tracking error is the smart risk-management strategy. Indeed, the further the manager deviates from the average, the greater the risk that his or her performance will deviate from that of peers and thus potentially disrupt client relationships.

Although such positioning makes a great deal of sense in a pretax, or tax-oblivious, business model, it's potentially quite damaging for someone who needs to worry about taxes. Figure 1.2 tells us that by the time we're in the murky middle, we have more than likely reached almost minimal tax efficiency and have stopped substantially short of maximum potential value added. We pay taxes on total return and not solely on value added. Therefore, assuming average market returns, it would not be unusual for a murky-middle manager to produce positive pretax value added and negative after-tax value added at the same time. Assume, for example, that the equity market has returned 10 percent and that our murky-middle manager has produced a pretax value added of 2 percent. Further assume that the portfolio's tax efficiency is around 70 percent. The after-tax return on that portfolio is 8.4 percent, since we will have paid 30 percent of 12 percent in taxes, or 3.6 percent. Assuming that the index has a tax efficiency of around 98 percent, which is probably unkind to the index, the after-tax return on the index would be 9.8 percent. Our murky-middle manager has done a great pretax job and cost us 1.4 percent relative to the index—even before we tack on the difference in management fees between the active murky-middle manager and the manager of an index fund.

An Alternative Design

Suppose we think instead in terms of "barbelling" the portfolio. Rather than placing all our eggs in the basket located in the middle of the portfolio-activity spectrum, we divide our portfolio into two strategic baskets, which, as we'll see later, don't need to be the same size. Indeed, the relative sizes of these two "extremes" of the portfolio will help determine the degree of overall average portfolio activity sought by the investor. The first subportfolio aims to produce the highest possible tax efficiency, and its design therefore includes the possibility that no value added will be generated at all. The second subportfolio aims to produce the highest reasonable value added and is therefore designed to be very tax inefficient. **FIGURE 1.3** illustrates that alternative design, which resembles a barbell.

A numerical example helps illustrate the difference such a design can make. As in our earlier example, assume that an index fund generates 9.8 percent after-tax returns and that a satellite strategy will have a 60 percent tax-efficiency. (Sixty percent is a good approximation of average minimum tax efficiency for individuals living in states with a 5 percent or so state tax rate; indeed, adding that 5 percent to the maximum 35 percent federal tax rate yields an expected 40 percent tax rate on returns made up of interest and realized short-term capital gains.) It follows that any satellite able to generate 16.3 percent pretax returns, or a 6.3 percent value added, will match the after-tax performance of the index. This reinforces two impor-

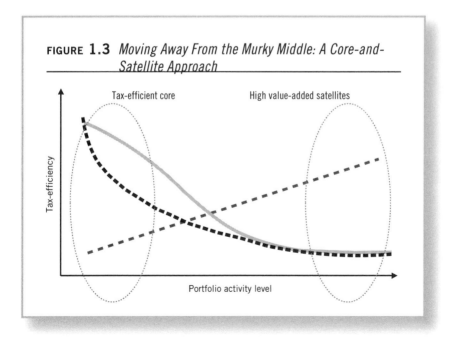

FIGURE 1.3 *Moving Away From the Murky Middle: A Core-and-Satellite Approach*

Tax-efficient core

High value-added satellites

Tax-efficiency

Portfolio activity level

tant points. First, you need a lot of pretax value added to beat an index after tax, but we already knew that. Second, combining a tax-efficient core and a tax-inefficient satellite might produce a higher risk-adjusted after-tax return than a murky-middle alternative would. Although that satellite would have a higher risk than the index, it would offer potential tax-efficiency benefits over time because that volatility would produce opportunities to use realized capital losses to offset some of the gains.

The core-and-satellite design further illustrates the importance of thinking in terms of the total portfolio. Imagine that instead of using a standard passive index fund, we invest in an active tax-managed strategy, such as the one described in 1999 by David M. Stein and Premkumar Narasimhan in the *Journal of Private Portfolio Management.*[5] Such a strategy potentially has a tax efficiency greater than 100 percent, since it generates net realized capital losses while matching the performance of the index. Even after accounting for dividend income, it's not unreasonable to aim for a 101 percent tax-efficiency ratio, given the approximate 2–3 percent net realized capital losses that Stein and Narasimhan—and later Arnott in his 2001 article in the *Journal of Wealth Management*[6]—reported in their experiments, at least in the earlier years, on average. If we aim only to beat the 9.8 percent after-tax return of the index, we can afford to combine a "hyper tax-efficient" passive structured strategy with some less-efficient subportfolio, with a high expected value added. **FIGURE 1.4** illustrates

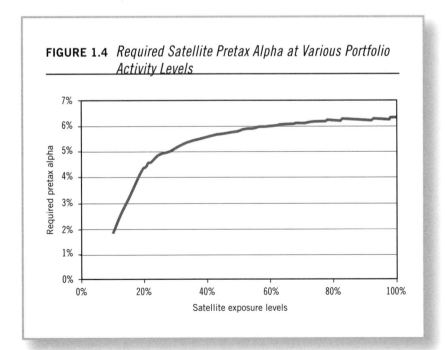

FIGURE 1.4 *Required Satellite Pretax Alpha at Various Portfolio Activity Levels*

the different combinations of expected satellite value added and satellite portfolio exposure needed to match the after-tax performance of the index. Note that the hyper tax efficiency of the passive structured approach allows the satellite strategy to offer minimal alpha at very low levels of portfolio exposure to that strategy. Yet, at higher levels of satellite portfolio exposure, the required alpha quickly becomes very imposing.

Arguably, this design is even more compelling when considered in the context of a multi-asset class or strategy portfolio. There, examples of strategies one might find in the core portion of the portfolio would include passive portfolios, actively tax-managed portfolios, municipal bonds, or private equity funds. By contrast, the tax-inefficient satellite portion of the portfolio might comprise taxable bonds, concentrated portfolios, or hedge funds—directional or nondirectional.

Making the Core/Satellite Decision

How does an investor decide on the relative sizes of the two subportfolios?[7] Two considerations can help—one is philosophical; the other relates to whether the investor prefers static or dynamic tax efficiency. An individual who doesn't believe that managers can add value through active portfolio management will tend to privilege tax efficiency at the expense of active strategies. For instance, that individual may decide that the only management activity reasonably likely to produce significant, risk-adjusted value added lies in hedge funds. Yet that person might also believe that the nonmarket risks associated with hedge funds—possibly their lack of liquidity—militates in favor of capping his or her total portfolio exposure to that sector to, say, 20 percent. Such an investor would end up with a portfolio 80 percent allocated to the tax-efficient core.

The question of philosophical focus on static or dynamic tax efficiency is somewhat subtler. Let's highlight the critical element of that debate, on which substantial additional research is needed to arrive at a meaningful conclusion. Static tax efficiency is focused on minimizing tax drag over the immediate term, accepting the potentially adverse consequences associated with the risk of "portfolio freezing," as discussed, for instance, in 1996 in the *Journal of Portfolio Management* by Roberto Apelfeld, Gordon Fowler, and James Gordon.[8] Again, that risk involves either forfeiting the potential to keep earning after-tax value added as trades become increasingly difficult to justify—because the level of unrealized gain in each position makes it increasingly hard to justify any sale—or accepting higher portfolio tracking error. This situation arises because the portfolio, which by definition is different from the index, will keep drifting away from the index as its individual holdings generate different returns from those of the index. When the portfolio freezes, it becomes impossible to rebalance it closer to the index, and the risk inherent in that drift becomes increasingly significant over time. Though Robert Jeffrey might argue, as he did in the *Journal of Wealth Management* in 2001,[9] that this is not an important issue, it must still be factored in, because it's a risk for which one is not compensated and can be very significant, particularly when considered in a multigenerational context. After all, the ultimate incarnation of this problem is known as low-basis portfolio concentration.

A dynamically tax-efficient process would look to balance tax efficiency, risk management, and the potential to earn value added over the long term. A dynamically tax-efficient investor would be concerned with the risk of too wide a gap developing between the portfolio's market value and its tax basis. He or she may thus be potentially more willing to incur some short-term tax drag, provided a fair after-tax and risk-adjusted compensation is expected to be earned over the long term. Such an investor might be therefore more inclined toward having a greater proportion of the portfolio in tax-inefficient satellite strategies, which will over time allow greater flexibility to adjust the portfolio's balance.

These two issues, as well as asset-location questions, can be incorporated into the appropriate quantitative portfolio optimizer. Indeed, a well-designed optimization tool should provide for individual preferences in terms of tax sensitivity, while your own return and risk expectations for each asset class or strategy will inevitably reflect your philosophical beliefs in terms of the ability of active managers to create value added. Yet it's important to segregate these issues conceptually, because each will help the investor understand why an optimizer provides solutions that may otherwise appear quirky or strange, and they'll help the investor make simple decisions when there's no compelling need to use a complex quantitative tool.

Considering Asset Location

Portfolio construction must finally be looked at in the context of the structure through which the wealth is held. In terms of asset location, it's fundamental for each investor to look at and assess the opportunities made available by the differences in the principles embedded in the income and transfer tax codes.[10] These can encourage investors to balance their choices more judiciously, offering alternatives that are painted in shades of gray rather than in the black and white that characterizes the barbell approach.

Indeed, one must always be careful, when attempting to create a delicate equilibrium, that one does not become overly "cute." Consider the case of an investor who doesn't feel comfortable opting for a fully tax-managed portfolio approach or for a fully active strategy. The logical way out of the dilemma, superficially, seemed to have some of both. Unfortunately, that solution exposes the individual to significant "wash sale" risk because the chances are high that at some point a net-loss realization sale in one subportfolio will be offset by a value purchase in the other, creating a tax-accounting nightmare, particularly if it's not caught early on. Asset-location considerations might allow locating one strategy in one "pocket" and the other in a different holding structure.

An Unintended Benefit

Interestingly, this core-and-satellite approach also helps in determining the amount of assets to be allocated to hedge funds.[11] By requiring the investor to look at the tax efficiency of each strategy—whether it be viewed as traditional or as belonging to the alternative world in which hedge funds typically fall—the core-and-satellite approach requires that nontraditional strategies such as hedge funds be considered as part of the satellite portion of the portfolio. That's because most hedge funds are notoriously tax inefficient, unless held through special structures such as variable life insurance or derivative contracts. But before going further, let's recognize that the term "hedge fund" is at best imprecise and at worst simply misleading.

At the AIMR conference in 2003,[12] I presented initial research findings on hedge fund allocations, offering three main themes. First, the traditional classification "hedge funds" is not terribly helpful. Second, it's better to think of hedge funds as investment processes involving a higher degree of activity than traditional, long-only approaches. Third, a mean-variance optimization model should be revised and appropriate constraints designed to allow investors to get a better sense of how incorporating hedge funds into their portfolios should lead to other changes within their traditional asset and strategy exposures.

That the term "hedge fund" is at best unhelpful should not surprise: a review of ten-year risk-return scattergrams of the various indices that appear in the Hedge Fund Research Index database[13] demonstrates that the universe is indeed very wide. In fact, there's more difference between the least and most risky points over that period than there is between short-term investment-grade bonds and emerging-market equities. And yet no one would be tempted to aggregate the latter two strategies or asset classes under a common label, other than possibly "financial assets," which wouldn't be terribly helpful either. More careful analysis of the data suggests that a number of clusters of hedge fund strategies share a number of characteristics. At least three such clusters can be identified: absolute-return strategies, which behave like high-octane fixed-income instruments; semidirectional long-short equity strategies, which behave like lower-risk equities; and highly concentrated portfolios (comprising individual equities or selected macrobets), which share the risk of the riskier strategies available to long-only investors.

A closer look at these clusters, particularly the first two, shows that the investment activity carried out by the hedge fund managers can be placed on the standard continuum, which starts with indexing and moves to enhanced indexing, core investment approaches, concentrated portfolios, opportunistic portfolios, and strategies incorporating both long and short positions (these being isolated or considered in pairs or groups). Interestingly, a substantially higher share of manager risk relative to market risk induces an abnormality in the distribution of returns, which is often negatively skewed and subject to a high kurtosis.

One can see the implication of such an analysis to the traditional strategic asset-allocation question for investors who want to combine traditional and less traditional strategies. The standard answer has been to constrain the potential exposure to nontraditional strategies, arguing that if not constrained, they would be chosen by the optimizer in excessive quantities. This begs the question: why? And if the answer is that the traditional risk/return/correlation framework does not appropriately represent them, then the question should be: how can it be made to represent them?

A simple solution is to force each asset class or strategy under consideration through a model that will produce two additional pieces of information: the share of the risk of that strategy accounted for by manager risk and some measure of liquidity. This allows the investor, among others, to constrain the total portfolio in terms of total acceptable exposure to manager risk and not preordain where and how that manager risk is taken. Interestingly, the model finds itself also creating a core-and-satellite portfolio structure—with strategies having little or no manager risk found in the core and high-manager-risk strategies (including nontraditional investments such as those usually classified under the "hedge fund" label) making up the bulk of the satellite exposure. Note that the decision is based on exposure to manager risk rather than on tax efficiency. The reason these two problems—total portfolio tax efficiency on the one hand and the allocation to manager risk on the other—would be solved with the same solution simply reflects the fact that the relationship between manager risk taking and expected value added is also nonlinear: good managers can be considerably more efficient in using risk than managers who feel somewhat bound by the overall risk in the asset class within which they operate. Thus, tax inefficiency rises quickly once a manager departs from a benchmark-replicating strategy. Similarly, the potential manager alpha increases more rapidly once the manager focuses on that potential rather than on minimizing his tracking error relative to the benchmark.

A more complex solution, but one considerably more elegant, would involve incorporating into the mean-variance analysis some constraint on total portfolio skewness and kurtosis. Though this would require creating coskewness and cokurtosis matrices for all strategies and calculating portfolio skewness and kurtosis at each iteration, it would be a more robust approach to the same problem. I doubt that it would provide significantly different results from those mentioned above, since the intellectual process and overall investment insights are strikingly similar.

The Bigger Picture

The core-and-satellite strategy illustrates one of the most significant differences between tax-oblivious and tax-sensitive portfolio management. The need to focus on the total portfolio forces investor and manager alike to reconsider long-practiced approaches. Interestingly, the core-and-satellite design echoes practices encountered years ago among European and Asian investors: having a high proportion of a portfolio in virtually risk-free assets and a small part exposed to the risk of total loss. The intriguing aspect of that coincidence is that these barbell practices were designed to help the investor manage risk, which was then ostensibly defined in terms of absolute downside risk. The conceptually similar core-and-satellite approach is, however, designed to enhance total portfolio tax efficiency. Thus, while one could argue that a barbell-inspired risk-management approach is not always appropriate, using a barbell approach to enhance tax efficiency is likely to be considerably harder to disprove.

Chapter Notes

1. The first part of this article is heavily inspired by Jean L. P. Brunel, "A Tax-Efficient Portfolio Construction Model," *Journal of Wealth Management* (Fall 2001): 43–50; and Jean L. P. Brunel, *Integrated Wealth Management: The New Direction for Portfolio Managers* (Institutional Investor Books, 2002), chap. 6, pp. 102–111.

2. Jean L. P. Brunel, "Why Should Taxable Investors Be Cautious When Using Traditional Efficient Frontier Tools?" *Journal of Private Portfolio Management* (Winter 1998): 35–50.

3. Jean L. P. Brunel, "Active Style Diversification in an After-Tax Context: An Impossible Challenge?" *Journal of Private Portfolio Management* (Spring 2000): 41–50.

4. Robert D. Arnott and Robert H. Jeffrey, "Is Your Alpha Big Enough to Cover Its Taxes?" *Journal of Portfolio Management* (Spring 1993): 15–26.

5. David M. Stein and Premkumar Narasimhan, "Of Passive and Active Equity Portfolios in the Presence of Taxes," *Journal of Private Portfolio Management* (Fall 1999): 55–63.

6. Robert D. Arnott, Andrew L. Berkin, and Jia Ye, "Loss Harvesting: What's It Worth to the Taxable Investor?" *Journal of Wealth Management* (Spring 2001): 10–18; Stein and Narasimhan (1999).

7. A quantitative approach to address this problem in the context of an equity portfolio was proposed and solutions discussed by Clifford H. Quisenverry, Jr., "Optimal Allocation of a Taxable Core and Satellite Portfolio Structure," *Journal of Wealth Management* (Summer 2003): 18–26.

8. Roberto Apelfeld, Gordon Fowler Jr., and James Gordon Jr., "Tax-Aware Equity Investing," *Journal of Portfolio Management* (Winter 1996): 18–28.

9. Robert Jeffrey, "Tax-Efficient Portfolio Management: Easier Said Than Done," *Journal of Wealth Management* (Summer 2001): 9–15.

10. Jean L. P. Brunel, "Asset Location—The Critical Variable: A Case Study," *Journal of Wealth Management* (Summer 2001): 27–43.

11. This is arguably true, whether the investor pays or does not pay taxes.

12. Jean L. P. Brunel, "A New Perspective on Hedge Funds and Hedge Fund Allocations" (Association for Investment Management and Research conference, "Investment Counseling for Private Clients V," 17–18 March 2003, Atlanta, GA).

13. Clearly, any analysis of historical data in the hedge fund world is even more exposed to survivorship bias issues than would be the case with strategies with greater stability. Yet, once understood and appropriately adjusted for, this risk of bias seems worth taking, considering the benefit it provides: a new way of looking at hedge fund strategies. For more information on this topic, see Harry M. Kat, "10 Things That Investors Should Know About Hedge Funds," *Journal of Wealth Management* (Spring 2003): 72–81.

CHAPTER 2

Death to the Policy Portfolio

WILLIAM W. JAHNKE

Peter Bernstein caused an uproar in 2003 with his article in *Economics and Portfolio Strategy* when he proclaimed that "policy portfolios are obsolete."[1] The policy portfolio is the term Bernstein uses to describe the common practice in financial planning of setting a fixed asset-allocation mix as part of investment policy and avoiding market timing. In challenging the policy portfolio, Bernstein is challenging the core belief that supports it: "Equilibrium and central values are myths," he says, "not the foundations on which we [should] build our structures." Bernstein is calling for flexible asset allocation that recognizes the changing investment opportunities and risks, evaluates the prospects for extreme financial outcomes from an economic perspective instead of a statistical one, and hedges some of the risks associated with extreme outcomes.

Bernstein is ruffling all kind of feathers. For many financial planners the policy portfolio is a cornerstone of investment practice. How could something with such wide appeal and acceptance in the financial-planning community be ideologically wrong? How can the policy portfolio, with its seemingly irrefutable theoretical and empirical credentials, be judged obsolete by one of the foremost authorities on investing? The answers have been there from the start. Indeed, the story behind the policy portfolio and its rise to prominence in the practice of financial planning—a chronicle as troubling as it is fascinating—is one worth telling.

Faulty Assumptions

The theoretical foundation of the policy portfolio is the random-walk model. As first conceived by Louis Bachelier (1900), the random-walk model assumes that successive price changes are independent, identically distributed, and normally distributed.[2] "Independent" means that no investor can use his knowledge of past data to increase his expected profit. "Identically distributed" means that the means and standard deviations from sample period to sample period will converge on being identical as the sample sizes get larger. "Normally distributed" means that the distribution of the time series of returns can be described by the well-known bell curve. For the assumptions of the random-walk model to hold, the process that generates returns across time must be stable.

The common practice of forecasting returns and portfolio volatility based on historical mean returns and standard deviations requires the belief that the return-generating process is stable and the assumptions of the random-walk model are valid. If the return-generating process is not stable or does not conform to the random-walk model assumptions, then the practice of forecasting future returns from historical returns is unreliable, because investment opportunities vary from period to period and thus the appropriate investment solution is subject to change. Without the random-walk model, there is no foundation for the policy portfolio.

Confusion abounds among academics and financial writers when it comes to terminology. By "random walk," some writers simply mean that future steps in the market can't be predicted. This is the definition that Burton G. Malkiel uses in *A Random Walk Down Wall Street*.[3] Malkiel's definition of random walk is better suited to defining the term "efficient market." According to the efficient-market model, the market is a "fair game," where prices are set fairly and there are no market inefficiencies for investors to exploit. The efficient-market model says nothing about stability in the return-generating process. The random-walk model is a special and more restrictive case of the efficient-market model, which carries the added assumptions that successive returns be independent and identically distributed. Malkiel is not alone; other financial writers confuse financial advisers with their use of the terms "random walk" and "efficient market." It's little wonder that many financial advisers have been confused in thinking that the policy portfolio is supported by efficient-market theory or that studies in support of the efficient-market model necessarily support the random-walk model and the policy portfolio.

While the random-walk model requires the return-generating process be stable, the efficient-market model does not require stability in the return-generating process. If the return-generating process is unstable, then statisticians cannot forecast mean returns and standard deviations from historical returns. If the return-generating process is stable and produces normal distributions, then statisticians have an easy job. If return distributions are stable but non-normal, then statisticians have their work cut out for them because the standard statistical tool kit assumes that return distributions are normal. It's common for statisticians to assume that distributions are normal when the empirical data do not appear to be normal, because of the lack of tools to work with non-normal distributions. When Bernstein observes equilibrium and central value myths, he is implicitly challenging the assumption that successive returns are being generated from a stable return-generating process.

The efficient-market model can claim theoretical legitimacy in classical financial theory even if empirically it does not perfectly fit the real world. However, no economic theory supports the random-walk model. The assumptions that successive returns are independent and identically distributed are among the most extreme and implausible assumptions in all of economics. The idea that returns are drawn from a stable return-generating process defies any appreciation of the instability, discontinuities, and inflection points common in the real world of business, finance, and investing.

What's troubling is that few financial planners know that the assumptions underpinning the statistical work on the policy portfolio have been under attack practically from inception a century ago. The evidence that asset-class returns do not behave in accordance with the normal distribution is overwhelming and conclusive. Virtually all of the early researchers observed that empirical return distributions had "fat tails." The solutions to the fat-tail problem varied: some researchers ignored the fact, some threw out the offensive outliers, some adjusted the numbers, some rejected the random-walk model, and some tried to salvage the model by replacing the normal distribution assumption with another stable distribution that better fit the data.

Just how poorly the random-walk model fits empirical data can be gleaned from the Ibbotson Associates publication *Stocks, Bonds, Bills, and Inflation*. Among the derived statistics are asset-class returns and standard deviations by decade, and rolling sample mean returns, standard deviations, and correlations. How can anyone looking at the tables and charts not be struck by the lack of stability? How can anyone believe that the average return, standard deviation, and cross correlation computed with all the data, whether inflation adjusted or not, provide accurate forecasts for the purposes of financial planning and asset allocation?

According to Benoit Mandelbrot (1967), the father of fractal geometry, all of the assumptions supporting the random-walk model "are working assumptions and should not be made into dogma." Mandelbrot pointed out that Bachelier, writing in 1914, made no mention of his earlier claims of empirical evidence for the random-walk model and noted the existence of empirical evidence contrary to the random-walk model: standard deviations vary from sample period to sample period, and the tails of the distributions are fatter than those predicted by the normal distribution. Mandelbrot gave Bachelier credit not only for being the first to propose the random-walk model but also for being the first to expose its major weaknesses.[4]

Mandelbrot was well aware that empirical data for many financial time series do not conform to the normal distribution assumption. Mandelbrot (1967) noted that virtually every student of price series has commented on the fact that empirical return distributions are fat tailed. In discussing stationarity, he stated, "One of the implications of stationarity is that sample moments vary little from sample to sample, as long as the sample length is sufficient. In fact, it is notorious that price moments often 'misbehave' from this viewpoint (though this fact is understated in the literature, since 'negative' results are seldom published)." Mandelbrot's stated goal was to save the random-walk model by accounting for the fat tails with a family of stable non-normal distributions called stable paretian. He acknowledged that there are other explanations for fat tails, including distributions that are not stable but "haphazard." According to Mandelbrot, if sample returns distributions from period to period are haphazard, that is, not capable of being treated by probability theory, "why bother to construct complicated statistical models for the behavior of prices if one expects this behavior to change before the model has time to unfold?" Bachelier believed he was looking at haphazard distributions. Mandelbrot's mission was to prove Bachelier wrong.

Bad Science?

The random-walk model languished in obscurity until Leonard Jimmie Savage rediscovered Bachelier's work in about 1954. Savage, a gifted statistician at the University of Chicago, introduced Bachelier's random-walk model to U.S. academics, including Paul Samuelson. The first American to win the Nobel Prize in Economics, Samuelson was enamored of Bachelier's work and believed in the theory that market prices are the best gauge of intrinsic value. He published a paper in 1965 called "Proof That Properly Anticipated Prices Fluctuate Randomly." Much has been made of Samuelson's proof; indeed, Bernstein devotes a chapter in his book *Capital Ideas* to it. Bernstein quotes Samuelson's reservations: "The theorem is so general that I must confess to having oscillated over the years in my own mind between regarding it as trivially obvious (and almost trivially vacuous) and regarding it as remarkably sweeping."[5] Samuelson's proof that prices fluctuate randomly is not a proof of the random-walk model but rather a proof that in an efficient market, prices fluctuate randomly.

Mandelbrot joined the faculty at the University of Chicago, where he influenced his student Eugene Fama, who was to become the leading academic advocate for the random-walk model. Fama discusses, in an article "Mandelbrot and the Stable Paretian Hypothesis" (1963), the issue of fat-tailed distributions and Mandelbrot's fix for the random-walk model.[6] The stable paretian distribution defines the distribution of returns in terms of four parameters instead of the normal distribution's two (mean and standard deviation). The four parameters of the stable paretian distribution determine the mean of the distribution, the symmetry of the distribution (skewness), the tails of the distribution (kurtosis), and the scales of the distribution. The normal distribution is a special case in the family of stable paretian distributions. Fama noted that the stable paretian distribution has "extreme" implications. Unless the return distribution is normal, the sample standard deviation is probably a meaningless measure of dispersion, and statistical tools such as least-squares regression will be at best considerably weakened and may in fact give very misleading answers. Fama warned, "Before the hypothesis can be accepted as a general model for speculative prices, however, the basis of testing must be broadened to include other speculative series."

The fact that the stable paretian can "explain" the existence of fat tails and other complexities observed in empirical data does not mean that the return-generation process actually conforms to the stable paretian hypothesis. How realistic is it that returns from one period to another are governed by a fixed set of four numbers? An alternative explanation for the fat tails is that the process that generates returns is unstable. A periodic reading of the *Financial Times* and the *Wall Street Journal* does not suggest an underlying mathematical order in the return-generating process; rather it suggests that investing offers an ever-changing set of risky bets with variable rewards for risk taking. After proposing the stable paretian hypothesis, Mandelbrot was never able to make good on his goal of successfully demonstrating the value of his work in forecasting returns. Later, he moved on to more fertile applications of non-normal stable distributions in the natural sciences.

The random-walk model was a marketing success due in large part to Fama's efforts. Fama's Ph.D. thesis, "The Behavior of Stock Market Prices" (1965), dealt extensively with the violations of the normality assumption in the random-walk model and Mandelbrot's attempt to salvage the random-walk model by introducing the stable paretian distribution.[7] Fama presented his own research that finds fat tails in the time series of returns for stocks listed in the Dow Jones Industrial Average. He also reviewed some of the studies he found to support the independence assumption over short time horizons as well as the inconsistency in performance in one mutual fund performance study and comes to number of conclusions: a large and impressive body of research supports the random-walk model; the stable paretian distribution fits empirical data better than the normal distribution; statistical tools using variance and standard deviations are invalidated.

In 1965, Fama confronted the investment profession when he published "Random Walks in Stock Market Prices" in the *Financial Analysts Journal*.[8] Fama not only challenged the practice of technical analysis; he attacked the usefulness of fundamental analysis. Fama limited his discussion of the random-walk model to whether the independence assumption fits the empirical data. He never referred to fat tails, non-normal distributions, or whether the return-generating process is stable. In the article, Fama concluded, "The evidence to date strongly supports the random-walk model."

One of the early works for which Fama is known in the investment community is his paper "Efficient Capital Markets: A Review of the Theory and Empirical Work" (1970), which sorted the empirical work into weak, semistrong, and strong form tests of efficient-market theory.[9] Here, Fama clearly distinguished the efficient-market model from the random-walk model and reaffirmed his support for efficient-market theory. "For the purposes of most investors, the efficient-markets model seems a good first (and second) approximation to reality. In short, the evidence in support of the efficient-markets model is extensive and (somewhat uniquely in economics) contradictory evidence is sparse." Fama claimed to be surprised that the evidence against the independent assumptions of the random-walk model was as weak as it was.

In his survey of the theory and empirical work, Fama avoided discussing instability in empirical return distributions, choosing to focus instead on the evidence of fat tails. In the section on distributional evidence, he again presented his 1965 conclusion that "non-normal stable distributions are a better description of the daily returns on common stocks than the normal distribution." He cited Osborne, Moore, and Kendall as having found fat tails in the distribution of returns in violation of the normal (Gaussian) distribution. Fama observed that the non-normal stable distribution is not more widely assumed in modeling: "Economists have, however, been reluctant to accept these results, primarily because of the wealth of statistical techniques available for dealing with normal variables and the relative paucity of such techniques for non-normal stable variables." He did not bring up the possibility that an alternative explanation for the fat tails is that the return-generating process is unstable.

Consultants' Payday

Fama's endorsement of the random-walk model and the promotion of the model by others coincided with a movement in the United States to improve the defined-benefit pension system. In 1974, Congress passed the Employee Retirement Income Security Act (ERISA) to curb abuses and to encourage the setting of investment standards. The influence of the efficient-market model was evidenced by the portfolio standard replacing the individual investment standard as a measure of prudence. This opened the door for defined-benefit plans to invest in index funds.

The consulting community responded to ERISA with a framework for pension fund investment management that included assigning investment managers to specialized roles where performance was measured against predefined benchmarks. In this framework, short-term market timing was not generally viewed favorably by consultants. Consultants did not feel comfortable giving short-term market-timing advice themselves, and they felt uncomfortable recommending short-term market timers. Market timing obscures the categorization of portfolio style allocations and makes it more difficult to apply the new set of tools with which to create normal portfolio benchmarks, evaluate portfolio risk, and determine whether or not a specialized investment manager was adding value (alpha). Given the extensive work on performance measurement, it became clear to institutional investors how difficult it was to beat performance benchmarks, and in the next decade came a general acceptance of quantitative risk management and performance-attribution tools.

One thing the "quant tools" had in common was the assumption that the underlying process generating the factor model returns is stable and the distribution of returns to risk factors is normal. It appears that Mandelbrot and Fama lost the argument.

In the new world of specialized investment management, both short-term market timing and active strategic asset allocation were largely rejected. Short-term market timing has a long record of being shunned by many of the old-school masters of investing.[10] Arguably, in traditional investment management, a distinction was drawn between trying to call short-term moves in asset-class returns (mostly a bad thing) and repositioning the strategic asset allocation on occasion (a good thing). In the era of the policy portfolio, short-term market timing and active strategic asset allocation were lumped together. One reason for this is that the introduction of efficient-market theory brought with it the idea that asset-class returns conform to a normal, long-term equilibrium, even though there was no theoretical or empirical support for the idea. Active asset allocation based on changes in long-term forecasts was relegated by consultants to an alternative investment category. In the post-ERISA world, pension funds usually set asset-allocation targets and narrow ranges based on portfolio simulations using historical returns. Although market timing had not been completely eliminated, in the new world of institutional investment management, it was fairly well contained.

While the motivation for reorganizing the institutional investment-management practice was largely pragmatic, a number of consultants adopted efficient-market views, ultimately influencing the financial-planning community's adoption of the policy portfolio. The consultant Douglas Love, for example, wrote in 1974 in the *Financial Analysts Journal*, "The client should base his policy decisions on an 'efficient market' approach, assuming that current market prices reflect what's known about the future, and concentrate on the long-term trade-off between expected return, risk, and liquidity. Stocks, bonds, and bills have different amounts of risk, and investors require average returns commensurate with these differences. To have a market outlook is to have an investment strategy. To have an investment policy is to have no outlook." [11]

The determination of the asset-allocation policy target and ranges was generally based on a study of historical asset-class returns. Roger Ibbotson and Rex Sinquefield (1976) published a study on how to forecast long-term asset-class returns based on the random-walk model. [12] "We assume in our simulation model that successive returns are independent and identically distributed. Our random-walk assumption for the three risk premia implies a world where both the unit price of risk (the distribution mean divided by the dispersion) and the level of risk (the dispersion of the distribution) are constant through time." It's interesting that Ibbotson and Sinquefield were willing to assume that returns are normally distributed in the face of Fama's indictment of the normal distribution, and they did not feel it necessary to comment on the issue in their paper. Nor did they provide any evidence of the forecasting effectiveness of their model.

Ibbotson founded a business offering the Ibbotson-Sinquefield building-block asset-class forecasting model and a mean-variance optimization tool. According to Ibbotson, their approach to forecasting asset-class returns became the standard for forecasted investment returns in the finance industry. In 1999, Ibbotson took credit for the accuracy of his 1976 twenty-five-year forecast, noting the Dow had an annualized rate return of 16.3 percent versus the 13 percent forecast. Ibbotson failed to mention that his 5th percentile forecast rate of return was 5.2 percent and the 95th percentile forecast rate of return was 21.5 percent. In 1999, Ibbotson made a new twenty-five-year forecast that the Dow would reach 100,000, based on his forecast of an 11.6 percent rate of return.[13] At the time some respected members of the investment community were forecasting a return of 6 percent or lower, based on dividend yield, forward-looking earnings growth rates and, in some cases, concerns about high valuation levels. Many financial advisers following the policy portfolio doctrine were not influenced by the disconnect between building-block forecasts and "supply side" forecasts for the stock market.

A Misunderstanding?

The last nail in the coffin for active asset allocation was not an academic study but a flawed empirical study authored by two investment advisers and a consultant, who set out to determine the relative importance of investment policy, market timing, and security selection in determining portfolio performance. "Determinants of Portfolio Performance," by Gary P. Brinson, L. Randolph Hood, and Gilbert L. Beebower (BHB), published in 1986, reported that investment policy, which they measured as the average quarterly exposure to stocks, bonds, and cash, explained 93.6 percent of the variation of quarterly portfolio returns, whereas, on average, market timing explained only 1.7 percent of the variation in portfolio returns and reduced portfolio performance by 0.66 percent per annum.[14] Based on these findings, BHB advised that the selection of asset classes and normal, long-term weights should be established as investment policy. The significance of the BHB study cannot be overstated. It became the most-cited, least-understood study in the financial literature. Pie charts demonstrating the overwhelming importance of investment policy became standard in marketing presentations. Though other articles had questioned the practice of market timing, the BHB study was the first to cast the issue of market timing clearly in investment policy terms.

Based on their findings, BHB proposed a hierarchy of investment decision making. The first two steps are properly part of investment policy: "deciding which asset classes to include and which to exclude from a particular portfolio" and "deciding upon the normal, or long-term, weights for each of the asset classes allowed in the portfolio." According to BHB, altering the investment-mix weights away from normal in an attempt to capture excess returns from short-term fluctuations in asset-class prices (market timing) resides in the sphere of investment strategy.

While not an immediate hit with the financial-planning community, the consulting community seized on the study to validate its having de-emphasized active asset allocation. It was a short step from BHB's definition of the investment policy to what Bernstein refers to as the policy portfolio: a fixed asset allocation with no market timing. BHB left the door open for the policy portfolio when they defined investment policy as the selection of "long-term classes weighted by their long-term weights," leaving it to the imagination of the reader whether and on what basis it's ever appropriate to engage in market timing or to actively adjust the long-term investment-policy allocations. Providing ammunition for the policy portfolio was the fact that the BHB study assumed the investment-policy allocations were fixed over the ten-year period studied.

As authoritative as BHB appeared to be on the subject of asset allocation and the importance of investment policy, there was a big problem with the study that seemingly no one had identified—not the authors, not the award committee at the *Financial Analysts Journal* that bestowed the prestigious Graham & Dodd award on BHB, not the consulting community that promoted the policy portfolio, not the marketing departments of financial advisers, not academia, and not members of the financial-planning community. The BHB study is seriously flawed; the study focused on the wrong thing, drew misleading conclusions about the relative importance of investment policy, market timing, and security selection, and ultimately confused investors facing the decision of how best to invest their assets to achieve their long-term financial objectives.

BHB's mistake was to focus their attention on their analysis of the variation of quarterly returns rather than on their calculation of holding-period returns. An analysis of the variation of quarterly returns tells us practically nothing about the prospects of clients achieving their financial objectives. Funding financial objectives comes from portfolio contributions and the compounding of returns over time. An analysis of the variations of returns is not a substitute for an analysis of the determinants of returns.

BHB failed to recognize the significance of their own study's calculation of the cross-sectional ten-year-holding-period returns; a simple calculation using the results of BHB's study indicates that investment policy explained only 15 percent of the realized cross-sectional standard deviation of ten-year-holding-period returns. While BHB made the case that market timing and security selection played minor roles in portfolio performance, they in fact played a larger role in investment outcomes over time than BHB led financial planners to believe. It's still commonplace for a financial adviser to make the statement that investment policy explains more than 90 percent of portfolio performance, when the consequences of active management decisions and cost usually explain well over 50 percent of cumulative investment returns.

Given the flaws in the BHB study design, it's surprising that the first real challenge to the study's validity occurred more than a decade after its publication.[15, 16] Criticism of the BHB study was not well accepted by some members of the consulting, investment-management, and financial-planning communities, as is to be expected when an embedded set of beliefs is challenged. A number of articles, including one by Ibbotson, appeared in journals and financial publications defending BHB and castigating the critics.[17] In defending BHB, Ibbotson was also defending the institution of the policy portfolio because of the commonly perceived role that BHB played in its formulation.

In "Does Asset Allocation Policy Explain 40, 90 or 100 Percent of Performance?" Ibbotson and Kaplan addressed the widespread misinterpretation of BHB.[18] According to Ibbotson and Kaplan, BHB were not addressing the questions "When choosing between two asset allocations, how much difference does it make?" and "What portion of my total return is due to asset allocation?" Instead, BHB answered the question, "How much of the movement in a fund's returns over time is explained by its asset-allocation policy?" Ibbotson and Kaplan pointed out, "Much of the recent controversy over the importance of asset allocation is due to a misinterpretation of the Brinson studies." If Ibbotson and Kaplan want people to believe that the readers of BHB are responsible for any misunderstanding, questions left to be addressed include: Why was the article titled "Determinants of Portfolio Performance" and not the "Determinants of the Quarterly Variation in Portfolio Performance"? What is the relevance of an analysis of the determinants of the quarterly variation in portfolio returns for an investor with long-term financial objectives? Are there other considerations besides the quarterly variation in returns that should be considered in determining an investment policy?

Although supportive of BHB, Ibbotson and Kaplan found in their empirical study that investment policy explained only 40 percent of the cross-sectional variation of ten-year-holding-period returns. They confirmed that investment policy explains approximately 90 percent of the quarterly variation in portfolio returns. They also found, not surprisingly, that investment policy explained 100 percent of the collective returns across all investors. According to Ibbotson and Kaplan, the answer to the question regarding the importance of investment policy depends on the question asked. However, of the three questions posed by Ibbotson and Kaplan, only one has much relevance for a long-term investor, and it's not the one Ibbotson and Kaplan say BHB addressed. A careful read of BHB and their 1991 follow-up article, "Determinants of Portfolio Performance II," raised questions that should be of interest to financial advisers who base their acceptance of the policy portfolio on BHB. Were the authors confused as to the significance of their own work? How much responsibility do they have for not clarifying the confusion regarding their study's role in promoting the policy portfolio? Had the financial-advisory community understood better that BHB's article is misleading, the policy portfolio would not likely have emerged as the dominant asset-allocation paradigm in the 1990s.

Investment Policy

In advocating the setting of an investment policy, BHB provided several footnotes of interest. One is Love's 1974 opinion piece, cited earlier, in which he stated that investment policy should be based on the efficient-market theory with no outlook on the market. The second was a reference on how to go about formulating an investment policy, written by Gary P. Brinson, Jeffery J. Diermeier, and Gary G. Schlarbaum, in the same year the BHB study was published. In the article "A Composite Portfolio Benchmark for Pension Plans," the authors recommend constructing an investment policy based on the assumption that plan sponsors desire portfolios that are Markowitz mean-variance efficient.[19] Determining an investment policy requires forecasts of return, standard deviations, and correlation coefficients, which can be based on historical long-term equilibrium rates of return. According to the authors, equilibrium rates of return are appropriate in determining a "normal" policy.

At about the same time BHB were conducting their study on pension fund performance, Charlie Ellis (1985) published his now classic *Investment Policy: How to Win the Loser's Game.*[20] Although the primary focus of Ellis's consulting business was the institutional investor, the book influenced forward-thinking financial planners, who were interested in elevating the standards of their profession. Ellis provided content, process, and policy recommendations to Love's concept of setting an investment policy based on efficient-market theory. Ellis incorporated the idea that markets are efficient and, over time, returns are the product of a normal equilibrium in the return-generating process. "In investing, the patient observer can see the true underlying patterns that make the seemingly random year-by-year or month-by-month or day-by-day experiences not disconcerting or confusing but rather splendidly predictable—on average and over time.... In weather and investments, larger and more numerous samples enable us to come closer and closer to understanding the normal experience from which the sample is drawn. It is this understanding of the normal experience that enables us to design our own behavior so we can take advantage of the dominant normal pattern over the long term and not be thrown off by the confusing daily events that present themselves with such force.... The single most important dimension of investment policy is asset mix, particularly the ratio of fixed-income to equity investments.... The trade-off between risk and reward is driven by one key factor: time."

According to Ellis, the crucial investment problem is not forecasting asset class; it's managing risk. "Recognition that risk drives returns instead of being simply a residual of the struggle for higher returns transforms the concept of investment policy. We now know to focus not on the rate of return but on the informed management of risk. The rate of return obtained in an investment portfolio is a derivative of the level of market risk assumed." Here Ellis provides the argument that an investor's risk tolerance is defined by how well he sleeps at night given the portfolio volatility inherent in his investment policy. Financial advisers accepted Ellis's definition of risk: It was no longer the possibility of a failure to achieve the long-term financial objectives, but how much volatility the investors suffer and whether they will hold on to their investment policy.

In the chapter "Beating the Market," Ellis advised planners to set an investment policy with maximum exposure to the stock market, subject to the client's tolerance for portfolio volatility, and to avoid the costly mistakes of attempting to add value by active investment management in any of its guises. The appropriate allocation to stocks, according to Ellis, can be determined from the historical asset-class return and the client's investment horizon. Ellis was not alone in these views but was among the key thought leaders in investment practice.

Ibbotson, collaborating with Gary Brinson, provides advice on how to go about determining asset-class investment-policy weights, "the weights that would be maintained in the absence of any information about the short-term performance of the various asset classes."[21] Implementing an investment policy "requires information about the performance characteristics of the asset classes and how they interact.... This information allows an investor to adopt a policy mix that, over time, would be expected to achieve the specified objectives.... The most common approach to establishing customized policy weights is the mean-variance portfolio-optimization procedure that was developed by the Nobel Prize–winning economist Harry Markowitz. The inputs necessary for this procedure are the expected returns and standard deviations for each asset class and the matrix of expected correlations of the returns for each asset class with every other. The output is a set of alternative portfolios, each having a minimum possible risk for a given expected return. The set of such portfolios, called optimal portfolios, describes a curve called the efficient frontier.... The asset-allocation policy decision involves selection of the efficient portfolio that best fits the investor's situation."

Ibbotson and Brinson then stated the assumption that underpins the mean-variance asset allocation: "This approach reflects the belief that the long-term relationships between asset classes are stable and that deviations from the policy mix are appropriate only when the expected returns differ from those used to generate the policy allocation. Therefore, an active asset allocation implies a situation in which the expected asset-class returns are in a temporary state of disequilibrium."

Judging from their business activities, Ibbotson and Brinson apparently have not agreed on the likelihood that returns temporarily deviate from equilibrium. Ibbotson Associates markets the random-walk model in its building-block forecasting model to be used in its mean-variance asset-allocation optimizer. Brinson's firm managed active asset-allocation strategies based on the premise that asset prices are at times in a state of disequilibrium.

Misrepresentation

The case for the policy portfolio often references Markowitz and Sharpe along with BHB. When Harry Markowitz and William Sharpe were awarded a share of the 1990 Nobel Prize in Economics, advocates for the policy portfolio got a welcome boost, claiming the prize further validated the scientific rigor behind the policy portfolio. That conclusion was false. There is nothing in Markowitz mean-variance optimization or in Sharpe's capital assets pricing model that is based on the random-walk model, suggests that historical returns should be used in formulating return expectations, or suggests that the asset allocation should be fixed.

Markowitz (1952) presented portfolio selection as an active, not static, practice based on future return expectations and the investor's tolerance for portfolio variance.[22] Markowitz's conception of mean-variance portfolio optimization was applied to the selection of securities, not of asset classes. Markowitz warned that portfolio selection at the asset-class level requires care in interpreting relationships among aggregates, which he noted presented problems and pitfalls. The common practice in the application of mean-variance optimization has been to rely heavily on the historical time series of asset-class returns to generate the inputs. Indeed, Markowitz warned against the practice of extrapolating returns. "When past performances of securities are used as inputs, the outputs of the analysis are portfolios which performed well in the past. When beliefs of security analysts are used as inputs, the outputs of the analysis are the implications for better or worse portfolios."[23]

The idea of investing in the capitalization of the market portfolio was proposed by Sharpe (1964). With Sharpe's capital assets pricing model (CAPM), the most attractive investment solution for an investor is the market portfolio with borrowing or lending based on the investor's tolerance for portfolio volatility. Sharpe's solution is based on the efficient-market model—not the random-walk model. According to Sharpe, an investor's investment policy would vary over time along with changes in the constituents of the market portfolio.

As a business proposition in the 1990s, the policy portfolio had many things in its favor, including a strong secular bull market with modest volatility. One thing it no longer had in its favor was Fama's support. In "Capital Markets II," Fama (1991), in a remarkable change of view, pulled the rug out from under the random-walk model.[24] "In brief, the new work says that the returns are predictable from past returns, dividend yields, and various term-structure variables. The new tests thus reject the old market efficiency–constant expected returns model that seemed to do so well in the early work.... Moreover, the early work concentrated on the predictability of daily, weekly, and monthly returns, but the recent tests also examine the predictability of returns for longer horizons. Among the more striking new results are the estimates that the predictable component of returns is a small part of the variance of daily, weekly, and monthly returns, but grows to as much as 40 percent of the variance of two- to ten-year returns. These results have spurred a continuing debate on whether the predictability of long-horizon returns is the result of irrational bubbles in prices or large swings in expected returns." Among the more damaging evidence Fama cited against the random-walk model are Fama and French (1988), who found "large negative auto-correlation for return horizons greater than one year";[25] Poterba and Summers (1988), who showed that "the ratio of one-year return variance to eight-year return variance is one half that predicted by the random-walk hypothesis";[26] and Fama and French (1988), who showed that "the increasing fraction of the variance of long-horizon returns explained by dividend yield is due in large part to slow mean reversion of expected returns."[27]

While holding to his belief in market efficiency, Fama states, "Market efficiency per se is not testable" because such tests are by their nature joint tests of market efficiency and an asset-pricing model. "In the pre-1970 literature, the common equilibrium-pricing model in tests of stock market efficiency is the hypothesis that expected returns are constant through time. Market efficiency then implies that returns are unpredictable from past returns or other past variables, and the best forecast of return is its historical mean.... Examining the forecasting power of variables like dividend yield and earnings yield over a range of return horizons nevertheless gives striking perspective on the implications of slow-moving expected returns for the variation of returns.... All of which shows that dealing with whether return predictability is the result of rational variation in expected returns or irrational bubbles is never clear-cut.... The fact that variation in expected return is common across securities and markets, and is related in plausible ways to business conditions, leans me toward the conclusion that if it is real, it is rational."

Absent from Fama (1991) is a discussion of Mandelbrot and stable non-normal distributions, which were such an important part of his early work; Mandelbrot doesn't even receive a footnote. Absent also is any discussion of fat tails and the challenge they present to statisticians. Gone is the certitude of Fama (1970) regarding the efficiency of the market. In its place, Fama offers his belief in market efficiency and his conviction that market bubbles do not exist. For Fama, the scientific case for market efficiency is now ambiguous from a scientific standpoint: "In short, a ubiquitous problem in time-series tests of market efficiency, with no clear solution, is that irrational bubbles in stock prices are indistinguishable from rational time-varying expected returns." Regardless of how one comes down on the question of market efficiency, the implications for the policy portfolio are clear: expected returns are not constant, and the variation in returns is not constant. In a world with changing return expectations, asset-allocation solutions should not be static regardless of where one comes down on the question of market efficiency.

There is something troubling about Fama's 1991 about-face on the random-walk model. In his 1965 *Financial Analysts Journal* article "Random Walks and the Stock Market," Fama concluded, "The evidence to date strongly supports the random-walk model." And in his 1970 *Journal of Finance* article "Efficient Capital Markets," he stated, "Indeed, at least for price changes or returns covering a day or longer, there isn't much evidence against the 'fair game' model's more ambitious off-spring, the random walk." Andrew Lo and Craig MacKinlay in their book *A Non-Random Walk Down Wall Street* indirectly challenge Fama's claim that there was not much evidence against the random-walk model before 1970.[28] "We also discovered that ours was not the first study to reject the random walk and that the departures from the random walk uncovered by Osborne (1962), Larson (1960), Cootner (1962), Steiger (1964), Niederhoffer, and Osborne (1966) ... were largely ignored by the academic community and unknown to us until after our own papers were published. We were all in a collective fog regarding the validity of the random-walk hypothesis, but as we confronted the empirical evidence from every angle and began to rule out other explanations, slowly the fog lifted for us." Lo and MacKinlay proceed to indict academic objectivity at the University of Chicago, in quoting a story in Niederhoffer's (1997) autobiography. "One of the students was pointing to some output while querying the professors, 'Well, what if we really do find something? We'll be up the creek. It won't be consistent with the random-walk model.'

The younger professor replied, 'Don't worry, we'll cross that bridge in the unlikely event we come to it.'"

To appreciate Niederhoffer's story, one needs to understand that support for the random-walk model and the efficient-market model was politically correct at the University of Chicago. The economics and finance departments were largely populated by professors who were true believers in classical economic theory, in the virtue of free markets, and in a limited role for government in economic affairs. The random-walk and efficient-market models were on the ideological front line. Those who chose to challenge the random-walk or efficient-market models were not warmly received. Anyone presenting a paper at seminars at the Center for Research in Security Prices (CRSP) in Chicago had to face what became known as "murderers row"—professors at the University of Chicago Business School who did not take kindly to naysayers on the efficient-market and random-walk models.

Paul Cootner (1964) published *The Random Character of Stock Market Prices,* in which he introduced, commented on, and reprinted important papers on the subject.[29] What is striking about Cootner's book is the number of unresolved statistical issues cited, the number of findings that were inconsistent with the random-walk model, and the need for more research on the subject before drawing any hard conclusions. In chapter 1, Harry Roberts (1959) stated, "In another sense, the reaction against 'chance' is sound. Much more empirical work is needed, and it seems likely that departures from simple chance models will be found—if not for stock market averages, then for individual stocks: if not for weekly periods, then for some other period; if not from the independence assumption, then from the assumption of a stable underlying distribution. Indeed, the analytical proposals of this paper are based on the assumptions that such departures will occasionally be found. Holbrook Working had discovered such departures in his commodity market research."

Among the more serious issues from the policy portfolio perspective that Cootner raised in his book was the independence assumption. In the introduction to part 3, "The Random Walk Hypothesis Reexamined," Cootner cited a number of cases where the random-walk model diverges from reality. Here Cootner cited Alexander (1961), Larson (1960), Cootner (1962), Steiger (1963), Osborne (1942), Fama (1963), and Mandelbrot (1963). Cootner (1962) began his article "Stock Prices: Random vs. Systematic Changes" by saying, "The subject matter of this paper is bound to be considered heresy. I can say that without equivocation, because whatever views anyone expresses on this subject are sure to conflict with someone else's deeply held beliefs." Cootner went on to challenge the independence assumption and, among other things, introduced the idea that the dispersion of returns expands with time at a slower rate than predicted by the random-walk model. This has all sorts of implications for asset allocation.

Cootner's book also included his colorful response to Mandelbrot's attack on the normal distribution: "Mandelbrot, like Prime Minister Churchill before him, promises us not a utopia but blood, sweat, and tears. If he is right, almost all of our statistical tools are obsolete.... Almost without exception, past econometric work is meaningless. Surely, before consigning centuries of work to the ash pile, we should like to have some assurance that all of our work is truly useless. If we have permitted ourselves to be fooled for so long into believing that the Gaussian assumption (normal distribution) is a workable one, is it not possible that the paretian revolution is similarly illusory?"

While Cootner voiced his doubts about Mandelbrot's four-parameter fix to the random walk, what remains was the failure of the normal distribution to explain the time series of returns. An even greater problem for statisticians was the prospect that there was no stable return-generating process to model. Cootner and several other contributors to the book raised the question. For example, Kendall (1953) said, "A comparison of the variances of the two parts of the series suggests that there has been an increase in variability since World War I.... It will also be noticed [that the time series in returns] is not a stationary process. There is no reason why it should be. No economic system yet observed has been stationary over long periods of time."

Although the academic side of the random-walk debate is pockmarked with controversy, contradictory evidence, methodological conundrums, and in some cases wishful thinking, the random-walk model presented to the financial-planning community was one of clear and overwhelming evidence, unassailable analytical methods, and scientific objectivity.

Conventional Wisdom

One of the most influential voices from within the financial-planning community has been Roger Gibson (1989).[30] "Most research evidence is that markets are reasonably efficient," Gibson told us. "In an efficient capital market, security prices are always fair. Given this, modern portfolio theory stresses that it is wise to simply 'buy and hold' a broad array of diverse investments. These concepts were later given legislative endorsement in the Employee Retirement Income Security Act of 1974, which stressed the importance of diversification within a broad portfolio context.... Designing an investment portfolio consists of several steps: Deciding which asset categories will be represented in the portfolio, determining the long-term 'target' percentage of the portfolio to allocate to these asset categories.... The first two steps are often referred to as investment policy decisions.... Dramatic support for the importance of asset allocation is provided by a study of 91 large pension funds.... The study dramatically supports the notion that asset-allocation policy is the primary determinant of investment performance, with security selection and market timing playing a minor role."

In the chapter on market timing, Gibson ends with a quote attributed to Charlie Ellis: "In investment management, the real opportunity to achieve superior results is not in scrambling to outperform the market but in establishing and adhering to appropriate investment policies over the long term, policies that position the portfolio to benefit from riding with the main long-term forces in the market." In the chapter on managing client expectations, Gibson provides advice on how to formulate return expectations: "The expected return for the S&P 500 can be estimated by adding the historical risk premium of 6 percent (rounded to the nearest percentage point) to the current Treasury bill yield." In discussing money management, Gibson defines the asset-allocation policy: "A client's investment policy decisions define a 'normal asset mix.' The normal asset mix is often referred to as the strategic asset allocation. The normal asset mix is, by definition, the most appropriate portfolio balance to maintain on average over time, given the client's risk tolerance and investment objectives. For the adviser advocating a passive asset-allocation approach, the normal asset mix is the fixed percentage allocations to be closely maintained in managing the portfolio."

Gibson provides a lens through which to view the world of financial planning, where leaders of the community were endeavoring to improve its standards of practice. Unfortunately, many of these industry standard-bearers were taken in by bad science. Given the influence of Gibson and other highly regarded members of the financial-planning community, the policy portfolio took root. It became the dominant asset-allocation paradigm in the 1990s, despite rejection at the time of the random-walk model in the highest academic circles. Financial planners were comfortable with the policy portfolio. The idea of setting an asset allocation in accordance with the client's ability to sleep at night and sticking with it became dogma. It was not until the market correction that began in March 2000 created an awareness that historical returns can overstate what investors can expect from the stock market in the future that financial planners began to question the soundness of the policy portfolio. What financial planners should find disturbing is how easily the community was persuaded by faulty academic arguments and by the commercial interests of consultants.

Fresh Start

As for determining an investment policy and asset-allocation strategy, we're pretty much back to where we were before the policy portfolio took over, except we now have more computing power that permits more complex simulation of investment strategies in relation to long-term financial objectives. We also have an expanded set of investment vehicles to implement active asset-allocation decisions. Forecasting asset-class returns is still as difficult as it has always been, but making forecasts with fundamental variables provides more realistic inputs for asset allocation than extrapolating historical risk premiums. This will lead to better investment solutions, more realistic financial plans, and more successful financial outcomes for many clients. In a world where stable equilibriums and central values are myths, the policy portfolio is a crutch for those who prefer to operate in a fantasy world. Its proposition is not just obsolete; it was invalid from the start. The policy portfolio deserves to be buried.

Chapter Notes

1. Peter L. Bernstein, "Are Policy Portfolios Obsolete?" *Economics and Portfolio Strategy* (March 1, 2003).

2. Louis Bachelier, *Theory of Speculation* (Gauthier-Villars, 1900).

3. Burton G. Malkiel, *A Random Walk Down Wall Street* (Norton, 2003).

4. Benoit Mandelbrot, "The Variation of Some Other Speculative Prices, *Journal of Business* (October 1967).

5. Peter L. Bernstein, *Capital Ideas* (Free Press, 1992).

6. Eugene Fama, "Mandelbrot and the Stable Paretian Hypothesis," *Journal of Business* (October 1963).

7. Eugene Fama, "The Behavior of Stock Market Prices," *Journal of Business* (January 1965): 34–105.

8. Eugene Fama, "Random Walks in Stock Market Prices," *Financial Analysts Journal* (September/October 1965).

9. Eugene Fama, "Efficient Capital Markets: A Review of the Theory and Empirical Work," *Journal of Finance* (May 1970).

10. Charles D. Ellis and James R. Vertin, *Classics* (Business One Irwin, 1979), and *Classics II* (Business One Irwin, 1991).

11. Douglas Love, "Opinion," *Financial Analysts Journal* (December 1974).

12. Roger G. Ibbotson and Rex A. Sinquefield, "Stocks, Bonds, Bills, and Infla-

tion: Simulations of the Future (1976–2000)," *Journal of Business* (July 1976).

13. Roger G. Ibbotson, "Predictions of the Past and Forecasts for the Future: 1976–2025" (posted March 1999), www.ibbotson.com.

14. Gary P. Brinson, L. Randolph Hood, and Gilbert L. Beebower, "Determinants of Portfolio Performance," *Financial Analysts Journal* (July/August 1986).

15. William Jahnke, "The Asset Allocation Hoax," *Journal of Financial Planning* (February 1997).

16. John Nuttall, "The Importance of Asset Allocation," uwo.ca/~jnuttall/asset.html (accessed May 25, 2004).

17. William Jahnke, "The Asset Allocation Chronicles," www.4CWM.com (accessed May 25, 2004).

18. Roger G. Ibbotson and Paul D. Kaplan, "Does Asset Allocation Policy Explain 40, 90, or 100 Percent of Performance?" *Financial Analysts Journal* (January/February 2000, vol. 56, no. 1).

19. Gary P. Brinson, Jeffery J. Diermeier, and Gary G. Schlarbaum, "A Composite Portfolio Benchmark for Pension Plans," *Financial Analysts Journal* (March/April 1986): 15–24.

20. Charles D. Ellis, *Investment Policy: How to Win the Loser's Game* (Business One, 1985).

21. Roger G. Ibbotson and Gary P. Brinson, *Global Investing* (McGraw-Hill, 1993).

22. Harry Markowitz, "Portfolio Selection," *Journal of Finance* (March 1952): 77–91.

23. Harry Markowitz, *Portfolio Selection* (Wiley, 1959).

24. Eugene Fama, "Capital Markets II," *Journal of Finance* (December 1991).

25. Eugene Fama and Kenneth French, "Permanent and Temporary Components of Stock Prices," *Journal of Political Economy* 96 (1988): 246–273.

26. James Poterba and Laurence Summers, "Mean Reversion in Stock Prices: Evidence and Implications," *Journal of Financial Economics* 22 (1988): 27–59.

27. Eugene Fama and Kenneth French, "Divident Yields and Expected Stock Returns," *Journal of Financial Economics* 22 (1988): 3–25.

28. Andrew W. Lo and Craig MacKinlay, *A Non-Random Walk Down Wall Street* (Princeton University Press, 1999).

29. Paul H. Cootner, *The Random Character of Stock Market Prices* (MIT Press, 1964).

30. Roger C. Gibson, *Asset Allocation* (Dow Jones Irwin, 1989).

CHAPTER 3

A Holistic Approach to Asset Allocation

WILLIAM W. JENNINGS AND WILLIAM REICHENSTEIN

B ooks for professional advisers are intended to make life easier by answering questions or addressing difficult issues. This chapter may make your life harder by raising questions on asset allocation that you haven't considered and challenging the approach you take to it. But the answers that result are likely to make you a better financial planner.

Personal financial planning regularly adopts sophisticated techniques developed for institutional money managers, yet individual portfolios are different from institutional portfolios in at least two important ways: First, individuals pay taxes, whereas many institutions, like endowment funds and pension plans, do not. Second, it's clear what assets belong in institutional portfolios, but the same is not true for individual portfolios. This chapter explores those differences. We'll also consider how focusing on after-tax valuation of the extended portfolio interacts with mean-variance optimization.

Most of these ideas are included in our book *Integrating Investments and the Tax Code*.[1] In the process of working on that book, we developed a holistic approach—one based on after-tax valuation of the extended portfolio—that we believe represents an improvement to the traditional approach to managing individuals' portfolios.

Distinguishing Pretax Funds
From After-tax Funds

Our holistic approach to managing individual portfolios makes two modifications to the traditional approach to asset allocation. First, we distinguish pretax funds from after-tax funds. We convert all account values to after-tax values and then calculate the asset mix based on *after-tax* values. Second, when addressing retirement preparedness, we believe financial planners should manage an *extended portfolio* that contains both financial assets and other off-balance-sheet assets that affect the individual's financial well-being, including things like the present value of projected income from Social Security and defined-benefit (DB) plans. In short, we calculate the current asset mix based on after-tax values of an extended portfolio.

Sam Smythe's Portfolio

Sam Smythe, age sixty-five, recently retired and asked Jan Jones, his financial planner, for advice. His financial assets include $400,000 in a 401(k) plan and $600,000 in taxable accounts. In addition, he'll receive $1,400 a month from Social Security, an amount that will increase with inflation.

Like most financial planners, Jan Jones believes that the choice of asset allocation is an investor's most important decision. In reaching her recommendation, she follows these three steps, which we call the *traditional approach* to setting the asset allocation.

1 She calculates the value of his portfolio. Following tradition, she includes only the financial assets in his portfolio. Henceforth, this is called his *traditional portfolio,* and it contains funds in the 401(k) and taxable accounts worth $1 million.

2 She determines the optimal asset allocation and applies it to the traditional portfolio. For simplicity, assume there are only two asset classes—stocks and bonds. Given six parameter estimates—expected return and risk of stocks, expected return and risk of bonds, correlation between stocks and bonds, and Sam's risk tolerance—she determines the optimal asset allocation. Later in this chapter, we examine this step in detail. For now, assume the optimal allocation is 60 percent bonds and 40 percent stocks.

3 After determining the asset allocation, she determines the asset location. That is, to the degree possible should stocks be held in the 401(k) plan and bonds in taxable accounts, or vice versa? Following conventional wisdom, she places stocks in the tax-deferred account and bonds in the taxable account.[2]

FIGURE **3.1** *Sam Smythe's Traditional Portfolio*

ASSET CLASS	AMOUNT	SAVINGS VEHICLE
Bond funds	$600,000	taxable accounts
Stock funds	$400,000	401(k)

Once these steps are completed, Jan recommends and Sam adopts the portfolio in **FIGURE 3.1**. It has the desired 60 percent bonds/40 percent stocks asset allocation and the desired asset location.

Many financial planners use this traditional approach to asset allocation, but as we shall see, it ignores taxes. Moreover, it's based on the traditional portfolio, which, we argue, is the wrong portfolio when addressing retirement preparedness.

The 401(k) plan contains pretax funds, while the taxable account contains after-tax funds; the book value and market value of the bond funds are equal. If Sam is in the 25 percent tax bracket and withdraws $1,000 from his 401(k), he pays $250 in taxes and can buy $750 of goods and services. If he withdraws $1,000 from this taxable account, he can buy $1,000 of goods and services. Since retirement planning concerns the client's ability to buy goods and services, it must distinguish between pretax funds and after-tax funds.

We have yet to talk to a financial planner who thinks taxes should be ignored; that is, we have yet to talk to someone who thinks the traditional portfolio, which ignores taxes, is correct. Consequently, the question seems to be *"How* should we adjust for taxes?" and not *"Should* we adjust for taxes?"

We recommend converting all funds to after-tax funds and then calculating the asset mix based on after-tax funds. To convert qualified retirement accounts such as 401(k)s, 403(b)s, simplified employee pension individual retirement accounts (SEP IRAs), traditional (deductible) IRAs, and Keogh accounts to after-tax funds, we simply multiply the pretax value by $(1 - t_r)$, where t_r is the expected tax rate during retirement. If Sam expects to be in the 25 percent tax bracket during retirement, his $400,000 of pretax 401(k) funds converts to $300,000 of after-tax funds. Since the profession now treats these pretax funds as being equivalent to after-tax funds, it implicitly assumes t_r will be zero. Although the expected tax rate during retirement is unknown, any reasonable estimate should improve on the traditional approach's implicit estimate of zero.

Taxable accounts sometimes contain both after-tax and pretax funds. Suppose a taxable account contains stocks with a market value of $14,000, including $4,000 of unrealized capital gains. In this case, we would advocate adjusting the $14,000 market value to reflect anticipated taxes.

No single procedure is always the best one for converting unrealized gains into after-tax dollars. If the gain will be realized immediately and taxed at 15 percent, the account's after-tax value is $13,400, where $600 is the capital gains tax. In *Integrating Investments and the Tax Code,* we argue that the $13,400 estimate is usually reasonable since most investors realize gains within a few years.

However, in some circumstances, this treatment may be inappropriate. The tax rate on the unrealized gain would be zero if the gain were realized after receiving a step-up in basis at death or if the appreciated asset were given to charity. For example, suppose an elderly couple in Texas, a community property state, owns stock with a cost basis of $20,000 and a market value of $120,000. If they plan to realize the gain after the death of the first to die, there will be no taxes. Or they could plan to give the appreciated asset to charity without paying taxes. In these cases, there is no embedded tax liability on the unrealized gains. By talking with Sam and informing him about the tax consequences of his decision on the timing of capital gains, Jan provides a valuable financial-planning service.

A nonqualified tax-deferred annuity is a hybrid account that contains pretax and after-tax funds. Someone may invest $40,000 of after-tax funds at age sixty, and fifteen years later it may be worth $75,000, including $35,000 of pretax deferred returns. In that case, taxes must eventually be paid on the deferred returns. Although this strategy is not perfect, the account could be converted to after-tax funds by assuming that the $35,000 is taxed immediately at the tax rate in retirement. (For further discussion of converting market values to after-tax values, see *Integrating Investments and the Tax Code.*)

Following the traditional approach, Jan first determines the optimal asset allocation and applies it to the traditional portfolio without adjusting for taxes, and then determines the asset location. This procedure is inappropriate because, as the following examples show, the asset location affects the *after-tax* asset allocation. In Figure 3.1, Sam's portfolio contains $400,000 in stocks in the 401(k) and $600,000 in bonds in taxable accounts (with market value equal to book value). So his after-tax asset allocation contains $600,000 in bonds and $300,000 in stocks, or 33 percent stocks. Instead, suppose his asset location placed bonds in the retirement account. If he had $400,000 in bonds in the 401(k) and $400,000 in stocks and $200,000 in bonds in taxable accounts (with market values equal to book values), his after-tax asset allocation would contain $500,000 in bonds and $400,000 in stocks or 44 percent stocks. In both examples, the traditional portfolio has a 60/40 bond/stock mix, but the after-tax asset allocations differ significantly.

The traditional approach to calculating the asset allocation tends to overstate the true exposure to the dominant asset held in tax-deferred retirement accounts. For example, in Figure 3.1, Sam holds stocks in the retirement account and the traditional approach says he has a 40 percent stock exposure when his after-tax stock exposure is only 33 percent. In practice, a dollar of funds in a taxable account is worth more after taxes than a dollar of funds in a qualified retirement account.[3] It follows that since Sam holds only stocks in his retirement account, he overstates his portfolio's true stock allocation as measured using after-tax values.

The lessons are clear: The two-stage procedure of first determining the traditional asset allocation and then determining the asset location is inappropriate. Traditional asset allocation overstates the true value of retirement accounts and thus overstates the asset weight of the dominant asset class held in retirement accounts.

The Right Assets for the Family Portfolio

Which assets belong in a family portfolio? The answer: It depends. If the question concerns estate taxes, last-to-die insurance and the personal residence count. In this chapter, we're concerned about whether the family has enough resources to meet its retirement needs. To that end, we adopt Maria Crawford Scott's criterion for deciding what belongs in the extended portfolio.[4] Scott includes items that produce cash flows, either now or later, that can be used to finance retirement needs. As such, we exclude last-to-die insurance and the personal residence. But let's consider some examples that suggest that the traditional portfolio of financial assets is not the best portfolio to consider when estimating a family's optimal asset allocation.

Inheritance. Suppose Sam's aunt recently died and left him $200,000 that should be available after probate. A financial planner should not include an inheritance in the extended portfolio unless that inheritance is virtually certain. If there's little question that the aunt's estate will pass smoothly through probate, we believe it should be included in Sam's portfolio. Obviously, to provide optimal advice, Jan must be managing the appropriate portfolio. We believe the extended-portfolio view is correct and the traditional-portfolio view is suspect.

Lottery. Assume the Dorr family wins a lottery that pays $1 million a year for ten years. The traditional portfolio would exclude the value of the lottery because it is not a financial asset. In many states, a lottery winner can sell the future payments. But even if a state could prevent a family from selling the future payments, we believe the after-tax present value of the payments should be included in the portfolio. Lack of marketability means only that the asset cannot be sold; it does not mean that the asset has no value. The present value of the after-tax cash flows from the lottery should be included as an asset in the extended portfolio, and it should be treated as a bond.

An immediate annuity. Suppose Mary, age sixty-five, just retired with $1 million in financial assets. All assets are in taxable accounts, and the market values and book values are equal. Following the advice of Gary, her financial planner, she invests $600,000 in stocks funds and $400,000 in bond funds. She will withdraw $2,400 automatically each month from her bond funds.

One month later, Mary asks Gary about the advantages and disadvantages of an immediate fixed annuity with a lifetime payout option and no guaranteed certain period. He explains that the major advantage is that this payout annuity would provide a monthly payment for the rest of her life. The major disadvantage is that, after her death, the annuity would be worthless, so there would be no remaining value to bequeath. Since both of her parents lived into their nineties and Mary has no children, the trade-off appeals to her. At Gary's recommendation, she purchases an immediate fixed annuity with the proceeds from the bond funds. It pays her $2,400 a month.

What is Mary's asset allocation after the annuity purchase? Should the payout annuity be included in her extended portfolio? We believe it should. Her financial position after the purchase of the annuity was similar to what it was before. With the payout annuity, she will never run out of money, but after her death there will nothing left from the proceeds of the bond funds for her beneficiaries. If she invests in the bond funds and withdraws funds each month, they will probably be depleted in about twenty-five years. But if she dies within twenty-five years, there will probably be funds available to leave to her beneficiaries. The choice between the immediate annuity and bond fund with monthly withdrawals involves the trade-off between longevity risk and bequest motive. However, we believe that the traditional portfolio is wrong when it ignores the annuity and says she had a 60 percent stock exposure before the annuity purchase and a 100 percent stock exposure after the purchase.

Social Security and pension plans. We recommend that the after-tax present value of projected payments from Social Security and defined-benefit pension plans be included as bonds in the extended portfolio. If the annuity counts, then it's logical that the present value of projected payments from pensions should count too. In the previous example, the payout annuity provided Mary with $2,400 a month for the rest of her life. If her company's defined-benefit plan pays her $2,400 a month for the rest of her life, it should count, too. The defined-benefit income is taxable, so we would include its after-tax present value. Similarly, income from Social Security should count in the portfolio. In *Integrating Investments and the Tax Code,* we present separate models that value income from Social Security, defined-benefit plans, and military retirement.

Mortgage. In her *AAII Journal* article, Maria Crawford Scott includes in the portfolio all assets that produce a cash flow either now or later. Based on this criterion, we believe the mortgage should be considered a short bond position in the family portfolio. Suppose Sam has the same portfolio as in Figure 3.1, but he also has a $100,000 mortgage. He could liquidate $100,000 in bonds and pay off his mortgage. When the mortgage is included in the extended portfolio and viewed as a short bond position, his net bond position is $500,000 before prepayment and $500,000 after prepayment. If the mortgage is ignored, it is as if he has a smaller net bond position and higher stock allocation after prepayment than before.[5]

Personal residence. In general, we do not believe the extended portfolio should contain the value of the residence. If the family continues to live in the residence, it will not produce cash inflows. The exception is if the family expects to downsize its residence. In this case, the value of the freed funds could be viewed as part of the portfolio and counted as real estate.

Sam's Extended Portfolio

FIGURE 3.2 presents Sam's extended portfolio. It contains the after-tax values of financial assets and projected Social Security payments. The extended portfolio is worth approximately $1,088,000 after taxes and contains 28 percent stocks and 72 percent bonds.

Recall that Jan Jones estimated an optimal asset allocation of 40 percent stocks and 60 percent bonds. To be clear, we are not saying that the optimal asset allocation of Sam's extended portfolio should be 40 percent stocks. Rather, we believe Jan (and the financial-planning profession) has been thinking along these lines. "For someone with Sam's risk tolerance, with typical income from Social Security and no other extended assets, the *traditional portfolio* should be approximately 60/40 bonds/stocks, which translates into a smaller stock allocation in the extended portfolio." That is, the profession has implicitly recognized the value of Social Security for a typical family, but it has not recognized that Social Security's value is atypical for some families. Moreover, the profession has not recognized the value of other, nonfinancial assets in the extended portfolio.

Consequently, the allocation of the after-tax traditional portfolio should be affected by the amount of *extended assets*—that is, assets beyond

FIGURE **3.2** *Sam Smythe's Extended Portfolio*

ASSET	ASSET CLASS	PRETAX VALUES	AFTER-TAX VALUES	SAVINGS VEHICLE
Stock funds	stocks	$400,000	$300,000	401(k)
Bond funds	bonds	600,000	600,000	taxable amount
Social Security	bonds	$239,000	188,000	
			$1,088,000	

The $239,000 pretax present value assumes $16,800 ($1,400 monthly) will be received each year for 17.6 years, the life expectancy of an average 65-year-old male, and a 2.7% annual discount rate, where the latter is the real yield on Treasury Inflation-Linked Securities. The $188,000 is approximately $239,000 (1 − .2125), where 21.25% is the effective tax rate assuming 85% of Social Security income is taxed at 25%. See chapter 11 of *Integrating Investments and the Tax Code* for a more detailed model.

the traditional portfolio. If Sam has a high level of retirement income—perhaps receiving income from defined-benefit plans or a fixed-payout annuity in addition to Social Security—then, with everything else the same, his traditional portfolio should contain more stocks. In contrast, if Sam has a low level of retirement income, then, with everything else the same, his traditional portfolio should contain more bonds. (See **FIGURE 3.3**.)

To recap, we recommend that an individual's extended portfolio include, at a minimum, the after-tax present value of projected income from Social Security, defined-benefit pension plans, and payout annuities. In addition, it may include the after-tax present value of other near-certain cash flows.

Mean-Variance Analysis

Let's look again at the second step in the traditional approach to asset allocation, in which the financial planner determines the client's optimal asset allocation. Often, the prescribed optimal asset allocation is the end product of mean-variance analysis.

The planner uses *traditional mean-variance analysis* to determine the optimal asset allocation. In this traditional analysis, the inputs in mean-variance optimization are pretax risk and pretax returns; taxes are ignored.

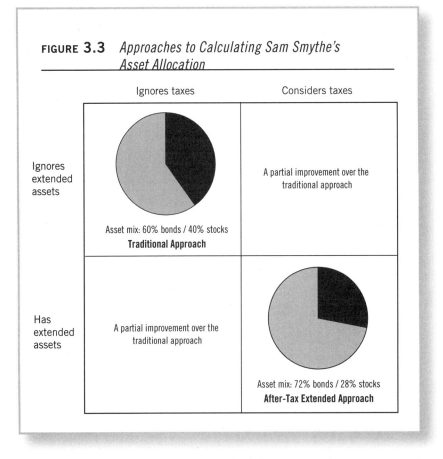

FIGURE **3.3** *Approaches to Calculating Sam Smythe's Asset Allocation*

	Ignores taxes	Considers taxes
Ignores extended assets	Asset mix: 60% bonds / 40% stocks **Traditional Approach**	A partial improvement over the traditional approach
Has extended assets	A partial improvement over the traditional approach	Asset mix: 72% bonds / 28% stocks **After-Tax Extended Approach**

The planner estimates the pretax standard deviation and pretax expected return for each asset class, the correlation coefficient between each pair of asset classes, and the client's risk tolerance. Given that input, the optimal asset allocation can be calculated.

Some financial planners perform constrained optimization, where the allocation to each asset class may be constrained within a range.[6] Other planners implicitly apply mean-variance analysis; that is, they recommend allocations that reflect the principles behind Markowitz's Nobel-laureate work, but because of the potential for errors in estimation, they prefer not to use explicit estimates. Each example, whether based on explicit or implicit estimates, is an instance of traditional mean-variance analysis. The key characteristic is that the analysis does not adjust for taxes.

FIGURE 3.4 presents input in the mean-variance analysis when adjusted for taxes. For simplicity, we assume two asset classes, but now these two assets can be held either in the 401(k) or in a taxable account. In essence, this produces four assets: bonds held in the 401(k), stocks

FIGURE **3.4** *Mean-Variance Analysis Applied to Sam Smythe's Traditional Portfolio*

ASSET CLASS	AFTER-TAX EXPECTED RETURN	AFTER-TAX STANDARD DEVIATION	MATRIX CORRELATION	PORTFOLIO WEIGHT
1. Bonds in 401(k)	4.6%	10%	1	W_1
2. Stocks in 401(k)	7	15	.2 1	W_2
3. Bonds in taxable accounts	3.45	7.5	1 .2 1	W_3
4. Stocks in taxable accounts	5.95	12.75	.2 1 .2 1	W_4

Constraints

$W_1 + W_2 = 0.333$ *401(k) is 1/3 of financial portfolio*

$W_i \geq 0$ for all i *No short selling*

$W_1 + W_2 + W_3 + W_4 = 1.0$ *Fully invested*

held in the 401(k), bonds held in a taxable account, and stocks held in a taxable account.

In this optimization, we use the *after-tax return* and *after-tax risk* of each of these four asset classes. In Figure 3.4, we assume that bonds' pretax return and pretax standard deviation are 4.6 percent and 10 percent and stocks' pretax return and pretax standard deviation are 7 percent and 15 percent.

For funds held in 401(k) and other qualified retirement accounts, after-tax return and after-tax risk are the same as the pretax return and pretax risk. Recall that today's after-tax value of $1 in the 401(k) is $1(1 − t_r), where t_r is the tax rate in retirement. If the $1 is withdrawn n years later after earning a geometric average pretax return of i percent per year, the after-tax ending wealth is $1(1 + i)^n(1 − t_r)$. It grows from $1(1 − t_r)$ today to $1(1 + i)^n(1 − t_r)$ in n years. The after-tax value grows at the pretax rate of return. On funds held in a qualified retirement account, the individual investor receives all of the returns and bears all of the risk.

Next, consider the after-tax risk and after-tax returns on bonds held in taxable accounts. Interest income is taxed each year. If $1 is invested in bonds yielding i percent, after n years its after-tax value will be $1[1 +

$i(1-t)]^n$, where t is the marginal tax rate for the next n years. When held in taxable accounts, bonds earn an $i(1-t)$ percent after-tax rate of return. If the pretax return is 4.6 percent, the bond investor earns 3.45 percent after taxes. In essence, the government taxes 25 percent of the returns and assumes 25 percent of the risk. The individual investor receives 75 percent of the returns and bears 75 percent of the risk.

When stocks are held in taxable accounts, the government taxes some of the stocks' returns *and assumes some of the stocks' risk.* For stocks, the amount of returns taxed and risk borne by the government depends on whether returns are in the form of dividends or capital gains and how quickly the individual investor realizes gains. If the individual realizes gains within one year, they are taxed at the ordinary income tax rate. At the other extreme, there are no taxes on the gains if the individual awaits the step-up in basis or gives the appreciated asset to charity. In Figure 3.4, we assume Sam realizes gains each year (technically, in one year and one day) and pays taxes at 15 percent on both dividends and capital gains. Sam earns 5.95 percent, or 7 percent $(1-.15)$ after taxes, on stocks and his risk is 12.75 percent. The government takes 15 percent of the returns and bears 15 percent of the risk. Sam receives 85 percent of the returns and bears 85 percent of the risk. The key insight is that the government shares some of the risk and returns on stocks held in taxable accounts.

Again, *the asset location affects an asset class's risk and returns. Because of taxes, the government shares in risk and returns of taxable assets.* Figure 3.4 presents input in the optimization for Sam Smythe. He chooses among four assets—bonds in the 401(k), stocks in the 401(k), bonds in taxable accounts, and stocks in taxable accounts. Since his *after-tax* asset allocation contains $300,000 in a 401(k) and $600,000 in taxable accounts, his portfolio is constrained to have one-third of financial assets in the 401(k) assets. The weights in each asset class must be greater than or equal to zero, and the sum of the four weights must equal 100 percent.

Let's review the errors in the *traditional mean-variance analysis* as applied to an individual's *traditional portfolio.* When addressing the question of retirement preparedness, we believe the expanded portfolio properly includes, at a minimum, the after-tax present value of retirement income streams. For simplicity, we suppress expanded portfolio thinking to focus on the errors in tax-oblivious traditional mean-variance analysis. By failing to consider taxes, traditional mean-variance analysis results in the following errors:

❑ The traditional asset allocation does not distinguish between pretax and after-tax funds, so it says Sam has $400,000 in a 401(k) and $600,000 in taxable accounts. After adjusting for taxes, his 401(k) is worth $300,000 and his taxable accounts are worth $600,000.

These after-tax values should be used in the calculations of his asset allocation.

❑ Stocks' and bonds' *expected returns* and *risk* depend on whether they're held in the 401(k) or a taxable account. The same asset held in a taxable account is effectively a different asset when an individual holds it in a qualified retirement account.

❑ The asset-location decision affects the asset-allocation decision. The traditional two-step procedure of first making the asset-allocation decision and then the asset-location decision is inadequate. Only the integrated, concurrent optimization of asset allocation and asset location uses all available information to determine the best portfolio for a client.

In chapter 14 of *Integrating Investments and the Tax Code,* we demonstrate after-tax mean-variance analysis more fully.

SINCE 1998, we have spent considerable time thinking about these differences between personal and institutional portfolios and examining the implications. There remains much work to be done. Over the next decade, we believe and hope leading professionals and academics will spend considerable effort addressing the shortcomings of the traditional approach to asset allocation. In the process, some of our suggestions will be modified, and some may be rejected. But we suspect most of our suggestions and insights will remain valid.

One thing is certain. Taxes matter to clients. The traditional approach of ignoring taxes is inadequate. So, too, are approaches to asset allocation that ignore nonfinancial assets. Our profession has a lot of work to do to integrate investment and the tax code.

Chapter Notes

1. W. Reichenstein and W. W. Jennings, *Integrating Investments and the Tax Code* (Wiley, 2003).

2. John B. Shoven and Clemens Sialm, "Long-run Asset Allocation for Retirement Savings," *Journal of Private Portfolio Management* (since renamed *Journal of Wealth Management*) (Summer 1998): 13–26; W. Reichenstein, "Calculating a Family's Asset Mix," *Financial Services Review* 7(3) (1998): 195–206; S. M. Horan, "After-tax Valuation of Tax-sheltered Assets," *Financial Services Review* 11(3) (2002): 253–276; J. Poterba, "Valuing Assets in Retirement Saving Accounts" (MIT working paper, 2003).

3. Recall that to convert the value of qualified retirement accounts to after-tax funds, we multiply the pretax value by $(1 - t_r)$. Even if the book value of the asset in the taxable account was zero and the gain would be realized immediately, we would calculate the asset's after-tax value by multiplying its pretax value by $(1 - t_{cg})$, where t_{cg} is the capital gains tax rate. Since t_{cg} is generally less than t_r, it follows that \$1 of pretax funds in a taxable account is worth more after taxes than \$1 of pretax funds in a qualified retirement account.

4. Maria Crawford Scott, "Defining Your Investment Portfolio: What Should You Include?" *AAII (American Association of Individual Investors) Journal* (November 1995): 15–17.

5. W. Reichenstein "Rethinking the Family's Asset Allocation," *Journal of Financial Planning* (May 2001): 102–109.

6. H. Evensky, *Wealth Management: The Financial Advisor's Guide to Investing and Managing Client Assets* (McGraw-Hill, 1997).

CHAPTER 4

Professional Portfolio Design

HAROLD EVENSKY

A t the end of the 1990s and in early 2000, practitioners and academics began to revisit their expectations for equity returns. Their analyses brought them to a consensus that investors would be facing an investment environment of low equity returns during the decade ahead. These expectations led me [Evensky (2001)] and others to argue that retail investors needed to revise their equity portfolio design. As reported in the media and reflected in professional surveys, however, few practitioners have done so. Still, the consensus regarding equity-return expectations remains unchanged. Consequently, the need for a major revision of retail portfolio design remains critical. In fact, if a practitioner's equity-return assumption is consistent with the consensus, blind adherence to the traditional multi–asset class, multistyle model verges on professional malpractice.[1]

Expectations of an investment environment with lower returns do not challenge our profession's basic investment philosophies, that is, a belief in the tenets of modern portfolio theory, the importance of diversification, the value of market factors (for example, size and value), and the potential value of active management. Consequently, a successful alternative portfolio design for retail investors must remain philosophically consistent with these beliefs while incorporating the effects of expenses and taxes. A review of alternative design strategies[2] shows clearly that the most effective portfolio structure is a variation of a strategy generally called "core and satellite."[3]

The core-and-satellite structure has been elegantly described as "harmony through separation."[4] In its simplest manifestation, the strategy combines "core" tax- and expense-efficient investments with small tracking error relative to market benchmarks and satellite investments designed to provide net alpha.

Current Portfolio Design

Portfolio design of retail client equity portfolios[5] evolved from the design process used by institutional investors.[6] The result—multi–asset class, multistyle (MAMS)—has been a commitment to multiple active managers in individual portfolios. Best represented by the now classic Morningstar Style Box, portfolios generally include allocations to all or most of the nine categories.[7] In addition, it's common to find multiple managers in one specific style box (for example, two or more large-cap domestic growth managers). These basic allocations are often supplemented by specialty allocations (for example, real estate investment trusts, sector funds). As a result, it's not uncommon to find ten to twenty active managers represented in the equity allocations for a single portfolio.

The design and implementation of portfolios with so many components has been justified by the expectation of adding small elements of alpha for each allocation while, at the same time, improving the portfolio risk profile through diversification. Whether this expectation has been met in the past is not the question here; the issue at hand is, "Will the traditional strategy add alpha in the future?"[8] And, if not, what portfolio design strategy is appropriate for the retail portfolio? If we accept the premise that portfolio design should be based on historically low real future equity returns, then we must consider the consequences, for retail investors, of a lower return environment and find a solution.

The Equity Risk Premium

The debate over the equity risk premium has continued unabated for the last two decades. The early focus was on explaining the premium; during the mid- to late 1990s, the emphasis was on justifying the historically high returns epitomized by "new era" markets. As the world entered the twenty-first century and the equity market began its long and painful retrenchment, both academics and practitioners began to redirect the discussion to focus on what investors might expect from equity returns over the next decade. Adjusting for varying interpretations of "equity premium" and translating the estimates into expectations for real returns, the broad consensus in mid-2002 for forward-looking real returns was 3–6 percent.[9]

Some practitioners, upon considering the need for a change in portfolio design, acknowledge that in a low-return environment, the traditional

Professional Portfolio Design | 55

model is inappropriate. However, they argue that the consensus on lower returns was developed at a time when the market was still significantly overvalued, and the market losses subsequent to the studies noted above mitigate or eliminate the low-return expectations; hence, no changes are necessary. Unfortunately, the expectations for low equity returns remain substantively unchanged. Although the credibility of prognosticators is no guarantee of accuracy, the representative list emphasizes the heavy burden of justification required of a professional designing portfolios based on higher return expectations.[10]

Low Returns and Portfolio Design

Retail investors face innumerable issues that are of little or no importance for institutional investors. These include taxes, expenses, and alpha.

Taxes

- ❑ Numerous forms of taxation
- ❑ Tax consequences influenced by unique cash flow and tax basis
- ❑ Numerous "pockets" of investments (for example, taxable, tax deferred, and tax free)
- ❑ Tax payments that do not necessarily come from the portfolio generating the taxable event

Some effort has been made during the last few years to address the impact of tax erosion for retail investors. The predominant strategy has been to use "tax-efficient" funds and separate account management. Although the efficacy of these strategies is debatable,[11] even if an investor successfully selects all tax-efficient asset class or style strategies, for the total portfolio, the result would be suboptimal. As Brunel (1999) demonstrated, in a tax-aware environment, sequential optimization is ineffective. The combination of an individual manager's insensitivity to the tax impact on overall after-tax portfolio performance, rebalancing, manager replacements, and client cash flows can quickly destroy overall portfolio tax efficiency. Stein and McIntire (2003) demonstrate that the first two issues alone can cost 30–60 basis points annually.

Expenses

- ❑ It is costly for retail clients to have access to active-management skills.
- ❑ Retail custodial and related costs are significantly higher than institutional costs.
- ❑ Retail rebalancing costs are more expensive.

❑ Implementation costs via packaged products are often expensive for retail clients.

As a consequence, unlike institutions, which invest in a two-dimensional universe (that is, risk and return), the retail client must consider a third dimension—taxes and expenses. As discussed below, it's the performance drag of this third dimension that overwhelms the attempt to capture alpha.

Alpha

If the benefit of the MAMS design provided adequate alpha to cover the friction of taxes and expenses, the "third dimension" might be comfortably ignored.[12] Unfortunately, that result is extraordinarily unlikely with a lower equity returns.

Alpha has two potential sources: the alpha contribution of active managers and the factor alpha contributed by allocations to specific asset classes and styles (for example, small cap and value). As consistently reported in studies evaluating the magnitude of these contributions, the absolute magnitude of consistent alpha, net of fees and expenses, is modest.

The Third Dimension

Even if one were to argue that an individual adviser or investor could, as a result of superior ability, continuously add significant alpha, that individual too would be humbled by the counterintuitive math of a low-return environment. The key to understanding the problem is to focus on the net benefit sought by the retail client; namely *real* after-tax, after-expense returns. "Real" is the crux of the issue, because as nominal returns drop, the expense and tax drag associated with inflation mushroom (see **FIGURE 4.1**).

The results are sobering. Although return expectations have been reduced by less than one-half and alpha remains unchanged, the net-net real return to the client has dropped from 9.7 percent to 3.7 percent. Eliminating alpha from the analysis (for most portfolios, a very realistic assumption), the real net-net is only 2.8 percent.

Given that alpha is an unknown and not guaranteed, whereas fees and taxes are known and manageable, the consequences for portfolio design are dramatic and clear. In a high-return environment, modest additional expenses or taxes may be appropriate in the search for uncertain alpha. In a low-return environment, the risk of failure is significant; the benefit of modest savings in expenses and taxes is significant.[13] Professionals, acting in a fiduciary capacity in relation to their clients would do well to heed the sage advice of Peter Bernstein (2002): "Your [that is, our clients] future wealth isn't a game." As a consequence:

FIGURE 4.1

During the period that advisers were developing portfolio design criteria based on institutional portfolio design, nominal total return expectations for equities were about 15 percent. Today, a reasonable (and, according to many, optimistic) forward-looking expectation is 8 percent. The following example, factoring in a generous alpha, compares the net real return available to the investor after expenses and after taxes in a 15 percent nominal return environment to that available in an 8 percent nominal return environment.[14]

	MARKET RETURN	
	15%	8%
Nominal market return	15.0%	8.0%
Gross alpha	4.0	4.0
Gross nominal portfolio return	19.0%	12.0%
Taxes [15]	2.9%	1.8%
Expenses		
Basic portfolio	1.0%	1.0%
Alpha management & expenses	2.5	2.5
Total expenses	3.5%	3.5%
Net nominal return	12.7%	6.7%
Inflation	3.0%	3.0%
Net-net real return	9.7%	3.7%

In a low-return environment, management of expenses and taxes must be a primary aspect of the portfolio-design process. Ignoring this issue in the pursuit of alpha may be malpractice.[16]

The question for the professional wealth manager is, How do we meet this new challenge?

Core and Satellite: An Alternative Design

At Evensky, Brown & Katz, which concluded that planning for the firm's clients should be based on the assumption of low returns, it was clear that as a result of expenses and taxes (that is, the third dimension), the MAMS portfolio design was no longer appropriate. The core-and-satellite (C&S) strategy had been in use since the 1990s[17] but until 2003 was discussed only intermittently in professional wealth-management publications and, with rare exception,[18] has been ignored by the popular press. However, a number of highly respected retail financial market participants provide strong intellectual support for the strategy;[19] according to Barclays (2002), "many—if not most—large pension plans utilize C&S framework"; and C&S is well recognized and implemented throughout the world.[20]

An Efficient Solution

The investment-decision process has been well documented by such professional icons as Brinson, Hood, and Beebower (1986) and Charles Ellis (2000). The process they delineated is consistent with current wealth-management practice and can be described as

- ❏ setting the long-term asset allocations (for example, bond/stock allocation)
- ❏ establishing the investment policy and rebalancing parameters
- ❏ determining active/passive allocations
- ❏ selecting managers
- ❏ assessing ongoing management—performing tactical activities, monitoring and replacing managers

In his seminal article on C&S, Stein (2001) points out that the first two decisions are the most important. They're also relatively inexpensive and tax efficient compared with the other decisions, yet they receive the least attention. Therein lies the opportunity for an alternative portfolio design. To provide a viable option to the traditional MAMS model used by retail investors and their advisers, an alternative strategy must resolve a number of issues:

Expense management
- ❏ Trading costs (commissions and spreads)
- ❏ Rebalancing expenses
- ❏ Management fees
- ❏ Manager hiring/firing expenses

Tax management
- ❑ Alpha tax (that is, the tax generated by active-management decisions)
- ❑ Rebalancing tax
- ❑ Manager hiring/firing tax
- ❑ Multiple-manager tax (that is, the tax related to the inefficiency of non-tax-coordinated investment allocations)
- ❑ Benchmark reconstitution tax

Risk management
- ❑ Market risks—diversification
- ❑ Behavioral risk

With these issues in mind, Stein concludes that the opportunity for retail investors is to focus on the equity portfolio structure.

Brunel (2001), in the second seminal article (and the inspiration for the first part of Brunel's chapter; see page 10), confirms Stein's insights and provides a simple but elegant justification for selecting a C&S design as an optimal equity portfolio structure. Specifically, Brunel addresses the issue of the relationship between portfolio activity and expected value added. As he demonstrates in chapter 1, a *murky-middle manager, adding 2 percent pretax alpha, delivers to the taxable investor a portfolio return 1.4 percent* less *than the index (not including the cost of the active manager's fees)*. He proposes an alternative design—"barbelling" the portfolio into two strategic baskets (that is, core and satellite)—as an effective one.

I obviously agree. But the strategy presents issues for advisers and their retail investor clients. What follows are some specific solutions to the practical design of a C&S portfolio.

Issues and Solutions

In developing a new portfolio design structure for the retail investor, a number of issues, some unique to the retail investor, need to be considered; they include:

General issues
- ❑ Management of expenses
- ❑ Management of taxes

Issues unique to the retail investor
- ❑ Retail expense levels (significantly higher than institutional expenses)
- ❑ Limited retail product choices (for example, funds and wrap accounts versus institutions' direct access to managers; limited access to short investing strategies and other alternative investment strategies)

❑ Uncertain and generally short holding periods
❑ Investors' behavioral characteristics—for example, an aversion to realizing losses impedes rebalancing, a need for "bragging rights" and excessive optimism encourages investing in "hot" investments and frequent trading; mental math results in a focus on nominal return

There are practical design solutions for these issues.

The Core

The decision to seek greater potential returns by allocating funds to the equity market presumes a belief in an equity market premium; that is, a premium independent of any active-management skills. Having decided on an allocation to the equity market, investors may also seek additional passive-return premiums by looking to capture the size and value (BtM) factors first described by Fama and French (1992). "Core" describes that portion of the equity allocation primarily designed to capture these three market factor returns (that is, beta, size, and BtM).

The structural design and implementation of the core portfolio is based on the management of the general issues, hence the primary attributes of the core are cost and tax efficiency and Fama-French factor returns. The design of the core is a four-step process that mimics the traditional asset-allocation process now used by most professionals.

Step 1—equity allocation. This is the determination of the allocation between fixed income and equities. Implementation of a C&S strategy in no way conflicts with whatever system the investor or adviser may use to make this decision (whether Markowitz mean-variance optimization, professional experience, or dartboard), therefore no change is necessary.

Step 2—determination of the equity allocation between core and satellite. We'll defer the discussion of this step to the next section, "The Satellites."

Step 3—selection of the investment(s) and allocations to be used for the core. This decision is analogous to step 1. A simple and rational approach, especially for an investor who does not believe in factor returns, would be to allocate 100 percent of the core to a broad-based market index (for example, the Russell 3000). Incorporating the Fama-French factors would suggest additional core allocations to small-cap and value equities. In any event, the core allocations should consist of a relatively few positions primarily designed to capture market-factor returns. The determination of the allocation between investments within the core should be determined in a manner consistent with the process used to determine the overall portfolio allocation.

Step 4—determination of the rebalance parameters for the core investments. The determination of the rebalancing criteria is a critical factor in the management of expense and tax drag. In general, the bias should be in favor of the widest possible rebalance bands consistent with the practitioner's goal to manage portfolio risk exposure. Recent papers on this issue by Masters (2003) and Abeysekera and Rosenbloom (2002) provide useful guidelines in making this decision.

The Satellites

The sole goal of satellite investments is to add net-net alpha (that is, after expenses and taxes). Although, by their very nature, they will tend to be poorly correlated with the core, risk reduction via satellite diversification is a secondary benefit and need not be a factor in satellite selection. In fact, although counterintuitive to professionals, satellite investments need not be style consistent, low (or even moderate) risk, liquid, or cost or tax efficient. The only criteria for consideration of a satellite investment are:

❑ The investment vehicle or strategy is fundamentally sound (that is, not a gimmick).
❑ The expected net-net real return exceeds that of the core.

Obviously, with such a broad universe of choices, combined with the potentially high volatility of satellite investments, there is a need to balance opportunity and risk in the decision regarding the number of satellite investments to include. Based on discussions with those now using this strategy and the experience in my own practice, the recommendation is to consider two to four satellite positions. Having fewer satellites significantly increases the risk (to both the total portfolio return and the client's emotional state) of a wrong choice. It also limits the behavioral benefit of bragging rights (too few good stories to tell their friends about). Larger numbers of allocations may add little to the net satellite alpha, because additions are more likely to reduce risk than increase returns. Finally, given the effort necessary to select and monitor satellite investments, the effort of incorporating more satellite managers may outweigh the benefit.

Satellite Allocation

The decision regarding the allocation between core and satellite investments is one of risk budgeting. Risk budgeting refers to the trade-off between market risk and active risk.[21] Although theoretically a quantifiable process, implementation requires significant professional "art" because so many factors are to be considered, each with its own level of uncertainty. Fortunately, there are a few good resources to assist in this process.

Stein and Quisenberry (2003) provide an excellent guideline in "Core-and-Satellite Portfolio and Taxes," in *Investment Advisor*. They suggest that "many taxable investors would be well served by core allocations that exceed 50 percent." The article is based on Quisenberry's paper "Optimal Allocation of a Taxable Core and Satellite Portfolio Structure" in the *Journal of Wealth Management*. Quisenberry demonstrates that the decision process is sensitive to four issues, and advisers may allocate more to the core,

- ❏ the lower the alpha of the satellite managers
- ❏ the higher the tracking error of the satellite managers
- ❏ the higher the turnover or gain realization of the satellite managers
- ❏ the higher the expected market return

Barclays Global Investors makes available to professionals a powerful analytical program known as the Core/Satellite Hypothetical Tool to assist in allocation decisions. A discussion of C&S portfolio construction and the tool can be found under "Tools: Core/Satellite Hypothetical" at the Barclays Global Investors iShares site (www.ishares.com).

Based on Stein and Quisenberry's work, simulations with the Barclay tool, and discussions with the firm's clients, I recommend that an initial satellite allocation be set between 20 percent and 30 percent. This range provides the best balance between the theoretical efficient allocation and clients' desire to "earn something" and have bragging rights, as well as their tolerance for the volatility associated with satellite investments. Details of Evensky, Brown & Katz's current C&S portfolio design are detailed in the appendix on page 65.

Net Results

Core-and-satellite portfolio design elegantly meets the criteria for efficient solutions in all three problem areas.

General Issues

Management of expenses

- ❏ As core investments are designed to capture market returns, there is little or no additional cost associated with management fees and trading costs.
- ❏ For the same reason, there is little or no need to incur the cost of replacing poor-performing active managers.
- ❏ Cost effectively capturing market returns through core investments and focusing the investment on alpha for satellite investments significantly reduce wasted management fees.[22]
- ❏ Unlike the traditional MAMS portfolio design, the C&S design reduces movement of positions between managers (for example, stock

in a successful and growing small company being sold by a small-cap manager only to be purchased by the mid-cap manager, then sold by the mid-cap manager and concurrently purchased by the large-cap manager, etc., etc.) and, consequently, reduces trading and tax costs.

Management of taxes (in addition to the items noted above)
❏ Minimization of active management reduces the portfolio exposure to alpha tax.
❏ Core investments can be effectively managed to minimize taxes without the risk of reducing alpha.
❏ Elimination of manager replacement also eliminates the need for early realization of gains, as is often the case when, after a successful period, the decision is made that a manager needs to be replaced (for example, the fund has grown too big or has attracted too much hot money).
❏ Traditional design, incorporating multiple managers, results in a frequent need for rebalancing. Although rebalancing is an important and integral element of portfolio management, it's an inherently tax-inefficient strategy; the process always realizes gains and defers losses. With a very limited number of core allocations and reasonably broad rebalance parameters, the need for rebalancing is significantly reduced.

Unique Issues

Retail expenses
They are significantly higher than institutional expenses.
❏ Core allocations can make effective use of low-cost index funds and exchange-traded funds for the majority, if not all, of the equity allocation.
❏ Concentration of a significant percentage of the equity allocation to the core results in the opportunity to invest more frequently at quasi-institutional rates (for example, $500,000 threshold versus $50,000).

Retail product choices
Choices include funds and wrap accounts versus direct access to managers, and limited access to short investing strategies and other alternative investments.
❏ Concentration of a significant percentage of the equity allocation to the core may result in allocations large enough to qualify for direct access to managers, bypassing the need and associated costs of separate account platforms.

Uncertain and generally short holding periods

❑ Having fewer positions makes the process of providing for unplanned additions or withdrawals of capital from a portfolio much more cost-effective.

Client preferences

❑ Having fewer active positions reduces the probability that a position will cause a client to be concerned.

❑ A significant core allocation reduces the risk that clients will perceive market-tracking error (that is, think that they're doing poorly while the market is doing well).

❑ Conversely, the availability of satellite allocations allows the practitioner to consider and incorporate managers whose styles may have excluded them from consideration in the past (for example, eclectic, concentrated, "too risky"). This gives rise to both a wider universe of investment alternatives and an opportunity to include in the portfolio a number of behaviorally appealing "good stories," the latter providing clients with bragging rights and a perception (and perhaps the reality) of superior returns.

In With the New

Advisers have the professional responsibility of providing investment advice based on thoughtful and well-reasoned market assumptions. If those assumptions significantly change, advisers have the professional responsibility to modify or change, if necessary, their recommendations for portfolio design.

The broad consensus of sophisticated institutional managers and academics is that reasonable expectations for real equity market returns over the next decade are in the range of 3–6 percent. In such a low-return environment, for retail investors, the expense and tax drag on net-net real portfolio return overwhelm the enhanced return benefits associated with traditional multi–asset class, multistyle portfolio design. Very simply, for retail clients, the old way (that is, MAMS) will not work in the future. As a consequence, advisers must revisit and revise their investment policy design. A viable alternative is core and satellite.

APPENDIX
Core and Satellite: A Live Example

Evensky, Brown & Katz has implemented C&S portfolios for its clients. The following is an example of the policy now implemented for an all-equity allocation. The primary investment vehicles for core allocations are exchange-traded funds (for example, the Barclay Russell 3000 iShare for the Broad Domestic Core). In larger taxable portfolios, the firm has directly employed a quant-based tax manager. This appendix is included not as a recommendation but solely as an example of how a C&S policy might be implemented.

	CURRENT ALLOCATION	TACTICAL BAND
Core	79%	70%–90%
Broad domestic core*	45	
Large/mid cap domestic value	6	
Small cap domestic value	12	
International developed	16	
Satellite	21%	10%–30%
Micro cap domestic growth	7	
Emerging markets	7	
Alternative	7	
Rebalance parameters		
Fixed/equity	8%	
Broad domestic core	7	
Large/mid cap domestic value	3	
Small cap domestic value	4	
International developed	5	

*As of April 2004, our firm's investment committee is considering the allocation of 15–20 percent of the "broad core" to an absolute-return "fund of funds."

Active satellite investments are carefully monitored monthly on a "by exception" analysis and report. If the analysis indicates that a satellite investment has violated any one or more of a series of preset criteria, the report notes the exception and the investment committee, at its next monthly meeting, must make a decision to keep or replace the investment.

Attributes monitored against preset standards include cash positions, turnover, standard deviation (three, six, and twelve months), and performance. Performance is measured against a variety of criteria including a predetermined satellite benchmark, the satellite's historical return, and the satellite's return versus the core's return. Performance triggers are set for upside as well as downside variations and are based on both absolute and relative criteria. The upside triggers are based on a philosophical belief in investment regression to historical returns.[23]

The core allocations reflect the firm's philosophy of modest overweighting in value and small-cap positions to capture BtM and size factors and its belief that nondomestic positions should be incorporated in a core portfolio. The determination of the percentage of the allocations is based on a classic Markowitz mean-variance optimization, constrained and then tested for acceptable suboptimal performance (that is, OpSop, Evensky [1997]). The rebalance parameters are absolute percentages and are set based on a number of factors, including the standard deviation of the asset class, the size of the commitment to the class, and the estimated correlation between investments.

References

Abeysekera, S. P., and E. S. Rosenbloom. "Optimal Rebalancing for Taxable Portfolios." *Journal of Wealth Management* (Winter 2002): 42–49.

Arnott, Robert, and Robert Jeffrey. "Is Your Alpha Big Enough to Cover Its Taxes?" *Journal of Portfolio Management* (Spring 1993): 15–26.

Bernstein, Peter. *Pensions and Investments.*

Brinson, Gary, L. Rudolph Hood, and Gilbert Beebower. "Determinants of Portfolio Performance." *Financial Analysts Journal* (July–August 1986): 39–44.

Brunel, Jean. "A Tax-Aware Approach to the Management of Multiclass Portfolios." *Journal of Private Wealth Management* (Spring 1999): 57–70.

Brunel, Jean. "A Tax-Efficient Portfolio Construction Model." *Journal of Wealth Management* (Fall 2001): 43–50.

Cestnik, Mark. "Balancing Act." In *Quantitative Capital.* TD Asset Management, 2003.

Chamberlain, Mark, and Jay Jordan. "Core/Satellite Portfolio Construction." *Senior Consultant* (January–February 2002): 1–4.

Chamberlain, Mark, and Jay Jordan. "Core/Satellite Portfolio Construction," Barclays White Paper (http://www.ishares.com/material_download.jhtml?relative Path=/repository/material/downloads/intermediary/active_risk_budgeting.pdf).

Common Fund News (Spring 2000).

Ellis, Charles. "Levels of the Game." *Journal of Portfolio Management* (Winter 2000): 12–15.

Evensky, Harold. *Wealth Management.* McGraw-Hill, 1997.

Evensky, Harold. "Heading for Disaster." *Financial Advisor* (April 2001): 65–69.

Fama, Eugene, and Kenneth French. "Cross-Section of Variation of Expected Stock Returns." *Journal of Finance* (June 1992).

Futrelle, David. "Stock Research: The Search for Objective Ratings." *Money* (February 2003): 69.

Gibson, Roger. *Asset Allocation: Balancing Financial Risk.* McGraw-Hill, 2000.

Hunt, Lacy, and David Hoisington. "Estimating the Stock/Bond Risk Premium." *Journal of Portfolio Management* (Winter 2003): 28–34.

Ibbotson, Roger, and Peng Chen. "Long-Run Stock Returns: Participating in the Real Economy." *Financial Analysts Journal* (January–February 2003): 88–98.

Ilmanen, Antti. "Expected Returns on Stocks and Bonds." *Journal of Portfolio Management* (Winter 2003): 7–27.

Jeffrey, Robert. "Tax-Efficient Investing Is Easier Said Than Done." *Journal of Wealth Management* (Spring 2001): 10–18.

Leibowitz, Martin, forum chair. TIAA-CREF/AIMR Equity Risk Premium Forum, New York. November 8, 2001.

Masters, Seth. "Rebalancing." *Journal of Portfolio Management* (Spring 2003): 52–57.

Merrill Lynch. "The Great Portfolio Divide: Updating Our Global Portfolio Strategy Themes." *Global Portfolio Monthly* (November 4, 2003): 2–5.

Milligan, Jack. "The New Face of Investing in the 21st Century." *CFA Magazine* (January–February 2003): 33–35.

Picerno, James. "The Equity Risk Premium Has Been Drying Up: How Long Will the Drought Last?" *Bloomberg Wealth Manager* (May 2003): 85–87.

Quisenberry, Cliff. "Optimal Allocation of a Taxable Core and Satellite Portfolio Structure." *Journal of Wealth Management* (Summer 2003): 18–26.

Reichenstein, William. "Prospects for Long-Run Stock Returns: Implications for Individual Investors." Presentation to TIAA-CREF Financial Advisor Advisory Board. New York. August 2001.

Santoli, Michael. "Unreal Expectations." *Barron's* April 21 2003, 27.

Stein, David. "Equity Portfolio Structure and Design in the Presence of Taxes." *Journal of Wealth Management* (Fall 2001): 37–42.

Stein, David, and Greg McIntire. "Overlay Portfolio Management in a Multi-Manager Account." *Journal of Wealth Management* (Spring 2003): 57–71.

Stein, David, and Cliff Quisenberry. "Core-and-Satellite Portfolio and Taxes." *Investment Advisor* (April 2003): 95–96.

Vanguard Investments, Financial Intermediary Services. *How Do You Get to Investment Excellence?* Vanguard Investments, 2002.

"Creating Value Through DB Outsourcing." News feature, Vanguard Group, 2003.

Chapter Notes

1. The reference to malpractice, while dramatic, is included to emphasize the importance of the issue. This chapter suggests neither that practitioners must modify their portfolio design nor that failure to do so is malpractice. It does argue that professional practice standards and relevant law (detailed in note 16) require practitioners to have a reasonable basis for their professional recommendations. Consequently, a practitioner who concludes that equity returns are likely to be significantly less than the assumption used as the basis for current portfolio design must consider whether a change in design is necessary. A revised return assumption without consideration of the consequences—that is, "blind adherence"—would be inappropriate.

2. Alternatives include the "spectrum" strategy, described in "Rethinking the Barbell," Goldman Sachs (August 2002); "wholestock" portfolios, described in Ennis Knupp + Associates Research, "The Case for Wholestock Portfolios: Failure of the Multiple-Specialist Architecture," *Journal of Portfolio Management* (Summer 2001); Kevin Means's proposal for an "active long portfolio" in "A Proposal for Tax-Efficient Active Equity Investing," *Journal of Wealth Management* (Winter 2002); and the "all capitalization and style tax-aware" models proposed by Douglas Rogers in "Tax Aware Equity Manager Allocation: A Practitioner's Perspective," *Journal of Wealth Management* (Winter 2001).

3. Also known as "core and explore," "core and edge," and "tax-aware equity allocation."

4. Bernard Scherer, "Core Satellite Investing: Harmony Through Separation," Risk Management for Investors, www.risknet.com, September 2001, pp. S21–S25.

5. This chapter focuses on the design of retail equity portfolios. The discussion separates the investor universe into two major categories, retail and institutional. The primary demarcations between categories are portfolio size and tax status. The chapter defines "retail" as taxable portfolios of less than $50 million and sheltered portfolios of less than $20 million. This criterion is based on my studies estimating the point above which asset size and related market efficiencies may overcome the drag of taxes and expenses. Although investors' needs and resources are unique, the investment portfolios of most individual investors and advisers' clients fall well below these thresholds.

6. Gibson (2000) and Evensky (1997).

7. Large, mid-, and small capitalizations; growth, core, and value styles.

8. As Evensky (2002) noted, "Wealth managers are faced with the unnerving prospect that the institutional conventions of portfolio design may soon be reduced to nothing more than a shimmering mirage—at least for portfolios that hold taxable investments. The prospect of substantially diminished equity risk premium is a 'malignancy' that threatens the very foundations of contemporary wealth management."

9. See Reichenstein (2001), Leibowitz (2001), Deutsche (2001), and Bernstein (2002).

10. The returns referenced below are generally nominal. Real returns estimates are 2–3 percent lower.
• *CFA Magazine,* "Based on interviews with a cross-section of investment professionals, projected returns for U.S. equities over the next five years generally range between 5 percent and 10 percent." Milligan (2003)
• *Financial Analysts Journal,* "To summarize, the long-term supply of equity return is estimated to be 9.37 percent (6.09 percent after inflation)." Ibbotson and Chen (2003)
• *Money,* "We figure that investors can expect a long-term return of 7 percent or 8 percent, not 10 percent, on equities." (2003)
• *Journal of Portfolio Management,* "All three considerations affecting relative stock and bond returns—the inflation rate, the dividend yield, and the P/E ratio—suggest that we are coming into a time when stock returns will be considerably diminished relative to the return on bonds." Hunt (2003)
• *Journal of Portfolio Management,* "A moderately constructive case is that feasible and subjectively expected long-run equity returns are in balance near 7–8 percent. The deliberately optimistic assumptions … give rise to 8 percent feasible (nominal) return." Ilmanen (2003)
• *Bloomberg Wealth Manager,* "The Financial Executives International latest polling of 400 executives (CFOs) in March reveals an average equity risk premium forecast of 3.7 percent over the next ten years." Picerno (2003)
• *Barron's,* "If today's stubbornly high valuations indicate that investors are more willing to accept somewhat smaller gains, 7 percent to 8 percent [nominal] a year isn't unreasonable, according to Asness. That would still mean stocks are a decent bet for the long run but are nothing like the great bargain they've been for most of modern times." Santoli (2003)

11. For example, Jeffrey (2001).

12. For this discussion, alpha is used to describe return in excess of the broad market.

13. For example, in the 15 percent return environment, an additional 1 percent in expenses and taxes would reduce the net-net real return to 8.7 percent—a modest 11 percent reduction and still a significant return. One percent of additional

costs in the 8 percent environment would reduce the net-net real return by *almost* one-third to a depressing total of 2.7 percent. Viewed in terms of savings, a 50 basis-point reduction in expenses and taxes, in the low-return environment, may increase the client's net-net real return by almost 20 percent.

14. Although unsubstantiated, investors and practitioners incorporate generous assumptions of alpha. For illustrative purposes, the example assumes a gross alpha of 4 percent (independent of the level of nominal returns), with a total alpha expense of 2.5 percent (trading costs, spreads, management fees). All returns are assumed to be taxed at 15 percent. Basic core investment costs are conservatively estimated at 1 percent.

15. I believe that the assumption of an effective 15 percent tax rate is conservative. As Jeffery (1993) demonstrated, taxes are a function of holding period, not of turnover. As a consequence, traditional active management, even with modest turnover, is inherently tax inefficient. Evensky (2002) demonstrated that even most index funds are subject to an effective tax rate of more than 20 percent (that is, at least equal to the effective long-term capital gains rate).

16. Malpractice is herein used to describe a violation of professional standards causing harm (also see note 1). For an investment adviser/wealth manager, the primary applicable standards would include AIMR Standards, CFP Board Ethics and Practice Standards, ERISA, and the Third Restatement of Trusts (and related prudent investor acts). Selected sections applicable to the issues discussed in this paper include:

AIMR Standards: Reasonable Basis and Representations. Members shall
• exercise diligence and thoroughness in making investment recommendations or in taking investment actions
• have a reasonable and adequate basis, supported by appropriate research and investigation, for such recommendations or actions

CFP Board: Rules That Relate to the Principle of Competence Rule 301:
• A CFP Board designee shall keep informed of developments in the field of financial planning

ERISA: Prudent-Man Standard of Care: A fiduciary shall discharge his duties with respect to a plan solely in the interest of the participants and beneficiaries and for the exclusive purpose of
• providing benefits to participants and their beneficiaries and
• defraying reasonable expenses of administering the plan
with the care, skill, prudence, and diligence under the circumstances then prevailing that a prudent man acting in a like capacity and familiar with such matters would use in the conduct of an enterprise of a like character and with like aims.

Third Restatement
• Realistic, cautiously evaluated return expectations of active investment programs must justify these extra costs and risks. The greater the trustee's departure from one of the valid passive strategies, the greater is likely to be the burden of justification.
• Trustees have a duty to avoid fees, transaction costs, and other expenses that are

not justified by needs and realistic objectives of the trust's investment program.
• If the trustee possesses a degree of skill greater than an individual of ordinary intelligence, the trustee is liable for a loss that results from failure to make reasonably diligent use of that skill.

17. According to Ohio State, it was pioneered in the early 1990s by Jim Nichols, the university treasurer.

18. The two exceptions uncovered during a literature search were Jonathan Clements's December 14, 1999, *Wall Street Journal* article, "Making the Most of Your Weakness," in which he wrote, "Investors should consider a 'core-and-satellite' approach in which index funds are held along with actively managed funds"; and Jim Jubak's June 27, 2000, Web journal, in which he wrote, "A portfolio with a core of long-term holdings orbited by riskier equities seems just right for today's volatile market…. I've heard it called 'core and explore' and 'core and satellite,' among other things. I like to call it 'core and edge.' "

19. For example, Merrill Lynch: "Building investment portfolios that separate a core strategy allocation from an opportunistic allocation is the most efficient and effective way of taking advantage of any investment environment." (2003); Vanguard Investments: "Vanguard believes that, for most investors, a sure way of allocating assets to protect and grow wealth is a core-satellite approach" (2002) and "Plan sponsors are gravitating toward a core-satellite approach in their DB plan investment lineups" (2003); and TD (Waterhouse) Asset Management: "A great way to help you avoid short-term knee-jerk reactions that can destabilize your portfolio and let you stray from your carefully constructed asset mix is to invest the core portion in a balanced fund … complemented by one or more specialty funds. This type of strategy is often referred to as 'core and satellite' approach, and is intuitively appealing."

20. Legal & General, U.K. (in excess of $200 billion under management), Tom Breedon, director of investments: "I believe that people should have 'a core and satellite' approach to structuring their investments"; Old Mutual, South Africa: "core-and-satellite approach is adopted for the South African equity portfolios"; Commonwealth Bank, Australia (second largest retail fund manager in Australia): "pursues a core and satellite philosophy of investment management"; other international examples include Mvelaphanda Asset Managers, South Africa; Family Money, Westminster Portfolio Services, Thailand; Dresdnerbank Investment Management, Germany; CI Global Advisors, Canada.

21. In this discussion, the expression "market risk" refers to the risk taken to earn market returns, that is, the returns attributable to the three Fama-French factors (beta, size, and BtM). Active risk is the risk an active manager takes to achieve active return. As Waring (2000) notes, "An active manager will always have an active return; only the sign is in doubt."

22. For example, a search of the Morningstar database (Principia April 30, 2003) screened for unique active managers with 80 percent or more in U.S. equities

resulted in a list of 2,228 funds. The average R^2 was 70. In effect, 70 percent of the manager fee was wasted, because that portion of the return would have been captured by a core market allocation.

23. John Campbell and Luis Viceira, winners of the TIAA-CREF 2002 Paul A. Samuelson award for their study *Strategic Asset Allocation,* maintain that "investors can benefit from ongoing reassessment of market conditions by reducing holdings of risky assets when they appear overvalued relative to historical norms, and increasing them when they appear undervalued."

PART TWO

STRATEGY

Contributors to "Part One: The Portfolio" enter the realm of widely held theory and throw mud on the icons, but our strategists prefer not to dwell too long on the head of the pin. Only solid deliverables are discussed here. This "practical potpourri" is a collection of wide-ranging contributions related only by their references to issues of investment implementation and practical strategic solutions for the issues raised; hence the catchall rubric "Strategy."

Tim Kochis begins the section with insights on strategies related to the thorny issue of concentrated stock positions. David Stein considers the global question of tax-efficient management of multimanager equity portfolios. Bob Gordon and Tom Boczar, specialists in inventive tax strategies, correlate the goal of tax efficiency with appropriate strategies. And Gobind Daryanani considers the oft-debated question of how to most efficiently and strategically use the tax advantages of a client's sheltered account.

However, instead of choosing traditional sides in the battle (for example, stocks in or out of the IRA), he proposes a new and powerful alternative approach.

From start to finish, a most productive journey.

S. Timothy Kochis

Tim Kochis, a longtime friend, is president of Kochis Fitz Tracy Fitzhugh & Gott. He is one of the country's most respected wealth managers. As someone who has been in the trenches for decades (in fact, he designed and built many of the trenches), there's no one better suited to mapping out specific and practical solutions to a very common problem faced by practitioners—concentrated equity positions. My guess is that even advisers quite familiar with tax-implementation strategies will find something in Kochis's discussion that they wish they'd encountered sooner.

David M. Stein

David Stein and Jean Brunel (see "Part One: The Portfolio") are crusaders in the reformation under way for managing investments in a taxable environment. Here, Stein addresses one of the most misused investment catchphrases—"tax efficiency." Ever since Jeffrey and Arnott demonstrated that management of the holding period, not turnover, drives tax efficiency, tax sensitivity has been a hot subject in the professional press. Unfortunately, the focus of discussion has gotten stuck on individual investments. You need only consider, for example, the marketing material extolling tax-efficient funds and the tax efficiency of separate accounts. From a retail adviser's perspective, clients don't just own investments; they own portfolios consisting of multiple investments (for example, funds and separate accounts). Stein keeps our attention from wandering away from the tax efficiency of the entire portfolio and focusing instead only on its components.

Robert Gordon and Thomas Boczar

Bob Gordon is chief executive officer of Twenty-First Securities, and Tom Boczar, his associate, is a chartered financial analyst and vice chairman of the Private Wealth Management Committee of the New York Society of Security Analysts. For the last decade, Evensky, Brown & Katz has turned to Gordon and Boczar whenever it faced a complex client tax issue. Just as we live and breathe financial planning, Gordon and Boczar live and breathe tax planning. That's good news, because keeping abreast of tax-planning strategies is a full-time job. When we asked them to contribute a chapter to *Think Tank*, we encouraged them to be as comprehensive in their coverage as possible, because most planners may be familiar with one or two strategies but few are familiar with the wide range of approaches now available. Also, from our own experience, we recognized that even basic familiarity does not necessarily mean a complete or even accurate understanding of how the strategy may be implemented. Gordon and Boczar delivered as expected—a wonderfully comprehensive, up-to-date, and practical chapter on tax strategies and investing.

Gobind Daryanani

Because most retail investors have both sheltered accounts (for example, IRAs, 401(k)s) and taxable accounts, a significant investment issue is deciding what investments to place in each of the accounts. Although innumerable papers have been written on the subject, there is no consensus as to the "right" solution, and most practitioners either use simple defaults (for example, shelter bonds first or allocate pro rata) or (in true seat-of-the-pants tradition) custom allocate each client. Daryanani suggests a very logical "difference method," which he describes as a "generic framework for finding the optimal location for multiple asset classes." His difference method provides a strategy that's quantifiable and sensitive to the client's unique tax and investment constraints. Daryanani's studies indicate that the strategy can provide a net annual 20-basis-point return premium over traditional methods. Whether the use of the difference method will generate this alpha in your client's portfolios is unknown. What we do know is that the thought process and strategy he proposes is too important to ignore.

CHAPTER 5

Managing Concentrated Stock Positions

S. TIMOTHY KOCHIS

H aving a large position in one stock isn't always a problem. In fact, it may even be essential if the objective is to maintain or acquire control of a small company. And when the size of the total portfolio is large enough, the risk of one part being concentrated may be completely tolerable. At Kochis Fitz, we work with a client, the chief executive officer of a public company, whose company stock makes up more than 85 percent of his net worth. The balance, however, is more than $30 million and is broadly diversified across an array of assets not closely correlated to that company stock. If concentration like that is a problem, it's one most people would love to have.

More typically, however, concentration is at least theoretically unwise because of the risk. Mainstream investment theory holds that one is not compensated for taking risks that can be reduced. Since diversification of a concentrated position would mitigate its risk, failing to diversify means one is accepting risk for no reward.

The classic "efficient frontier" diagram in **FIGURE 5.1** shows that a concentrated stock position, A, has the same expected return as portfolio C but more risk—or as much risk as portfolio B but with less expected return. The situation can be ameliorated by diversifying either toward portfolio C, with lower-risk alternatives, or toward portfolio B, with higher-return alternatives.

Most people, of course, are eager to maximize their risk-adjusted investment returns. But some can't easily do so because of concerns over tax liability. Particularly for corporate executives, the alternatives for addressing the problem are often constrained by post–initial public offering "lockups," specific

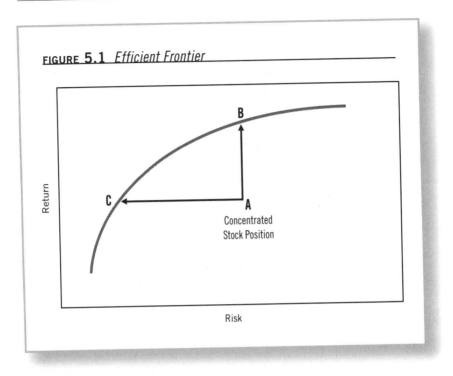

FIGURE 5.1 *Efficient Frontier*

employer-mandated shareholding requirements, and, hardly least, Securities and Exchange Commission (SEC) restrictions on short-term trading or the use of inside information. Limitations notwithstanding, techniques exist—some very simple, others quite elaborate—for easing this concentration risk.

Sale and Diversification

Early in 2002, I met with prospective clients who were in their late fifties. The husband had just retired from a long and successful career with a very large public company. Their largest individual holding was more than $8 million in his employer's stock. Its price had been falling, and the couple was quite agitated about what to do next to preserve this large value. They had already been to see other advisers and were confused. "Some people say we should do puts or buy a collar. Another told us to do something called a 'prepaid forward.' Frankly, I didn't understand that. I hope you can help."

"All of those things, and others, could be appropriate," I explained, "but let's start with the simplest steps. We could just sell it. Even if your basis were zero, the worst that happens is a capital gains tax of about 25 percent." (When the 2003 tax law changed the federal capital gains rate to 15 percent, the total for a California taxpayer went to about 20 percent.) "With the remaining 75 percent, you get to do whatever you want," I said. "Things get better if you have any basis at all."

"We don't have any net gains in this holding," the husband shot back. "Overall, it's at a loss!"

"Well, then, why don't we just sell it—today?" I responded. At that suggestion, the wife jumped up, came around the conference table, and planted a big kiss on my cheek—and I had a new client.

The advice this couple had been offered as they shopped for an adviser demonstrates that too frequently advisers are so in love with fancy strategies that they fail to inquire about the most basic facts of clients' circumstances —such as the tax basis—and fail to gauge clients' appetite for complex solutions. The simplest solutions are often the best in terms of controlling costs, reducing delay, and gaining clients' confidence in the outcome. Now that maximum federal capital gains tax rates are only 15 percent, many more clients will opt for the simple sale even if their tax basis is very low. And if the size of the gain is fairly modest, say, 25 percent or so, the tax toll may be well under 5 percent of the total value. Diversified proceeds don't have to perform particularly well to quickly compensate for such a low transition charge.

Stock Options

Many corporate executives with concentrated long positions in a company's stock also have substantial holdings of stock options. Here, the diversification strategy can have a two-pronged approach. To protect against the risk, we recommend that they sell the long shares but perhaps keep the options unexercised to preserve the upside potential. In our experience, this approach is the direct opposite of what most clients would intuit. They consider the long shares "real," and having developed a kind of loyalty to them, they're reluctant to part with "their" shares, already in hand. Option shares, in contrast, are seen by many option holders as only a prospective asset, and it's psychologically much easier for them to cash in those shares.

To reverse this perspective, apply some economic logic. First, from the tax standpoint, the risk of long shares is much worse than that of options. A dollar loss in the stock price costs as much as $.85 (after 15 percent federal tax, assuming no state tax) for a long share but only $.6355 (after 35 percent federal ordinary income tax plus 1.45 percent Medicare tax) for a share under option. Second, from the standpoint of investment leverage, option shares are much more powerful on the upside. Because of the fixed bargain price, an option's performance can be *less* than other, diversified investments and still produce more value. The higher the exercise price is in relation to the market value (that is, the smaller the spread), the truer this is. Low exercise prices have less leverage and behave much like long shares. A long share in any event has no such leverage; it must perform at the same rate as diversified alternatives or it will produce the problem that raised the issue of concentration risk to begin with.

That's not to say that it's necessarily safe for clients to hold large option positions. The concentration risk is still there; option shares may need to be diversified as well. It means only that when the client has both long shares and options, the long shares should be the first to go.

Diversification and Deferred Compensation

We often encounter a very powerful element in many executives' compensation package: a deferred-compensation plan that permits an investment measure tied to a diversified equity portfolio, like the Standard & Poor's 500 stock index, for example. Participating in such a plan can provide a strong investment opportunity that serves as an attractive destination for diversification proceeds. Although such a plan can't accept proceeds of the sale of long shares and usually can't directly accept the results of options transactions, the desired results can be accomplished indirectly. Clients can heavily defer salary and bonus payments into the deferred-compensation plan and live instead on the proceeds of stock sales or option exercises and sales of the resulting stock.

This strategy usually requires a commitment far in advance, in that many deferred-compensation plans require an irrevocable election in the year before the income would otherwise be paid. Since the decision usually can't be easily changed, it adds an important element of discipline to actually getting the concentrated stock option positions liquidated. Often, clients will acknowledge the wisdom of diversification, but they just can't bring themselves to pull the trigger when the time comes. In this deferred-compensation strategy, having money to live on provides an imperative.

Section 10b5-1 Plans

For corporate directors and senior corporate executives with access to information about the company that may not be available to the public, virtually any sale of the company's stock can enter the realm of illegality. Many corporations establish a relatively brief trading window each quarter, following the release of quarterly data, during which it's presumably safe for these executives to transact in the company stock. Recognizing that such brief and infrequent windows could unfairly limit legitimate diversification strategies, the SEC promulgated Rule 10b5-1 in 2000. This rule permits transactions under prearranged plans or by independent third-party discretion, even if material, nonpublic (inside) information exists at the time of the actual transaction. As long as no inside information was known when the plan was put in place and no amendments or countervailing strategies are adopted, a 10b5-1 plan provides an affirmative defense. These plans can cover sales of long shares and options transactions and can have very elaborate parameters—for example, sell X number of shares on the first trading day of each quarter, as long as the price is above $Y/share and average trading volumes for the prior five trading days is greater than Z shares/day—to improve the prospect of actually achieving the desired result.

These plans are becoming common, and we expect that before long, most public companies will *require* their officers and directors to have such plans in place. One excuse for failing to diversify—the SEC won't let me do it—could soon fade away.

Misused Section 83(b) Elections

An obvious but important way to manage a concentrated stock position is to avoid buying even more shares. To the surprise of many employees and their advisers, that's exactly what happens in making the Section 83(b) election. Just as grants of restricted stock have become popular once again in the wake of supposed stock option abuses, the opportunity to make an election under Section 83(b) will also attract heightened attention.

Restricted shares generally aren't taxable when granted because they carry, usually for a specified time, a substantial risk of forfeiture. Consequently, tax liability doesn't arise until the restrictions lapse. But one can, within thirty days of the grant, make an election to take the current value into ordinary income, hoping that later, when the stock is eventually sold, the value will be higher, with the subsequent gain taxable as capital gain. This prospect is so seductive that many make the Section 83(b) election without considering its consequences.

First, the client must be confident that the risk of forfeiture will not in fact occur. Next, the client must be confident that the stock will rise in value at least enough to compensate for the opportunity cost of the actual taxes to be paid under the election. But if the client is confident both that the risk won't occur and that the required minimum appreciation will, then there's an even better course of action: forgoing the election and taking the amount of the would-be tax payment to buy more of the stock on the market. That strategy *will* yield a better overall result.[1] So if a client wouldn't buy more of what is already a concentrated position, they most certainly shouldn't make an election under Section 83(b) for that same stock. Recall what the fundamental issue here is. It's not that the stock's value might go *up* at a handsome rate. If we could be certain of that, diversification would make no sense. Rather, diversification makes sense because the stock's value might go *down*—and the client realistically has neither foreknowledge nor control over what direction that price movement might take.

Gift Strategies

When direct sales—or avoided purchasing—can't thoroughly manage a concentrated position, gifts of the stock can be the next best solution.

Gifts to Family

Gifts to a client's family have the obvious benefit of potentially lower tax rates. Under the new tax law, lower-bracket taxpayers may pay as little as 5 percent federal capital gains tax and, as scheduled for the year 2008, a zero tax may even apply. More important than this advantage may be the psychic distance a gift can provide. The client might be very reluctant to part with a concentrated position. The children (or their trustees or custodians) probably have no such problem.

In addition to these advantages, gifts to family can, of course, also minimize the overall costs of family wealth transfers. That's especially true if the transfer is to a family limited partnership, where potentially substantial discounts may be available due to the recipients' lack of control and, possibly, the assets' lack of marketability under the terms of the partnership.

Similar discounts can apply when the gift is the transfer of a non-qualified stock option. So when the option is for stock of the concentrated position, such a gift not only removes the option's value from the donor's concentrated holding, it also removes that value from the donor's estate—as well as the income tax that will be incurred when the option is exercised. Similarly, if an appreciated position is transferred to a defective grantor trust, the asset value is removed from the estate, but the income tax liability at sale remains (intentionally) with the donor, removing that gains tax amount from the estate as well, with no transfer tax incurred on that additional transfer of value to the trust's beneficiaries.

Gifts to Charity

Gifts of highly appreciated assets to charity are generally a well-understood and broadly used strategy. The gift of long-term capital gain assets (the amount of any short-term gain is *not* deductible) removes that appreciation from income tax liability and generates a deduction for the full market value of the donated property. Certain limits apply. When appreciated assets make up the gift, the charitable deduction is limited to 30 percent of adjusted gross income (AGI). If the gift is to a private foundation, that limit is further reduced to 20 percent of AGI. In either case, any amounts not used in the year of contribution may be carried over for the next five years.

It's important to recognize that gifts to charity are not free. They all have an actual cost in the form of the net consumable wealth forgone. If the assets had been sold, net proceeds would be available to spend or reinvest. The gift's tax savings from the charitable deduction are the only "proceeds" that come from making a charitable gift instead. The difference between these two results is the net cost of the charitable gift. There is *always* such a cost. So genuine philanthropic intent is always an essential component of a wise gift strategy.

As is necessarily the case when tax rates are reduced, the cost of charitable contributions was substantially increased by the 2003 tax law. Not only has the available after-tax proceeds from a sale alternative been increased (only 15 percent federal capital gains tax instead of the former 20 percent), but the tax benefits of the deduction have been reduced (35 percent versus the former 38.6 percent). Consequently, even for a concentrated position with zero basis, the lowest cost of a charitable contribution has gone up from 41.4 percent of the asset's value (80 percent after-tax sale proceeds less the 38.6 percent tax savings) to 50 percent of that value (85 percent proceeds less the 35 percent tax savings). Philanthropic intent is now even more important as a motivator for the charitable gift.

Charitable remainder trusts (CRTs). The CRT is a favorite device of many wealth managers because it seems to offer the best of both worlds, achieving a substantial tax deduction while retaining the benefit of an income stream derived from the diversified proceeds of the sale of the concentrated position. It's crucial to recognize, however, that the CRT merely postpones the tax; it does not eliminate it. The CRT's payment stream carries out not only the current tax consequences of the CRT assets' yield and transactions but also the accumulated gains from the initial sale of the original donation. Further, the benefit to charity is delayed for perhaps many years until that interim payment period comes to an end. Together, these drawbacks could significantly compromise the client's real objectives, both frustrating the owner's access to the assets and postponing the intended benefit to charity. Considering the alternative of an outright sale of some of the position and an outright charitable gift of the rest, many clients conclude that CRTs are not worth the effort.

Gifts of nonqualified stock options to charity. As explained regarding gifts to family, some stock option plans permit gifts of options. Some plans also permit them to be given to charity, in which case there is an opportunity to use the Internal Revenue Service's "safe harbor" valuation to significant advantage. The option's value, calculated using the Black-Scholes option-pricing model, is likely to be substantial, giving rise to a large charitable deduction. Note that potentially large mismatches could arise among the amount of the client's charitable deduction (Black-Scholes value), the benefit actually received by the charity, and the corresponding additional AGI actually incurred by the donor (the spread, at the *charity's* exercise, between the stock's market value and the option's exercise price).

There could also be a mismatch in timing: the charitable deduction arises in the year of the gift; the increment to the client's AGI attributable to the exercise occurs when the charity actually exercises the option.

Transferring stock options to charity, where permitted, can be an effective technique, but it may make even more sense for the client to cash in those options, freeing up liquid, spendable—or investable—proceeds and instead transfer *other* appreciated assets to charity.

Lowest-basis shares first. In almost all cases, it will be most appropriate for clients to give away their *lowest*-basis assets first, since they have the greatest capital gains tax liability. Some clients want to hold on to assets with the *very lowest* basis, in anticipation of a step-up in basis at their death. With the scheduled major changes to the *amount* of basis change that will be permitted, the merits of this delay have been greatly reduced. Those merits were rarely compelling even under the old estate tax law. Given the lower risk of the diversified sale proceeds, it never takes very long for the benefits of predeath sales to overcome the prospective benefits of even an unlimited step-up opportunity.

Alternative Strategies

If neither sales nor gifts thoroughly solve the concentration problem, many additional strategies remain.

Margined Diversification

The use of margin has always carried a somewhat dangerous reputation among planners, and many clients have an almost visceral distaste for this technique. Nevertheless, within manageable parameters, margin can *reduce* the risk in an otherwise concentrated position. If the client is unwilling or unable to sell the concentrated position, that position may still serve as collateral for margin borrowing. The proceeds of that margin can then be placed in a broadly diversified supplement to the undiversified position to yield an aggregate portfolio that becomes less risky—and more liquid—than the undiversified holding was.

Although margin has a generally poor reputation, its judicious use can be highly advantageous. As long as the after-tax return from the assets purchased on margin exceeds the after-tax cost of that borrowing, that positive portfolio leverage can substantially improve net investment results, especially over time. If investment returns achieve just a 5 percent after-tax rate, there could be a 3 percent advantage over the after-tax cost of margin prevalent in late 2003 to early 2004 (about 2 percent). For every $100,000 invested on margin, that's an *incremental* after-tax return of $3,000—every year that the relationship applies.

FIGURE 5.2

ACTUAL DECLINE IN CONCENTRATED POSITION (LESS TAXABLE GAIN)	TOLERABLE DECLINE IN MARGINED POSITION (TAX LOSSES)
20%	26.5%
30	16.5
40	6.5

This strategy is not without risk. Margin magnifies both the upside and the downside potential of the margined portfolio. The upside, of course, is no problem. To protect against the downside, we generally limit our clients' margin to no more than 25 percent of the premargin balance. This will avoid margin calls that could force the client to sell assets at precisely the wrong time, when markets are down. At that modest rate of margin use, the aggregate portfolio (some diversified, some not) could decline by nearly 70 percent before a margin call would arise. Even if a client were to use 100 percent margin (the maximum at the outset) by acquiring diversified assets equal to the undiversified collateral, either or both segments of the aggregate can decline substantially before the aggregate portfolio's violation of the typical 35 percent net equity ("maintenance margin") requirement forces a sale (see **FIGURE 5.2**).

If any such losses did occur, any reluctance to sell because of capital gains tax could disappear. If the concentrated position loses value, the feared taxable gain is reduced. If the diversified portfolio supplement loses value, there would now be capital losses to offset gains in the concentrated position.

Tax-Managed Index-Proxy Accounts

Another device, developed relatively recently, for managing concentrated positions involves the use of an index-proxy account that mimics an index, typically the S&P 500, with low (1 or 2 percent) tracking error. These accounts select a large sample of the actual index to achieve a very close approximation of the index's performance, but the positions are actively managed both to avoid further exposure to the already concentrated position and to harvest tax losses as they occur in some of the positions while generally retaining gains to reduce the overall tax exposure of the very-near-index performance.

This strategy can be very attractive even when there's no concentrated position to manage. If an index exposure is a component of the overall investment plan, the advantageous tax consequences of this technique can substantially overcome its higher management costs (65–100 basis points versus 15–20 basis points for an index fund, or even less in the case of an exchange-traded fund).

But these tax-managed accounts are especially appealing when a concentrated position has a substantial tax liability that makes an outright sale unattractive to the client. Here, the harvested tax losses in the *other* components of the index-proxy account can offset periodic sales and diversification of the low-basis, concentrated stock position. Over time, the client achieves a more broadly diversified portfolio and minimizes the tax cost of getting to that result.

Exchange Funds

Exchange funds might be described as a much cruder but long-tenured antecedent to the index-proxy account. In an exchange fund, a large number of different investors' concentrated stock positions are assembled to eventually achieve a more diversified portfolio. The tax exposure of the individual contributions is not softened, even gradually, and no ongoing effort to diversify is undertaken within the fund. At the end of the exchange fund's duration (usually at least seven years), each initial contributor receives a pro rata portfolio made up of pieces of all the initial contributions, with a tax basis equal to the original tax basis of the contributor's initial position. Thus, the tax exposure is merely postponed, not reduced. Further, the diversification is itself usually very limited. The stocks in the fund are almost always very large domestic stocks in sectors that have simultaneously enjoyed exceptional performance. Exchanging one's highly appreciated Oracle shares for a basket of highly appreciated shares of Microsoft, Sun Microsystems, et cetera, is not really solving the problem.

Further drawbacks include the long holding period, typically high costs (1.5–2.5 percent for a portfolio that remains virtually untouched over that span), and, hardly least, the tax law requirement that at least 20 percent of the fund involve illiquid assets. This is very often some suboptimal real estate asset that can't be sold separately. In our experience, the benefits of an exchange fund seldom justify its costs and inefficiencies.

Derivatives

For clients willing to purchase derivative securities, additional strategies for managing concentration risk become available.

Selling covered calls. The simplest of these strategies is to *sell* a call option (that is, the right to buy at a higher price for some time up to the expiration of the option). Selling calls, like other derivative securities, can be highly profitable—or very risky if one doesn't already own the shares subject to the call. To satisfy the purchase right, one might have to either buy the shares necessary to settle or buy back the much-appreciated call option—in either case, at a potentially substantial loss.

But in this situation, the client already owns a position that he's reluctant to sell—because of tax exposure, for example. Selling a call against that position has two large benefits. The premium received for selling the call can itself be invested in diversified assets. Second, the higher future call price sets a psychologically significant trigger for a future sale, rewarded, if it occurs, with greater proceeds than can be achieved today. Put another way, if the client is reluctant to sell at today's price, would he be more inclined to sell later, at a higher price, and get an additional payment for waiting? In our experience, many clients find this argument compelling and use this strategy to commit to an eventual sale.

Buying puts. The reverse of the call strategy is to *buy* a put option (that is, the right to sell at some lower price for some span of time). This strategy can ensure that the risk of concentration has at least some limit. Unlike the call strategy, this approach has no direct, immediate diversification benefit (no premium to invest) and, in fact, involves additional cost (the price of the put purchased) that's indirectly being invested in the already concentrated position. The best that can be achieved with this strategy is to set a limit on losses, and the client has to pay for that limit. Once clients see the put strategy in this light, initial reluctance to sell just because of taxes often disappears. If the reason for not selling now is *not* about taxes, but because of securities law constraints, puts are of little help. Certain officers and directors, as Section 16b insiders, are not permitted to purchase puts in their company stock.

Collars. The two derivative strategies discussed above are often combined to create a "collar" of prices above and below the current price to ensure a relatively narrow range of price exposure. Sometimes, this collar can be structured to be "costless": times and prices are selected so that the premium to be received for selling the call equals the price to be paid for buying the put. Although this maneuver has no net cost to the client, it also generates no net currently diversifiable proceeds.

Since options generally extend no more than nine months, this can serve only as a temporary holding pattern. Still, it can be long enough to span some anticipated change in tax exposure or some anticipated career event, after which a more comprehensive or permanent resolution of the concentration risk becomes possible.

Prepaid forward contracts. The prepaid forward (or variable delivery) contract is similar to a collar. These contracts provide downside protection in exchange for limiting upside gains. One attraction of a prepaid or variable forward is that it permits the client to immediately convert a large part of the position to cash and thus provide liquidity to diversify the position or to fund near-term consumption goals. However, that liquidity can come at a steep price. Prepaid forwards pay the client only a discounted percentage of the current stock price, the up-front payment, in the form of a loan. These discounts can be quite large, ranging from 15 percent to 25 percent, but all of that up-front payment can be reinvested immediately in diversified assets, with taxes postponed to the end of the contract. Aside from an outright sale, this can still be the best cash flow alternative and is often used by corporate executives following an IPO. They may be eager to sell but cannot do so because of a lock-up period agreed upon with the company's investment bank.

The initial loan is repaid when the contract closes, usually in two years. But the amount to be repaid is at the counterparty's risk. If the stock's value falls below the initial discount amount, no cash is repaid but all the shares are delivered to the counterparty. If the position has appreciated, the client repays (delivers) enough of the shares to repay the loan and give all the appreciation above a threshold to the counterparty. Taxes are reckoned when the contract closes.

CLEARLY, THERE'S A wide range of approaches to addressing the problem of concentrated stock positions, and wealth managers should have all of them in their repertory. The simplest solutions are often the best, and a combination of techniques usually makes the most sense. And even partial solutions are better than none. Wealth managers should coordinate the management of concentrated stock positions as a component of a client's overall financial plan. Awareness of the client's objectives, priorities, and time frames is as important in this area as it is in any other.

Chapter Notes

1. There are two exceptions to this general rule: (1) there is no public market for the stock, so an election under Section 83(b) is the only way to "acquire" the stock; and (2) the client's ordinary income tax rates would increase by more than 6 percent (say from 28 percent to 35 percent) from the current tax year to the year when restrictions lapse. Note, however, that the election could raise the current year's rate by virtue of bringing in the extra income. Even in these cases, clients must still be confident *both* that the risk of forfeiture won't occur *and* that the minimum appreciation to compensate for opportunity cost will occur.

CHAPTER 6

Managing the Taxable Equity Portfolio

DAVID M. STEIN

T ax-sensitive equity portfolio management covers a lot of ground. It's best discussed from a strategic, coordinated perspective that integrates planning, asset allocation, asset location, and tax-sensitive portfolio management. But in this chapter, we'll narrow the focus and discuss how to manage an equity portfolio in the face of taxes. We'll also assume that the investments are for the long term and that the goal is to preserve wealth rather than to create it.

The taxable portfolio is a place where a great deal of value can be inadvertently and carelessly lost.[1] Compared with an institutional pension fund, a private investor has a more limited lifespan and incurs higher costs for borrowing, transactions, and advice; his financial situation is less stable and likely to undergo significant changes, and of course he pays taxes. What's good for the General Motors pension plan is not good enough for him.

Indeed, taxes represent a very large performance drag, often larger than transaction costs, management fees, or inflation. Many advisers believe that investors should not allow tax considerations to dominate their investment decisions. Although there is truth to this, tax considerations do significantly affect investment returns, and failing to understand taxes can be expensive, particularly if taxes are allowed to erode returns over the long term.[2]

Incorporating taxes into the investment decision is not easy. Taxes impose additional complexity, both conceptual (rethinking the strategy) and pragmatic (requiring customization). And the issues they raise are relatively boring, distracting the adviser from more interesting topics such as the state of the economy or the valuation of individual companies. Yet taxes affect both return and risk, and their management cannot be tacked on as an afterthought.

The field of tax-sensitive investment management is still quite immature, although it's developing quickly. In the mid-1990s, few equity managers gave more than lip service to tax issues, but that's changing. More and more investors and their advisers are concerned with taxes: wealthy investors are expecting advisers to produce after-tax reports; regulators are requiring after-tax reports for mutual funds;[3] and in 2002, the CFA Institute revised its standards for after-tax performance reporting.[4] It's now common for fund advertisements in the popular press and on billboards to tout tax efficiency. The separate-account industry, offering tax-advantaged customization, is growing.[5] There is increased attention in both academic and practitioner journals: a new publication, the *Journal of Wealth Management,* was launched in 1998, and in 2003, the *Financial Analysts Journal* published what might be its first article relating to the tax management of portfolios.[6]

Still, there are holdouts. Parts of the consulting community are reluctant to embrace the subject and still focus exclusively on pretax performance, and many managers do not want to report after-tax performance.

The Four Stages of Tax Sensitivity

The distance between the holdout and the tax-sensitive manager covers a broad territory, and it's useful to classify investment managers by the degree of their tax sensitivity. There are four stages to developing the skills required. Moving from one stage to the next often entails a conceptual shift or a willingness to add complexity to the management process. Stages 1 and 2 require a philosophical shift from pretax approaches. Stages 3 and 4 require a technological infrastructure.

Stage 1: The measurement of after-tax return and the evaluation of performance. A manager who does not measure after-tax performance does not quantify how his decisions affect the portfolio. After-tax reporting is the starting point for tax-sensitive investment management. This stage is one of understanding taxes.

Stage 2: The development of a tax-sensitive investment strategy. Once a manager understands after-tax performance, he's necessarily driven to an investment strategy that differs from a tax-exempt strategy. The articulation of this strategy is the manager's next step. This stage is one of adapting to taxes.

Stage 3: The customization of a portfolio to the investor's tax issues and active tax management. Since one size does not fit all, the portfolio needs customized management, often in a separate account. This stage is one of proactively embracing the management of taxes.

Stage 4: The coordination of tax management among managers and broader investor issues. Returning to the realization that true tax management requires a coordinated strategy and that tax decisions are not made in isolation, the tax-sensitive adviser or manager desires to coordinate his decisions with those of other managers. This stage is one of transcending local issues in the portfolio.

Stage 1: Measuring After-Tax Return and Evaluating Performance

The first stage of tax sensitivity requires understanding after-tax performance. Ultimately, it's after-tax performance that matters; pretax performance is an unattainable illusion. A manager or consultant who does not report after taxes does not have a good sense of what has been accomplished, nor does his investor.

The Securities and Exchange Commission (SEC) regards after-tax performance as necessary investor information for mutual funds. The CFA Institute has defined standards for separate accounts and for manager composite reporting. By making simplifications (as is done in all performance reporting), the subject becomes reasonably straightforward and computations are not complex. Both the SEC and the CFA Institute measure taxes using a simplified rate (the maximum marginal federal rate or an "anticipated tax rate") and deduct taxes when they're realized. Disclosures are designed to explain, clarify, and prevent misleading interpretations. These are major improvements over pretax performance measurement with its assumption of zero taxes.

But after-tax performance reports can be tricky and must be interpreted with care. First, since return measures a rate of change in value, we need to value the taxable portfolio. The value of a portfolio with an unrealized tax liability needs to be defined.[7] Second, because after-tax performance depends on investor cash flows and other decisions, not all investors realize the same after-tax performance. Some practitioners seem to become confused by this, but the concept is central to after-tax performance: an individual investor's after-tax performance is idiosyncratic, and his portfolio requires customization. Well-managed, tax-efficient portfolios within a single investment firm will necessarily have different holdings with different cost bases. While tax-exempt managers can achieve a low dispersion of returns, a tax-sensitive manager who treats each client individually will have a relatively high dispersion of returns.

And how should we evaluate after-tax return? Determining whether a manager is good or bad requires comparison with an after-tax benchmark. This is a more complex issue, and the industry has not addressed standards yet, though there are some interesting proposals.

Clearly, we're evading a precise definition of "tax efficiency." Efficiency, an engineering term, implies measurable performance relative to an ideal. Some like to quantify tax efficiency by measuring after-tax performance relative to pretax performance. Because pretax performance is unattainable, this measure is not directly relevant. When after-tax performance exceeds pretax performance, as is common, efficiency by this definition exceeds 100 percent. That's not meaningful, so I prefer to use the term "efficiency" informally, referring qualitatively to the focus that the manager places on taxes.

Some in the industry want to avoid reporting after-tax returns. That choice is not always responsible.

Stage 2: Developing a Tax-Sensitive Investment Strategy

Once a portfolio manager understands how taxes affect performance, he usually adapts his management discipline so as to be aware of taxes. The primary issue is that the portfolio is exposed to taxation (the realization of capital gains) every time the manager or investor changes his mind.

Active portfolio management concentrates the mind. The fundamental tax-management decision that an active manager faces is that of determining how much alpha (excess return) he needs to justify his trade. Here's a simple illustration. Suppose we hold security A, with a market value of $100 and a cost basis of $50. We're indifferent to A, expecting it (and the market) to appreciate by 8 percent per year (no dividends) for twenty years. We prefer security B, which we expect will appreciate 10 percent per year for the next three years and thereafter to behave like the market. In **FIGURE 6.1** we compute the expected final value after twenty years, showing both preliquidation and postliquidation values, for the two decisions—either to do nothing or to trade.[8]

In this case, it would be preferable to hold the security; to justify the trade we would need an alpha of 2.6 percent per year for three years. More

FIGURE **6.1** *Comparison of Two Decisions—Do Nothing or Trade —After 20 Years*

	PRELIQUIDATION	POSTLIQUIDATION	AVERAGE
If we do nothing	$466	$404	$435
If we trade	456	401	428

FIGURE **6.2** *Alpha (Excess Return) Required to Justify a Capital Gain as a Function of Cost Basis and Holding Time*

						COST BASIS						
		0	0.1	0.2	0.3	0.4	0.5	0.6	0.7	0.8	0.9	1
HOLDING TIME	1	17.2	15.2	13.3	11.4	9.6	7.9	6.2	4.6	3.0	1.5	0
	2	8.3	7.3	6.4	5.6	4.7	3.9	3.1	2.3	1.5	0.7	0
	3	5.5	4.8	4.3	3.7	3.1	2.6	2.0	1.5	1.0	0.5	0
	4	4.1	3.6	3.2	2.8	2.3	1.9	1.5	1.1	0.8	0.4	0
	5	3.2	2.9	2.5	2.2	1.9	1.5	1.2	0.9	0.6	0.3	0

generally, **FIGURE 6.2** shows the alpha required to justify the capital gain on a sale. The alpha will depend on the cost basis of the initial security and on the "holding time," the time over which we expect the replacement stock to outperform.

Since the trading decision depends on the cost basis, that is, on the individual investor's cash flow, the decision will generally differ for each investor.

The realization of capital gains is a drag on equity performance. If we can build a buy-and-hold portfolio, we can avoid realizing gains and defer them instead. This is the main reason why cap-weighted indexed portfolios are well known as being tax efficient: most cap-weighted indexed portfolios require only small amounts of trading to keep them aligned with their target.[9]

Of course, it's almost impossible to imagine an investment scenario in which we will not change our minds. We're all subject to uncertainties, our investment and financial situations change over time, and tax rates are sure to change. Yet realizing that there's an expense incurred in changing our minds, we need to make our decisions so as to reduce the cost of taxes when they do become necessary. The higher the tax on changing your mind, the more necessary it is to seek what's known as a *dynamic decision-making policy*.[10]

After an extended market rise, a low-turnover tax-efficient portfolio becomes "locked up," that is, its value grows to be much larger than its cost basis. For the investor with a taxable portfolio, this is not necessarily a bad thing; it's evidence that taxes have been deferred and have not been paid unnecessarily and that the portfolio has increased in value. But it becomes costly to change the portfolio.[11] This is a special case of the fundamental tax-management decision. Lockup is a necessary cost of seeking tax deferral.

An even more extreme example of lockup is the concentration of low-basis holdings. Many investors, after building their wealth, find themselves with concentrated holdings and are reluctant to diversify because of the tax cost of doing so. But the risks of too much concentration are high. There are numerous approaches to diversifying, some using derivative strategies or exchange funds,[12] but it's often best to simply bite the tax bullet.[13]

Clearly, the notion of tax deferral can be taken too far. Taxes should not be avoided; they should be managed. R. H. Jeffrey and R. Arnott (1993) recognize lockup as a critical issue, and they talk of the "pruning decision" in terms of how managers earn their keep.[14] An active manager's pruning decision will be closely related to his alpha projection. A passive manager's pruning decision will be related to his tracking risk and the manner in which the universe he's targeting evolves over time. Some tax-managed portfolios are pruned almost continuously.

The portfolio manager's goal, then, is to become locked up with a portfolio that's desirable rather than one that's risky. The expert tax manager recognizes this at the start and sets an investment policy with this in mind. Some strategies—for example, value strategies or small-cap strategies—are particularly sensitive to lockup; higher taxation is an implicit cost of these strategies.

In seeking a portfolio that realizes gains at a low rate, one needs to consider also the structure of the equity investment.[15] After-tax value is often lost through poor structure—for example, an equity portfolio that's partitioned into style and cap subsets, with overlap among managers that change frequently. Such a design requires expensive maintenance and undermines tax efficiency. In addition to the portfolio manager's alpha tax, many types of capital gains taxation lurk to trap the unwary investor: a rebalancing tax, a manager-selection tax, and a benchmark-reconstitution tax. To avoid these costs, structure the equities with a broad core equity investment that's passive and tax managed in cooperation with satellite-concentrated active managers. The satellites can be relatively small portfolios that are unconstrained with respect to risk and not too focused on taxes.

Stage 3: Customizing a Portfolio

Having reduced taxation by seeking to defer capital gains, the portfolio manager reaches the third stage in tax sensitivity when he realizes that individual portfolio performance can be improved through customization by taking into account the cost basis of the investor's tax lots. The management of the individual portfolio then depends on that portfolio's investment flows. This means embracing the concept of taxes and adding value by actively managing them.

Commingled accounts such as mutual funds are at an inherent tax disadvantage since all investors are treated alike. Additionally, mutual funds cannot distribute capital losses. Exchange-traded funds are in only a slightly better position.[16] Customization requires a separate account.[17]

Such customized active tax management is what separates the pros from the amateurs. An active portfolio manager seeking to add value can do so either by selecting securities or by actively managing taxes, and these two approaches typically conflict with each other. The subject of active tax management has now been well documented and simulated.[18] The active tax manager maintains—and exploits—tax lot information in the portfolio every time the portfolio is rebalanced and every time there's a cash inflow or outflow. He transfers securities into or out of the portfolio and regularly harvests capital losses around his target holdings. He matches capital losses with gains whenever possible and avoids wash sales. He does this while managing the alpha expectations of his securities and balancing the trade-offs among tax costs or benefits, alpha expectations, and portfolio risks. Active tax management can be implemented in a portfolio that changes frequently, in a market-tracking portfolio, or in a customized core portfolio.

When the investor has capital gains tax liabilities and uses harvested losses to reduce them, the value of harvesting losses can be substantial. Loss harvesting can be worth 0.80–1.20 percent or more per year over a ten-year period above passive tax management at little incremental risk. These decisions can be worth as much as, or more than, stock selection. Usually the economic value added is "front-loaded" and declines over time; it depends on the market conditions (in weaker markets, the value is higher) and on the volatility of the securities. If the investor has substantial short-term gains he wishes to offset, the process can be turbo-boosted, realizing small amounts of long-term capital gains in order to increase the realization of the more valuable short-term capital losses.

Few managers are able to actively manage taxes well. Doing so requires a technological infrastructure for maintaining detailed tax information on the portfolios and for automating portfolio rebalancing. Automated portfolio-management systems are not yet widely available for doing this well, and those that are available require expert piloting. Because of the effort and costs of customization, some techniques are appropriate only for wealthier investors. The industry—and its technology—is always evolving to make these approaches practical at lower asset levels as well.

Stage 4: Coordinating Tax Management

Once an investor has embraced separate-account customization and employs multiple managers, it becomes clear that portfolio management needs to transcend its focus on the portfolio. Tax sensitivity is better addressed from a strategic, coordinated point of view. Let's look at some of the broader issues.

Others have discussed matters associated with uncoordinated multiple managers.[19] Inefficiencies creep into the management of multiple separate accounts. Multimanager accounts that combine the separate skills of a number of managers in a single account are becoming popular. They serve to avoid duplication of effort among the managers and coordinate trading, tax, and risk management. An effective multimanager account requires what the investment industry refers to as overlay portfolio management.

The overlay manager makes account-specific decisions. He coordinates the trading and seeks to add value through active tax management at lower account minimums. The value he adds comes from operational efficiencies (convenience, reduced paperwork, unified reporting) and improved after-tax performance. The value added by overlay tax management has been estimated at 0.3–0.6 percent and more, depending on the starting point and on the overall portfolio structure and design.[20] It requires a "mass customization" capability.

Overlay portfolio management in an equity portfolio is just one aspect of coordinating taxation. Other opportunities for coordination exist as well. There's the idea of tax-sensitive rebalancing among asset classes, but little has been published on this subject.[21] The *location* of assets addresses questions of coordinating between taxable and tax-deferred retirement accounts or tax-exempt charitable trusts.[22] Improved performance can be achieved by carefully determining where to hold highly taxed assets and where to hold more tax-efficient assets. Opportunities often exist for improving coordination among the investment manager, the tax accountant, and the trust and estate attorney.

In general, the focus needs to be on tax planning rather than on tax minimization. M. S. Scholes and M. A. Wolfson (1992) discuss tax planning in depth for corporations,[23] and as individual investors and their advisers become more sophisticated, we can probably expect them to apply some of these principles. Most tax planners typically assume that the current tax rate will remain in place indefinitely. Although we know that taxes will always exist, tax rates are uncertain and almost surely will change. Indeed, U.S. tax laws are scheduled for review in the future. Investment managers are in a position to place a bet on tax rate changes or to hedge against undesirable moves, and either can be a useful endeavor. Compared with forecasting security returns, changes in interest rates, or economic trends, forecasting changes in tax rates is relatively easy. Tax rates move slowly and are fixed only after a great deal of public debate. Anticipating tax law changes can lead to improved valuation of securities and to the intelligent timing of the restructuring and rebalancing of investments.

Tax laws may change slowly, but equity portfolio management has come a long way since the early 1990s, when it became evident that taxes matter a great deal, that they undermine many a portfolio manager's attempts at seeking return, and that they can be managed to advantage.

Chapter Notes

1. D. M. Stein, and J. P. Garland, "Investment Management for Taxable Investors," in *The Handbook of Portfolio Management,* edited by Frank Fabozzi (F. J. Fabozzi Associates, 1998).

2. This is still the case with the 2003 Jobs and Growth Tax Relief Reconciliation Act tax rates. Even though the opportunity to actively manage taxes is slightly lower than before, the cost of mismanaging taxes is still high: there are new requirements to manage dividends, and the difference between short-term and long-term capital gains rates is 20 percent.

3. SEC, "Disclosure of Mutual Fund After-Tax Returns," http://www.sec.gov/rules/final/33-7941.htm (2001; modified March 6, 2002).

4. AIMR "Performance Presentation Standards" http://www.aimr.org/pdf/standards/aftertax_changes.pdf (2002).

5. Cerulli Associates, *The Cerulli Edge, Managed Accounts Edition,* 3rd quarter (Cerulli Associates, 2002).

6. A. L. Berkin and J. Ye, "Tax Management, Loss Harvesting and HIFO Accounting," *Financial Analysts Journal* (July 2003): 91–102.

7. D. M. Stein, "Measuring and Evaluating Portfolio Performance After Taxes," *Journal of Portfolio Management* (Winter 1998): 117–124.

8. The model here is as follows. We're assuming a tax rate $t = 15\%$ on capital gains, cost basis/market value $c = 50\%$.

V_0 = initial value; L_0 = initial liquidation value;
$$L_0 = V_0 - (V_0 - cV_0)\,t = V_0\,[1 - t(1 - c)]$$

For *preliquidation value*, V:

Hold: $V_1 = V_0 \times (1.08^{20})$ *Trade:* $V_2 = L_0 \times (1.1^3) \times (1.08^{17})$

For *postliquidation value*, W:

Hold: $W_1 = V_1 - (V_1 - cV_0)t$ *Trade:* $W_2 = V_2 - (V_2 - L_0) \times t$

In determining the preferred decision above, we use the average of preliquidation and postliquidation values. For higher tax rates and particularly higher short-term rates, the alpha requirement is greater.

9. There are exceptions to this generalization.

10. D. M. Stein and A. F. Siegel, *The Diversification of Employee Stock Options, Investment Counseling for Private Clients IV* (AIMR Conference Proceedings, Phoenix, March 11–12, 2002).

The theory of statistical decision-making identifies a *decision policy* that specifies how a decision will be made at each point in time given the realization of future uncertain events. One can distinguish between decision policies that are *static* from those that are *dynamic*. A static decision is made now, using current information, and employs no knowledge of how future decisions will be made. A dynamic decision is made in full knowledge of how future decisions will be made; when you act, you do so knowing that you will act again in the future and anticipate how you will act given future events. Stein and Siegel provide an example of a dynamic decision as applied to the realization of employee options.

11. Although it's costly to change the portfolio at this point, this cost is less than it would have been had the taxes been paid at an earlier stage.

12. S. Welch, "Comparing Financial and Charitable Techniques for Disposing of Low Basis Stock," *Journal of Wealth Management* (Spring 2002): 37–46.

13. D. M. Stein et al., "Diversification in the Presence of Taxes," *Journal of Portfolio Management* (Fall 2000): 61–71.

14. R. H. Jeffrey and R. Arnott, "Is Your Alpha Big Enough to Cover Its Taxes?" *Journal of Portfolio Management* (Spring 1993): 15–25.

15. D. M. Stein, "Equity Portfolio Structure and Design in the Presence of Taxes," *Journal of Wealth Management* (Fall 2001): 37–42; H. Evensky, "Changing Equity Premium Implications for Wealth Management, Portfolio Design and Implementation," *Journal of Financial Planning* (June 2002).

16. Because of the way an exchange-traded fund distributes assets in kind to certain redeeming shareholders, it's able to distribute slightly fewer capital gains than a mutual fund with the same mandate.

17. There do exist commingled partnerships in which the actions of some investors provide advantages to other investors.

18. D. M. Stein, B. L. Langstraat, and P. Narasimhan, "Reporting After-Tax Returns: A Pragmatic Approach," *Journal of Private Portfolio Management* (Spring 1999): 10–22; R. D. Arnott, A. L. Berkin, and J. Yu, "Loss Harvesting: What Is It Worth to the Taxable Investor?" *Journal of Wealth Management* (Spring 2001): 10–18.

19. J. L. P. Brunel, *Integrated Wealth Management: The New Direction for Portfolio Managers* (Institutional Investor Books, 2002); D. M. Stein, and G. McIntire, "Overlay Portfolio Management in a Multi-Manager Account," *Journal of Wealth Management* (Spring 2003): 57–71.

20. Stein and McIntire (2003).

21. N. L. Jacob, "Taxes, Investment Strategy and Diversifying Low Basis Stock," *Trusts and Estates* (May 1995).

22. R. M. Dammon, C. S. Spatt, and H. H. Zhang, "Optimal Asset Location and Allocation with Taxable and Tax-Deferred Investing" (Social Science Research Network Electronic Library); G. Friedman, "Combining Estate Planning with Asset Allocation" (AIMR Conference Proceedings, Investment Counselling for Private Clients II, Philadelphia, November 9–10, 1999), pp. 68–74.

23. M. S. Scholes and M. A. Wolfson, *Taxes and Business Strategy* (Prentice Hall, 1992).

CHAPTER 7

Tax-Efficient Investing

THOMAS J. BOCZAR AND ROBERT GORDON

Over the years, Wall Street has been quite inventive in creating numerous ways to make the same investment. For astute investors, these choices create an opportunity for better value. That's because even though the investment vehicles' potential for gain or loss is essentially the same, the tax treatment each receives can differ considerably. By choosing investments strategically, investors can increase tax efficiency and enhance their after-tax returns. This chapter explores these divergent tax treatments—seen from both the point of purchase and the point of sale—of the investment choices available.

An S&P 500 Investment

Why are exchange-traded funds such as Standard & Poor's depositary receipts (SPDRs, or "Spiders"), which are listed on the American Stock Exchange and track the Standard & Poor's 500 stock index, such a big deal? The truth is they're not. Despite all the hype surrounding these index-based instruments, investors can achieve the investment performance these vehicles promise with greater tax efficiency and at a lower cost by using investment products that have been around for years.

Investors may be surprised to learn that low-expense, open-end index funds have outperformed SPDRs every year since SPDRs were created, according to a study by New York University professors Edwin Elton and Martin Gruber. According to the NYU study, the main reason conventional index funds outperformed SPDRs is that exchange-traded funds

(ETFs) can't lend out shares or reinvest money received from dividends. Open-end index funds can. Perhaps even more significant is the conclusion reached by Dr. James Poterba of the Massachusetts Institute of Technology, who found that open-end index funds outperform ETFs even after taxes. Although an ETF's ability to redeem in kind is a powerful tool for high turnover portfolios, the gains realized, at least thus far, have been minuscule.

Investors with time horizons of less than one year and who are bullish or bearish on the broader stock market should explore listed call or put index options, respectively, on the S&P 500 and other broad-based index options. Options such as these are "marked to market" at year-end, and any profits on these "Section 1256" contracts are automatically taxed at a 23 percent tax rate, no matter how long they're held, whether the investor is long or betting on the short side. By contrast, ETFs are not marked to market, and short-term gains are taxed at 35 percent.

Why the difference? The tax-favored options are those that are listed on an exchange; strangely, over-the-counter (privately negotiated) options do not get the same favorable treatment. The 23 percent tax rate for listed broad-based index options represents the legacy of a legislative victory by legendary Chicago Congressman Dan Rostenkowski. The rate derives from an assumption that 60 percent of any profits or losses are long term (taxed at 15 percent) and the other 40 percent of profits or losses are short term (taxed at 35 percent). Regardless of the interesting legislative history, the take-home message for investors is simple and compelling: If your time horizon is less than one year and you're seeking the returns of the broader stock market, you should explore listed call index options (or futures) on the S&P 500 and other broad-based indexes.

Many industry sector index options also qualify for Section 1256 treatment. A list of sector indexes and their classification as narrow or broad-based is available at www.twenty-first.com/exchange-traded_index_options.htm. Paradoxically, options on SPDRs and other ETFs do not get this favorable treatment. **FIGURE 7.1** compares the features of exchange-traded funds, open-end index funds, listed index options, and unlisted (over-the-counter) index options.

Investors who believe the stock market will be bearish for more than a year ahead should consider buying puts. Puts can be over-the-counter (non-exchange-traded) broad-based options, listed narrow-based index options, or options on ETFs or other mutual funds. If these puts are held for more than twelve months, profits will be taxed at the 15 percent long-term capital gains rate. In contrast, listed broad-based put options are marked to market each year and their profits are taxed at 23 percent. Short sales of ETFs are always considered short term and thus taxed at

FIGURE 7.1 *S&P 500 Investment*

	EXCHANGE-TRADED FUNDS	OPEN-END INDEX FUNDS	LISTED INDEX OPTIONS	UNLISTED INDEX OPTIONS
Management fee	Yes	Yes	No	No
Tracking error	Yes	Yes	No	No
Commissions on purchase/sale	Yes	No	Yes	Yes
Short-term gains taxes @	35%	35%	23%	35%
Long-term gains taxes @	15%	15%	23%	15%
Marked-to-market at year-end	No	No	Yes	No
Distribution of gains	Yes	Yes	No	No
Possible mispricing	Yes	No	Yes	Yes
Trades intraday	Yes	No	Yes	Yes
Taxable dividends	Yes	Yes	No	No

35 percent, no matter how long the short position was held.

Obviously, the different tax treatment of similar index products affords investors many choices. The investor's time horizon is usually the key to which investment tool to use. **FIGURE 7.2** may help investors simplify the decision. If the investor's time horizon is between one and five years, then the best tool is an equity swap. A swap could be structured so that the investor makes periodic payments (for example, a LIBOR-based fee for the cost to carry the position) but defers all payments and receipts with respect to dividends and price movement of the investment until the end of the swap agreement. The LIBOR-based fee should be a current ordinary deduction at the 35 percent rate. There may be some limitations on the deductibility of this expense.

As the swap nears maturity, the investor will have a choice. If the stock market has increased in value, the investor, by terminating the swap before its stated maturity, can recognize a long-term capital gain at the 15 percent rate. Conversely, if the stock market has decreased in value, the investor

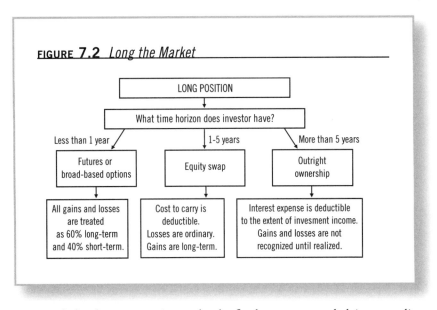

FIGURE 7.2 *Long the Market*

LONG POSITION

What time horizon does investor have?

Less than 1 year | 1-5 years | More than 5 years

| Futures or broad-based options | Equity swap | Outright ownership |

| All gains and losses are treated as 60% long-term and 40% short-term. | Cost to carry is deductible. Losses are ordinary. Gains are long-term. | Interest expense is deductible to the extent of invesment income. Gains and losses are not recognized until realized. |

can simply let the swap expire, make the final payment, and claim an ordinary deduction at the 35 percent rate, subject to the limitations discussed later in this chapter. In sum, by using a swap, an investor can potentially obtain current ordinary deductions for the carrying costs, ordinary deductions if the stock market decreases in value, and long-term capital gain if the stock market increases in value. Keep in mind that a swap can be used to gain exposure to a single stock as well as a basket of stocks.

For investments with an anticipated time horizon exceeding five years, swaps are harder to structure because dealers typically do not wish to enter into a transaction beyond that length. In addition, because the early termination or expiration of a swap will force recognition of gain, investors with an indefinitely long time horizon would likely do better investing in a SPDR or an open-end index fund. Here the investor has complete control over the timing of the recognition of gain or loss. If the investor holds the position until death, there should be no income tax imposed on the gain on the investment because of the step-up in basis.

Individual Stock Investments

An investment in the performance of the stock of a publicly traded company can be accomplished in at least four different ways. Although each method has similar potential for similar investment gains, each has different tax consequences.

The four methods of investing in the equity of a publicly traded corporation are:

❑ Purchasing shares of stock
❑ Buying call options and selling put options
❑ Entering into an equity swap
❑ Entering into a single-stock futures contract

Purchasing Shares of Stock

An investor's outright purchase of stock triggers numerous tax consequences. The investor begins to accrue a holding period on the day after the trade date. If the stock is held for longer than one year, any gain or loss on its disposition will be a long-term capital gain or loss. For individuals, the distinction between long term and short term is critical because long-term capital gains are currently taxed at 15 percent whereas short-term capital gains are taxed at 35 percent. Dividends that are considered qualified dividend income are taxed as ordinary income at the 15 percent rate and are no longer considered investment income.

Other rules come into play for individuals who leverage their stock purchases via margin loans. The interest they pay on such debt is an investment interest expense that they can deduct to the extent of investment income (for example, interest income, dividends that are not qualified dividend income, and short-term capital gains). Long-term capital gains and qualified dividend income are not normally included in the investor's investment income for this purpose. However, investors can elect to treat their long-term capital gains as short-term capital gains and their qualified dividend income as nonqualified dividend income in order to have such income treated as investment income. Foreign investors who purchase dividend-paying stocks are subject to U.S. withholding taxes on those dividends.

Perhaps most important, by owning the stock directly, investors can delay the payment of the capital gains tax until they dispose of the shares. Certain exit strategies can be used to further defer the imposition of the capital gains tax.

Buying Call Options and Selling Put Options

Instead of buying the shares of a company outright, an investor could buy a call and write (for example, sell) a put on a stock with identical strike prices and expiration dates. The difference between the premiums of the call and the put will be very close to the cost of financing the purchase of the stock, reduced by the dividend yield on the stock, taking into account the intrinsic value of the option position. Assume, for example, that ABC Corporation stock is trading for $100 per share, that the current price of a six-month call option with an exercise price of $100 is $8.72, and that the current price of a six-month put option with an exercise price of $100 is

$8.11. No dividends are expected over the next six months. This presents investors with two investment alternatives:

- ❑ The investor could buy the stock at $100, financing the entire price at a 1.50 percent interest rate. That would generate an interest expense of $0.75 over the next six months.
- ❑ The investor could buy six-month $100 calls at $8.72 and sell six-month $100 puts at $8.11. The net cost is $0.61 (and the options have zero intrinsic value).

In either case, the investor benefits or suffers dollar for dollar with any increase or decrease in the price of ABC Corporation stock. The cost of doing the transaction using the options is $0.61 versus a financing cost of $0.75 to buy the stock. By using the options, the investor gives up voting rights in the corporation.

From a tax perspective, the options transaction and outright stock purchase receive very different treatment. The call and put positions are not a straddle (see "The Straddle Rules" for the definition of a straddle) because the risk of holding one position does not substantially diminish the risk of holding the other position. Thus, any gain or loss resulting from closing the option positions will be taxed currently and treated as a capital gain or loss. The gain or loss on the call will be short term or long term, depending on the holding period of the call (for example, long term if held for more than one year), whereas the gain or loss on the put will be short term regardless of how long the position is held open. The economic effects of leveraging the stock and the expected dividend flows are incorporated into the pricing of the options and therefore will be capital in nature.

If an investor entered into the ABC Corporation option transaction, closing the option position in six months would result in a taxable gain or loss. Immediately entering into a new position with expiration dates in the future would be equivalent to maintaining a long stock position in ABC Corporation. Nonetheless, a taxable event will have occurred. In comparison, simply maintaining a position in the stock would not trigger a gain or loss. However, if a loss is recognized on the closing of the options, establishing the new option position would not be a wash sale. In contrast, an investor would be prohibited by the wash sale rules from selling the stock, immediately repurchasing it, and recognizing the loss for tax purposes.

If the investor exercised the call option, he or she would have a basis in the stock equal to the exercise price of the option plus the premium paid. No gain or loss on the call would be recognized. The holding period of the stock would begin on the date the call was exercised. If the put is exercised against the investor, the basis of the stock received is reduced by the proceeds received from writing the puts. No gain or loss would be recognized with respect to the puts. The holding period of the stock would begin on the date the put was exercised. In either situation (call or put), an unexercised option is given its tax effect on lapse or disposition.

Entering Into an Equity Swap

Entering into the long side of a total-return equity swap can provide an investor a potential gain or loss similar to that of a leveraged stock purchase. A swap could be structured so that the investor makes periodic payments (for example, a LIBOR-based fee for the cost to carry the position) but defers all payments and receipts with respect to dividends and price movement of the stock until the end of the swap agreement. During the term of the swap structured this way, all payments are ordinary expenses.

For individuals, the payments would be treated as investment expenses and would be subject to the 2 percent floor on miscellaneous itemized deductions, as well as the 3 percent limitation on itemized deductions. The timing of the recognition of loss on the swap is based on the frequency of payments due under the swap. If an investor terminates the swap before the expiration date, any gain or loss on the termination would be a capital gain. The holding period in the swap would begin on the date the swap is entered into. There is currently no withholding on swap payments even though a portion of the payment does reflect the value of a dividend that would otherwise be subject to withholding. This could be especially important for foreign investors who want to invest in U.S. dividend-paying stock.

Entering Into a Single-Stock Futures Contract

Futures contracts on a single stock now trade on exchanges in the United States. The holding period of a long futures contract will determine whether the gain or loss is short term or long term. However, all gain or loss with respect to a short position will be treated as short-term.

If an investor takes delivery of stock under the futures contract, there is no gain or loss on the contract, but the holding period of the stock will include the holding period of the futures contract, which is quite different from the exercise of a call that starts a new holding period for the stock.

For a U.S. taxpayer purchasing a high-yielding stock with a fairly long time horizon, direct ownership is probably the best tool. But for a nonresident who would otherwise be subject to U.S. withholding tax, a derivative might be the best tool. If the investor wants to use leverage but can't use the interest-expense deduction, a derivative might be the best tool. If the investor enters into a derivative and might want to take delivery at the expiration of the contract, futures can be better than options that restart the holding period.

Exiting a Stock Investment

The stock market's extreme volatility during the start of the decade caused many investors who hold a single concentrated stock position with a low cost basis to explore strategies to reduce their exposure to the stock.

Investors can eliminate or reduce the risk and reward of holding a single stock by:

❑ Selling the stock outright
❑ Establishing a short against the box position
❑ Selling call options and buying put options
❑ Entering into an equity swap
❑ Entering into a forward contract
❑ Entering into a single-stock futures contract

Ideally, an investor holding a concentrated position in an appreciated stock would like to

❑ hedge against a decrease in the value of the stock;
❑ defer and eliminate capital gains tax, that is, avoid triggering a current taxable event and still qualify for a step-up in basis at death; and
❑ gain liquidity—monetize the position (that is, receive in cash a substantial portion of the market value of the stock) to diversify into other investments.

Outright Sale

Selling a stock outright is clearly the easiest way to eliminate the exposure. However, because an outright sale triggers an immediate capital gains tax, investors often look for a more tax-efficient alternative.

Short Against the Box

Before the enactment of the Taxpayer Relief Act of 1997 (TRA '97) and Section 1259 of the Internal Revenue Code (IRC), commonly referred to as the constructive-sale rules, the short-against-the-box strategy (SAB) was the cheapest and most efficient method investors could use for achieving their objectives. In a SAB, the investor shorts the same number of shares that are held, creating a perfect inverse matching position.

Although the constructive-sale rules have generally eliminated the use of the SAB, it's still important to understand how it works. First, through certain forms of merger arbitrage, it remains possible for an investor to establish a SAB that should not be subject to the constructive-sale rules. Second, the SAB remains the paradigm that all financial-derivative-based hedging and monetization strategies attempt to replicate as closely as possible without violating the constructive-sale rules.

In a SAB, the investor is simultaneously long and short in the same number of shares of the same stock. The fully hedged position will earn close to the risk-free rate of return on 100 percent of its value through a short interest rebate (for example, interest that's earned on the short-sale proceeds). Because the position is fully hedged, the investor can typically borrow up to 99 percent of its value. Although there's a cost associated with this borrowing, the short interest rebate greatly offsets the cost of borrowing, making monetization very inexpensive.

Before enactment of the constructive-sale rules, the long and short positions were treated separately for tax purposes, therefore deferring the capital gains tax, and because the long shares qualified for a step-up in basis at death, an investor who kept the short against the box open until death completely eliminated the capital gains tax. Also, the SAB is specifically exempt from the straddle rules (even though economically it's a perfect straddle), so the interest expense that's incurred is currently deductible, that is, it need not be capitalized.

From a tax perspective, before enactment of the constructive-sale rules, the form of the transaction, rather than its economic substance, controlled. The constructive-sale rules focus on the economic substance, rather than the form, of a hedging transaction.

The Constructive-Sale Rules

Because of the constructive-sale rules, investors must engage in a three-pronged analysis to ensure that they use the most tax-efficient hedging strategy:

- ❑ Can the investor establish a short-against-the-box position that avoids the application of the constructive-sale rules? If so, that's clearly the preferred choice.
- ❑ If this isn't possible, can the investor synthetically (through derivative structures) replicate the cash flows and payoff profile of the SAB fairly closely without triggering a constructive sale?
- ❑ Are there alternative strategies (to a short-against-the-box or derivative-based solution) that might be appropriate in a particular case?

Escaping the Constructive-Sale Rules

It's common for one corporation to acquire another pursuant to a tax-free stock-for-stock reorganization (for example, a merger). Establishing a short position in the acquirer's stock in an announced stock-for-stock merger presents an intriguing investment opportunity for investors who own an appreciated stock position in the target. If the merger closes, the investor will have backed into a short-against-the-box position that should not be subject to the constructive-sale rules.

Under the constructive-sale rules, an investor is deemed to have made a constructive sale (which is a taxable event) of an "appreciated financial position" (for example, low-basis stock) if he or she enters into a short sale of the "same or substantially identical property." The term "substantially identical" is not defined in the IRC.

An investor who owns stock of the target enters into a short sale of the acquirer's stock at a time when the deal presents considerable risk (for example, before regulatory approvals are obtained and before the shareholders approve the transaction) should not be deemed, for tax purposes, to have entered into a short sale of substantially identical property. Further, the provisions of the TRA '97 that deny the step-up in basis to certain investors who have entered into a short against the box should not apply. On consummation of a stock-for-stock merger, long positions in the target's stock are automatically converted into long positions in the acquirer's stock. Thus, if the investor starts out with a long position in the target's stock and shorts the acquirer, the end result (if the deal closes) is a short against the box in the acquirer's stock, which could be kept open for a long-term period (for example, until death).

If an investor holds an appreciated stock position in a target corporation that is involved in a tax-free stock-for-stock merger, he or she could establish a short position in the acquirer's stock before the completion of regulatory approvals and shareholder votes (that is, at a time when the transaction is not yet a "done deal"). If the deal is consummated, the investor will have established a short-against-the-box position that should not be subject to the constructive-sale provisions of TRA '97. A similar opportunity exists if the investor is long in the acquirer and shorts the target. However, additional tax issues are raised in this "reverse" arbitrage context.

Replicating the SAB: Income-Producing Collars

If the merger arbitrage strategy is not available (and, obviously, in most cases it will not be), the investor must examine what type of derivative-based strategy will deliver the desired hedging and monetization economics, as well as the optimal tax treatment. An equity collar—the type that has become known as an "income-producing collar"—has emerged as the preferred strategy because it can fairly closely replicate the cash flows of the SAB while avoiding the constructive-sale rules. By structuring a collar that has a fairly tight band around the current price of the stock, an investor can minimize (within certain limits) exposure to price movement of the underlying stock and generate positive cash flow to offset the cost of monetization while deferring and possibly eliminating the capital gains tax (by qualifying for a step-up in basis at death). To avoid qualifying as a constructive sale, an income-producing collar should be no tighter than 15 percent around the current price of the stock.

The House and Senate committee reports on the constructive-sale rules both contain an example of what they deemed a standard collar. The example uses a 95 percent put and a 110 percent call. Although the committee reports express no view on whether this collar is abusive (and would therefore trigger a constructive sale), most tax practitioners believe this example was included to give investors some practical guidance as to what type of equity collar would *not* trigger a constructive sale. [See H.R. Rep. No. 105-148 (1997) and S. Rep. No. 105-133 (1997).]

The cash flows of this type of collar closely resemble a short-against-the-box strategy but should not trigger a constructive sale. An important corollary is that any derivative strategy that completely eliminates both the risk and the reward of holding the stock will be deemed a constructive sale.

The Straddle Rules

The economics of an equity collar (for example, hedging and monetization) can be achieved through the use of several derivative tools. Each of these tools, however, can result in very different tax consequences, depending on an investor's situation. Investors and their professional advisers (and especially fiduciaries who might have a duty to do so) should analyze the derivative tool to ensure that it's the one most likely to minimize the investor's after-tax cost of implementing the collar. *Whether or not the straddle rules of IRC Section 1092 apply is critical in the selection of the most appropriate tool.*

A straddle exists when holding one position substantially reduces the risk of holding another. Because a collar substantially reduces the risk of owning the underlying stock, the stock and collar together should be treated as a straddle for federal tax purposes. Investors face two negative ramifications when their stock and collar is deemed a straddle:

- ❑ Any loss realized from closing one leg of a straddle must be deferred to the extent there is unrealized gain on the open leg. Thus, as a collar expires, is terminated, or is rolled forward, any losses must be deferred. However, any gains are currently taxed.
- ❑ Interest expense incurred to "carry a straddle" must be capitalized (as opposed to being currently deductible). There has been (and continues to be) spirited debate about the methodology to be applied in determining the amount, if any, of the interest expense that must be capitalized under IRC Section 263(g).

Stock Acquired Before 1984

The straddle rules should not apply to stock that was acquired before January 1, 1984. Therefore, if stock was acquired before 1984, a collar can be implemented without triggering the straddle rules. This creates significant tax-planning opportunities.

The tools. The three hedging tools that can produce the economics of a collar are options (either listed or over-the-counter), prepaid variable forwards, and swaps with an embedded collar. Single-stock futures do not allow collar-like economics. Rather, by shorting futures the investor completely eliminates the risks and rewards of owning the underlying stock. Thus, the use of single-stock futures would constitute a constructive sale.

For stock acquired before 1984, in most situations the optimal tool to hedge an appreciated stock will be a swap, with collar-like economics built into it, monetized through a margin loan. The two other possible tools—an options-based collar monetized through a margin loan and a prepaid variable forward—produce less-favorable tax consequences.

Options. Options-based collars involve the simultaneous purchase of puts and sale of calls on the underlying stock. The options eliminate the potential for loss below the put strike price and for profits above the call strike price. For example, an investor holding ABC Corporation shares that currently trade at $100 might buy a put with a strike price of $95 and sell a call with a strike price of $110 and then borrow against the hedged position (or other publicly traded securities) to monetize the position.

Prepaid variable forward. A prepaid variable forward is an agreement to sell a security at a fixed time in the future, with the number of shares to be delivered at maturity varying with the underlying share price. The agreement effectively has the economics of a collar combined with borrowing against the underlying stock embedded within it. For example, an investor holding ABC Corporation shares trading at $100 might enter into a prepaid variable forward that requires the dealer to pay the investor $88 at the start of the contract in exchange for the right to receive a variable number of shares from the investor in three years pursuant to a preset formula that embodies the economics of a collar (for example, a long put with a $95 strike and a short call with a $110 strike).

The formula would require the investor to deliver all his or her ABC Corporation shares if the price of ABC in three years is less than $95. If the price of ABC is greater than $95 but less than $110, the investor would deliver $95 worth of shares. If the price of ABC is above $110, the investor would keep $15 worth of shares and deliver the remainder to the dealer.

Swaps. A swap is an agreement between an investor and a derivative dealer with payments referenced to the price of a particular stock and covering a particular dollar amount (called the notional amount). Under a swap agreement, the investor could agree to pay the dealer any appreciation above a specified share price (for example, the strike price of the embedded short call) plus any dividends paid on the stock. The dealer in turn could agree to pay the investor any depreciation below a specified share price (for example, the strike price of the embedded long put) plus an interest-based fee on the notional amount. For example, an investor holding ABC Corporation shares trading at $100 could enter into a swap agreement to pay the dealer any appreciation above $110 plus any dividends paid on the stock while the dealer could agree to pay the investor any depreciation below $95 plus a LIBOR-based payment on $100. The investor could then borrow against the hedged position (or against other marketable securities) to monetize the position.

Deductibility of interest expense. Because the straddle rules should not apply to stock acquired before 1984, there should be no question that the interest expense incurred in return for the use of the monetization proceeds is currently deductible against investment income (for example, nonqualified dividends, interest, and short-term gains) otherwise taxed at the ordinary rate.

Because both a swap with an embedded collar and an options-based collar can be monetized through a margin loan (secured by the hedged position and/or other marketable securities), the investor will incur investment interest expense that is currently deductible against investment income with a benefit of 35 percent. With a prepaid variable forward, however, the investor cannot achieve the same favorable tax result. Instead, the investor is required to defer and capitalize the net cost of borrowing with a maximum potential benefit of 15 percent.

In the example offered for variable prepaid forwards used for stock acquired before 1984, the investor holding ABC Corporation shares trading at $100 entered into a prepaid variable forward embodying the economics of a collar (that is, a long put with a $95 strike and a short call with a $110 strike) that required the dealer to pay the investor $88 at the start of the contract. The difference between the $95 put strike (that is, the sales price) and the $88 advance is mostly the net cost of borrowing. Unfortunately, a deduction for this very real expense cannot occur until the underlying shares are actually delivered to close out the contract. Because the forward in our example has a term of three years, the deduction will be deferred for at least this period.

In addition, because the expense of borrowing is capitalized into the forward price, the value of the deduction is slashed from the ordinary rate to 15 percent. Assume that three years from now the price of ABC is less than $95 and that the investor decides to physically settle the forward by delivering shares to the dealer. The investor would then be taxed on the difference between the advance received up front ($88) and his or her basis in the stock that was delivered. That is, the investor is not taxed on the difference between the sales price ($95) and the amount received up front ($88). If the investor had held the stock for a sufficiently long period before entering into the forward, the benefit of the deduction would have been dramatically reduced.

Tax disadvantage of swaps. Swaps have one slight potential tax disadvantage. Any payment received during the swap's term (whether an up-front payment or one received periodically) will be deemed ordinary income currently subject to tax. However, the only payment that the investor would be scheduled to receive (periodically) from the dealer during the term of the swap would be an interest-equivalent LIBOR-based fee based on the notional amount.

Proposed regulations. As discussed under "Deductibility of Interest Expense" above, the proposed regulations published by the IRS in January 2001, with respect to the straddle rules would change the ground rules for hedging stock acquired after 1983. These proposed regulations should not, however, in any way affect stock that was acquired before 1984.

Settling the collar. When it comes to settling an existing collar and rolling into a new one, if the stock price decreases, swaps with an embedded collar, options-based collars, and prepaid variable forwards are afforded essentially the same tax treatment. A decrease in the price of the stock below the put strike should create long-term capital gain, assuming the long-term holding period was met. Conversely, an increase in the price of the stock above the call strike should produce an ordinary deduction if a swap is used, a short-term capital loss if an options-based collar is used, but only a long-term capital loss if a prepaid variable forward is used.

In the example used for variable prepaid forwards, the investor holding ABC Corporation shares trading at $100 entered into a prepaid variable forward embodying the economics of a collar (that is, a long put with a $95 strike and a short call with a $110 strike) that required the dealer to pay the investor $88 at the start of the contract. Assume the stock increases to $200 at the expiration of the contract. Most likely, the investor will sell $90 of the underlying stock to fund the settlement obligation, assuming the investor wishes to roll into a new forward. If the investor has achieved a long-term holding period on the shares that were sold and those shares have a zero basis, the investor will recognize a $90 long-term capital gain. Under the netting rules for capital gains, the $90 long-term capital loss must first offset the $90 long-term capital gain. Here the $90 long-term capital loss cannot be used to offset other short-term gains or ordinary income that the investor might have generated. Thus, the value of the loss is only 15 percent.

Swaps receive more favorable tax treatment than prepaid variable forwards should the stock price increase above the embedded call strike. All payments made or received under the terms of a swap agreement should generate either ordinary income or loss. However, a termination of a swap agreement should generate either capital gain or ordinary loss. Thus, with proper planning an investor using a swap should be able to recognize either capital gain or ordinary loss.

For instance, if the underlying stock declines in value below the embedded put strike, the investor could terminate the swap before its stated expiration date, creating a long-term capital gain. However, if the stock increases in value above the embedded call strike, the swap could be allowed to run until its stated expiration. The resulting loss is treated as an ordinary loss that is deducted against ordinary income, which otherwise would have been taxed at the 35 percent ordinary rate.

Again, to be deductible, the loss on the swap plus all of the investor's other itemized deductions must exceed 2 percent of the investor's adjusted gross income (AGI). After this hurdle is met, the deductible amount is reduced by 3 percent of the taxpayer's AGI. The deduction is also disallowed for alternative minimum tax purposes. Therefore, if the stock price exceeds the embedded call strike near the swap's expiration, the investor must determine whether it's better to generate an ordinary deduction, subject to these limitations, or a long-term capital loss. The swap affords the investor this choice.

An investor who uses a swap should never be worse off than if he or she had used a prepaid variable forward. That is, if the 2 percent and 3 percent AGI limitations on miscellaneous itemized deductions prohibit the investor from receiving the full benefit of the ordinary deduction, he or she should simply terminate the swap before its stated expiration date and recognize a long-term capital loss, which is the same as if a prepaid variable forward had been used. Put another way, a swap should deliver only a potentially better result (never a worse result) than a prepaid variable forward.

Swaps: the superior tool. Swaps appear to be the superior tool for hedging and monetizing stock acquired before 1984. If the underlying stock depreciates in value, the gain on the swap should be long-term capital gain. If the stock increases in value, the loss on the swap can be ordinary or capital, whichever is more beneficial to the investor. In addition, because a swap is monetized through a margin loan, the investor will incur investment interest expense that is currently deductible against investment income. Options-based collars and prepaid variable forwards produce less-favorable tax treatment.

Options-based collars receive essentially the same treatment as swaps if the underlying stock decreases in value, and because monetization occurs through a margin loan, the investor will incur investment interest expense that is currently deductible against investment income. However, options receive less-favorable treatment than swaps if the stock increases in value (that is, no ordinary deduction is possible). Prepaid variable forwards receive essentially the same tax treatment as swaps if the underlying stock decreases in value, but receive less-favorable treatment if the stock

FIGURE **7.3** *Tax Treatment of Alternative Hedging/Monetization Techniques for Stock Acquired Before 1984*

Should carrying costs be currently deductible against investment income (35% benefit)?

If investor implements monetizing collar through:

Prepaid variable forward	No
Options and margin loans	Yes
Equity swap (with embedded collar) and margin loans	Yes

When *cash settling*, if stock price is *above* call strike, what is the character of the loss?

If investor implements monetizing collar through:

Prepaid variable forward	Long-term capital loss
Options and margin loans	Short-term capital loss
Equity swap (with embedded collar) and margin loans	Ordinary deduction or long-term capital loss at investor's discretion

When *cash settling*, if stock price is *below* put strike, what is the character of the gain?

If investor implements monetizing collar through:

Prepaid variable forward	Long-term capital gain
Options and margin loans	Long-term capital gain
Equity swap (with embedded collar) and margin loans	Long-term capital gain or ordinary income at investor's discretion

increases in value. Prepaid variable forwards also require the investor to defer and capitalize the net cost of borrowing.

Although all three tools achieve virtually the same economics, for an investor who acquired his or her stock before 1984, swaps should usually produce a superior after-tax result. **FIGURE 7.3** compares and contrasts the tax treatment of the three available financial-derivative-based hedging and monetization strategies—swaps, options, and forwards—for stock acquired before 1984.

When delivering stock, what is the character of the gain?

If investor implements monetizing collar through:

Prepaid variable forward	Long-term capital gain
Options and margin loans	Long-term capital gain
Equity swap (with embedded collar) and margin loans	Long-term capital gain

At what rates are dividends taxed?

If investor implements monetizing collar through:

Prepaid variable forward	35%
Options and margin loans	35%
Equity swap (with embedded collar) and margin loans	35%

Stock Acquired After 1983

The objective for the investor who owns stock acquired after 1983 is to mitigate the negative impact of the straddle rules as much as possible (see "The Straddle Rules," page 111).

Evolution of the single-contract collar. Investors can address the first negative ramification of the straddle rules (for example, getting "whipsawed") using an over-the-counter derivative contract that encompasses both a put and a call. Assume that XYZ Corporation stock is selling at $100 per share. The investor constructs a three-year zero-cost collar on the stock (with either listed or over-the-counter options), buying puts struck at $90 for $14 and selling calls struck at $160 for $14. If the collar expires with the stock price between $90 and $160, then the investor faces a tax of $4.90 (35 percent of $14 short-term capital gain) on each expired call; however, he or she cannot currently deduct the wasted $14 cost of the puts, which is a deferred long-term capital loss under the straddle rules. The investor created economic protection and some potential for profit, but the after-tax cost is about $5 per share (with no actual profits realized).

Suppose, however, that instead of buying and selling separate puts and calls, the investor hedges XYZ by employing a single-contract options-based collar. With this approach, he or she can create the same economic structure—effectively buying puts struck at $90 and selling calls struck at $160. However, when a zero-cost collar is documented using a single contract, the price of the collar for tax purposes should be zero even if the straddle rules apply. Thus, if the collar expires with the stock price anywhere between $90 and $160, the expiration should not create any taxable income or loss. The investor has created the same level of economic protection and potential for profit without being whipsawed for tax purposes.

Unfortunately, it's not possible to implement a single-contract collar for listed options, because the documentation that's used by the options exchanges treats the put and the call as separate contracts. Practitioners have been encouraging the exchanges to develop this type of collar. However, it is possible to implement a single-contract collar only with over-the-counter options.

With respect to a swap with an embedded collar or a variable forward, the amount received for the embedded call and the amount paid for the embedded put will also net against each other automatically because of the nature of those instruments. In this regard, an equity swap with an embedded collar is slightly tax disadvantaged compared with an options-based collar or a prepaid variable forward, because any payments received by the investor up front or during the swap's term will be taxed currently as ordinary income, whereas a single-contract options-based collar or a variable forward would allow such a payment to be part of an open transaction, with the tax deferred. During the term of the swap, the investor would be scheduled to receive an interest-equivalent fee periodically from the dealer, based on the notional amount. No matter where the stock price is on the expiration date, over-the-counter options documented as a single contract and variable forwards should receive essentially the same tax treatment when settling the collar.

Deductibility of interest expense. In addition to hedging, most investors with appreciated stock wish to generate liquidity in order to reinvest and diversify their investments. Often investors choose to monetize, or borrow against, their appreciated stock. Borrowing creates interest expense. If the borrowing cost occurs in conjunction with a straddle, the interest expense may need to be capitalized.

Proposed regulations published in January 2001, with respect to the straddle rules make it clear that if shares that are hedged by a collar are pledged as collateral for a borrowing, the interest must be capitalized. However, the proposed regulations do give an investor the right to specify which shares form a straddle and which are being leveraged. *A careful identification of collateral will preclude the IRS from allocating (and therefore capitalizing) any of the borrowed proceeds against the shares that have been collared.* Because of this "specific identification" rule, an investor who has liquid securities (other than the collared shares) to post as collateral should still be able to deduct some or all of the interest expense.

Assume, for example, an investor with $100 of XYZ Corporation stock wants to hedge the stock with an options-based collar and then monetize the maximum amount possible under the margin rules (Regulation T) in order to diversify. The investor could borrow $50 against the hedged XYZ position. If the investor diversifies into publicly traded securities, he or she could then finance the purchase of $100 of reinvestment securities through an additional $50 margin loan against the reinvestment portfolio. Under the proposed regulations, the interest expense incurred with respect to the borrowing against the hedged XYZ position must be capitalized, while the interest expense incurred with respect to the borrowing against the reinvestment portfolio is deductible.

Suppose instead that an investor with $200 of XYZ Corporation stock wants to hedge $100 of XYZ with an options-based collar and then monetize $100 in order to diversify. He or she could borrow $50 against the unhedged XYZ position. If the investor diversifies into publicly traded securities, he or she could then finance the purchase of $100 of reinvestment securities through an additional $50 margin loan against the reinvestment portfolio. Under the proposed regulations, both the interest expense incurred by borrowing against the unhedged XYZ position and the interest expense incurred by borrowing against the reinvestment portfolio are deductible because there was no borrowing against the collared position. Therefore, under the proposed regulations, investors can readily monetize options-based collars and swaps with embedded collars through margin loans and, in most instances, still achieve a current deduction for some or all of the interest expense incurred with respect to the monetization.

FIGURE **7.4** *Tax Treatment of Alternative Hedging/Monetization Techniques for Stock Acquired After 1983*

Should carrying costs be currently deductible against investment income (35% benefit)?

If investor implements monetizing collar through:

Prepaid variable forward	No
Options and margin loans	Yes, at least partially
Equity swap (with embedded collar) and margin loans	Yes, at least partially

When *cash settling*, if stock price is *above* call strike, what is the character of the loss?

If investor implements monetizing collar through:

Prepaid variable forward	Deferred long-term capital loss
Options and margin loans	Deferred long-term capital loss
Equity swap (with embedded collar) and margin loans	Deferred ordinary deduction or long-term capital loss at investor's discretion

When *cash settling*, if stock price is *below* put strike, what is the character of the gain?

If investor implements monetizing collar through:

Prepaid variable forward	Short-term capital gain
Options and margin loans	Short-term capital gain
Equity swap (with embedded collar) and margin loans	Short-term capital gain or ordinary income at investor's discretion

In certain instances, however, it might be necessary to use a prepaid variable forward to achieve the monetization level desired, because of margin rule limitations. Assume, for example, that an investor with $100 of XYZ Corporation stock wants to hedge the stock with a collar and then monetize the maximum amount possible in order to diversify into a portfolio of investments that the dealer cannot ascribe collateral value to (for example, hedge fund investments). If the investor hedges the XYZ position with either an options-based collar or a swap with

When delivering stock, what is the character of the gain?

If investor implements monetizing collar through:

Prepaid variable forward	Long-term capital gain
Options and margin loans	Long-term capital gain
Equity swap (with embedded collar) and margin loans	Long-term capital gain

At what rates are dividends taxed?

If investor implements monetizing collar through:

Prepaid variable forward	35%
Options and margin loans	35%
Equity swap (with embedded collar) and margin loans	35%

an embedded collar, a maximum of $50 could be borrowed against the hedged XYZ position under Regulation T. It will not be possible to borrow against the reinvestment portfolio because it consists of investments that are not publicly traded securities and, hence, cannot be given collateral value by a brokerage firm. Only $50 can be monetized, and under the proposed regulations all of the interest expense would need to be capitalized because the borrowing was incurred against a collared position.

If the investor instead used a prepaid variable forward, he or she would most likely be able to monetize between 85 percent and 90 percent of the value of the position, as the Regulation T limitations do not apply to prepaid variable forwards. Although the nature of a prepaid variable forward effectively converts interest expense into a deferred capital loss, in this instance there is no tax disadvantage, because if margin loans were used to monetize the position, the borrowing is against the collared stock, so the interest expense would have to be capitalized.

Investors have the right under the proposed regulations to specify the collateral pledged to secure margin indebtedness. If the interest expense is incurred by borrowing against unhedged securities, the investor can currently deduct such expense; otherwise, it must be capitalized. Therefore, the monetization structure that should deliver optimal after-tax results would be an options-based collar combined with a margin. A prepaid variable forward is tax disadvantaged because its structure ensures that all net borrowing costs are deferred and capitalized.

The optimal tool for post-1983 stock. To some degree, the proposed regulations level the playing field among the various derivative tools that are available to hedge and monetize stock acquired after 1983. If the proposed regulations with respect to the straddle rules become effective, a single-contract collar combined with a margin loan should in most instances deliver the minimum after-tax cost for stock acquired after 1983.

Listed options are clearly disadvantaged because of the inability to net the option premiums, which can easily be accomplished with over-the-counter derivatives. Prepaid variable forwards are clearly tax disadvantaged because of their structure, which gives the investor no choice but to defer and capitalize the net cost of carry.

Prepaid variable forwards do, however, have several nontax advantages. First, the cost of borrowing is fixed throughout its term, in contrast to a floating-rate borrowing typical of a margin loan. (Brokerages do, however, offer fixed-rate margin loans to their clients.) Second, because Regulation T is not applicable, a margin call would not be possible in the future. (A margin call is a possibility if margin loans are used.) Third, because Regulation T is not applicable, the investor is not limited to borrowing a maximum of 50 percent of the value of the hedged position if the purpose of the borrowing is to reinvest in other securities, as it would be if a margin loan were used. Fourth, because there are no "moving parts" (for example, no interest payments because the interest has been prepaid, no interest rate resets because it's fixed-rate debt, no mark to markets) until the expiration date, there are no monthly statements and other periodic communications from the brokerage firm (as there are with options and swaps) to confuse and potentially frustrate a private client.

FIGURE 7.4 compares and contrasts the tax treatment of the three available financial-derivative-based hedging and monetization strategies—swaps, options, and forwards—for stock acquired after 1983.

Recent Tax Developments

The provisions of the Jobs and Growth Tax Relief Reconciliation Act of 2003 affect investors who hedge and monetize a dividend-paying stock. The act lowered the tax rate on dividends to 15 percent for individuals if they hold the shares for at least sixty-one days. However, the new rules require that investors hold their dividend-paying shares unhedged during the sixty-one-day holding period. This requirement applies to every dividend period. If investors hedge the stock during this period, they will not be eligible for the reduced 15 percent tax rate. Therefore, if an investor hedges with an options-based collar, a swap-based collar, or a prepaid variable forward, any dividends paid will be taxed at the 35 percent rate, not the 15 percent rate. Thus, Wall Street's ultimate challenge is to devise a strategy that gives the investor the desired economics (hedging and monetization) while allowing any dividends received with respect to the stock to be taxed at the 15 percent rate and not be a straddle. Stay tuned.

Exchange Funds: An Alternative Solution

Over the past few years a number of bills have been introduced in Congress that would eliminate the use of exchange funds as a viable strategy to diversify highly appreciated securities. None has been passed into law.

Under current law, exchange funds can prove useful in two situations. First, if a derivative-based solution is not available because of the characteristics of a particular stock (for example, the stock is difficult to borrow or is subject to liquidity constraints), an exchange fund might be an acceptable solution. Second, if an investor's objective is to diversify out of all or a portion of a highly appreciated stock position and into a passively managed portfolio that tracks a certain index (for example, the S&P 500), certain exchange funds might prove particularly useful. Certain exchange funds historically have exhibited a very high degree of correlation with the index they were designed to track, and their "all-in" cost compares favorably against what it would otherwise cost to monetize through a derivative-based solution and redeploy the proceeds into an index fund.

Because of the constructive-sale rules, derivative-based solutions generally have a maximum length of five years, at which time they must be rolled over to maintain the benefit of the tax deferral. Whether or not an investor can enter into a similar derivative transaction five years from now will, of course, depend on the status of the tax law at that time. Exchange funds are often structured with an unlimited life, and even if they were legislated away, the legislation is unlikely to be retroactively applied.

Since exchange funds have periodically come under attack, investors considering an investment in an exchange fund might wish to act sooner rather than later to take advantage of the current opportunities.

Recapping the Choices

Before the enactment of the constructive-sale rules, hedging and monetizing a concentrated, highly appreciated stock position was fairly straightforward. The short against the box was the strategy that was most often used, and it was very cheap and extremely effective. The constructive-sale rules currently in place require a much more sophisticated analysis to ensure that the investor selects this strategy and tool that deliver the optimal after-tax result.

An investor who is fortunate enough to own highly appreciated shares of a company that's involved in an announced tax-free stock-for-stock merger would do well to explore the potential of establishing a short against the box that will not be subject to the constructive-sale rules through merger arbitrage. Successfully implemented, this strategy will clearly deliver the optimal tax result. If the merger arbitrage strategy is not available to the investor, an income-producing collar could be a more appropriate one. This strategy can be implemented through various financial derivative tools, including options, a swap with an embedded collar, or a prepaid variable forward.

If the investor acquired the stock before 1984, the straddle rules do not apply, and a swap with an embedded collar combined with a margin loan would be the most tax-efficient solution in most situations. If a swap is not executable (perhaps because of minimum-size requirements of the dealer), an options-based collar with a margin loan would be optimal.

If the investor acquired the stock after 1983, the straddle rules apply, and a single-contract, options-based collar combined with a margin loan should deliver the optimal after-tax result. If the client owned municipal bonds, a portion of the interest will not be deductible and a prepaid forward would be appropriate.

If the merger arbitrage strategy and the income-producing collar strategy are not available to the investor, consider an exchange fund.

CHAPTER 8

A Different Approach to Asset Location

GOBIND DARYANANI

Without question, the first step in managing a portfolio is de-termining the client's equity exposure and appropriate asset allocation. The next step—the placement of the asset classes in their various taxable and tax-deferred accounts—generates a lot of questions, and experts don't all agree on the best answers. Typically, the client's portfolio consists of four to fifteen asset classes, and the client will own a taxable account and a traditional individual retirement account (IRA). Asset location defines how much of each of these asset classes is placed in the taxable account and how much in the traditional IRA. More generally, these asset classes may need to be distributed among accounts with other tax characteristics, such as Roth IRAs, annuities, or trusts.

Formal studies on asset location have addressed the location of two asset classes, namely, stocks and bonds. One concluded that bonds should be located in the IRA before stocks;[1] another came to the opposite conclusion.[2] Trade journals have documented recommendations on asset location from leading planners and mutual fund companies. These opinions vary, with some managers favoring bonds in the IRA and others the opposite strategy of stocks in the IRA. Other leading planners use the same percentage of all asset classes in both the traditional IRA and the taxable accounts (called the pro rata approach). The pro rata approach is also prevalent in nonmanaged 401(k) plans and when multiple managers are involved.

But there may be a better way—the difference approach, a generic framework for finding the optimal location for multiple asset classes. The framework is based on comparing the relative value (defined as after-tax end wealth) when the asset class is placed in a traditional IRA versus when it's placed in a taxable account. The benefit of the approach is quantifiable and depends on the client's particular financial profile (taxes, cash flows), prevailing tax laws, and the tax characteristics of the asset classes in the portfolio. The difference approach can provide an after-tax return benefit of approximately 20 basis points per year over simply using identical allocations in the multiple accounts with different characteristics. The methodology is generic in that it can be extended to any number of asset classes and adapted to address other account types such as the Roth IRAs, annuities, and trusts. Note, however, that considerations other than maximizing end wealth, such as client preferences (for example, wanting their taxable accounts and IRAs to have similar performance) and fund constraints (certain funds cannot be held in a taxable account), are not accommodated in the analyses.

The Difference Method

Let's look first at the traditionally used sum approach to asset location, which has been explored in prior studies. Consider a client who has $500,000 in a taxable account and $500,000 in a traditional IRA. Her asset allocation is 50 percent in stocks and 50 percent in bonds. Let's assume the following for the client's tax profile and asset classes: ordinary tax rate = 30 percent, capital gains rate = 15 percent, stocks pretax return = 8 percent, bonds pretax return = 5 percent, horizon n = 30 years. Assume that all growth in the taxable account is long term and realized (taxed at 15 percent); the IRA grows at the pretax rate and taxes become due on the full account at liquidation in year 30. Given these assumptions, which location maximizes after-tax end wealth? Stocks in the IRA or bonds in the IRA? Using the sum approach, both scenarios are analyzed and the one that leads to higher after-tax end wealth is chosen:

Strategy 1: Stocks in IRA
Total end wealth = end-wealth stocks in IRA (SI) + end-wealth bonds in taxable (BT)

$$SI = \$500,000 * [1 + .08*(1 - .3)]^{30} = \$3,521,930$$
$$BT = \$500,000 * [1 + .05*(1 - .3)]^{30} = \$1,403,397$$
$$SI + BT = \$4,925,327$$

Strategy 2: Bonds in IRA
Total end wealth = end-wealth bonds in IRA (BI) + end-wealth stocks in taxable (ST)

BI = \$500,000 * (1 + .05)^{30} * (1 - .3) = \$1,512,680
ST = \$500,000 * [1 + .08 * (1 - .15)]^{30} = \$3,598,385
BI + ST = \$5,111,065

For this set of assumptions, strategy 2 results in greater end wealth, so the client should locate bonds in the IRA and stocks in the taxable account. Mathematically, bonds go into the IRA first if

$$BI + ST > SI + BT \tag{1}$$

With different assumptions, the order may flip—for instance, if the capital gains rate is 20 percent, stocks win; if the stock pretax return is 10 percent, stocks win; if the horizon is forty years, stocks win; or if the ordinary tax rate is 25 percent, stocks win again. By "stocks win" we mean stocks in the IRA do better than bonds in the IRA. Clearly, the results depend on the input assumptions.

What if she had three classes: A, B, and C? In that case, it's not a question of which class goes into the IRA and which doesn't, but rather which of the three classes goes into the IRA *first*. The three classes would somehow need to be rank ordered to determine the fill sequence into the IRA. A brute-force approach would be to compare A and B, A and C, and B and C, just as we did above. That would then lead to a rank order for the three classes. That would mean six analyses, since each analysis requires two comparisons. So, using the sum method, two asset classes require two comparisons, and three asset classes require six comparisons; and one can show that four asset classes require twelve comparisons, ten asset classes require ninety comparisons, and so on. In general, N asset classes require $N*(N - 1)$ comparisons. Doable but quite a chore.

Let's look at how the difference method would be applied. The thought process emanates from the question, How much *difference* does it make to end wealth whether an asset class is placed in an IRA or in a taxable account? If favoring the IRA makes a lot of difference, the asset class should be placed in the IRA. If favoring the taxable makes a lot of difference, it should be placed in the taxable account. If it makes little difference, it doesn't matter much whether the asset class is placed in the taxable or the IRA. Essentially, the approach can be summed up this way: Rank the asset classes based on the differences in end wealth between placing them in the IRA versus the taxable account. Fill the IRA using this rank ordering. For the two-asset-class problem the differences would be as follows:

SI − ST = \$3,521,930 − \$3,598,385 = −\$76,455
BI − BT = \$1,512,680 − \$1,403,397 = \$109,283

Mathematically, bonds go into the IRA first, since

$$BI - BT > SI - ST \qquad (2)$$

Equation 2 can be derived from equation 1 by simply subtracting BT and ST from both sides of the inequality. Thus the sum method is exactly equivalent to the difference method. The primary advantage offered by the difference method is that it requires fewer comparisons. In the difference method, for ten asset classes, we require ten comparisons to establish the rank order for filling the IRA; whereas in the sum method we would have required $10 * (10 - 1) = 90$ comparisons.

If there are N asset classes, the steps for determining the optimum asset location would be as follows. For purposes of rank ordering, assume the same amount of money in the taxable account and the IRA—say, $1. For the first asset class, compute the end wealth when placed in an IRA, then in the taxable account, and record the difference. Repeat

FIGURE **8.1** *Four Asset Classes Example*

Step 1: Establish rankings

	ALLOCATION	IRA	TAXABLE
Real estate	9.0	7.0	2.00
Corporate bonds	5.0	4.0	1.00
Short-term bonds	2.2	2.3	-0.10
U.S. large cap	7.0	10.0	-3.00

Step 2: Fill the IRA using rankings

	ALLOCATION	IRA	TAXABLE
Real estate	$100,000	$100,000	$0
Corporate bonds	$100,000	$100,000	$0
Short-term bonds	$300,000	$100,000	$200,000
U.S. large cap	$500,000	$0	$500,00
TOTALS	**$1,000,000**	**$300,000**	**$700,00**

this for each of the N classes, recording a total of N differences. Rank the asset classes based on the differences. This rank order establishes the sequence in which the IRA gets filled. That is the essence of the difference approach.

Let's illustrate these steps with an example using four asset classes. Suppose a client owns $1,000,000 split between two accounts: $300,000 in an IRA and $700,000 in a taxable account. The client's overall portfolio allocation is 50 percent ($500,000) in U.S. large stocks, 30 percent ($300,000) in short-term bonds, 10 percent ($100,000) in real estate, and 10 percent ($100,000) in corporate bonds. Using the difference method, how would these asset classes be located in the two accounts? The client's horizon is thirty years and the characteristics of the asset classes are known. The first step is to rank these classes based on end wealth for each. Assume that someone has done this analysis for you and that the end wealth of a dollar for each of the classes is as shown in **FIGURE 8.1.**

Step 1 in Figure 8.1 is read as follows: If a client had $1 of real estate, in thirty years it would grow to $9 after taxes in the client's IRA, and $7 after taxes in the client's taxable account. The difference is $2 in favor of the IRA. Thus you'd want to locate real estate in the IRA. A pro rata approach, placing $.50 in the taxable and $.50 in the IRA would result in $8, which is an inferior placement. The differences for the other classes are shown and ranked accordingly. Step 2 is to fill the IRA, starting with the top-ranked asset class (real estate) and continuing down until the $300,000 of the IRA is filled; the remaining funds are placed in the taxable account. This location of assets is optimal in that it maximizes after-tax end wealth for the client under the assumptions that have been made.

A Case Study

This case study applies to a client who owns ten asset classes and illustrates the complete model developed for studying asset location. The taxable account in the study was modeled for variable cash flows and tax rates and included the treatment of dividends, long-term gain (realized and unrealized), netting of losses, and step-up in basis. The IRA model included minimum required distributions, with any excess withdrawals being transferred to a taxable account. The portfolio would be rebalanced annually, and we included simulation capabilities to study the effects of volatility. Asset Locator, a software program developed by Digiqual Inc., is used for the analyses presented in this chapter.[3]

The baseline case study considers a client, age sixty, who has $500,000 in a taxable account (basis $450,000) and $500,000 in a traditional IRA

FIGURE **8.2** *Return Data for 10 Asset Classes Used in Baseline Study*

ASSET CLASS	MEAN	SD	DIV%	LTG%	LTG REALIZED%	ALLOCATION 60% EQUITIES
Short-term bonds	2.5%	2.79%	0.0%	0%	0%	32.0%
High-yield bonds	6.0%	7.72%	0.0%	0%	0%	8.0%
U.S. large stocks —active	11.0%	19.78%	1.5%	35%	15%	6.0%
U.S. large stocks	8.5%	17.38%	1.5%	100%	0%	18.0%
U.S. small stocks —active	11.5%	29.56%	0.5%	80%	60%	9.0%
International large stock	9.0%	18.72%	0.0%	80%	67%	6.0%
Emerging markets	12.0%	27.18%	0.0%	90%	60%	6.0%
Real estate (public)	10.5%	16.80%	0.0%	25%	10%	6.0%
Commodities	8.0%	20.95%	0.0%	0%	0%	4.5%
Absolute return	8.0%	7.00%	0.0%	10%	10%	4.5%

(no basis). The client's effective federal tax rate is 35 percent preretirement and 30 percent postretirement, and state tax is assumed to be 5 percent. The client retires at age sixty-five, and we assume a time horizon of thirty years (to age ninety). In the base case, we assumed no additions or withdrawals, except for required minimum distributions; no step-up in basis; and no carryforward losses. Realized capital gains and dividends are taxed at 15 percent.

As shown in **FIGURE 8.2**, the client's overall portfolio contains ten asset classes: 40 percent in bond classes (two classes) and 60 percent in equity classes (eight asset classes, with different tax-efficiency characteristics). This is a reasonably well diversified portfolio for a client with a moderate risk tolerance. Some classes, however, were selected specifically to illustrate the principles of location. The return characteristics of the asset classes are shown in Figure 8.2. The notes at the end of this chapter detail how this data was derived.[4] The return components of equity classes are read as follows: for example, for U.S. small stocks (active), assume a total return of 11.5 percent, of which 0.5 percent is dividends return and 11 percent is capital gains return; of the 11 percent capital gains, 80 percent is long term (8.8 percent) and 20 percent is short term (2.2 percent); 60 percent of the long-term capital gain is realized annually (6.6 percent); and 20 percent of the long-term capital gain is unrealized (2.2 percent).

Using the Asset Locator model, we first computed the difference in after-tax end wealth between the IRA and the taxable account for each of these classes. Note that the accounts are liquidated at the end of the horizons to establish the after-tax end wealth. The ranked differences are shown in **FIGURE 8.3** and graphed in **FIGURE 8.4**.

Observe that the high-return, low-tax-efficiency asset classes (real estate, U.S. large active, commodities, and absolute return) do much better in the IRA. The high returns enhance the benefits from tax deferral, and these classes would not benefit much from the lower capital gains tax rates in the taxable account since only a small portion of their return is subject to capital gains treatment. Such classes, with high returns and low tax efficiency, will generally do much better in an IRA.

FIGURE 8.3 *End-Wealth Differences for Baseline Case*

	IRA FACTOR	TAXABLE FACTOR	DIFFERENCE
Real estate (public)	10.33	8.21	2.11
U.S. large stocks—active	11.97	9.99	1.98
Commodities	5.29	4.45	0.83
U.S. small stocks—active	14.24	13.51	0.73
Absolute return	5.33	4.62	0.71
High-yield bonds	3.16	3.08	0.08
Emerging markets	16.01	16.06	-0.05
International large stock	7.41	7.63	-0.22
Short-term bonds	1.26	1.59	-0.33
U.S. large stocks—tax efficient	6.80	8.60	-1.80

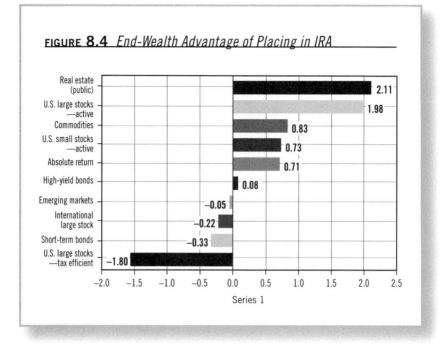

FIGURE 8.4 _End-Wealth Advantage of Placing in IRA_

On the other hand, the high-return, highly tax-efficient class (U.S. large efficient) does much better in the taxable account. That's because this class benefits from both the lower taxation of capital gains and the tax deferral of the capital gains (since these gains are not realized each year). Such high-return, tax-efficient classes will generally do much better in a taxable account.

Note also that the differences are relatively small for the low-return classes (short-term bonds and, to some extent, corporate bonds), making the penalty for mislocating these classes in one account versus the other small also. So it won't matter much where the low-return classes are placed. Emerging markets, international large, and U.S. small (active) have medium efficiencies and high returns. For such classes, for this particular client's profile, the benefits of tax deferral in the IRA are high, but so are the benefits of lower capital gains tax rates in the taxable account. These two opposing forces tend to cancel each other, resulting in a small difference between the IRA and the taxable end wealth. Changes in the client's profile, however, can swing the advantage in favor of the IRA or the taxable account. Such medium-return or tax-efficiency classes are swing classes in that their location will depend strongly on the client's profile. We'll see these guiding principles reinforced in the subsequent sections on sensitivity analyses.

FIGURE 8.5 *Asset Location for Baseline Case*

	ALLOCATION	IRA	TAXABLE
Real estate (public)	$60,000	$60,000	$0
U.S. large stocks—active	$60,000	$60,000	$0
Commodities	$45,000	$45,000	$0
U.S. small stocks—active	$90,000	$90,000	$0
Absolute return	$45,000	$45,000	$0
High-yield bonds	$80,000	$80,000	$0
Emerging markets	$60,000	$60,000	$0
International large stock	$60,000	$60,000	$0
Short-term bonds	$320,000	$0	$320,000
U.S. large stocks—tax efficient	$180,000	$0	$180,000
	$1,000,000	$500,000	$500,000

The asset-location process is completed by filling the IRA with these established rankings. The results are shown in **FIGURE 8.5**.

This difference location strategy was compared with three alternative location strategies: all bonds in the IRA (bonds in), all stocks in the IRA (stocks in), and a pro rata location strategy (using the same percentage asset allocation in both the taxable account and the IRA). The resulting end wealth for these four location strategies are shown in **FIGURE 8.6**. Annual rebalancing was assumed in this analysis.

The difference location strategy results in $5,485,881 − $5,118,229 = $367,652, which is more end wealth than the result for the pro rata location strategy. This difference translates to an after-tax benefit of 24 basis points per year over the pro rata location strategy, a 30-basis-point benefit over the bonds-in location strategy, and an 18-basis-points benefit over the stocks-in location strategy. The analysis shown in Figure 8.6 was based on a straight-line fixed return for the classes.

To study the impact of volatility on these results, we ran Monte Carlo simulations comparing the difference location strategy with the pro rata location strategy. The results, shown in **FIGURE 8.7**, indicate that the mean benefit

FIGURE **8.6** *Comparison of Location Strategies for Baseline Case*

Straight-line analyses with annual rebalancing

	START	AT END	RETURN
Pro rata	1,000,000	$5,118,229	5.59%
Bonds in	1,000,000	$5,035,322	5.54%
Stocks in	1,000,000	$5,208,722	5.66%
Difference located	1,000,000	$5,485,881	5.84%

FIGURE **8.7** *Comparison of Difference Located vs. Pro Rata Monte Carlo Analyses With Annual Rebalancing*

Straight line	0.24%
STATISTICAL ANALYSIS	
Mean	0.22%
25% Probability	0.19%
50% Probability	0.23%
75% Probability	0.26%
Total end wealth located	**$5,485,881**
Total end wealth pro rata	**$5,118,229**
Increase in end wealth	**7.2%**

is slightly lower (22 basis points versus 24 basis points), but the benefit is quite robust, in that it stays positive even for the 25th percentile of the simulations.

Clearly, the pro rata location of asset classes is suboptimal, leading to 7 percent less end wealth than the results with a difference location strategy.

	Benefit / (Loss)		
VS. PRO RATA	**VS. BONDS IN**	**VS. STOCKS IN**	**VS. LOCATED**
0.00%	0.06%	-0.06%	-0.24%
-0.06%	**0.00%**	-0.12%	-0.30%
0.06%	0.12%	**0.00%**	-0.18%
0.24%	0.30%	0.18%	**0.00%**

Sensitivity Analyses

Changes in the client's financial profile, tax laws, and the characteristics of the asset classes affect the ranking of asset classes in the portfolio and the location benefit. Sensitivity analysis can offer some general guidelines on location and help identify the parameters that are most critical in location decisions.

The parameters of a client's profile include tax rates, horizon, withdrawals, carryforward losses, percentage of assets in the IRA, and equity exposure. We'll look at tax law changes such as dividends tax rates, long-term gains tax rates, and step-up in basis rules. Asset-class parameters must also be considered, including total return, dividends, percentage of return that's long term or short term, percentage of long-term return that's realized annually, and assumed risk premium.

Client Profile

The location-analysis results for the base case are shown as scenario A in **FIGURE 8.8**. For this base case, remember, we assumed a preretirement tax rate of 35 percent, a postretirement tax rate of 30 percent, a time horizon of thirty years, no withdrawals, and no carryforward losses at the beginning of the study. The impact of changing postretirement tax rates (scenarios B, C), carryforward losses (scenario D), withdrawals (scenario E), and horizon (scenarios F, G) are shown in this table. The top part of the table shows the differences between placing asset classes in the IRA versus taxable accounts. The bottom part of the table shows the ranking for filling the IRA based on these differences.

For this set of client parameter variations, we see that the tax-inefficient, high-return classes (real estate, U.S. large active, absolute return,

FIGURE 8.8 *Sensitivities to Client Profile Parameters*

Difference between placing in IRA and taxable

SCENARIO SCENARIO DESCRIPTION	A BASE CASE	B TAX RATE 35%	C TAX RATE 15%
Real estate (public)	2.11	1.67	2.13
U.S. large stocks—active	1.98	1.39	2.31
Commodities	0.83	0.63	0.82
U.S. small stocks—active	0.73	-0.25	2.07
Absolute return	0.71	0.50	0.77
High-yield bonds	0.08	-0.04	0.16
Emerging markets	-0.05	-1.25	1.76
International large stock	-0.22	-0.73	0.58
Short-term bonds	-0.33	-0.39	-0.18
U.S. large stocks—tax efficient	-1.80	-2.35	-0.71
End wealth	5,485,881	5,135,019	6,782,134
Location benefit over pro rata	0.22%	0.22%	0.14%

Rank order for filling RA

Real estate (public)	1	1	2
U.S. large stocks—active	2	2	1
Commodities	3	3	5
U.S. small stocks—active	4	6	3
Absolute return	5	4	6
High-yield bonds	6	5	8
Emerging markets	7	9	4
International large stock	8	8	7
Short-term bonds	9	7	9
U.S. large stocks—tax efficient	10	10	10

D CARRYFWD LOSS 200K	E WITHDRAWALS 10K/YR.	F HORIZON 20 YRS.	G HORIZON 10 YRS.
1.00	1.37	0.49	-0.20
0.73	1.19	0.38	-0.24
0.16	0.26	0.19	-0.20
-0.43	-0.12	-0.13	-0.40
0.06	0.13	0.13	-0.23
-0.38	-0.40	-0.10	-0.26
-1.29	-0.93	-0.39	-0.45
-0.87	-0.88	-0.34	-0.39
-0.55	-0.70	-0.31	-0.32
-1.97	-2.40	-0.81	-0.47
5,705,910	4,032,677	2,949,678	1,547,559
0.17%	0.32%	0.23%	0.16%
1	1	1	1
2	2	2	4
3	3	3	2
6	5	6	8
4	4	4	3
5	6	5	5
9	9	9	9
8	8	8	7
7	7	7	6
10	10	10	10

and commodities) remain the first classes to fill the IRA. The high-return tax-efficient U.S. large is consistently the last class to fill the IRA, that is, the first class to fill the taxable account. The long-term tax-deferred benefits of placing this class into a taxable account far exceed all other considerations. Given a choice between filling the taxable account with short-term bonds or tax-efficient, high-return classes, the tax-efficient class is the clear winner.

Tax-efficient high-return classes gain a lot from being placed in the taxable account, but it doesn't make much difference which account holds the low-return, short-term bond class. For the other classes, the differences are relatively minor, and their IRA-fill priority depends on the scenario's parameters. General rules are difficult to come by, and a customized analysis is needed to find the optimal location for maximum end wealth. But since the differences are relatively small for these classes, the location decisions will usually not be as critical as for classes where the differences are large.

From scenario E we see that the benefit is greater and therefore more critical if the client will be withdrawing funds. That's not surprising, since we would intuitively expect a larger penalty for mislocation if the assets are withdrawn soon thereafter. Scenarios F and G show that the differences are relatively smaller when the horizon is shortened, which suggests that location optimization does not matter as much if the assets are going to be liquidated within a few years.

The final client parameter we'll discuss is the percentage of assets held in an IRA. Clearly, there would be no benefit due to location if all assets

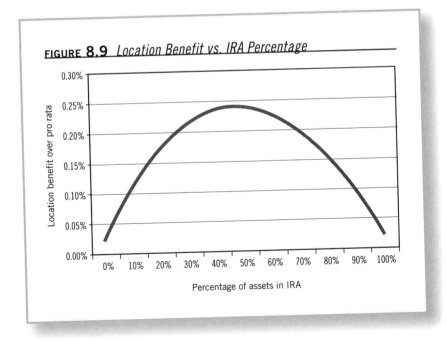

FIGURE 8.9 *Location Benefit vs. IRA Percentage*

were in a taxable account (0 percent in IRA) or if 100 percent of assets were in an IRA, since there would be nothing to cross-locate. The benefit of difference location over pro rata location increases as the percentage in the IRA departs from these extremes. This is depicted in **FIGURE 8.9**. For this client, we see that the location benefit ranges from 0 to 25 basis points, depending on the percentage of assets in the IRA.

In separate analyses, we observed that location benefits increase with the client's equity exposure. This is to be expected, since the equity classes contribute more to end wealth.

Tax Laws

This study of asset location was triggered by our need to understand the impact of reductions in the dividend taxation rates (from ordinary rates to 15 percent) and capital gains taxation rates (from 20 percent to 15 percent) that resulted from the Jobs and Growth Tax Relief Reconciliation Act (JGTRRA) of 2003. **FIGURE 8.10** shows the impact of these changes on location for our sample client.

The reduction in these tax rates has only a small impact on end wealth in the IRA (insofar as minimum distributions transferred to the taxable account got some tax benefits); however, the end wealth in taxable accounts increased significantly. Not surprisingly, assets with higher returns showed more of an increase. The top two classes and the bottom two classes remained in their respective bands, whereas the middle classes' rankings changed slightly. Emerging market is the only class that moved in rank by more than two positions, although the difference remained small. If this client had placed asset classes correctly—as shown in Figure 8.10—before JGTRRA became law, no major changes would have been required in the asset location as a result of the act. The reduction in tax rates did increase the projected end wealth by approximately 5 percent, and the benefit of difference location over pro rata location stayed the same.

Now, let's consider the impact of step-up in basis on location (see **FIGURE 8.11**). Because an IRA does not receive a step-up in basis, the increase in end wealth is small, being limited to the portion that was distributed to a taxable account due to required minimum distributions. Higher-return classes benefit a lot from basis step-up in the taxable account. As a result, we see that some equity classes drop in ranking (for example, the emerging markets asset class drops from 7 to 9) because it would do better in the taxable account. The end-wealth increases by approximately 5 percent, and the location benefit increases to 25 basis points per year. Note that U.S. large stocks (tax efficient) have held the last place firmly through a wide range of parameter variations.

FIGURE 8.10 *Sensitivities to Tax Rates*

	TAX RATES IRA FACTOR	
	ORD / 20%	15% / 15%
Real estate (public)	10.2	10.3
U.S. large stocks—active	11.6	12
Commodities	5.3	5.3
U.S. small stocks—active	13.7	14.2
Absolute return	5.3	5.3
High-yield bonds	3.2	3.2
Emerging markets	15.5	16
International large stock	7.2	7.4
Short-term bonds	1.3	1.3
U.S. large stocks —tax efficient	6.5	6.8
Location benefit over pro rata	**0.22%**	**0.22%**
End wealth	**$5,485,881**	**$5,204,866**

Ord / 20% means dividends taxed at ordinary rates; pre-JGTRRA capital gains taxed at 20% (pre-JGTRRA).
15% / 15% means dividends taxed at 15% and capital gains taxed at 15% (post-JGTRRA).

Asset-Class Parameters

We've seen that location of an asset class depends on the difference in end wealth when placed in the IRA versus the taxable account. If the difference is positive, the class will do better if placed in the IRA; if it's negative, the class will do better if placed in the taxable account. Mathematically, we can express this difference as:

$$\text{Difference} = (1 + \eta_{ira}*r)^n - (1 + \eta_{txbl}*r)^n \tag{3}$$

Here r is the pretax return, n is the horizon, η_{ira} and η_{txbl} are the tax efficiencies (= after-tax return / pretax return) in the IRA and taxable account,

TAXABLE FACTOR		TAX RATES DIFFERENCE		RANKING	
ORD / 20%	15% / 15%	ORD / 20%	15% / 15%	ORD / 20%	15% / 15%
8	8.2	2.3	2.1	2	1
8.8	10	2.8	2.0	1	2
4.4	4.5	0.8	0.8	5	3
11.7	13.5	2.0	0.7	6	5
4.6	4.6	0.8	0.7	3	4
3.1	3.1	0.1	0.1	8	6
14.1	16.1	1.4	-0.1	4	7
6.9	7.6	0.3	-0.2	7	8
1.6	1.6	-0.3	-0.3	9	9
7.2	8.6	-0.7	-1.8	10	10
5.40%					

respectively, $\eta_{ira}*r$ is the after-tax return in the IRA, and $\eta_{txbl}*r$ is the after-tax return in the taxable account. For the taxable account, tax efficiency is high if most of the return is long-term gain that's deferred; the account is inefficient if the return is taxed in the current year as short-term gain or long-term realized gain. We've seen that high-return classes are better placed in a taxable or tax-deferred account, depending on the efficiency of the asset class. Thus, neither return nor tax efficiency alone can be used to determine the best location of a class. The key metric for establishing location is after-tax end wealth, which depends on some combination of return and tax efficiency.

FIGURE 8.11 *Sensitivity to Step-Up in Basis*

	STEP-UP IN BASIS IRA FACTOR	
	NO STEP-UP	STEP-UP
Real estate (public)	10.33	10.44
U.S. large stocks—active	11.97	12.13
Commodities	5.29	5.29
U.S. small stocks—active	14.24	14.46
Absolute return	5.33	5.33
High-yield bonds	3.16	3.16
Emerging markets	16.01	16.40
International large stock	7.41	7.48
Short-term bonds	1.26	1.26
U.S. large stocks—tax efficient	6.80	7.25
Location benefit over pro rata	**0.22%**	**0.25%**
End wealth	**$5,485,881**	**$5,780,344**

FIGURE 8.12 depicts that combination for a client with a thirty-year horizon. In this analysis, we defined efficiency as 1 minus the percentage of total return that's not deferred and is taxed at a normalized 35 percent rate. Consider, for example, an asset class that has a pretax return of 7 percent, and suppose 20 percent of the return is taxed at ordinary tax rate of 35 percent and 40 percent is realized at a long-term rate of 15 percent. The normalized percentage of return taxed at 35 percent = 20 percent * 35/35 + 40 percent * 15/35 = 37.1 percent, and the efficiency = 1 − 37.1 percent = 62.9 percent. From the chart this class would be better placed in the taxable account. Similar generic charts could be developed for shorter and longer horizons.

We've shown that if the total returns are low (for example, short-term bonds), the differences will be small, and the location of such asset classes will not affect end wealth. Equity classes that are projected to have higher returns will make a larger difference to the end wealth, so their location is more critical.

TAXABLE FACTOR		STEP-UP IN BASIS DIFFERENCE		RANKING	
NO STEP-UP	STEP-UP	NO STEP-UP	STEP-UP	NO STEP-UP	STEP-UP
8.21	8.45	2.11	1.99	1	1
9.99	10.33	1.98	1.80	2	2
4.45	4.46	0.83	0.83	3	3
13.51	14.01	0.73	0.44	4	5
4.62	4.63	0.71	0.71	5	4
3.08	3.09	0.08	0.07	6	6
16.06	17.03	-0.05	-0.63	7	9
7.63	7.82	-0.22	-0.34	8	7
1.59	1.61	-0.33	-0.34	9	8
8.60	10.33	-1.80	-3.09	10	10

Since the placement of higher-return equity classes makes more of a difference to end wealth, we would expect location benefits to increase with the assumed risk premium, as shown in **FIGURE 8.13**. If the assumed risk premium is 1 percent, the returns from all the classes do not differ much and location benefits are seen to be relatively small. The ranking of classes was not found to change much with risk premium.

Summary of Case Studies

We tested our assumptions on location benefits over a range of client profiles and tax law variations, including client's age, tax rates, equity exposure, percentage in IRA, horizon, withdrawals and additions, changes in tax laws, and risk premium. More than seventy-five cases were explored. We found that the benefits are higher for longer horizons and higher assumed risk premium; they're lower for shorter horizons and when the

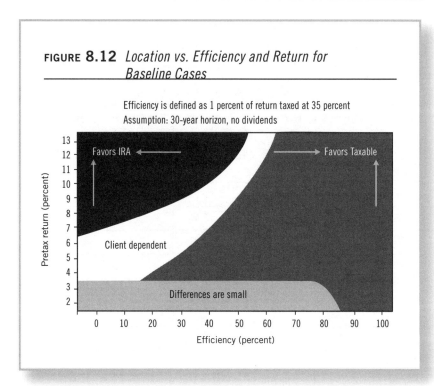

FIGURE 8.12 *Location vs. Efficiency and Return for Baseline Cases*

Efficiency is defined as 1 percent of return taxed at 35 percent
Assumption: 30-year horizon, no dividends

Favors IRA ← → Favors Taxable

Client dependent

Differences are small

Pretax return (percent)

Efficiency (percent)

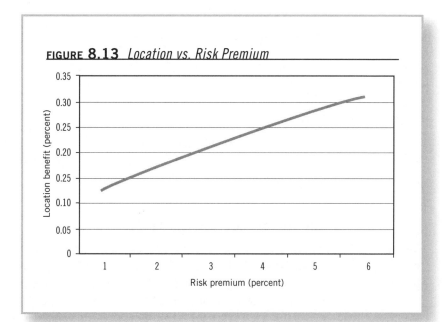

FIGURE 8.13 *Location vs. Risk Premium*

Location benefit (percent)

Risk premium (percent)

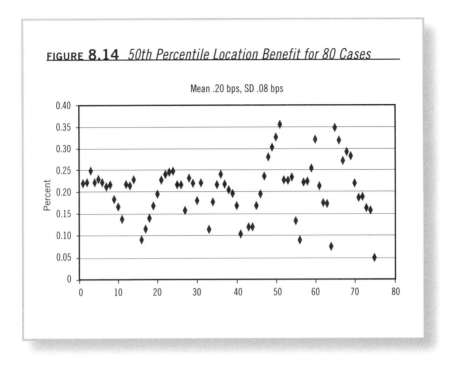

FIGURE **8.14** *50th Percentile Location Benefit for 80 Cases*

Mean .20 bps, SD .08 bps

percentage of assets in the IRA was close to zero or 100 percent.

FIGURE 8.14 plots the mean benefit of difference location over pro rata location for these cases, and **FIGURE 8.15** shows the results of simulations used to derive the 25th and 75th percentiles for these cases. The mean location benefit is 20 basis points per year after taxes, and the location benefits are robust, in that even the 25th percentile benefit is more than 10 basis points per year after taxes. This is in contrast with benefits from tax-loss harvesting[5] and rebalancing,[6] where the 25th percentile benefits are typically negative (which means that these tax-efficiency measures can hurt 25 percent of the time).

The location benefits for other pairs of account types for the baseline case were studied and are reported in **FIGURE 8.16**. The relative benefit of location increases with the difference in tax characteristics of the accounts. If the client had a Roth IRA and a taxable account, the difference location for asset classes would provide an advantage of 35 basis points per year over a simple pro rata location, which suggests that efficient location is even more important for this pair of accounts. Intuitively, one would want to fill the Roth with the higher-return classes. In contrast, for similar account types, such as an IRA and an annuity, the location benefits are relatively small (6 basis points per year), which suggests that even a pro rata location strategy should be quite acceptable. To date, our studies have

FIGURE **8.15** *Location Benefit Percentiles*

	MEAN	SD
25th percentile	0.15%	0.07%
50th percentile	0.20%	0.07%
75th percentile	0.24%	0.08%

FIGURE **8.16** *Benefit of Difference-Based Location Over Pro Rata Location for Different Account Pairings*

IRA + TAXABLE	ROTH + TAXABLE	ANNUITY + TAXABLE	ROTH + IRA	ANNUITY + IRA
0.21%	0.35%	0.27%	0.21%	0.06%

been limited to pairs of accounts; the study of location for the client with more than two account types has yet to be developed.

In Practice

Although there is a definite after-tax return benefit to locating assets properly, one needs to weigh them against certain costs of location. First, in contrast to pro rata location, where all account types have the same allocation, the rebalancing of asset classes becomes much more difficult when the client has different asset classes in the different account types. Some planners have chosen the pro rata approach primarily to minimize the administrative costs of rebalancing accounts with different asset classes. We believe the end-wealth benefits provided by difference location over the pro rata method justify those costs.

Be aware, too, that the relocation of asset classes—assuming the client's assets are not located correctly—may require the sale of assets with unrealized gains. One needs to assess the benefits of relocation versus the cost of recognizing those gains. As in the real estate business, relocation would not make sense if the horizon of the portfolio is relatively short.

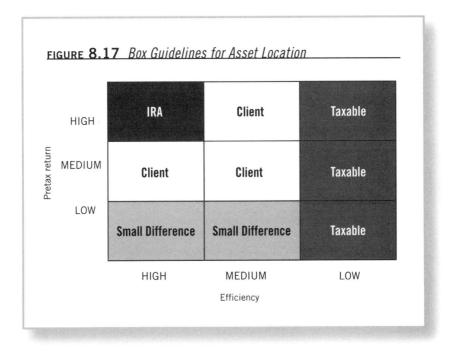

FIGURE 8.17 *Box Guidelines for Asset Location*

Our end-wealth location analysis did not consider restrictions that may preclude the location of certain asset classes in taxable or tax-deferred accounts, and we have not yet addressed the location when there are more than two account types. Optimizers may be required to accommodate such constraints.[7] Nor did we address the issue of client preferences, such as a desire to have all accounts provide similar returns. Such constraints may need to be considered in the location decisions.

But once you've decided to apply the approach, keep the following in mind (see **FIGURE 8.17**):

❑ The ranking of which assets to place in an IRA should be based on end wealth, not on return or efficiency alone.

❑ The client parameters that are most critical in this ranking are the horizon and tax rates.

❑ The asset-class parameter that's most critical is the percentage of long-term and short-term return realized annually.

❑ High-return, highly tax-efficient classes do much better in a taxable account; high-return, low-efficiency classes do better in an IRA.

❑ Low-return classes can be placed in either account, since the difference in end wealth will be small.

❑ Low-return and very-high-efficiency classes, such as municipal bonds, should be located in taxable account.

❑ General rules are difficult to come by for medium-return and efficiency classes, and a customized analysis would be needed to find the optimal location that maximizes end wealth

The framework we've described addresses optimal asset location using the difference in end wealth between two account types. This difference location approach leads to a robust advantage of approximately 20 basis points per year after taxes over the pro rata location strategy of using the same asset classes in the IRA and taxable accounts.

Chapter Notes

1. Robert M. Dammon, Chester S. Spatt, and Harold H. Zhang, "Optimal Asset Location and Allocation With Taxable and Tax-Deferred Investing," ftp://pareto .gsia.cmu.edu/pub/papers/retire.pdf (June 2003).

2. John B. Shoven and Clemens Sialm, "Long-Run Asset Allocation for Retirement Savings," *Journal of Private Portfolio Management* (Summer 1998): 13–26.

3. Asset Locator, a software program developed by Digiqual Inc.: http://www .taxefficientplanning.com.

4. This standard deviation and correlations (not shown) were based on historical data for the period 1970 to 2002. The projected arithmetic-mean return for the U.S. large efficient was assumed to be 8.6 percent, corresponding to a risk premium of 3.5 percent over long-term bonds return of 5.1 percent. The returns of the other equity classes were based on historical differences relative to the U.S. large efficient asset class. The dividends, percentage of long-term gain, and percentage of realized long-term gain were derived from Morningstar's data on the fifty largest funds in each asset class.

5. Robert D. Arnott, Berkin L., and Jia Le, "Loss Harvesting: What's It Worth to the Taxable Investor," *Journal of Wealth Management*: 84–94.

6. Robert D. Arnott and Robert M. Lovell, "Rebalancing: Why? When? How Often?" *Journal of Investing* (Spring 1993): 5.

7. PORTAX, a software tool developed by Windermere Investment Associates: http://www.windinvest.

PART THREE

INVESTMENTS

In investing, the nitty-gritty covers a lot of ground—far too much to cover in any single book. Rather than attempt to prepare a few chapters covering a long list of specific investments that have been addressed by innumerable authors in innumerable books, we selected a few specific investment categories that are (or should be) among those every adviser knows a good deal about: alternative investments, insurance investments, and those yet to be. Obviously, we've taken a bit of poetic license with the latter; however, when we asked people as thoughtful and forward-looking as Gary Gastineau and Craig Lazzara to write on a cutting-edge subject they consider important for advisers, we weren't surprised when they provided a chapter not on an investment that exists today but on one that practitioners are likely to be dealing with tomorrow—if we're lucky.

Gary L. Gastineau and Craig J. Lazzara

When pondering the future of investments, you can't do better than to ask those involved in the creation of earlier successful investments. That's why we invited Gary Gastineau and Craig Lazzara to participate in the *Think Tank,* and they delivered. Gastineau and Lazzara propose a new investment vehicle—the multiple-share-class fund, based on strategies to substantially reduce costs and improve the use of research information.

The chapter provides readers with immediate value by presenting a wealth of useful information regarding the current components of investment costs. This information will facilitate better evaluation and management of the investment products available to clients today. Longer term, although Gastineau and Lazzara acknowledge that they have no illusions that their creation provides all the elements of an ultimate fund structure, readers are sure to spread the word, and the ideas can only stimulate discussions and innovations that result in additional ways to improve fund performance for our clients.

Ben Baldwin

Ben Baldwin is recognized not only by the insurance industry but also by the legal, accounting, and planning professions as "Mr. Insurance." Whenever a complex issue regarding insurance arises at Evensky, Brown & Katz, the cry is "call Ben."

Although we remain skeptical about the propriety of the extensive use of insurance investment products, the sheer magnitude of their use by investors and the credibility of respected advisers such as Baldwin suggest that ignoring these investments may be detrimental to our clients' financial health.

As you'll quickly learn when you dip into Baldwin's offerings, he not only believes in insurance investment wrappers, he's passionate about them. Who better to learn from than a knowledgeable, respected, and dedicated practitioner? Whatever your bias, you'll be well rewarded as Baldwin shares with you his insights and wisdom on the efficacy of insurance-wrapped investment products.

Mark Hurley

Mark Hurley, a friend and member of our Alpha Group (a seventeen-member professional study group), is well known throughout the investment world for his broad-ranging and insightful knowledge of the profession and his prestigious wealth-management conferences. Hurley believes that although alternative asset classes are fraught with risks, advisory firms that want to remain successful will need to know how to invest effectively in them. Framing his discussion as a cautious approach to alternatives, Hurley nevertheless argues that before long, alternative investments, properly screened, will be considered not off the beaten path but rather as additional investment choices to be used in constructing optimal portfolios. Do we agree with Hurley's conclusion? Absolutely. After years of investigating, considering, and even rejecting the use of alternative investments in our clients' portfolios, our investment committee voted to incorporate a modest allocation of our core equity investments to an absolute-return fund. Hurley's chapter can assist you in incorporating these investments appropriately and successfully into the range of possibilities you consider for your clients.

CHAPTER 9

Reinventing the Investment Fund

GARY L. GASTINEAU AND CRAIG J. LAZZARA

I t's not hard to find strong, consistent, and well-reasoned criticism of investment products and services. From "insider" industry critics like John Bogle, founder of the Vanguard Group, to crusading journalists and high-profile politicians, proponents of change in the financial-services industry in general and fund management in particular are everywhere. Most reform rhetoric focuses on eliminating conflicts of interest and extracting large financial settlements from alleged offenders. Ironically, few of the changes wrought—or even proposed—will improve the efficiency or effectiveness of the investment process very much.

Reform can bring dramatic performance improvements—when reformers solve real problems. The late trading that New York Attorney General Eliot Spitzer revealed in September 2003 probably netted all the perpetrators—both identified and unidentified—about $400 million before any necessary payoffs and expenses in 2001.[1] The performance cost of late trading to investors was probably at least twice what the bad guys took home. Spitzer also came down on market timers, most of whom operate within the law. Market timers made about $5 billion from investors in 2001 and cost funds at least the same amount in additional expenses.[2] Eliminating the scope for both late trading and market timing and solving a myriad of other problems by simply requiring that fund share purchase and sale orders be received by 2:30 p.m. would augment ongoing fund shareholder performance by around $40 billion per year.[3]

This chapter is about keeping that $40 billion in investors' accounts and possibly improving their investment experience in other ways as well.

The changes we propose will reduce costs substantially, improve the use of research information in the fund-management industry, and ultimately improve investor performance. We describe how to build a better pooled investment fund product—the self-indexing fund (SIF)—by improving the structure of contemporary fund products. We measure, at least in an approximate way, the advantages of changing the structure of the various types of funds offered today and quantify the expected cost reduction and performance enhancement. The estimates of cost savings we've developed illustrate how third-party fund evaluators might improve the usefulness of their analyses.[4]

This new multiple-share-class fund structure can foster efficient and confidential use of investment information by controlling the release of trading information until the fund's managers and traders have had every reasonable opportunity to act on the information. With such changes in place, superior investment products and services can be packaged effectively. Of course, as with all grand conceptions, it has a few obstacles. But we offer some ideas for getting past them.

Structural Efficiency: Reducing Costs

A fund's structural costs can be reduced in at least five areas:

❏ *Shareholder accounting:* Mutual fund companies usually provide shareholder accounting at the fund level; for most closed-end funds and for all exchange-traded funds (ETFs), shareholder accounting occurs only in the investor's brokerage or advisory account.

❏ *Index fees:* Some benchmark index funds, especially ETFs, pay significant amounts to index providers as index-licensing and calculation fees.

❏ *Embedded transaction costs:* Some benchmark indices have become so popular that the announcement of index changes before the fund can change its portfolio increases the cost of implementing the index changes, thus penalizing index fund performance.

❏ *Last-minute creation and redemption of ETF shares:* By permitting creation and redemption notification until the market closes, exchange-traded funds restrict the portfolio manager's flexibility to implement portfolio changes, thus increasing the fund's transaction costs and discouraging aggressive implementation of changes.

❏ *Last-minute purchases and sales of conventional fund shares:* Traders can buy or sell most open-end mutual fund shares until just seconds before the market close. These traders often use conventional open-end funds as a source of liquidity—at considerable cost to the fund's long-term investors.

Each of these structural features has a distinct effect on the relative performance of certain funds. The structural concept we propose—a self-indexing fund—can be used both as a benchmark against which to compare the costs of current fund structures and as an illustration of how investors' costs can be minimized by thoughtful decisions about fund structure. Several important characteristics make the structure unusual:

- ❑ SIFs have a core ETF share class and are designed to be traded on an exchange. Like any current ETF, investors can buy and sell SIFs throughout the trading day at prices close to intraday asset value.
- ❑ Creations and redemptions of the core ETF share class take place once daily, at net asset value. Authorized participants, the dealers who create and redeem ETF shares, will not have until the market's close to declare their intention to create or redeem SIF shares but instead must "show their cards" by 2:30 p.m. eastern time.
- ❑ The SIF structure can accommodate active as well as passive strategies and multiple share classes. A passive SIF, however, would not attempt to match a conventional benchmark index.[5]

The unique features of the index fund version of the SIF illustrate some of the cost advantages of the self-indexing fund. Different stock market indices are designed to serve different purposes. The indices that underlie all current ETFs are standard, or benchmark, indices (for example, Standard & Poor's 500, Russell 2000, and Morgan Stanley Capital International Europe Australasia and Far East [MSCI EAFE]). We denote these as benchmark indices because they were originally designed to serve as standards against which investments and investment managers could be evaluated. Changes to a benchmark index must be publicly disclosed *before they become effective.*

Besides benchmarking active managers, in what other ways might indices be used? One obvious purpose is to serve as a fund template, that is, as a model to guide the investment of money. Benchmark indices were not designed to serve as fund templates. This fact was of little consequence in the early days of index funds. The value of indexed assets was small relative to actively managed assets, and indexing was concentrated in liquid, large-cap market sectors. As indexing has grown, the disadvantages of using a benchmark index as a fund template have become increasingly evident. Specifically, announcement of pending benchmark index changes means that the trading plans of benchmark index funds are announced in advance. The disclosure of benchmark index funds' expected trading produces significant transaction costs—perhaps as much as 50–100 basis points annually for large-cap index funds and much more for funds based on popular small-cap indices. No active manager would tolerate this performance penalty; in fact, active managers keep their trading plans secret because they don't want to give away information.

What characteristics would be desirable in an index designed to serve as a fund template? For starters, it would not disclose changes in advance of the fund's portfolio executions. Such a "silent" index is designed to serve *solely* as a fund template. Silent indices can cover the same market segments and subsegments as benchmark indices do. Unlike benchmark indices, however, changes to a silent index would be disclosed publicly only *after* the manager of a silent index fund has had the opportunity to incorporate the change into the silent index fund portfolio. Silent indices are the appropriate templates for index funds.

How would an ETF based on a silent index differ from today's benchmark index ETFs? Two adjustments would be required. One relates to the index itself. Obviously, a silent index fund cannot be based on any commercially available benchmark index. The fund manager/index compiler will need to define index membership rules and rebalancing schedules clearly enough for investors to understand what they're buying but ambiguously enough to keep opportunistic traders from front-running the fund.

The second adjustment is surprisingly simple: the self-indexing fund must impose an earlier deadline for authorized participants to declare their commitments to create or redeem fund shares. Now ETF authorized participants have until 4:00 p.m. eastern time (that is, until the market close) to reveal their intentions. This means that when an ETF manager changes his portfolio, he can't be assured of buying and selling the right quantity of stock. If, for example, there are net creations on the day in question, the manager will have sold too little of the stock being dropped from the portfolio and will have to clean up the residual the next day. Conversely, if a redemption occurs, the manager will have to reverse part of the trade, buying back enough of the liquidated stock to cover the redemptions.

Without an early cutoff on creation and redemption notices, opportunistic traders will realize that the ETF in question has to sell X and buy Y the next day, and they will attempt to trade ahead of the ETF, potentially increasing its transaction costs. Not so with a silent index fund, where index changes are not known until the portfolio's trading is complete. By requiring earlier notice of intentions to create or redeem, the fund can execute all trades required by index changes *in a single day*.[6] By the time the next day's creation basket reveals that the index has changed, the portfolio change will have been executed.

What is remarkable about the self-indexing fund concept is that the same structural change required by a silent index fund will also enable a SIF to accommodate many actively managed strategies. Like silent index managers, active equity managers do not want their trades—that is, their portfolio changes—to be disclosed in advance of execution. The early-notice provision will provide active managers the same trading confidentiality it gives to managers of a silent index fund.[7]

A Comparison of Fund Structure Costs

FIGURE 9.1 evaluates the operating cost disadvantage of competing fund structures relative to the self-indexing fund; index funds are compared with silent index versions of the SIF, and actively managed funds are compared with actively managed SIFs. Figure 9.1 highlights five fund structures:

- ❑ *Self-indexing fund.* This is the prototypical self-indexing fund ETF share class. It differs from ETFs now trading in that it requires commitment to create or redeem by 2:30 p.m. on normal trading days. Any index is a silent index—that is, changes are not disclosed until after the fund has had an opportunity to transact. All fund entries and exits are through the ETF share class.
- ❑ *Conventional index fund.* The Vanguard 500 fund serves here as an example of a large conventional benchmark index fund. Other conventional index funds are usually less efficient—sometimes much less efficient—than the Vanguard 500.
- ❑ *Benchmark index ETF.* The most numerous examples of benchmark index ETFs are the iShares equity funds issued and managed by Barclays Global Investors. These iShares funds have conventional ETF cost advantages and should have ETF tax efficiency, but they retain the transaction-cost disadvantages of benchmark index mutual funds.
- ❑ *New index ETF share class.* If a manager bases a fund on a newly designed benchmark index, the fund might be thought of as occupying an intermediate position between a self-indexing fund and a widely used benchmark index fund. Vanguard has changed the benchmark indices for its domestic index funds (other than its S&P 500 index fund) and has adopted indices developed for the U.S. market by Morgan Stanley Capital International (MSCI), apparently to Vanguard's specifications.[8] Vanguard's versions of these funds also have entry and exit through both a conventional share class and an ETF share class.
- ❑ *Conventional actively managed fund.* This is by far the most common type of conventional mutual fund.

In the following sections, we review the avoidable cost elements we've identified and how they affect the relative economics of the five fund structures.

FIGURE 9.1 *The Self-Indexing ETF Cost Advantage*

	FUND-LEVEL SHAREHOLDER ACCOUNTING	INDEX CALCULATION OR LICENSE FEES
Self-indexing fund ETF share class —active or silent index	——	Not material
Vanguard 500 conventional index fund	.06%	Not material
Benchmark index ETF	——	.015%–.05%
New index ETF share class	——	Not material
Conventional active mutual fund	.06+%	——

*An investor in a large-cap silent index fund using the SIF structure should enjoy an average annual pretax performance advantage over the Vanguard 500 fund of .06–.56 percent, or 6–56 basis points.

Fund-Level Shareholder Accounting

ETF shares and ETF share classes are fully Depository Trust Company–eligible securities, which means there are no shareholder accounting costs at the fund level for these shares. All funds are required to furnish periodic reports to their beneficial shareholders, but ETFs have a single registered shareholder, the Depository Trust Company's nominee, Cede & Co.

Fund-level shareholder accounting costs for conventional funds vary greatly from one fund company to another. For the most credible minimum estimates for fund-level shareholder accounting (and related costs incurred by the fund issuer), consider the difference between Vanguard's conventional index fund expense ratios for ordinary shareholders (investor shares) and the expense ratio for the VIPERs ETF share classes or for Admiral Shares (offered only to very large shareholders). The difference in each case is 6 basis points. For conventional active funds, note that in many cases shareholder accounting and related service costs are substantially higher, well into double (basis-point) digits.[9]

EMBEDDED TRANSACTION COSTS	LAST-MINUTE CREATION/ REDEMPTION	LAST-MINUTE CASH PURCHASE	NET COST DISADVANTAGE RELATIVE TO SIF*	RANK IN TAX EFFICIENCY
—	—	—	—	1
0–.50%	—	—	.06%–.56%	4
.20%–1.90%	See text and Figure 9.3	—	.22%–1.95%	2
.10%–.95%	Inadequate data	—	.10%–.95%	3
—	—	1.43±%	1.49+%	5

Index Calculation or License Fees

A self-indexing fund with a silent index will bear some costs associated with development and maintenance of its underlying index. Because silent index funds will lack meaningful retail index branding, they will almost certainly need to be launched with an institutional share class in place. An important purpose of this institutional class is to build the new index fund's credibility partly on the implied endorsement of the institutional shareholders. Given this "core" investment commitment, the net cost of any index licensing and calculation will not be material when measured against assets and will probably be less than 1 basis point for the fund as a whole.

Given Vanguard's current low index license fee structure (for example, $50,000 per year maximum to Standard & Poor's), most industry observers believe that the fee Vanguard pays for the new MSCI brand indices is similarly immaterial. Figure 9.1 indicates immaterial index license fees for both the Vanguard 500 and new index fund types listed. Most non-Vanguard conventional index funds pay annual license fees of 3 basis points or less.

Barclays Global Investors entered into an essentially uniform license fee arrangement with its principal equity index providers.[10] Under this

FIGURE **9.2** *Expense Ratio and Transaction Cost Differences —Silent vs. Benchmark Index Funds*

	(1) LARGE-CAP SILENT	(2) S&P 500	(3) SMALL-CAP SILENT	(4) RUSSELL 2000
Expense ratio	.15%	.10%	.30%	.20%
Embedded index transaction costs	.25%	.50%–1.00%	1.00%	2.00%–3.00%
Total	.40%	.60%–1.10%	1.30%	2.20%–3.20%
Net benchmark index fund disadvantage	.20%–.70%		.90%–1.90%	

licensing arrangement, most of their license fees fall in the range of 1.5–5 basis points, with most of the fund assets above the midpoint of that range. Most other large benchmark index ETFs pay annual license fees of 3–6 basis points, with one large fund apparently paying an effective license fee significantly above that range. Actively managed funds usually pay no index license fees.

Embedded Transaction Costs

Like benchmark indices, silent indices for self-indexing funds incur some market-impact transaction costs when a portfolio is changed, even if market impact is not exacerbated by publication of the index change before the fund has an opportunity to trade. Our estimates, based on the assumed annual expenses in **FIGURE 9.2**, show a minimum net disadvantage for large-cap benchmark index ETFs of 20 basis points (0.20 percent) and a maximum net disadvantage on small-cap index funds (for example, Russell 2000) of 190 basis points (1.90 percent). Other numbers in Figure 9.2 reflect expected differences in fund-management expense ratios, which may be slightly higher for a silent index fund's ETF share class. (The premium expense ratio may be justified by the expectation of premium fund performance based on savings in transaction costs with silent indices.) It's reasonable to assume in Figure 9.1 that the new index ETF share classes will face relative transaction cost penalties about half the size of those faced by established benchmark ETFs. Vanguard's MSCI index license is nonexclusive. Consequently, if the funds are successful, other funds can license the same indices. If the indices become popular, Vanguard will face embedded index change transaction costs, just as it did with the older benchmark indices it abandoned for the MSCI indices. Like other benchmark indices, the changes in these MSCI indices will be determined before the fund can trade to implement them.

In Figure 9.1, we estimate incremental embedded transactions costs for the Vanguard 500 index fund at 0–50 basis points. This comes from deducting a generous 50 basis points from both the minimum and maximum for large-cap indices in Figure 9.2 to reflect Vanguard's historical ability to recapture some of the embedded transaction costs in the S&P 500 Index and thereby improve performance. These estimates assume a continued level of embedded transaction costs close to the levels seen since 1993. If we had a Russell 2000 conventional index fund in this category, it would have much higher embedded index transaction costs than the large-cap S&P 500 fund.

A related aspect of ETF benchmark index fund portfolio management—ETFs' failure to beat their benchmark indices as some conventional index mutual funds do—merits some discussion and analysis. A number of managers of conventional benchmark index funds—Vanguard being the best known—and many institutional indexed portfolios have consistently beaten their benchmarks *after expenses.* In contrast, most ETFs have done little better than to track their indices *before expenses.* For example, the Vanguard Small-Cap Index Fund Investor Shares, which were shares in a conventional index fund benchmarked until mid-May 2003 to the Russell 2000 Index, beat that index before taxes and *after expenses* by an average of 76 basis points over the ten-year period ending December 31, 2001.[11] **FIGURE 9.3** shows that the Vanguard Fund beat the Russell 2000 Index by 61 basis points in the year ending December 31, 2001, whereas the iShares Russell 2000 ETF returned 53 basis points less than the index return in that same year. Both results include similar levels of reported fund expenses. A number of small-capitalization mutual fund and institutional portfolio managers have regularly beaten the Russell 2000 by 100 basis points or more before expenses, so Vanguard's degree of Russell 2000 Index outperformance after expenses was not unusual. This outperformance appears to come largely from timing the implementation of index changes to capture some of the transaction costs embedded in the annual index reconstruction process.

Few ETFs fall as far behind their benchmarks as the iShares Russell 2000 ETF did in 2001, but the principal managers/administrators of most equity index ETFs have not been aggressive in attempting to beat

FIGURE **9.3** *Fund Performance and Tracking Error in Two Russell 2000 Funds*

	2001		2002	
	PERFORMANCE	TRACKING ERROR	PERFORMANCE	TRACKING ERROR
Vanguard Small-Cap Investor Shares	+3.10%	+.61%	−20.02%	+.46%
Russell 2000 Index	+2.49%	——	−20.48%	——
iShares Russell 2000 ETF	+1.96%	−.53%	−20.52%	.04%
Vanguard outperformance of iShares	+1.14%.	——	+.50%	——

their benchmarks. Before 2003, most ETFs lagged their benchmarks by roughly the amount of the fund's expense ratio—the performance we would expect from an index fund manager who replicates index changes precisely.[12] Unfortunately for ETF investors, performance since the end of 2002 has featured negative tracking errors larger than expense ratios for most ETFs.[13]

Why have ETFs generally failed to beat their benchmark indexes? Partly because the transparency of the current equity index ETF structure may encourage disclosure of trade timing through the creation basket, correspondingly discouraging—or at least complicating—efforts to beat the benchmark.[14] This obstacle to improving returns relative to the benchmark index in an ETF is largely artificial, and it can be eliminated completely by simply setting the cutoff time by which an authorized participant must commit to create or redeem earlier in the trading day than the market close.[15]

Last-Minute Creations and Redemptions

Requiring early notice of intent to create or redeem fund shares can have a modest favorable impact on an ETF's performance. The manager of a self-indexing fund (or of any other ETF) wants to plan trades to get to a target portfolio at the end of the trading day. To do this, the manager needs to adjust her trading plans to reflect the fact that the size of the portfolio may change during the day because of creations and redemptions that will be effective at the market close. With early notice, the manager can hit the portfolio composition target by completing trades after 2:30 p.m. to reflect creations and redemptions to be made at that day's close.

Early notice is unlikely to have a readily measurable effect on a new index ETF share class because the ETF share class would be only one of at least two share classes that might affect trading plans. There are too many variables, including the relative size of the ETF share class, to pin the effect down in advance of a few years' operation of funds with these indices. Any movement toward early notice and recapture of embedded benchmark index trading costs should reduce the cost disadvantage experienced to date by benchmark index ETFs. In estimating embedded transaction costs, Figure 9.1 assumes that *all* benchmark index ETFs will require earlier cutoff times and will start to beat their benchmark indices—as the better conventional index funds currently do.[16] Our calculations suggest that the irreducible cost to ongoing shareholders from last-minute creations and redemptions in an otherwise well-managed ETF is typically less than 5 basis points annually.[17] The effect on benchmark ETF portfolio manager behavior is also real—but generally much larger than 5 basis points.

Last-Minute Cash Purchase of Conventional Fund Shares

One of the least appreciated yet most important advantages of the ETF structure over that of most conventional funds is that it protects ongoing shareholders from the impact of fund share traders. With very minor exceptions, the current issuers of ETFs have set the conditions for creation and redemption to place the *entire* cost of fund share turnover in the creation and redemption process and to protect ongoing shareholders from the impact of fund share trading completely.

An excellent 1999 academic study of fund trading estimated the net cost to conventional mutual funds of providing liquidity to investors at approximately 1.43 percent per year.[18] This study explored why various researchers have found that although fund managers appear to add value in market timing and stock selection, this performance does not flow through to fund shareholders. Performance is penalized by the funds' cost of providing liquidity to traders. The principal reason is fairly straightforward: fund traders tend to take advantage of momentum; they buy funds when the market is trending upward and sell funds when the market is trending downward. When a trader buys a fund at Monday's net asset value, the fund has cash to invest on Tuesday morning. If short-term momentum persists, the cash will be deployed at higher prices than those that determined Monday's net asset value, thereby subsidizing the fund share buyer. The same dynamics apply in reverse to fund share sales.

In contrast, a short-term trader does not affect the ETF portfolio unless his trades stimulate creation or redemption of ETF shares in kind. When creation or redemption occurs, the creating or redeeming dealer (or trader) pays all the costs of buying or selling portfolio shares as well as the creation or redemption fee that covers the administrative and processing costs of the transaction. The significance of this difference between conventional funds and ETFs is that, other things being equal, an ETF should outperform a comparable conventional fund by the conventional fund's net cost of providing liquidity to fund share traders. Figure 9.1 reflects the estimated cost difference of 143 basis points, or 1.43 percent.

In contrast to most actively managed funds, Vanguard used to protect its index fund shareholders from fund share traders by a process that, in effect, gave Vanguard's portfolio managers the functional equivalent of the early creation or redemption notice for the self-indexing fund. All funds should either use the former Vanguard process or else permit entry and exit exclusively through an ETF share class to protect ongoing shareholders.[19]

Net Cost Disadvantage Relative to the Self-Indexing Fund

This column in Figure 9.1 shows the total net cost disadvantage range of each of the alternative structures relative to the self-indexing fund. The relative advantage of the self-indexing fund structure is stated conservatively.

Rank in Tax Efficiency

The final column of Figure 9.1 shows an estimate of the relative tax efficiency of each fund or fund type. The market decline that followed the first quarter of 2000 makes this ranking less significant than it would have been before the market decline, but it remains of considerable long-term importance for shareholders who pay taxes. We use a ranking measure because the size of capital gains distributions depends on overall market performance.[20]

Silence Is Golden: The Stealth Index Fund

A silent index fund should outperform an index fund based on a benchmark index because, as noted earlier, benchmark index funds incur unnecessarily large transaction costs.[21] The multiple fund licensees of some benchmark indices, together with speculators and other investors, who acquire full (and costless) knowledge of benchmark index changes, impose a transaction cost penalty on funds using benchmark indices. Benchmark index funds are forced to make portfolio changes amid a flurry of market activity caused by the announcement of changes to an index—and often buy high and sell low during the blizzard of rebalancing and related speculation. Transaction costs associated with high-profile index changes are increasingly embedded in benchmark index performance.

A silent index is based on many of the same kinds of rules as a good benchmark index, but the specific silent index rules are not subject to use by multiple funds (or by speculators attempting to front-run trades by funds using the index). As a result of delayed disclosure of index changes, the silent index fund should outperform comparable benchmark index funds by anywhere from a few basis points to a few hundred basis points per year, depending largely on the benchmark index's rules, capitalization range, and popularity. The silent index will be less well known than similar benchmark indices and, consequently, may have a fund marketing penalty associated with it. However, the performance of the most popular benchmark indices is so adversely affected by embedded transaction costs that the silent index and its fund are very likely to outperform the benchmark over any reasonable time interval. A performance advantage based on the easily understood principle of confidential treatment of planned fund transactions should overwhelm any cachet attached to a branded index fund.

Occasionally, someone immersed in the minutia of today's benchmark index funds may be shocked by the suggestion that a silent index could be created and managed by the same organization that advises the fund. But who is more likely than the fund manager to have the interests of the fund in mind? Indeed, with actively managed funds, a single organization—sometimes even a single individual—is ultimately responsible for the whole investment process. One reason equity indices and equity index funds are so widely criticized today is that when indexing was in its infancy, the market impact of index funds trying to match index changes was not significant. This lack of market impact in the early years of indexing led to today's performance problems with benchmark index funds.[22] By the late 1990s, market impact costs had risen significantly and were drawing increased attention.[23]

The manager of a benchmark index fund is not permitted to know about changes in the index before anyone else does. Once announced, the changes are known to anyone who cares before the fund can trade. A benchmark index fund is the only type of fund that operates under such an information handicap. No one seems able to explain why such publication of a fund's trading plans makes sense for investors. Indeed, full advance disclosure sets up long-term index fund investors to be ravaged by front-running traders. Common sense suggests that we adjust procedures to serve the investor better rather than simply accepting tradition, but benchmark index funds continue to attract assets. Market-impact costs are hurting benchmark index fund investors—and the more assets invested in funds tracking a benchmark index, the greater the transaction-cost penalty associated with using that index. In this context, it's useful to describe a few features of silent index funds.

Rules to Minimize Turnover

There are a variety of ways indices can be constructed and reconstituted to minimize portfolio turnover costs in a fund based on the index. If, for example, an index is based on mid-cap stocks or small-cap stocks, turnover can be reduced by putting a buffer range above or below—or possibly at both ends of the capitalization range—to limit changes in the membership of the index that may be reversed on the next rebalancing date. If a stock gets far enough outside the index's desired company size range, for example, a full reversal becomes less probable and the stock can be dropped from the index with less likelihood of its reentering at the next rebalancing.

The Changing Role of the Index Fund Manager

Most of the fun of being a benchmark index fund manager comes from outperforming the fund's benchmark index. Index funds have attracted some excellent managers who demonstrate their skill by nearly always beating the benchmark *before the fund's costs* and often beating it *after reported costs.* Indeed, the defining quality of a good benchmark index fund manager has become the ability to trade better than the other market participants who attempt to profit from index changes. These managers simply recapture some of the transaction costs embedded in the benchmark index.

It will be harder for silent index fund managers to beat their indices, but their funds should perform better, on average, than comparable benchmark index funds—even if the manager simply matches the silent index—because many of the embedded transaction costs of the benchmark index can be avoided. In fact, simply matching the index was what the pioneers of indexing advocated. But matching a popular benchmark index today means accepting a performance penalty.

Just as the role of the index fund manager will change, the availability of an actively managed ETF-based fund structure offers a great opportunity to integrate actively managed portfolios in a way that preserves the value of an adviser's trading information.

An Integrated Investment Process for Actively Managed Portfolios

Most sizable investment-management organizations offer a variety of products to investors. These investment products are usually managed independently in that each portfolio is independent in composition relative to other portfolios. However, because funds and other products from the same adviser hold numerous securities in common and because the investment manager has a responsibility to the beneficial holders of each portfolio to treat them fairly, management of the products is partly integrated. In practice, this means that the firm often will purchase a particular security or group of securities for many or even all of the manager's accounts or funds. To manage conflicts of interest, investment-management organizations have developed techniques to handle purchases and sales for different accounts in a sequence or rotation. The rotation is designed to ensure that a particular account comes first on the list for some investment ideas, in the middle for some, and, inevitably, at the bottom of the list for others. The starting point for the purchase of a new position or the liquidation of an old position is selected at random, or the starting point simply moves from the top to the bottom of the list, a step at a time, recycling back to the top until a position has been either taken or liquidated for accounts as necessary.

Each type of account has characteristics that cause a manager trading in it to reveal different amounts and kinds of information, almost at random, to other market participants while the trading moves through account categories. A few examples will illustrate the range and nature of this disclosure—or leakage.

Actively managed ETFs will tend to reveal something of their trading implementations in the publication of creation or redemption baskets at the very least and, in some cases, from published changes in entire portfolios. It will be a while before the number of active ETFs is large enough for their role to affect the disclosure of an investment organization's trading activity. Posted changes in the initial funds will be high profile and might be expected to have a significant market impact when a fund is in the midst of a trading program. We expect the initial actively managed ETFs to report changes in the fund portfolio daily after the close of trading. Within a short time, the nondisclosure period should extend to at least two weeks. In today's markets, very little trading information has value after two weeks, so the active ETF disclosure issue should end at that point.

Of all the players in the poker game of trading, conventional mutual funds play it closest to the vest. Beginning in late 2004, they will have to report the major positions in their portfolios quarterly, but not until sixty days after the effective date of the reported portfolio. No other institutional portfolio composition stays relatively confidential for that long. The secrecy of conventional mutual funds is unusual and may, in practice, be illusory considering that the typical conventional mutual fund is just one client of a diversified adviser.

Many advisers of actively managed conventional funds also manage a variety of separate taxable accounts and other separate and pooled institutional accounts such as pension and profit-sharing plans. Any activity in one account has possible implications for other accounts handled by the same manager. If an investment manager is responsible for a number of separate taxable accounts for individual investors, the arrival of a trade confirmation in the investor's mail—and in the mail or e-mail of a financial planner or other adviser who monitors portfolio-management activities on behalf of the investor—reveals what has been done in the account. Many investment advisers manage wrap programs, and changes in the program's prototype portfolio are communicated by the adviser's investment personnel to financial counselors and consultants at brokerage firms who enter orders with their firms' trading desks to change positions in individually crafted, tax-sensitive accounts. The fee is usually shared by the introducing (selling) adviser and the investment manager. Disclosure of a portfolio change to advisers and to their firms' trading desks has the effect of disseminating the investment manager's transaction plans very widely.

The dissemination of information about changes in institutional portfolios is usually slower and more restricted than information dispersed in executions of separate-account transactions. Nonetheless, trading information is communicated to a variety of individuals and organizations when institutional accounts trade, partly because the accounts will typically use an independent executing broker and, in the case of pension accounts, because a consultant and fund trustees are apprised of transactions promptly. There's nothing malicious or problematic in any of these information transfers. The point is simply that they occur and that different individuals and organizations with different policies and regulatory constraints on how they treat trading information are involved in each category of account. Discreet handling and implementation of every trading decision are important, but one thing must be kept in mind when evaluating the confidentiality of an open-end actively managed ETF's trading activity: the investment manager and the executing broker may be discreet, but not everyone aware of every trade pending for a client of an investment manager is as obligated as a fund's manager and broker to protect that information.

Clearly, one of the weaknesses of the typical active manager's investment-management process—in which different types of accounts are buying or selling the same security in rotational sequence—is information leakage that could be eliminated if all of the manager's clients met in a single investment pool. With a single pool, there are no conflicts associated with the order in which transactions are made, and there would be no leakage to outside organizations from trade confirmations sent to owners of separate accounts and individuals associated with institutional and pooled portfolios. Pooling can be accomplished most efficiently with multiple-share-class funds.

Portfolio Management: Economics and Structure

An investment-management operation increases in efficiency as more positions are consolidated before they get to the ultimate investor's account statement. For example, the amount of programming, processing, human interaction, and paper generation associated with an account in which an investor owns shares in a fund is substantially less than the resources required to process a similar risk/reward position for an investor holding individual positions in hundreds of different companies. Investment decisions made and implemented within a more consolidated framework give every client the benefits of greater efficiency, tighter control of information leakage, and reduced cost.

The opportunities for cost savings from consolidating and simplifying trading and operations are substantial. A detailed comparative cost analysis of current investment-management options for a multiple-share-class ETF-based fund is outside the scope of this chapter, but a few comments are in order. **FIGURE 9.4** lists some costs for two broad categories of investors and indicates how these costs are likely to change with a pooled fund structure. The extent to which costs will change in the aggregate is largely a function of the success the fund enjoys overall and with each category of potential investors. The list is based on general expectations for each investor group and the principle that fixed expenses in the multiple-share-class fund structure will be higher initially and variable expenses much lower ultimately than the cost structure of an investment-management business that only partly integrates the portfolio-management process and has different operating structures for diverse accounts. The appropriate comparison for institutional investors is to an indexed or actively managed institutional account with an adviser who also manages separate retail products. The most appropriate comparison for individual investors is against a position in a conventional (non-ETF) indexed or actively managed mutual fund. Only a rudimentary effort has been made in

FIGURE **9.4** *Costs of the Multiple-Share-Class, ETF-Based Fund vs. Alternate Pooled Investment Management Structures*

TAX-EXEMPT INSTITUTIONAL ACCOUNTS

EXPENSES THAT WILL BE HIGHER

- SEC fee levied on incremental fund asset deposits (.0000809 x incremental assets, or about $81 per million dollars in net assets, the first year the fund assets increase)
- Some additional legal expenses inside the fund for early funds
- Cost of building and operating a multiple-share-class structure and software (one-time and largely fixed annual expenses)
- Trade-management costs for investors to get in or out of the fund

EXPENSES THAT WILL BE LOWER

- Index license fees
- Client-specific account records
- Account-related investment-management costs
- Transaction costs to get in or out of the fund
- Transaction costs from loss of trading confidentiality or to increase or reduce investments in the fund
- Fewer legal expenses relative to a separate or special-purpose pooled account
- Administrative, trading, and operations personnel costs in the fund

TAXABLE INDIVIDUAL ACCOUNTS

EXPENSES THAT WILL BE HIGHER

- Tax-lot cost-basis accounting

EXPENSES THAT WILL BE LOWER

- Index license fees
- Client-specific account records
- Transaction costs from:
—Shareholders entering and leaving the fund
—Loss of trading confidentiality
- Taxes, thanks to capital gains deferral
- Administrative, trading, and operations personnel costs

Figure 9.4 to distinguish costs chargeable to specific investors from general overheads, one-time costs from annual costs, or fixed costs from variable costs. One of the ideas behind this fund structure is to take advantage of economies of scale and the way the economies interact with most funds' largely fixed costs.

There will be initial software and administrative costs associated with a multiple-share-class fund. The start-up costs will be significant for the first fund constructed along these lines, but once the regulatory hurdles have been cleared, the process is in place, and the software has been developed, start-up and software costs for future funds should be similar to start-ups of simpler funds. After the first funds, start-up and fixed costs can be offset by savings from managing a single portfolio and eliminating most fund-level account services and record keeping.

The fund-trading desk will be concerned with tax-lot accounting largely for the benefit of taxable investors in the exchange-traded share class. Tax-lot management is a relatively straightforward and highly automated process. The small incremental cost of this process will be attributed to the ETF share class and any other share classes for taxable investors. Use of ETFs by taxable investors will not depend merely on tax efficiency in a single fund portfolio. Most multimanager overlay techniques will work with diversified portfolio sector ETFs at lower cost than accounts composed of individual securities.

The trading that the active investment manager would ordinarily have to do to invest cash coming in or going out of the fund will be done by the authorized participants who create and redeem ETF shares and who, in effect, manage the fund size increase and decrease transactions. The fund portfolio-management process itself will deal only with portfolio composition changes. The trading staff required will be much smaller than the trading staff needed to handle the same level of assets for diverse types of accounts.

To many investors, the principal attraction of exchange-traded funds has been the low expense ratios the funds have posted relative to expense ratios of most similar conventional funds. Major institutions make only occasional or limited use of ETFs for specific applications because the fees institutions are accustomed to paying for index fund management are even lower than the exchange-traded funds' expense ratios. One of the principal reasons for offering different share classes is to give investors who are putting $100 million or $1 billion into an indexed (or actively managed) portfolio approximately the same fee structure they've enjoyed in the past. A special share class of a silent index fund should deliver superior performance at a comparable or even lower cost.[24]

Corresponding cost advantages and disadvantages will apply to indexed and actively managed portfolios in most cases, aside from the research and stock selection behind the active-management process. The net fee realized by the investment manager *after operating costs* per-dollar of retail or institutional assets would be at least as high, even allowing for lower gross fees from both retail and institutional clientele, because the impact of a number of cost items have been reduced or, in some cases, eliminated by offering participation in a single investment pool.

The initial institutional investment commitment to these new funds will be extremely important because institutions provide a degree of credibility comparable to the branding that sometimes comes from an index license in a conventional benchmark index fund. Branding for an actively managed fund usually comes from a well-known investment manager or a fund sponsor that can exploit media name recognition in money-raising activities. To the extent that an institutional investment organization sees value in an index process or in an active manager, the institution's implied endorsement could have significant marketing value, and the institutional investor could benefit from that value in the form of a lower fee or participation in the profit of the enterprise.

So far, we've offered few details on relationships among share classes. The exchange-traded share class will be exchangeable into other share classes on request and probably tax-free. The non-ETF share classes will have varied expense ratios. In some cases, a share class will have embedded sales charges to permit the investor to pay a financial planner or other adviser tax-efficiently out of the fund's investment income. In-kind creation and redemption will dominate, but there will be some partial cash redemptions for purposes of realizing losses within the fund. Notices of creation or redemption will be tendered by 2:30 p.m. each day to give the portfolio manager an opportunity to complete any desired portfolio changes by the market close.

The portfolio basket used as an intraday valuation proxy for trading purposes will be the actual fund portfolio as it existed at the opening of trading on that day. To protect the interests of the fund's ongoing shareholders, the intraday fund valuation publication frequency should be reduced from every fifteen seconds to once an hour.[25] This will protect long-term shareholders' confidentiality in trading and will provide an adequate frame of reference for market makers and investors interested in judging the appropriateness of fund share bids and offers in the marketplace. Less-frequent intraday valuation proxy publication will frustrate efforts to use the valuation publication to determine precise portfolio composition and portfolio changes in progress. We would expect research organizations—and perhaps even the investment manager—to publish information on the risk characteristics of the portfolio as a supplement to intraday values and the end-of-day net asset value.

In a silent index fund, the index changes—except in unusual circumstances, such as a bankruptcy or a tender offer with a limited period of effectiveness—would be concentrated when possible. They might occur largely in the first ten or the last ten trading days of the month or largely at a set time during the calendar quarter or year. Under ordinary circumstances, investors and authorized participants could count on full portfolio transparency a large part of the time. Actively managed funds will need greater flexibility in terms of their trading pattern, but we would expect all these funds to adopt a more open policy on disclosure of portfolio composition than conventional funds, perhaps publishing the actual portfolio every ten trading days with a ten-trading-day lag, in contrast to the requirement for conventional funds with actively managed portfolios to publish holdings every quarter with a sixty-day lag.

Obviously, if an exchange-traded fund holds a portfolio that's very different from what's been revealed to the public, the fund's tracking error relative to the published portfolio will affect the trading spread adversely in the secondary market for the fund shares. Each issuer should be able to make decisions based on the characteristics of the fund offered and the investors to whom it's offered. Apart from a general framework, such fund features should not be a regulatory issue.

Everything we've presented so far is related to traditional investors—a typical individual investor and a typical institutional investor. There are a variety of investor subtypes that might prefer to do slightly different things with the same underlying portfolio, such as buying share classes with leverage and with embedded derivatives. Subject to regulatory and tax considerations, it might be possible to have share classes that feature leverage or risk modification with derivatives. Market timing and asset allocation might be incorporated into special share classes, though these might work best in an ETF-of-ETFs holding-company structure. Levels and types of service and who provides them will evolve with time and regulatory consent. **FIGURE 9.5** illustrates some possible share class expense-ratio relationships.

Many, but not all, types of marketing arrangements used by today's open-end funds could be used with appropriate share classes inside the dominant ETF share class. Sales charges would be more transparent with the new fund structure because comparisons of special share classes with embedded marketing fees would be an almost inevitable, and certainly a natural, part of the trade confirmation. This new structure is certainly a natural way to meet demands for marketing-fee transparency. Other cost estimates could be developed by third-party analysts from more extensive trade data released periodically by the fund.

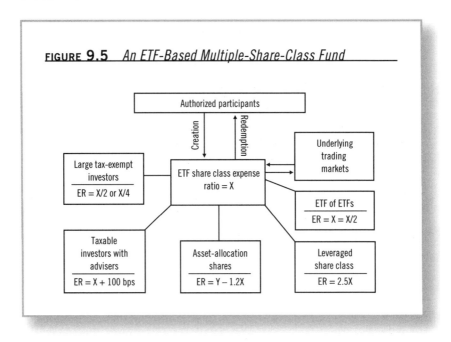

FIGURE 9.5 *An ETF-Based Multiple-Share-Class Fund*

The greatest obstacle to success for the new fund structure is finding the right place for it in the fund industry's marketing framework. The funds will be different in some important ways from what investors are used to, and those differences will require an explanation along the lines of a highly simplified version of the material in this chapter. If marketing groups and fund evaluators who care about their investor clients' performance and want to add value will help deliver the necessary information, the new funds will succeed on their merits.

The key points for investors are readily capsulized: The structure of the self-indexing fund is very much like existing funds in many respects, but it reduces costs and protects the value of the investment manager's research information. Portfolios and expenses will be more transparent, but trading will be done with less short-term transparency, and there is scope for a wide range of sales plans and marketing charges. Because all entries and exits will be through the core exchange-traded share class, the additional or reduced fees for special share classes will be easier for all parties to understand. A useful selling point for most users may be a cost structure that's easier to understand than the cost structure of most other funds. The most important feature of the new funds, though, is their cost and probable performance advantages over existing funds.

The self-indexing fund may not have all the features of an ideal fund structure, but we hope it stimulates others to find additional ways to improve fund performance for investors.

References

Blake, Rich. 2002. "Is Time Running Out for the S&P 500?" *Institutional Investor* (May): 52–64.

Blume, Marshall E., and Roger M. Edelen. 2002. "On Replicating the S&P 500 Index." Working paper, Wharton School, University of Pennsylvania.

Chalmers, John M. R., Roger M. Edelen, and Gregory B. Kadlec. 2001. "On the Perils of Financial Intermediaries Setting Security Prices: The Mutual Fund Wild Card Option." *Journal of Finance* (December): 2209–2236.

Edelen, Roger M. 1999. "Investor Flows and the Assessed Performance of Open-End Mutual Funds." *Journal of Financial Economics* 53: 439–466.

Gastineau, Gary L. 2002a. "Comments on SEC Concept Release: Actively-Managed Exchange-Traded Funds." S7 20-01, http://www.sec.gov/rules/concept/s72001/gastineau1.htm, January 14.

———. 2002b. "Equity Index Funds Have Lost Their Way." *Journal of Portfolio Management* (Winter): 55–64.

———. 2002c. "Silence Is Golden." *Journal of Indexes* (Second Quarter): 8–13.

———. 2003a. "Estimating the Cost of Accepting Creation Redemption Orders." Working paper, http://www.etfconsultants.com/Estimating%20Cost%20of%20Accepting%20Creation%20Redemption%20Orders.pdf.

———. 2003b. "Mutual Fund Conversion." ETFR (December): 8.

———. 2004a. "An Exchange-Traded Fund or a Conventional Fund—You Can't Really Have It Both Ways." *Journal of Indexes* (First Quarter): 32–34.

———. 2004b. "The Benchmark Index Exchange-Traded Fund Performance Problem." *Journal of Portfolio Management* (Winter): 96–106.

———. 2004c. "Protecting Fund Shareholders From Costly Share Trading." *Financial Analysts Journal* (May/June): 22–32.

———. 2004d. "Is Selling ETFs Short an Extreme Sport?" In *The Theory and Practice of Short Selling: Risk, Reward, Strategies,* edited by Frank J. Fabozzi (John Wiley & Sons, 2004).

Goetzmann, William N., Zoran Ivkovic, and K. Geert Rouwenhorst. 2001. "Day Trading International Mutual Funds: Evidence and Policy Solutions." *Journal of Financial and Quantitative Analysis* (September): 287–309.

Greene, Jason T., and Charles W. Hodges. 2002. "The Dilution Impact of Daily Fund Flows on Open-End Mutual Funds." *Journal of Financial Economics* 65: 131–158.

Mazzilli, Paul J., and Dodd F. Kittsley. 2004. "Most ETFs Have Exhibited Low Tracking Error." Morgan Stanley Equity Research Report, January 22.

————. 2003. "Low Historical Tracking Error for Most ETFs." Morgan Stanley Equity Research Report, February 27.

Quinn, James, and Frank Wang. 2003. "How Is Your Reconstitution?" *Journal of Indexes* (Fourth Quarter): 34–38.

Zitzewitz, Eric. 2003a. "Who Cares About Shareholders? Arbitrage-Proofing Mutual Funds." *Journal of Law, Economics, and Organization* (October): 245–280.

————. 2003b. "How Widespread Is Late Trading in Mutual Funds?" Working paper, September.

Chapter Notes

1. Zitzewitz (2003b).

2. Zitzewitz (2003a).

3. Gastineau (2004c). The necessary order receipt rules for foreign equity funds are a little more complicated.

4. The more fund analysts look for these kinds of data, the easier it will become to collect and refine them.

5. Much of this material is discussed at greater length in Gastineau (2002a, b, and c).

6. See Gastineau (2004b).

7. Some examples of situations where the self-indexing fund structure will not work well include illiquid markets and deep-value portfolio styles characterized by gradual accumulation and gradual sale of large, illiquid positions, or, more generally, situations where other ETF-based structures will not work well. The name "self-indexing fund" was chosen to indicate that the fund's trademarks may be licensed for derivatives and other trading to offset some fund expenses. The structure is suitable for many actively managed funds as well as improved index funds. The self-indexing fund is the subject of a U.S. patent application, and it is described more fully in Gastineau (2002a). Additional features of actively managed SIFs are discussed later in this chapter.

8. Information on these new indices is available at www.msci.com/us/index.html.

9. There is evidence that ETF shareholders use other fund shareholder services less extensively than conventional fund shareholders do. For example, the cost of 800-number services is anecdotally much lower for ETF shareholders than for conventional shareholders. Many conventional funds pay fees to proprietors of fund supermarkets to service shareholders who carry their fund shares in accounts at these firms. Fees of 40 basis points annually are common. These fees support marketing as well as shareholder accounting-cost reimbursement.

10. The license fee is typically 16.25 percent of each fund's posted expense ratio. If the expense ratio is 30 basis points, the annual index license fee would be .1625 times 30, or 4.875 basis points.

11. The benchmark index for this fund was changed to an MSCI index on May 16, 2003.

12. Mazzilli and Kittsley (2004) show historical tracking-error data for U.S. ETFs operating for more than a year as of December 31, 2002. Although not a complete basis for comparison, this is a good start for evaluation of ETF efficiency. Ultimately, all fund performance comparisons should be to a standard benchmark index in each fund category.

13. Mazzilli and Kittsley (2004).

14. The arguments against trying to outperform the index are (1) the index fund is supposed to track the index and (2) institutional investors want consistent tracking. See, for example, Blume and Edelen (2002) for an interesting discussion of these arguments. As Blume and Edelen put it, the conclusion that implementing S&P 500 stock index changes as soon as possible after the change is announced rather than waiting for the official index change date is "almost a case of stochastic dominance." Although the issues are outside the scope of this chapter, the best strategy for investors is clearly to go for the best possible performance. You cannot necessarily eat a low tracking error, but you can eat a large *positive* tracking error.

15. This mechanism is explained in detail in Gastineau (2004b).

16. If fund advisers continue to manage funds to minimize tracking error rather than to maximize performance, this assumption obviously will not be valid.

17. For details on this calculation, see Gastineau (2003a).

18. See Edelen, Roger M (1999). For a more detailed interpretation of Edelen's work, see Gastineau (2004b).

19. The importance of earlier cutoff times for fund share purchase and redemption orders and the former "Vanguard process" are discussed at length in Gastineau 2004(b).

20. Vanguard's new index, multiple-share-class approach can have adverse implications for tax efficiency relative to competing ETFs. See Gastineau (2004a) for a more comprehensive evaluation of the VIPERs multiple-share-class structure.

21. More detailed information on silent index funds is available in Gastineau (2002a) and Gastineau (2002c).

22. Gastineau (2002b).

23. Gastineau (2002b), Blake (2002), and Quinn and Wang (2003).

24. See Gastineau (2002a) and (2002c) for more detail. We note here that institutional investors who trade with other investors in a manager's pooled invest-

ment account do not—as they're often told and sometimes believe—trade for free. There may be no commission, but one party to the trade is highly likely to pay a market-impact cost. If a "free" exchange is possible, it should be equally possible into or out of the silent index ETF. There may also be some interesting securities-lending opportunities for institutional investors in ETF shares. See Gastineau (2004c).

25. The fund adviser should be permitted to choose any interval between fifteen seconds and one hour.

CHAPTER 10

The Cost and Consequences of Insurance Wrappers

BEN G. BALDWIN

W hen economist Peter Bernstein has an investment epiphany, as we learned in the September 2003 issue of *Pensions and Investments,* it's bound to get some attention. "Instead of creating a policy asset allocation based upon return forecasts," Bernstein concludes, "the investor must figure out a mix with the highest probability of being able to pay for the groceries when the time comes."[1] Indeed, Bernstein tells us, "The goal of any investor, institutional or individual, is to fund a stream of liabilities."[2]

Bernstein credits Kevin Kneafsey, an investment strategist with Barclays Global Investors, with helping him attain this enlightenment. The work of Kneafsey and Bernstein seems to conclude that whereas in the past we based the asset allocation of an individual portfolio on an account owner's risk tolerance and objectives—seeking the greatest growth based on the past performance of various asset classes—this thinking was arrogant. "When we never know what the future holds, how can we kid ourselves into believing we can estimate long-run rates of return and covariances for a broad menu of financial assets?" Bernstein asks. Rather, "under the new approach, the policy portfolio is where risk management takes place."[3] The role of risk management is to protect the portfolio if the assumptions turn out to be wrong.

These investment gurus are advising us to get our alpha—our return in excess of market returns—anywhere we can find it. Indeed, now that professional money managers have apparently discovered risk management and the importance for individual investors to protect against downside risk so that they can pay for the groceries when the time comes, it's time to review what costs and benefits insurance wrappers, such as life insurance and annuities, offer in regard to investment capital.

Life Insurance Wrappers

An insurance wrapper is an insurance contract wrapped around capital to protect against loss or damage by a contingent event. Insurance contracts are risk-management tools. Financial advisers recommend that clients exposed to the risk of fire, theft, accident, and liability purchase adequate insurance to protect against those risks. The products we're discussing here use either a life insurance contract or an annuity contract as the wrapper. The question the informed client deserves to have answered is, Does this wrapper, the insurance contract, provide enough value in the form of protection against loss of capital to justify its cost? Advisers sometimes fail to understand that once one of these contracts is wrapped around a block of capital, the legal nature of that capital changes in many important ways. Advisers need to understand the costs and features of insurance wrappers and to be able to explain them to clients so that they can make informed decisions about whether to use them.

Managing client money tax-efficiently has many challenges, and investment theory on how to provide the most efficient after-tax, after-expense rate of return continues to evolve. As a starting point for a decision, advisers need to determine what it costs to manage taxable portfolios in their practice. **FIGURE 10.1** presents a set of cost assumptions that can be adjusted according to your own information.

The gross return of 10 percent assumes an asset allocation with a large proportion of equities, which means that tax-free municipal bonds may protect the bond portfolio from some taxation but leaves the equities exposed to taxation. Indexing can minimize the cost of outside managers, but to the extent it's successful in an asset-allocated account and some rebalancing is used to stay within risk parameters, income taxes could at times exceed the average of 2 percent per annum. (Advisers who are able to keep their clients' tax burden under 2 percent per annum will want to adjust Figure 10.1.) Although many advisers are moving from charging for assets under management to charging retainers, we translated the adviser's long-term compensation—be it an asset-management fee, retainer, or commission—to about 1 percent.

If this capital is moved into an adviser-managed variable life insurance policy, how is the cost structure likely to compare? (See **FIGURE 10.2**.)

To answer that question, the critical adviser will ask:

FIGURE 10.1

	TAXABLE PORTFOLIO	ADVISER-SPECIFIC TAXABLE PORTFOLIO	ADVISER-SPECIFIC VARIABLE LIFE INSURANCE
Gross return	10%		
Income taxes	−2%		
Management fees	−1%		
Adviser fee/commission	−1%		
Cost of life insurance	N/A		
Net to investor	6%		

1 Can you find a variable universal life policy with subaccount management fees and mortality and expense (M&E) charges of 2 percent or less?

2 Can you keep adviser-management retainers, fees, or commissions down to 1 percent of policy capital?

3 Is there a possibility of keeping the monthly applied administration fees and the cost of life insurance down to 1 percent of policy capital per annum?

The answer to question one is yes, although it may take some contract hunting and subaccount selection. Typically, low-load products without surrender charges are more acceptable to advisers. The answer to question two is adviser driven and, with substantial capital in a life insurance contract, appropriate fees can be a great deal less than 1 percent of the capital in the policy. As for question three: In a single-life policy designed to retain all of the income tax benefits of life insurance, getting the monthly deducted cost of insurance and administrative expenses down to 1 percent of policy capital on an annualized basis is not likely to happen in the first years of the policy because of the government constraints on how much can be put into the contract during those years. With survivorship, or second-to-die, policies it will happen earlier because the costs of insurance are about a tenth of what they are for a first-to-die policy. Also, more money can be put into the contract, relative to the death benefit, in the early years of a contract if the policy owner is willing to forgo the ability to withdraw cost basis or take

FIGURE 10.2

	TAXABLE PORTFOLIO	TAXABLE PORTFOLIO EMBEDDED IN VARIABLE LIFE
Gross return	10%	10%
Income taxes	–2%	0%
Management fees and M&E	–1%	–2%
Adviser fee/commission	–1%	–1%
Cost of life insurance	N/A	–1%
Net to investor	6%	6%

policy loans from the policy without incurring immediate income taxation to the extent of gain in the contract and 10 percent Internal Revenue Service penalties on gain removed before age fifty-nine and a half.

In the single-life policy, retaining all of the tax benefits including the right to withdraw cost basis without taxation and to take policy loans without taxation, it would take five years for a sixty-five-year-old insured male to embed $500,000 in a $1 million policy. Whereas if the income-tax-free withdrawal/loan feature was not needed and modified endowment contract (MEC) status was acceptable, $500,000 could be put into the policy in year one. The MEC case could drive the cost of insurance and administrative costs down to 1 percent in year two, whereas in the slower five-year funding method, it could take five years to get to that point, depending on investment returns on the capital. Capital losses can drive up the cost of the life insurance, whereas capital gains can drive down the cost of the life insurance as a percentage of the capital in the policy.

Once cost questions are adequately addressed, the next questions have to do with how the life insurance wrapper around this capital changes the nature of the capital and whether those changes have positive or negative value for the particular client situation under study. The comparison table "How Variable Life Insurance Differs From Taxable Portfolios" (see Web address www.bloomberg.com/thinktank) may be helpful in determining the applicability and the positive or negative value in basis points of various variable life insurance features. To be as complete as possible, the list is extensive. Some features, of course, may be marked "not applicable" (N/A) for an individual client.

The adviser can use the blank portions of this table to evaluate a specific client situation, putting a check in each box, indicating positive, negative, or no value. Tallying the checks will indicate whether there is a preponderance of negatives or points of no value, so that further consideration is not required. If there are a significant number of positive checks, however, quantifying the value of the positive features versus the negative features may be warranted.

Annuity Wrappers

Annuity contracts (deferred, immediate, fixed, and variable) are financial tools intended to address the risk-management issues surrounding retirement capital. Annuities must, net after expense, prove to be credible and efficient financial tools capable of accomplishing client goals as well as, or better than, other alternatives.

The Nonqualified Annuity

Annuities compete for the consumer's investment dollars in an environment of changing and expanding investment opportunities and complex and changing personal needs. A nonqualified annuity is a financial tool that can help accomplish retirement financial goals using after-tax capital. The nonqualified annuity is constructed—and enabled by the tax code—to encourage long-term accumulation and long-term distribution of retirement capital while permitting the deferral of taxation until distribution. Under current federal law, distributions are taxed as ordinary income.

Many advisers regard it as a disadvantage for clients to use after-tax capital to accumulate in a nonqualified annuity and have distributions taxed as ordinary income, because they feel alternatives would offer their client better tax advantages. In a world where dividends and capital gains may be taxed at 15 percent or less, that's an understandable conclusion; however, state and local taxes may drive up a taxpayer's concern. High-tax-bracket clients typically want to lower current taxes on current investments. That could mean some of their non–15 percent tax bracket investment capital may be placed in nonqualified, deferred annuities to shift earnings to the future, when they expect to be in a lower tax bracket and may—they fear—have insufficient income. In discussing this issue, many clients say that if an adviser helps them have so much income in retirement that their biggest complaint is income taxes, they'll be very happy. In fact, those who do end up in this enviable situation find ways to mitigate their income taxes by giving to the charities they'd always wanted to be able to support.

An expert specializing in any type of investment can point out the products in their field they find consumer friendly and those that aren't. The distinction between consumer-friendly and consumer-unfriendly products is determined in the competitive marketplace. We all know and appreciate that for the manufacturer, the distributor, the intermediary, and the consumer, these products are a for-profit business and there is only so much juice in the orange, so to speak. If the manufacturer, distributor, or intermediaries choose to squeeze out more than their fair share, the consumer gets hurt. We all know that there are unfriendly annuity products on the market. There's no defense for the too-much-margin, too-large-a-commission, or "gotcha"-priced annuity products that some companies manufacture and some intermediaries choose to sell to an unsuspecting public.

But we're discussing the competitive position of the win-win-win products—those that are good for the manufacturer, the distributor, the intermediary, *and* the consumer. Of course, if we could cut two profit centers out of the lineup and go directly from the manufacturer to the consumer, as is done by the so-called low-load manufacturers, we should be able to save more juice for the consumer. Theoretically, that would be possible if the consumer could purchase this product without help and if the manufacturers staffed up and adequately served as both distributor and intermediary. But if a low-load product is used and an individual not paid by commissions is used to facilitate the sale and service of the contract, this individual has to be compensated for his or her efforts and for dealing with the applicable state laws regarding giving advice on the sale and service of insurance products. The quality of advice and assistance is very important, but no generalization can be made as to whether fee-compensated or commission-compensated advice is better for any individual client. Clients must decide which they're most comfortable with and which can represent their interests with integrity and low cost.

Fixed Deferred Annuities

Fixed deferred annuities compete with other investment alternatives that generate interest for the long-term investor. Interest-bearing investments compete on the basis of return and safety. Investors who agree to lend their money for longer periods of time demand to be paid more than those who lend their money for shorter periods. The long-term investor is taking more risk because of the length of time their money is at risk and the fact that they're giving up the right to invest those proceeds elsewhere in the interim, during which time interest rates and inflation could have a negative effect on their real return. Borrowers (insurance companies selling fixed annuities) do not expect to have their loans called early by their lenders (annuity buyers) and will pay a higher rate of interest to make sure the loan is not callable. Lenders (annuity buyers) who have a right to call a loan normally will have to pay some sort of penalty, contingent deferred sales charge, or market-value adjustment for doing so, as a result of the extra costs to the insurance company.

Deferred annuities are long term because tax law motivates purchasers to be long term by providing for the application of income taxes to the extent of gain, and a 10 percent penalty on withdrawals before age fifty-nine and a half, for using income from the annuity before that time. They're also long term because the pricing structure usually includes a contingent deferred sales charge, or surrender charge. Ideally investors should be very sure they will not need to access the funds from an annuity before age fifty-nine and a half and until after the surrender charge no longer applies. Therefore, annuities do not compete for the consumer's near-term cash, which belongs in checking accounts, savings accounts, money market funds, or even short-term bond funds, which provide instant liquidity with little, if any, market risk.

Consumers need to be aware that annuities are not a deposit, not insured by the Federal Deposit Insurance Corporation or by any federal government agency, and not guaranteed by any bank or savings association. In an annuity product, consumers are depending on the claims-paying ability of the insurance company for their guarantees. As a result, investigation of the financial position of the insurance company is necessary because the guarantee is only as good as the insurance company behind it. And we are all aware of insurance companies that have failed.

Variable Deferred Annuities

Weighing in on the ongoing discussions of the relative merits of the variable deferred annuity and inexpensive, tax-efficient mutual funds, we have the PricewaterhouseCoopers (PWC) study, *Variable Annuities and Mutual Fund Investments for Retirement Planning: A Statistical Comparison,* which was prepared for the National Association for Variable Annuities (NAVA) and published in October 2000. Although the study was prepared by a well-known accounting firm, it was done for NAVA, and that has caused some to discount the information because NAVA overtly promotes annuities. Others who have reviewed the study believe that in anticipating this type of criticism, NAVA and PWC went to extremes to be objective. Either way, the methodology and assumptions in the study are valuable to those trying to determine whether mutual funds or subaccounts inside of a variable deferred annuity contract would provide the highest after-tax return for retirement savings held outside of qualified retirement accounts.

Note that the PWC study deals only with the accumulation of capital outside of qualified plans. The implication here, as in most similar studies, is that consumers generally should take advantage of any and all qualified plan opportunities, including individual retirement accounts (IRAs) and Roth IRAs, to the full extent that regulations allow. The objective of that advice is not necessarily "the highest after-tax return for retirement savings" since a great deal of retirement income from qualified plan capital will be subject to ordinary income taxes when taken by the owner or beneficiaries.

The conundrum in the well-meaning objectives we set for people accumulating money for retirement is the marginal difference in security they'll feel on retirement day, depending on whether their retirement accumulations are after-tax or before-tax. By the highest after-tax return for retirement savings definition, $1 million of after-tax capital is worth more because the government has no income tax claim against it. But if two retirees have worked hard to accumulate $1 million in capital at retirement and one has $1 million of after-tax capital and the other has $1 million of entirely pretax capital, how much more net after-tax income could be generated by the after-tax $1 million than by the pretax $1 million without eroding principal? How much more secure income-wise would one of these retirees feel than the other?

If the retirement objective is to replace 70–100 percent of a person's gross income, our real objective is to build capital to be an income generator in retirement, a "capital wheel," as it were. To illustrate this concept in **FIGURE 10.3**, the figure inside one wheel generating income through personal efforts is replaced by the capital wheel generating the income when the individual no longer can or chooses not to.

The financial community used to feel fairly confident that it could generate $50,000 of taxable income—5 percent—from a $1 million capital wheel, regardless of whether it was pre- or posttax capital, and provide an inflation-adjusted income. After the 2000–2003 bear market, most believed that a reasonable assumption for taxable income was $35,000 per $1 million, or 3.5 percent. If we accept the 3.5 percent assumption, to generate taxable income of $50,000 per year, we now need about $1,430,000 in our capital wheel—43 percent more. Let's assume that an investor, because of financial constraints, needs to take advantage of all pretax accumulation opportunities to meet the goal of $1,430,000 retirement capital and to do so by his retirement date. This taxpayer also is aware that after his death and that of his spouse, the income tax liability on this pretax block of capital could be as high as $430,000 for their children, the beneficiaries of this account. True, the after-tax wealth is only $1 million, but by avoiding prepaying the income tax, this couple had an interest-free loan of $430,000 from the government on which to earn taxable income during their retirement years.

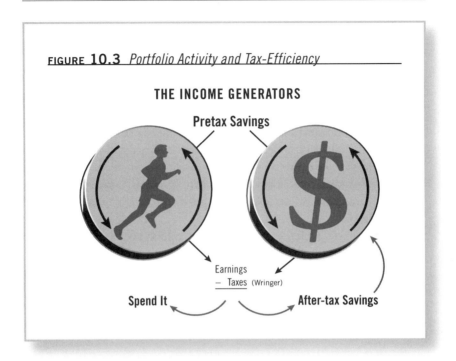

FIGURE 10.3 *Portfolio Activity and Tax-Efficiency*

THE INCOME GENERATORS

Pretax Savings

Earnings
− Taxes (Wringer)

Spend It   After-tax Savings

The taxpayer trying to make an informed decision about buying a variable deferred annuity should consider the financial goal. Is the objective to get the highest after-tax return for retirement savings, or is it to have the largest amount of capital available to generate income during retirement? If it's the latter, then security has been redefined from after-tax accumulations—the size of the pile of after-tax assets—to the size of one's ever-replaceable income. Once the destination is defined, it's easier to adopt the appropriate tools to get consumers there in the most practical, hassle-free, and efficient way possible. The function of capital is to generate income in retirement. In his paper "A Model of Desired Wealth at Retirement,"[4] Charles B. Hatcher frames the retirement goal by saying, "If I had X dollars per year for the rest of my life, guaranteed, I would retire." It really does seem to be all about ever-replaceable income.

The PricewaterhouseCoopers study, however, concentrates on whether a variable deferred annuity or a mutual fund provides the investor with the highest after-tax return for retirement savings.[5] The study was based on Morningstar data on 8,433 mutual funds and 10,499 variable deferred annuity subaccounts for the period 1987–1999, which, in light of the 2000–2003 bear market, cannot be viewed as typical anymore. But the assumptions and methodology of this study of mutual funds and annuities provides a framework for comparison of the two that can serve as a checklist of value for consumer and adviser.

Although the results of the study—which indicated that annuities are preferable to mutual funds under the specifications of the study—are interesting, they can't be used for individual decision making. The specifications and the assumptions are unlikely to fit the actual situation and current client requirements, but the comparison table "Discussion Points: Mutual Fund vs. Nonqualified Deferred Variable Annuity" (see Web address www.bloomberg.com/thinktank) provides an agenda for client discussion and an opportunity to compare the differences in product costs and taxation under current circumstances, rather than the circumstances in 1999 laid out in the PWC study. Some of those circumstances have changed considerably:

❑ Return assumptions in 2003 dropped to about 50 percent of 1999 assumptions.

❑ Long-term capital gains taxes and dividend taxation dropped to a maximum of 15 percent.

❑ Average annuity costs increased as consumers voluntarily purchased more portfolio insurance, in the form of enhanced guaranteed death benefits and enhanced guaranteed income, or account-value insurance.

The table is designed to be a checklist for testing an adviser's assumptions against the PWC assumptions in order to quantify the value of the taxable mutual fund selection versus the deferred variable annuity selection. A third column can be added to incorporate the adviser's alternative to these two selections.

With dividend and long-term capital gains taxes limited to 15 percent, isn't it much easier now to accumulate after-tax capital, thereby making deferred variable annuities less desirable? William Reichenstein, CFA, a professor of investment management at Baylor University, has been critical of annuities. Reichenstein is the coauthor, with William W. Jennings, of *Integrating Investments and the Tax Code* (Wiley, 2003), and the two have made available the Excel spreadsheets they used in their research. The spreadsheets are posted at www.wiley.com/go/reichenstein.

Reichenstein is also critical of a book called *Investing With Variable Annuities* (Parker-Thompson, 2002), by John P. Huggard, JD, CFP, who is very much in favor of variable deferred annuities. Since Reichenstein has been critical of Huggard's calculations, I used Reichenstein's Excel spreadsheet and assumptions to compare the mutual fund with the annuity as both capital accumulator and distributor. The spreadsheet I used is identified on the website as "Appendix 5.3 Calculations of Constant Annual Income From a Passive Stock Fund Held in a Taxable Account."

The following are the taxable mutual fund assumptions Reichenstein selected:

❏ Gross stock return was 8 percent.
❏ Made up of 1.2 percent dividend yield reduced by the fund's management fee of .3–.9 percent. The capital gain portion of the return is 6.8 percent, of which 5 percent was realized and taxable each year (34 basis points). The balance of the capital gain, 6.46 percent, was deferred until liquidated during a twenty-five-year retirement period, following a ten-year accumulation period.
❏ Net stock return for the mutual fund was 7.7 percent.
❏ Personal income tax rate during accumulation and distribution was 25 percent.
❏ I changed the capital gains and dividends rate to 15 percent for both.

By entering $100,000 of capital as the initial investment in the mutual fund and a like amount into a low-load annuity, with a total expense ratio of 1 percent (a tax-deferred return of 7 percent), the spreadsheet displayed what we could expect in ten years using the rule of seventy-two—a quick way to estimate how long it will take capital to double (dividing seventy-two by the given interest rate). At the end of those ten years, the capital in both had just about doubled, as shown in **FIGURE 10.4**.

We could conclude from Figure 10.4 that if this investor's objective is to maximize after-tax capital, the efficient mutual fund would be the way to go. But how prepared will the investor be when he's seventy years old to rely on this mutual fund for income for the next twenty-five years? This model says two things: First, theoretically, it's possible that the mutual fund could provide the income. Stochastic modeling would be much more likely to expose the risks involved so that a consumer could make an informed decision. All those who have friends and relatives who have lived to age ninety-five have to think of what life might be like for this person during the last five years of the plan, as the fund is rapidly being depleted of income while the individual lives on with more costly needs. Second, annuities are about assurance. Insurance companies relieve people of the risks they choose not to take personally, and they charge for it.

Some believe insurance companies have charged too much for insignificant promises. But insurance companies are increasing reserves and prices for promises that must be kept despite the unanticipated depth of the 2000–2003 bear market and a period of extremely low interest rates. Insurance regulators are insisting that they do so.

Mutual Funds and Commissioned Sales

Because of the way the fund industry is structured and the way funds are priced, registered representatives paid by commission have to deal with

FIGURE 10.4

	MUTUAL FUND	ANNUITY
Gross value at end of 10 years	$204,328.22	$196,715.14
Cost basis	$128,268.94	$100,000.00
Untaxed gain	$76,059.28	$96,715.14
Mutual fund taxed at 15%	-$11,408.89	
Annuity taxed at 25%		-$24,178.79
Net after-tax mutual fund (if liquidated)	$192,919.33	
Net after-tax annuity (if liquidated)	$172,536.35	
Mutual fund estimated after-tax income (if the mutual fund performs as assumed)	$15,178.27	
Annuity income after-tax for life (no ifs)		$16,518.44[6]

a myriad of rules and regulations in providing suitable mutual funds for their clients in taxable accounts. Some funds cost the consumer more and make the representative more money. As a result, a few representatives put their personal interests ahead of those of their clients. Regulators, fulfilling their duty to protect the consumer, write regulations and create forms and administrative procedures to try to make sure that registered representatives put their clients' interests first and sell only what's suitable and appropriate rather than what results in unwarranted sales charges or expenses.

In selecting mutual funds for their clients, it's not unusual for advisers to consult Morningstar Principia for independent research, as well as whatever material they're able to obtain. There were 16,513 funds in the Morningstar Principia database in the spring of 2004, with twelve different pricing designations. Of those funds, almost 3,000 were front-loaded, typically called A shares, with loads ranging from 8.67 percent to 1 percent. Another 2,700 were back-loaded, typically called B shares, with loads between 6 percent and .5 percent. Another 2,500 were C shares, or level load, meaning a sales charge is applied each year and typically a

SHARE CLASS	TYPICAL INVESTMENT EXPENSE	AVERAGE LONG-TERM EXPENSE RATIO	SUITABLE FOR
A	Front load as much as 5.75%, amounts are invested down to 0%	1.39%	Investors with large amounts to invest over long periods of time
B	Back loaded as much as 5%, reducing over 6 years to 0%	2% reducing to about A share after 8 or 9 years	Investors with an amount to invest less than any A class breakpoints, with a very long-term time horizon
C	No up front and no back load after one year	2%	Investors with limited amounts of money who will be taking it out within 10 years
Annuities	Most often no front load; back loads average 6% reducing for 7 years	Approximately 2.26%	Long-term investors who value the annuity contract features and are accumulating retirement capital (see www.bloomberg.com/ thinktank).

1 percent back load if liquidated within the first year. The average long-term expense ratios of the A, B, and C classes in 2004, according to Ibbotson Associates, are shown in **FIGURE 10.5**. There are also shares classified as ADV Inst, Inv, M, N, other retirement S, and T. It is no wonder that the regulators are concerned about the difficulty of knowing the cost of owning mutual funds.

NASD Rule 10b-10 requires the disclosure of compensation at the point of sale. In 1979, a "no action" letter was promulgated that said that if a fund's prospectus adequately disclosed compensation, that would be sufficient disclosure. However, that 1979 letter was prior to the proliferation of at least a dozen different ways in which to charge customers for mutual fund costs and did not address trading costs and other expenses that mutual fund owners may be paying. The only place to dig out information on trading costs may be the prospectus supplement. The fact that mutual funds may cost the consumer more than the expense ratio listed in the prospectus has been generally overlooked by the financial-planning community, the media, and the consumer. Under the new regulatory environment, this is unacceptable. Proposed new rules are likely to eliminate the 1979 letter permitting prospectus disclosure only and require disclosing the amount at the point of sale. Such a requirement is likely to make the multiple share classes impractical and encourage the manufacture of low-load and no-load mutual funds.

Next, the representative may consult (to the extent his or her broker-dealer will allow) what Morningstar Principia calls in its database "true no-load funds." In this list we find 6,187 funds, some of which charge a 12b-1 fee. Some require a minimum initial investment, and they have expense ratios ranging between 10 percent and .02 percent. To comply with the expense-reducing tools of breakpoints, reinstatement opportunities, letters of intent, rights of accumulation, and all other cost-effective pricing alternatives, including the choice of A, B, C, or no-load shares, many representatives try to find one family of funds within which to diversify a client's taxable investment accounts. To avoid the sins of inappropriate switching, excessive transactions, and churning, they're constrained to stay within this family even when they believe the client may be better served in a different fund family. This constraint has caused many advisers to use various levels of fees—similar to C shares for mutual funds—for their clients, which typically increase client costs relative to the long-term holding of A shares.

Many financial advisers have chosen to go "fee only" and charge a fee for assisting their clients in choosing from "no-load" and "low-load" funds, and they provide ongoing service, assisting clients in managing their portfolios. Charging fees has become more and more popular among advisers, but not necessarily less expensive for the consumer. Sometimes low-load products also offer fewer features to make the decision process easier for consumers who are trying to do everything on their own. This can be a disadvantage for consumers.

Annuities and Commissioned Sales

Out of 696 annuity contracts in the Morningstar Principia database updated through February 2004—three of which are closed to new business—only sixteen charge a front load. Clearly, a front load is a consumer-unfriendly feature that the buyer can choose to avoid. If the front load provided value with offsetting expense reductions or unique features, it might be justified, but such value in the cases reviewed is not apparent. Similarly, annual contract charges for account values in excess of $50,000 may not be competitive, and total base annuity expense ratios above 2.5 percent may not be competitive. But annuity purchasers can elect to buy investment insurance features at extra cost, to the extent that these features add value based on the individual purchaser's desire, risk tolerance, and circumstances.

Within an annuity total expense ratio of 2.5 percent, such as mentioned above, we've included the contract's mortality and expense (M&E) charge (which includes the basic features of an annuity and the insurance features, such as a guaranteed minimum death benefit of the account value, or the amount that's been invested in the contract less withdrawals), a guaranteed interest account, and guaranteed annuitization factors.

Another M&E feature is the minimum interest rate guarantee under annuity contracts, which generally has provided a minimum interest rate of at least 3 percent. In the 1990s, this guarantee was perceived to have little value. During those years, many who disparaged annuities said M&E was just another profit center for insurance companies. By 2004, the consumer could see that interest rate guarantee had great value. Indeed, in an interest rate environment in which 10-year Treasuries are paying 3.53 percent—as they were in 2003—insurance companies have a great deal of difficulty trying to maintain a spread between what they can earn on money as opposed to what they've promised to pay to their contract owners.[7]

The guaranteed annuity factors are coming under scrutiny not only because of low interest rates but also because of increasing longevity. Reserves created by the M&E charges are now seen by both insurance companies and insurance regulators as insufficient to deal with the low interest rates of today. It means that you can expect new annuity contracts to charge higher M&Es, provide lower guaranteed interest, or both.

The bottom line is that the average M&E insurance cost in variable annuities in the Morningstar database is 1.31 percent, which is included in the average total asset charge of 2.26 percent in variable annuities. The 16,513 mutual funds in the Morningstar Principia database in February 2004, which have an average total expense ratio of 1.44 percent and no insurance features, are the nearest competitor to the subaccounts of a variable deferred annuity. Consumers who wish to avoid insurance charges can do so and save an average of 82 basis points by using taxable mutual funds.

But investors can't make a sound decision based on these averages. They're better off picking out the mutual fund alternative for taxable capital. That choice may be the elusive low-cost, tax-efficient fund or a credible low-cost, deferred variable annuity that represents the reasonable alternative. Identify the actual costs to which the investor will be exposed in the mutual fund, then determine the cost differential for having the capital invested within the subaccounts of the annuity wrapper. Assuming that the annuity will have extra costs, have the investor evaluate whether the annuity's features have positive, negative, or no value. You can use the comparison table "How the Nonqualified Variable Annuity Differs From Taxable Mutual Funds" (see website address www.bloomberg.com/thinktank) to guide the discussion. Although many of the features may be inapplicable to a particular client, if those of positive or negative value are valued using basis points, it may help clients to know why they're opting in or out of a deferred variable annuity.

Fixed Immediate Annuities vs. Alternative Income Generators

"A synthetic pension is starting to look a lot better than no pension at all," read the lead sentence in a December 2002 *Wall Street Journal* article.[8] The stock market had been down for three years by that time, and interest rates were falling through the floor. By the spring of 2004, interest rates were hitting fifty-year lows.

The ever-replaceable income for retirees typically is provided from the following sources:

❑ Social Security: This is a particularly good source in that it does increase with the cost of living over the years. People twenty years away from qualifying for benefits, however, feel less sure of its reliability than do current retirees.

❑ government pensions

❑ civil service pensions

❑ teacher retirement system pensions

❑ employer-provided pensions

Recipients of adequate income from these sources generally survived the stock market decline of 2000–2002 and also are relatively unfazed by the interest rate decline that started in 1981 and culminated in the dramatically low interest rates of 2004. For those without sufficient support from these ever-replaceable sources of income (which were disparaged during the days of the roaring stock market and relatively higher interest rates), maintaining a standard of living has become difficult and stressful. Many employees took lump-sum settlements from their employers in lieu of the pension plans offered, confident that they could generate a 6–7 percent rate of return from the equity portfolio inside of their rollover IRA, only to see their capital base reduced by as much as 50 percent, and their expectation of a "safe" withdrawal rate drop from 7 percent to 3.5 percent.

Fixed Annuity vs. a Bond Portfolio

A theoretical bond portfolio has a beginning value of $100,000, the same as the capital to be placed into an immediate fixed annuity contract. The

FIGURE **10.6** *Immediate Life Annuity or Fixed Payments From a Fixed-Interest Investment Portfolio*

Assumptions: $100,000 investment, age 65, life expectancy 87, net return 5%

INVESTMENT OPTION	PAYOUT PERIOD	INCOME EXPECTED	PROBABILITY OF OUTLIVING THE LIFE EXPECTANCY
Single-life annuity	Life	$7,484	Not a concern
Fixed withdrawal	25 years	$6,969	?
Fixed withdrawal	30 years	$6,414	?
Fixed withdrawal	35 years	$6,041	?
Fixed withdrawal	40 years	$5,778	?
Interest only	Life	$5,000	Not a concern

Inputs:

- Retiree's current age
- Retiree's life expectancy from www.livingto100.com or similar site
- Retiree's assumed net long-term interest rate assumption (from retiree's and financial adviser's judgment of alternative investment opportunities)
- Current immediate annuity quotes from www.immediateannuities.com or similar site
- Income expected, based on the number of years to use up capital, calculated by constructing a spreadsheet using the capital sum invested and the assumed interest rate (compounding it and varying income withdrawals until the amount left in the account in the final year is equal to the amount of the annual withdrawal).

theoretical bond portfolio earns a steady 5 percent, from which $7,500 per year is extracted to match what the annuity contract will pay out to our sixty-five-year-old male retiree. It appears, according to the mortality tables, that the bond fund will be exhausted before the retiree's death. Choosing between these two investments depends on the investor's view of the risks involved.

FIGURE 10.6 is a decision guide that can be used by prospective retirees and their advisers. The numbers in the table are hypothetical and appropriate for the time that the guide was put together. The adviser should update them with current, client-specific numbers. The objective is to quantify the cost of risk reduction under the personal and economic circumstances at the time it's being used.

There are two ways to relieve clients of their concern about running out of money during their lifetimes—annuitization or taking earnings only. Taking earnings only leaves the principal to the beneficiaries, but in this case, a 50 percent increase in income is provided by annuitization. If the retiree's focus of concern shifts from living too long to dying too soon, a twenty-year minimum guarantee of income can be purchased for $752 per year, reducing the annuity income from $7,484 to $6,732. Since the choices for the retiree concerned with outliving his or her assets are either to annuitize or use interest only, then we must look at costs. Using interest only costs about $2,500 per year. Annuitization costs the possible loss of capital due to an early death or the insurance premium of $752 per year to assure annuity payments for at least twenty years, the assurance of a minimum annuity payout of $134,640 (20 years × $6,732 per year). The cost of choosing self-liquidation depends on how well the retiree can stand watching his or her capital diminish. The more conservative the client wishes to be in retaining capital, the more expensive it is in reduced income. The bottom line is that clients who are concerned about outliving capital can join with many others who have the same concern and shift some of that risk to an insurance company for a price. That money is pooled with the price paid by others to pay the claims of those who experience a loss—in this case, those who live an inordinately long life.

The Earnings-Only Alternative: Stock Dividends or Interest Only

A 1972 retiree enjoyed stock dividend yields above 4 percent (and as high as 6 percent) until 1985. After that time, yields moved precipitously downward to about 3 percent by 1994 and continued to decrease to about 1 percent in the year 2000.[9] As a result of more favorable taxation of dividends in the tax legislation of 2003, dividends from common stocks are tending to increase.

For consumers seeking income from an investment portfolio, professional management is probably essential for success. Mutual funds, such as the Franklin Income Fund or the Income Fund of America (American Funds) have long-term records of generating income if the investor can accept their volatility. For larger portfolios, individually managed portfolios may be economically feasible and can be better tailored to the individual's needs.

Annuitization: A Portfolio Stress Reliever

In the previous examples, we've seen that a portfolio of assets intended to provide financial security and income in retirement gets in trouble when market conditions make it impossible to generate enough income and assets have to be liquidated during unfavorable markets. Losses that occur at that point may be losses from which the retiree may never recover.

One approach to this problem could be to relieve the stress on the portfolio of providing income during these difficult periods. For example, in mid-2003, it would have taken approximately $58,893 in capital to relieve a portfolio of the requirement to pay out $1,000 per month for a five-year period, or $105,374 for ten years.[10] The payment amounts are based on an average of sixteen companies in the database of WebAnnuities.com. Although the interest earnings are not impressive in these examples, interest rates in general were not impressive as of that date. Fixed-amount or fixed-period annuity payments such as this are purchased because the relative interest rate is better than what can be attained elsewhere, and they provide the convenience of having one monthly required payment of $1,000 to cover living expenses rather than having to do piecemeal liquidations from a volatile investment portfolio. This type of annuitization also allows the balance of the portfolio to be managed for growth during the period it's not being called on to provide income. All annuity payments rely on the full faith and credit of the insurance company making those payments, so the insurance company's financial strength is extremely important to the payee.

These fixed-period or fixed-amount non-life-contingent annuities frequently are used in what are called structured settlements, required as a result of litigation, and also by the state lotteries, which typically promote their prize money as the arithmetic sum of the payments they will provide over twenty years. Winners usually accept a discounted present value of those payments.

Life contingent annuities were more expensive in 2003, when interest rates were low, than they were in 1987. My book *The Life Insurance Investment Advisor*, published in 1988, provides the costs for $1,000 per month for a sixty-five-year-old male at that time (see **FIGURE 10.7**).

A consumer in need of $1,000 per month in 2003 had to pay approximately $160,000 for a single-life annuity, whereas in 1987 the same income cost only about $110,000. The annuity payout percentage in 1987 was more than 10 percent ($12,000 / $110,000), whereas in 2003 it was about 7.5 percent ($12,000 / $160,000). The $50,000 increase in cost represents a 45 percent increase in the cost of income as interest rates decreased.

For those with known medical conditions, who are not concerned about the financial impact of a very long life, fixed-period or fixed-amount annuities can be used to relieve the stress of generating consistent income on a portfolio. This is done by taking part of the capital and annuitizing

FIGURE **10.7** *Costs for Single-Life Annuities Providing $1,000 per Month for a Male Annuitant Age 65*[11]

TYPE OF ANNUITY	COST TO PURCHASE 1987	COST TO PURCHASE 2003
Life annuity/pure annuity	$109,990	$158,203
Life annuity 10 years certain	$116,940	$163,773
Life annuity 20 years certain	$128,131	$178.342

it over the expected period of difficulty. Another alternative for those who question their potential longevity is to have an insurance company that issues medically underwritten immediate annuities examine them and make an offer of income based on their limited longevity expectations.

Variable Immediate Annuities

"How much can I take from my accumulated retirement capital and spend to maintain my lifestyle without running out of money before I run out of breath?" A question like this from a client can, and ought to be, an intimidating one for a financial adviser. Coming up with an answer may be an almost theoretical exercise for the young, healthy, and fairly well-off client about to retire, but for the ninety-year-old, fairly healthy retiree rapidly sliding down the steep and slippery slope toward exhaustion of assets in the early part of the twenty-first century, getting it right is critical. One organization that continues to do a great deal of research on retirement income issues is the TIAA-CREF Institute. "People spend a lot of time configuring retirement portfolios to hedge market risk," says John Ameriks, a senior research fellow economist at TIAA-CREF, "when they should be more concerned about maintaining their income levels for life."[12]

The Systematic Withdrawal Plan

The Ibbotson Associates PowerPoint presentation *Variable Annuity Investing,* published in the spring of 2003, offers an excellent example of the frailty of trying to use a diversified investment portfolio as an income generator. The portfolio used in the example had a value on December 31, 1972, of $500,000, invested 50 percent in the Standard & Poor's 500 stock index and 50 percent in 5-year U.S. government bonds. The consumer price index was used as the measure of inflation, and the income to be provided was 5 percent of the initial portfolio value, inflation adjusted with each monthly payment. The portfolio also was to be rebalanced monthly to the 50 percent S&P index and 50 percent 5-year Treasuries ratio. The calculations did not include any adjustment for taxes or transaction costs. **FIGURE 10.8** shows that the portfolio was entirely used up twenty-two years later, in about 1994.[13] An individual retiring at age sixty-five with this portfolio would have been broke, but not dead, at age eighty-seven.[14] The dramatic decline in the nest egg between 1988 and 1994 would have made those years very unpleasant in terms of economic security, especially since both the stock and bond markets were doing so well during those years.

Obviously, the example is highly theoretical, but it's instructive, because even if an adviser had had accurate projections of how two of the three factors—large company stocks and 5-year Treasuries—were going to perform, those projections would still have misled the client. Figure 10.8, taken from the Ibbotson Associates 2002 Yearbook, presents the annualized returns of these classifications and of other asset classes, as well as the inflation rate. If this adviser had known in 1972 that large-cap stocks would average more than 12 percent and that intermediate-term government bonds would average more than 9 percent, it's highly likely that he or she would have concluded that a 5 percent (even inflation-adjusted) withdrawal rate had little chance of exhausting this portfolio. Not factored in was the devastating effect that the negative returns on equities had on the portfolio in the first two years of retirement and the incredibly high demands that inflation adjustment on the income stream had in those same years, forcing liquidations in a down market.

In real life, the client and adviser would surely have tried to alter client behavior to avoid this crash-and-burn ending. But the 2000–2002 bear market has taught many advisers that, generally speaking, the risk tolerance of most retirees makes excessive dependence on systematic withdrawal plans exceedingly risky. Monte Carlo or stochastic modeling may help us understand the likely outcome and dramatically point out the impact of the negative outliers. It is the negative outliers that cause dramatic capital reductions during the withdrawal phase and that dictate the need for strategies to counter them.

In December 2001 in the *Journal of Financial Planning*, John Ameriks, Robert Veres, and Mark J. Warshawsky presented the results of a study and concluded that for thirty-year retirement periods, a 4.5 percent withdrawal rate succeeds more than 90 percent of the time, but only if the asset mix is heavily weighted toward stocks. "Retirees who select a more conservative (less stock-heavy) retirement mix might be able to achieve slightly more consistency if they expect a short retirement, but the probability of failure

FIGURE **10.8** *Annual Returns and Inflation, 1973–1994*[15]

	RETIRE	LARGE COMPANY STOCK	INTERMEDIATE TERM GOVERNMENT BONDS	INFLATION
1	1973	−14.66%	4.61%	8.80%
2	1974	−26.47%	5.69%	12.20%
3	1975	37.20%	7.83%	7.01%
4	1976	23.84%	12.87%	4.81%
5	1977	−7.18%	1.41%	6.77%
6	1978	6.56%	3.49%	9.03%
7	1979	18.44%	4.09%	13.31%
8	1980	32.42%	3.91%	12.40%
9	1981	−4.91%	9.45%	8.94%
10	1982	21.41%	29.10%	3.87%
11	1983	22.51%	7.41%	3.80%
12	1984	6.27%	14.02%	3.95%
13	1985	32.16%	20.33%	3.77%
14	1986	18.47%	15.14%	1.33%
15	1987	5.23%	2.90%	4.41%
16	1988	16.81%	6.10%	4.42%
17	1989	31.49%	13.29%	4.65%
18	1990	−3.17%	9.73%	6.11%
19	1991	30.55%	15.46%	3.06%
20	1992	7.67%	7.19%	2.90%
21	1993	9.99%	11.24%	2.75%
22	1994	1.31%	−5.14%	2.67%
Run out of money		12.09%	9.10%	5.95%

FIGURE 10.9

PORTFOLIO DESCRIPTION	STOCKS	BONDS	CASH	PERCENTAGE OF PORTFOLIOS MAKING 4.5% INFLATION-ADJUSTED INCOME PAYMENTS FOR 30 YEARS
Conservative	20%	50%	30%	32.6%
Balanced	40%	40%	20%	76.3%
Growth	60%	30%	10%	87.4%
Aggressive	85%	15%	0%	91.6%

will be dramatically higher over periods of twenty years or longer."[16]

The idea of counseling retirees to take more risk in their portfolios so that there will be less at risk in their long-term income stream is going to take some doing. **FIGURE 10.9** lists the assumptions used in the study, spanning the riskiness of a portfolio from conservative to aggressive.

Keep in mind that this paper was written by two academics with no ax to grind and one admittedly skeptical financial writer. It did not leave us with the conventional conclusion that the only answer for retirees likely to need income for thirty years or more was to adopt more equity-based, volatile portfolios. Rather, it brought annuitization into the mix of retiree assets as a credible alternative. The risk being addressed is the risk of a long life. The only way people can share that common risk is to pool assets with an insurance company in return for a promise of lifetime income.

The study also implied that for asset-allocation purposes, the annuity can be considered a type of bond. The mission of the bond portfolio is to generate income, which certainly is the task of immediate annuities. This may mean that some advisers will, depending on interest rate assumptions, consider the flow of $40,000 to $50,000 of ever-replaceable annual income (be it from Social Security, pensions, or annuity income) to be equivalent to a $1 million bond portfolio and will treat it as such in a client's overall asset-allocation strategy. It will be interesting to see how variable immediate annuities are treated in this context.

Annuities can relieve the stress on an investment portfolio to generate a certain level of income. **FIGURE 10.10** shows the impact on a portfolio's ability to generate the 4.5 percent inflation-adjusted income first, when 25 percent of the portfolio was used to buy annuity income and when

FIGURE **10.10** *Likelihood That a Portfolio Can Survive 30 Years While Providing a 4.5% Inflation-Adjusted Income Stream With and Without an Allocation of Assets to Purchase an Immediate Annuity[17]*

PORTFOLIO DESCRIPTION	NO-ANNUITY 30-YEAR SURVIVAL PERCENTAGES	25% ANNUITY 30-YEAR SURVIVAL PERCENTAGES	50% ANNUITY 30-YEAR SURVIVAL PERCENTAGES
Conservative	32.6%	53.3%	81.3%
Balanced	76.3%	85.1%	94.5%
Growth	87.4%	92.2%	96.7%
Aggressive	91.6%	94.6%	97.5%

50 percent of the portfolio was used to buy annuity income.

The addition of lifetime annuity income as a part of the retiree's asset allocation not only increases the chance that the portfolio will last for thirty years but also makes it impossible, during the retiree's lifetime, to lose the income stream provided by the annuity. The economic conditions of the early twenty-first century are increasing the appeal of immediate annuities, both fixed and variable. The next debate among advisers is likely to be about how much of a portfolio to allocate to annuities and how that allocation should split between fixed and variable annuities. Since immediate variable annuitants can now select and change the asset allocation of their annuity capital even during the income period of their variable immediate annuity, some advisers are likely to recommend a 100 percent variable immediate annuity with an asset allocation among subaccounts designed to provide a steady, level income and the balance to be more equity-based to offset the effects of inflation. This could reduce the annuitant's exposure to general account risk that exists in fixed annuities.

Immediate Annuity Implementation Decisions

Jim Otar, author of *High Expectations and False Dreams,* discusses an annuity ladder concept in which the client and financial adviser determine what percentage of a client's retirement capital will be needed to sustain the desired standard of living. (For Otar's latest thinking on this subject, go to his website at www.cotar.org.) If that percentage withdrawal is not likely to diminish the amount of capital, income needs are comfortably satisfied and no annuitization is needed. Otar calls this a retiree with "abundant savings." If, however, there is some likelihood that principal will be used to provide for income needs, leaving less capital available to provide for future income needs, then some annuitization is needed. For some this will be a "bright line" test of whether annuities must be considered. Although Otar uses a very specific formula to guide the decision about how much to annuitize, the formula is based on assumptions on which individual advisers and clients may not necessarily agree.[18]

Still, the formula may be helpful as a starting point when tempered with individual judgment, considering pertinent economic and client circumstances along with annuity purchase factors. For example, Otar defines the annuity payout rate as the annual annuity payment divided by the single premium required to buy the annuity. In the extremely low interest rate period of 2003–2004, this was generally about 7 percent for a male, age sixty-five, purchasing a fixed-life annuity with a ten-year-certain minimum guarantee. For one client, it may be appropriate and competitive to provide for minimum income requirements. For another, whose basic needs are sufficiently taken care of but who is interested in more discretionary income and concerned about future inflation, a variable immediate annuity may be more appropriate. A third may be just as happy taking all of the income from the Franklin Income Fund.

The focus of an article in the *Journal of Financial Planning* in June 2003[19] was the search for a coherent and formal model for how much wealth to allocate to longevity insurance (the insurance provided by an insurance company that a capital sum will provide a given amount of income for life no matter how long an annuitant lives). The authors point out that longevity insurance is not only appropriate to hedge against the risk of outliving one's wealth but also serves to relieve the stress on retirement portfolios caused by the need for systematic withdrawals. If these authors were counseling an individual with $100,000 who needed $7,000 in income, they would likely point out that locking in a fixed annuity is implicitly a market-timing play, that is, locking in at today's interest rates for the rest of the annuitant's life. In 2003–2004, for example, with interest rates reaching lows not seen since 1958, it would have been wise to buy a fixed, non-life-contingent, five-year period annuity providing $7,000, which would cost $34,000, and leave the $66,000 invested in a diversified equity account. In five years, when the retiree is seventy years old, he would be entitled to more income from a newly purchased life-contingent annuity as a result of increased age. Interest rates may be higher in 2008 than they were in 2003–2004 (which also would increase the income provided by a life annuity) and, with a little luck, the $66,000 left in the diversified equity account could grow back to the $100,000 level.

With the life-annuity plan, our sixty-five-year-old knows what the situation will be in 2008, whereas under the five-year, fixed-period plan, he'll be accepting risk on a number of fronts in hopes of higher rewards. The authors would ask this client to describe the balance between his desire to bequeath and his desire to consume. The implication is that if the client's desire is to leave an inheritance, then there is no place for an annuity, whereas if the client's first priority is to consume, then, "because the returns on annuities are always higher than the returns on traditional assets—conditional on the retiree being alive—the immediate annuities get 100 percent of the allocation."[20]

The Last Word

During the bull market, as many people acquired both fixed and variable deferred annuities, the industry generated a lot of criticism from the media, many financial advisers, and even the regulators, all of whom felt the cost of the annuities surpassed their value. Yet the public kept investing in them. Although some annuity contracts are in fact overpriced and overcommissioned, it's turning out that the people who placed their money in high-quality, consumer-friendly deferred annuity contracts were much wiser than the critics. The contractual provisions in their deferred annuity contracts, for which they paid extra and which are not available in any alternative investment, are going to be used to their great advantage in retirement as they convert these contracts into income generators, using the very provisions that many experts kept telling them were not worth the price.

When comparing annuity contracts to other ways to invest, the annuity product is an insurance contract providing insurance-protection features that may not be necessary in good times, but they sure do come in handy in tough times and provide peace of mind along the way. Not many investments let you rest that easy. The baby-boom generation, as they buy deferred variable annuities loaded with minimum guarantees, is proving that they value these contracts as a risk-management tool that allows them to allocate assets in their retirement capital in the volatile yet often more rewarding equity market, with guarantees that offer protection against downside risk.

Chapter Notes

1. Joel Chernoff, "Bernstein Amends Policy Portfolio Mantra," *Pensions and Investments,* September 1, 2003, 3, 34.

2. Peter Bernstein's August 15, 2003, client newsletter, as reported in ibid., n. 3.

3. Ibid.

4. Charles B. Hatcher, "A Model of Desired Wealth at Retirement" (Association for Financial Counseling and Planning Education, University of Georgia, Athens, GA, 1997), 57–64.

5. PricewaterhouseCoopers, *Variable Annuities and Mutual Fund Investments for Retirement Planning: A Statistical Study* (prepared for the National Association for Variable Annuities, October 12, 2000).

6. This net after-tax life annuity income for a seventy-year-old male was quoted from a highly rated insurance company in May 2003, a time when low interest rates had driven up the cost of life-income promises from insurance companies. The gross income quoted was $17,925.60, 68.9 percent of which would not be subject to income taxes because it is considered a return of the purchaser's cost basis, leaving $5,828.64 subject to a 25 percent income tax as per the model assumptions, or a tax of $1,407.19, bringing after-tax income down to $16,518. If this annuitant could accept $14,955.84 of after-tax income instead, he could have a ten-year-certain minimum guarantee of income, live or die, along with the promise of life income no matter how long.

7. Rachel Koning, "Ten-Year Yield Punches Through to New Low," *CBS Market-Watch,* May 14, 2003, http://cbs.marketwatch.com/.

8. Kathy Chu and Kaja Whitehouse, "Money Matters: Pensions From Scratch," *Wall Street Journal,* December 16, 2002, R4.

9. Ibid., p. 52, graph 3-1, "Large Company Stocks, Return Indices, Returns and Dividend Yields."

10. "Immediate Annuity Quotations," www.immediateannuities.com/rates.asp (accessed May 31, 2003).

11. Ibid.; and Ben G. Baldwin and William G. Droms (Probus, 1988), 164.

12. "Can Investors Make Retirement Income Last a Lifetime?" *TIAA-CREF Quarterly* (Winter 2002): 10–12, www.tiaa-crefinstitute.org.

13. Ibbotson Associates, *Asset Allocation Library PowerPoint: Variable Annuity Investing* (Ibbotson Associates, 2002), image no. 5.

14. Life expectancy in 2003 for a sixty-five-year-old is seventy-eight for males and 81 for females.

15. Ibbotson Associates, *Stocks, Bonds, Bills, and Inflation® 2002 Yearbook, Market Results for 1926–2001* (Ibbotson Associates, 1983–2002), p. 37, table 2-5, "Basic Series, Annual Total Returns (in percent) from 1971 to 2001."

16. John Ameriks, Robert Veres, and Mark J. Warshawsky, "Making Retirement Income Last a Lifetime," *Journal of Financial Planning* (December 2002): 60–76.

17. "Can Investors Make Retirement Income Last a Lifetime?" *TIAA-CREF Quarterly* (Winter 2002): 10–12.

18. Jim Otar, "The Perfect Mix," *Financial Planning Interactive,* February 3, 2003. http://www.cotar.org.

19. Peng Chen and Moshe A. Milevsky, "Merging Asset Allocation and Longevity Insurance: An Optimal Perspective on Payout Annuities," *Journal of Financial Planning* (June 2003): 52–62.

20. Ibid., 58.

CHAPTER 11

Alternative Investments

MARK HURLEY

The financial advisory industry grew up during the greatest bull market in history. Throughout the 1990s, long-only investments such as mutual funds and separate accounts were more than sufficient to meet clients' performance expectations. The global economy was developing just slowly enough to enable long-only diversification strategies to succeed.

For most of the first three years of this decade, however, advisers suffered through one of the worst bear equity markets on record. The Nasdaq fell nearly 70 percent, and virtually every major equity index dropped precipitously. The cornucopian 1990s were clearly over. But does this less-than-soft landing mean that advisers need to rethink their traditional approach to investment management?

The long-term historical returns of the financial markets suggest that it does. Although no one can predict the returns of any market for the next five minutes, much less the next five years, the equity market's returns for the 1990s were nearly 11 percent higher than their average from 1961 to 1990. Should the returns of the equity markets migrate back to their historical mean during the next ten years, many advisory firms' current approach to investment management may be inadequate.

At the same time, the globalization of the world's economy—a change even more important to address—is undermining many advisory firms' historical approach to investment management. As companies compete more frequently in a worldwide market for labor, materials, and sales, sector and country characteristics are less dominant factors in stock performance. The correlation coefficient of the returns of the Standard & Poor's 500, Nasdaq, Morgan Stanley Capital International Europe Australasia and Far East, and Russell 2000 indices has jumped significantly from 1991 through 2000, increasing the systematic risk of diversified long-only portfolios. Advisers must now look beyond traditional asset classes to find ways to reduce risk.

A Cautious Approach to Alternatives

To meet these investment challenges, many advisory firms have turned their attention to alternative asset classes—hedge funds, managed futures, private equity, and real estate. Historically the sole province of institutions and wealthy investors, alternative investments have enhanced investors' returns while reducing overall portfolio risk. These benefits have made alternative asset classes standard allocations of many major institutional investors; indeed, several leading universities have allocated more than 20 percent of assets to these products.

Alternative investments, however, are not a panacea for advisory businesses. They're similar in many ways to prescription drugs. Correctly prescribed and taken, they offer marvelous benefits to those who need them. Used incorrectly, they can be fatal.

Alternative asset classes are fraught with risks for the uninformed investor:

❑ Alternative asset classes comprise largely unregulated products. And there are numerous examples of fraud and even outright theft by some alternative investment managers.

❑ Manager evaluation and selection is as much an art as a science. Unlike open-end mutual funds that must disclose their investment performance in a statutorily prescribed manner, alternative investments are mostly private partnerships that have no legal reporting requirements. Consequently, accurate and publicly available data are limited.

❑ Including alternative asset classes in a portfolio is complicated, and determining allocations to these products requires an extensive understanding of their investment strategies and risks. Unlike traditional mutual funds and private accounts, alternative investments—in terms of a portfolio's construction—are not designed to be stand-alone assets. Instead, successful institutional investors use several different alternative strategies at once, which, in the aggregate, produce a desired return pattern.

❑ Access to the best managers is critical to such strategies because the difference between a first- and fourth-quartile alternative-investment manager can often be the difference between success and disaster. Successful manager selection of traditional asset classes can boost returns by as much as 3 percent annually over time. By comparison, many first-quartile venture-capital partnerships since 1998 delivered returns exceeding 1,000 percent, whereas several fourth-quartile funds generated net losses for their investors.

❏ Advisory clients are typically semiaffluent investors (with net worth of $1 million to $10 million). Unlike institutions or the super-wealthy, semiaffluent investors can invest only limited amounts in such products and have a greater need for liquidity. The risk profile of many alternative products may make them unsuitable for this kind of investor.

❏ Advisers must also address a series of legal, tax, and operational issues before they can include alternative asset classes in their clients' portfolios.

Advisers have faced similar problems before, however, and overcame them. The 1970s produced a prolonged period of dismal equity returns. A handful of today's most successful advisory firms ventured into the realm of alternative investments by necessity back then to counteract the malaise of traditional markets. Their ability to learn how to invest effectively in alternative asset classes was a key factor in their success, not to mention their survival.

Advisory firms that succeed into the future are likely to share an ability to invest effectively in alternative asset classes. Correctly used, these products can improve risk-adjusted performance for investors, and successfully including alternative asset classes in portfolios will distinguish the top advisory businesses from the second tier. Much like their institutional counterparts, successful advisory organizations do not even think of alternative asset classes as "alternative." These investments instead serve as simply additional choices that can be used in constructing optimal portfolios.

Alternative Roles

Alternative investments can be separated into three broad categories: absolute-return products, private-equity investments, and real estate investments. Absolute-return products include hedge funds and managed futures. Private equity comprises venture capital, mezzanine financing, and leveraged buyouts. Real estate covers private real estate investments and real estate investment trusts (REITs). Each of these asset classes plays a different role in a portfolio and can potentially provide different return and diversification benefits.

Most absolute-return products serve as portfolio diversifiers. They're designed to provide annual returns equal to the long-term performance of equities (8–10 percent) with very low (<0.20) correlation to traditional asset classes. They're effective portfolio diversifiers because the sources of their returns are investment strategies unrelated to the movements of the market.

Investments in real estate also provide diversification benefits to portfolios. And they can serve as a form of insurance against either inflation or deflation. An asset class with both equity and fixed-income return characteristics, real estate historically has generated lower returns than do absolute-return strategies.

Above-market-level returns are largely sought through higher-risk private-equity investments and some absolute-return strategies. These products often rely on financial leverage and derivatives to generate exceptional investment performance.

By combining the different aspects of alternative investment products in their portfolios, investors have historically increased returns and decreased risk (as measured by standard deviation). Using historical return data from 1990 to 2000 for traditional asset classes and the three alternative investment strategies, we created five sample portfolios to use as examples. As shown in **FIGURE 11.1**, in every sample portfolio, adding an allocation to alternative investments produced higher overall returns with lower volatility.

For an aggressive investor, we used a portfolio with an 85 percent allocation to equities (50 percent U.S. large cap, 20 percent U.S. small cap, and 15 percent international) and a 15 percent allocation to U.S. fixed income. We compared that portfolio's returns with those of a portfolio that included a 25 percent allocation to alternative investments, made up of 12.5 percent to absolute-return products, 10 percent to private equity, and 2.5 percent to private real estate.

The average annual return during the eleven-year period for the traditional equity and fixed-income portfolio was 12.36 percent, versus 14.53 percent for the portfolio with a 25 percent allocation to alternative investments. This increased return was achieved with almost 20 percent less volatility, thereby dramatically improving the risk/return characteristics of the portfolio.

For a more conservative portfolio (55 percent equities and 45 percent fixed income), a 7.5 percent allocation to alternative investments (5 percent absolute-return products and 2.5 percent private equity) would have had similarly beneficial effects. Its overall returns would have risen from 11.48 percent to 12.31 percent, and its volatility would have been about 9 percent less.

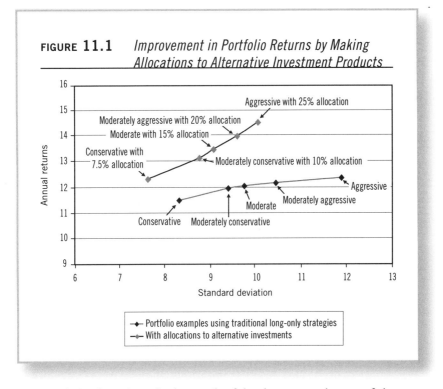

FIGURE 11.1   *Improvement in Portfolio Returns by Making Allocations to Alternative Investment Products*

Now let's take a closer look at each of the three general types of alternative investments.

Absolute-Return Strategies

The primary reason institutional investors have flocked to absolute-return products is diversification. During the last ten years, globalization has stripped away much of the diversification benefit from investing in different regions and sectors of the long-only market. The returns of long-only assets, regardless of an issuer's geographic location or market capitalization, are increasingly correlating.

Many absolute-return products, by comparison, generate their returns from factors unique to their investment strategies instead of the overall moves of the market. Consequently, their returns have a very low correlation to traditional asset classes. Because of this low correlation, adding an allocation to certain absolute-return strategies reduces a portfolio's overall systematic risk. Institutional investors have also shifted into hedge funds because of skepticism on the part of many pension, foundation, and endowment fiduciaries about the ability of traditional, long-only active money managers to add value to a portfolio.

Although each absolute-return manager has a unique style or approach, we've divided the thousands of potential investments into three major categories: relative value, event driven, and opportunistic.

Relative-Value Strategies

Relative-value strategies are generally portfolio diversifiers that profit by buying undervalued securities and selling short overvalued securities. Long/short strategies aside, the returns from this subgroup of absolute-return products result largely from relative changes in the pricing of similar securities. Relative-value managers identify these mispriced or undervalued securities by studying statistical and historical information and fundamental analyses. Under ideal circumstances, a manager will identify comparable overpriced and underpriced securities and take offsetting positions.

The fund profits when the securities return to their fair value. Turbulent markets and major corrections provide the most opportunities for relative-value strategies to succeed. The resulting mispriced securities create numerous arbitrage opportunities. For example, even during the worst stock market collapse in history—1929 to 1930—many arbitrageurs were very profitable.

A key limitation to any relative-value strategy is managing basis risk. Price movements of long and short positions are not always perfectly parallel. Unpredictable, exogenous variables can substantially alter the pricing of one side of a hedged position without changing the other, resulting in significant losses. With the exception of true, or risk-free, arbitrages, it's often impossible for a manager to construct a hedge that completely eliminates all basis risk.

Managing basis risk becomes harder during financial crises, when hedging is most needed to protect a position's value. It's almost impossible to predict how the price of one security will change relative to another when financial markets are gripped by panic. Failure to effectively manage basis risk has helped cause some of the greatest financial fiascos during the last twenty years, along with the demise of billion-dollar corporations.

Event-Driven Strategies

Event-driven strategies serve primarily as portfolio diversifiers. They capitalize on corporate events such as mergers, takeovers, spin-offs, bankruptcies, and reorganizations. The uncertainty of the outcomes of corporate events—and the resulting mispriced securities—is the primary source of returns for this subgroup of absolute-return strategies.

Event-driven managers are the scavengers of the financial markets. In the animal kingdom, creatures such as vultures, hyenas, and jackals prey on the defenseless—sick, old, very young, or tired animals—or try to seize part of the carcass of some other predator's conquest. In true scavenger style, event-driven managers attempt to gain advantage from the distress of weak entities or try to benefit from the takeover of healthy organizations by other companies.

They profit by correctly anticipating or at times even forcing a resolution to a corporate event. Analyzing potential investment opportunities can be complicated, however, and typically involves a three-step process. The first step is determining a company's true intrinsic value and comparing it with the market price of its outstanding securities. The second step of the analysis is to estimate the time until some sort of "catalyst" changes the market's perception of the company and reduces the gap between the intrinsic and current market value of its securities. The longer it might take for a distressed security situation to be resolved, the greater the likelihood of an unpredictable outcome and potential loss. As part of the analysis, managers assign probability weightings to potential resolutions of the event.

The third step of an event-driven manager's analysis concerns the manager's ability to influence potential outcomes. Although such actions are more common with distressed securities, risk arbitrageurs have also at times assumed significant control positions in merger and acquisition transactions.

Mispricing. Hedging can play a pivotal role in event-driven strategies. The greater a security's mispricing on an absolute basis, the more likely the manager will invest without hedging. For smaller disparities, the manager will probably take both long and short positions to capture relative differences in value.

But event-driven strategies often involve very complex transactions that have risks that can't be hedged. For example, a company management's desire to remain independent, shareholders' distrust of potential acquirers, and regulatory intervention can all disrupt event-driven strategies. Each is a noneconomic factor and, thus, very hard to hedge against.

Opportunistic Strategies

Opportunistic strategies are generally used to enhance overall portfolio returns. The broad changes across markets that often result in response either to governmental intervention or to speculative bubbles that appear during different market cycles are the primary sources of their returns. Managers in this field include many of the world's greatest and best-known speculators, such as George Soros and Julian Robertson. They take large market bets—often unhedged and highly leveraged—that can earn their investors exceptional returns or result in large losses.

Notable opportunistic investments have involved national governments that were attempting to artificially fix their currency values relative to some benchmark or to another country's currency. By selling these currencies short in large volumes and forcing their devaluation, the speculators reaped huge returns. Opportunistic strategies, however, encompass a far broader range of investments than currency speculation. Global macro, short sellers, emerging markets, and long-only substrategies fall into this category. And opportunistic managers often switch among strategies and markets as they deem necessary. It's not unusual for a manager to employ several strategies simultaneously.

Immense systematic risk is a common link in all such strategies, albeit short sellers are negatively correlated to traditional asset classes. And although short-seller strategies are sold to investors for the purpose of enhancing returns, their negatively correlating returns allow them also to serve as portfolio diversifiers.

Private Equity

Private equity is the second major alternative investment asset class. Its goal is to generate substantially greater returns than the long-term historical equity markets have, enhancing overall portfolio returns. Achieving such performance comes at a price: greater risk, very little liquidity, and limited diversification benefits. Most private-equity pools require long investment horizons (at least five to seven years) and do not distribute cash flow in the early years of the investment. Investors have been attracted to private equity because it has delivered exceptionally high levels of absolute return, particularly during the 1990s. The Venture Economics Private Equity Performance Index generated an average annual return of 22.1 percent during the ten years ended December 2000. Another benchmark, the Cambridge Venture Capital Index, returned 43.43 percent during the same period—nearly twice as great as the Nasdaq, its closest competitor among traditional benchmarks.

Unlike many absolute-return strategies and real estate investments, however, private equity has not been an effective diversifier of portfolios. The correlation of returns between private equity and the S&P 500 has been fairly high. Studies have also shown that during periods of crisis, private-equity strategies exhibit even higher levels of correlation with the S&P 500 and Lehman Aggregate Bond indices.

Investment activities of private-equity firms encompass every aspect of the life cycle of an organization, ranging from start-ups to mature businesses. There are three types of private equity: venture capital, mezzanine, and leveraged buyouts (LBOs). Within this broad spectrum of investments, there's a great deal of specialization among firms. Few organizations are exceptional at investing in more than a few stages of a company's development.

Venture capitalists typically provide capital at the earlier stages of a company's life. They usually take direct equity ownership in portfolio companies, although they may also receive warrants. Mezzanine firms typically invest in the middle stages of a company's life. Investments are often structured as subordinated debt—senior to the equity investors but junior to banks or normal bondholders. The compensation for the risk that they assume is usually the high level of interest paid on their debt. LBO firms usually invest in the later stages of a company's life. Using a combination of equity and debt financing provided by commercial and investment banks, LBO firms acquire undervalued public companies. Their investment usually takes the form of equity in the acquired companies.

The distinct difference between venture capital investing and LBO investing is important to recognize. Each targets very different companies and requires very different skills to analyze and add value after the transaction.

Venture capitalists are the epitome of growth investors. Experts at turning concepts into successful companies, they sometimes invest in a company before it begins operations and always invest before the company's success is established. They have to understand new technologies and how to turn them into products that the market will demand. Successful venture capitalists are also able to bring together capable management teams and guide them through the business's developmental stage.

LBO investors, by comparison, are the ultimate value investors. They invest in companies that have already passed through the start-up and developmental stages to become mature businesses. Their goal is to identify undervalued and poorly performing businesses that they can help turn around by helping the business create efficiencies and scale. Success in this arena requires extensive background in business operations, mergers and acquisitions, and defining core businesses.

Real Estate

Real estate is the third general category of alternative investments and constitutes nearly 10 percent of the investable assets in the United States. As of December 31, 1998, the real estate market was estimated at more than $3.5 trillion, making it the third-largest market segment, behind bonds/cash and stocks. The absolute size of the real estate market makes it difficult for investors who want to own a portfolio representative of the larger market to ignore this asset class.

Real estate as an asset class offers investors two potential benefits that most other asset classes do not. First, it provides significant diversification benefits to an overall asset allocation, along with fairly predictable long-term returns. Second, it can serve as a potential hedge against both inflation and deflation.

Diversification

The best argument for including real estate in a portfolio is diversification. Selecting assets with noncorrelating returns can improve the risk-adjusted performance of a portfolio. And there are very few asset classes that provide as much diversification benefit as real estate. During the ten-year period ending December 31, 2000, private real estate produced a 0.02 correlation versus U.S. stocks and a –0.14 correlation to U.S. bonds. REITs, publicly traded stocks of companies that invest in real estate, produced correlations of 0.29 versus stocks and 0.23 versus bonds. According to studies done in 1992 and 1997, investors seeking to optimize their portfolios should have included real estate in their portfolios at least 85 percent of the time.

To achieve real estate diversification benefits, allocations to this asset class must also be diversified from the perspective of three major factors. Similar types of property—regardless of location—often correlate in their returns. Consequently, property type is an important diversification factor. Geographic region is likewise important because real estate valuations within specific geographic regions can correlate fairly closely. Finally, allocations to real estate must be diversified by economic sector—that is, technology companies, financial services firms, et cetera—of the properties' tenants.

Inflation and Deflation Hedges

In theory, investments in real estate have attributes similar to both equities and bonds. They typically will have leases that provide a stream of fixed payments to the property owner that are similar to the coupon payments of a bond. The fixed nature of lease payments provides a measure of protection against deflation similar to that of long-term bonds.

The underlying value of the property, on the other hand, is similar to an equity investment in that it can appreciate or depreciate in value over time. The ability to appreciate in value provides a degree of protection against inflation.

In reality, private real estate returns have more closely resembled those of bonds than those of equities during the past ten years. From 1991 to 2000, the NCREIF Property Index (NPI) produced an average annual return of 6.69 percent with a standard deviation of 3.91 percent. The Lehman Aggregate Bond Index returned 7.96 percent with a standard deviation of 3.74 percent. The S&P 500, by comparison, returned 17.46 percent with 13.37 percent volatility.

These bondlike returns over an extended period of time have sparked widespread debate about the benefits of owning real estate in multi-asset-class portfolios. According to one popular academic theory, because real estate acts as insurance against inflation and deflation, it should have expected returns that are lower than those of equities. The investor is paying a "premium" for the insurance.

Recent research found conflicting evidence as to whether real estate truly helps hedge a portfolio against unanticipated inflation. One all-encompassing study in the *Journal of Real Estate* by Jack Rubens, Michael Bond, and James Webb looked at residential real estate, business real estate, and farmland. It examined whether these properties acted as hedges against actual inflation, expected inflation, and unexpected inflation. The study concluded that only residential real estate is a quantifiable hedge against actual inflation, only business real estate and Treasury bills are complete hedges against expected inflation, and only farmland and residential real estate were complete hedges against unexpected inflation. The study concluded that real estate is itself hedged against inflation, but that there are many better alternatives, such as commodity indices, to hedge a portfolio against inflation. A 1999 study by Kenneth Froot in *The Handbook of Alternative Investment Strategies* found that some property types perform better during inflationary environments than others. But it concluded that vacancy rates were the primary determinant of a property's ability to serve as a hedge against inflation. They must be low for the hedge to be effective.

This dependency on a correct balance between the supply and demand for real estate has been problematic in the United States at certain times during the last couple of decades. A series of factors unrelated to the actual demand for real estate have created supply/demand imbalances that have been disastrous for investors.

A large part of the boom in real estate development in the 1980s resulted from tax laws that gave inordinately high tax benefits to investors in real estate limited partnerships. Numerous federally insured financial institutions, such as banks and savings and loans, also embarked on commercial real estate lending binges in an attempt to generate enough high-yielding assets to offset their high costs of funding. The combined effect of these two factors resulted in a flood of new commercial and multifamily real estate properties that far exceeded the market's ability to absorb them. It also led to a collapse in real estate valuations as well as of hundreds of financial institutions.

The potential for forces not related to the actual demand for real estate to create major disruptions has led some institutional investors to view real estate investing in a more opportunistic fashion. Unlike their approach to fixed-income or equity allocations, these organizations in effect rely on some element of market timing in deciding to shift assets to the real estate sector. They also make their investments within narrow sectors of the real estate market instead of taking a broad investment approach.

Real Estate Investment Choices

Investments in real estate can be divided into two categories—private real estate and real estate investment trusts. Although both provide diversification benefits in varying degrees, they differ dramatically in their return patterns and the circumstances in which they are most appropriate for a portfolio allocation to real estate.

Private real estate. The private real estate market is considerably larger than the REIT market. As of the end of 2000, the private real estate market totaled nearly $3.5 trillion, whereas the public REIT market had a cumulative market value of $140 billion. The two primary means of investing in private real estate is through direct investments in individual properties and through pooled investments such as real estate limited partnerships. Direct investments in real estate require substantial expertise in evaluating individual properties, efficient property management, and real estate markets in general. They also are concentrated investments with returns tied to a single property.

Real estate limited partnerships are pooled investment vehicles managed by people specializing in different types of real estate investing. The pool's assets are invested across several properties to provide a degree of diversification to their investors' overall returns.

Property selection is a critical factor in generating good returns when investing in private real estate. A study in 1996 by Michael Young and Richard Graff concluded that investment performance tends to persist among top-quartile-performing properties and bottom-quartile-performing properties. In other words, if a property performs well over a period of time, it's likely to continue to deliver good returns for an extended period. Conversely, properties that have performed poorly for a period of time are not likely to see improvements in the near term.

Identifying investment properties that will perform well, however, can be very challenging. Only limited public information is available on individual real estate markets. Properties are traded infrequently, and sales are usually made through privately negotiated transactions instead of public auctions. Each property is also unique, and both property type and location affect valuation.

Beyond the difficulties in obtaining adequate diversification, a chief limitation to all private real estate investing is a lack of liquidity. Partnership investments usually have seven- to ten-year lives. Direct investments in individual properties are also extremely illiquid. Trades occur infrequently, and no organized market of buyers and sellers exists to allow investors to get in and out of positions immediately. A measure of the lack of liquidity in the real estate markets is reflected in the high transaction costs in this asset class. Real estate transaction costs typically range from 6 percent to 10 percent of the property's sale price, as opposed to 1 percent on mutual funds or 2–4 percent on alternative investment vehicles.

Real Estate Investment Trusts

REITs were first created in 1960 and were designed to provide real estate investors with a measure of liquidity. REITs are publicly traded companies whose shares are normally listed on the New York Stock Exchange. Most of them are equity REITs, which own and manage commercial real estate such as apartments, offices, and shopping centers. A few REITs are mortgage REITs, which lend on real estate or invest in mortgages. REITs are similar to closed-end mutual funds—where investors must sell shares to other partners as opposed to redeeming the assets from the fund to get liquidity—in that they allow investors to diversify their holdings, receive professional management, and are not taxed at the corporate level. Shares are publicly traded and priced daily. However, many REITs are active businesses that sell, acquire, and develop new real estate.

The publicly traded REIT market has seen rapid growth. It grew from less than $6 billion in total assets in 1990 to more than $140 billion by the end of the second quarter of 2001. Nearly 200 REITs currently trade on national stock exchanges and the increased liquidity of these vehicles is reflected in their average daily trading volume, which increased from about $28 million per day in 1992 to more than $400 million as of April 2001.

A great deal of debate continues, however, as to whether investments in REITs are analogous to investments in real estate. Although they own real estate, many REITs may be viewed as operating businesses whose performance can drive stock prices. The higher correlation of REITs (in comparison to private real estate) to traditional asset classes in large part reflects how these vehicles' earnings depend on their operating businesses, capital-allocation strategies, and broad-based fluctuations in the equities markets.

Consequently, for many institutional investors, REITs are an additional asset class, separate and distinct from real estate itself. REIT share prices can also be much more volatile than those of private real estate. A 1999 study by Dean Gatlaff and David Geltner suggests, however, that much of private real estate's low volatility is due to appraisal-based valuations. This reliance on appraisal valuation methodologies creates a "smoothing" effect on private real estate prices that does not necessarily represent the actual value of the underlying properties had they been sold on that date.

The Advisory Firm's Role

In addition to figuring out which types of alternative investments, if any, may be appropriate for their clients, advisory firms must also determine the role their organizations will accept in harnessing the benefits of these three broad asset classes. The decision will reflect the firm's investment and operational capability, as well as its willingness to incur additional liability. For example, some organizations will develop proprietary funds of funds and directly invest client assets into investment partnerships or transactions. Others will subcontract these investments to third-party organizations that specialize in selecting and monitoring alternative asset class managers. Regardless of which path is chosen, advisory firms must develop an expertise on these asset classes and how they're most effectively used in client portfolios.

Sophisticated advisory firms recognize that alternative investments offer their clients potential benefits that cannot be gotten from traditional long-only equities and bonds. However, alternative classes can be complicated and even risky products. So advisers face a dilemma. They can't simply ignore these asset classes. Nor can they consider using them without first devoting a considerable amount of time and resources to developing an understanding of them.

Unsuccessful or improper use of alternative investment products will also be a distinguishing factor among advisory firms. Organizations that fail to complete the lengthy and complicated due diligence process on the asset classes—as well as on individual products and managers—prior to investing will inflict irreparable harm on their clients' portfolios and on the future of their advisory businesses.

PART FOUR

PRACTICE AND THEORY

Think of this section as food for thought, a potpourri of vital investment discourse. The authors here—three professors, a world-renowned money manager, the voice of the fund industry, and the voice of the consulting world—have no trouble maintaining the standards of intellectual firepower set in the previous sections. Don Phillips provides guidance on improving our investment decision making by focusing on portfolio construction. John Brynjolfsson speaks the language of financial planners when he makes a case for real-return investments in a framework that recognizes that "investment performance is a means to a real end, not an end in itself," and "in investment chasing, some win, many lose, but all take unwarranted risks." David Nawrocki's contribution continues the discussion on risk, underscoring the risk our clients care most about—downside risk.

Roger Ibbotson, Michael Henkel, and Peng Chen, looking at risk from another perspective, make a strong case for the inclusion of lifetime payout annuities in retirement portfolios. Moshe Milevsky's chapter complements the work of the Ibbotson team by presenting the case for incorporating human capital into portfolio design. But all of the theory, knowledge, and strategies offered by these writers are of little use if they're not delivered to clients in a comprehensive, cohesive, and professionally responsible manner. That's why we saved Steve Winks's contribution for the wrap-up. Winks shares the accumulated wisdom of participants in the High Net Worth Standards Initiative, an initiative to define the processes, technology, and investment and administrative values necessary for financial advisers to fulfill their responsibility to clients.

Moshe A. Milevsky

Moshe Milevsky is a tenured professor at the Schulich School of Business at York University and the author of numerous articles and books on issues of importance to practitioners, including *Money Logic: Financial Strategies for the Smart Investor, The Probability of Fortune* (U.S. edition), and *Insurance Logic*. Through frequent media appearances and extensive consulting work, Milevsky continues to apply the lessons of academic research to the daily problems of investors.

In posing the question "Is that client a bond or a stock?" Milevsky brings front and center an issue many practitioners may give lip service to but either ignore or rarely incorporate into their planning. "The concept of human capital is a powerful one that can guide many decisions in personal finance," Milevsky concludes. We expect that this chapter will serve as an important wake-up call to professionals to actively incorporate into the planning process the vital but repeatedly overlooked investment—human capital.

David Nawrocki

As practitioners, we're continually talking about risk—evaluating it, measuring it, managing it. These discussions implicitly assume a normal distribution of returns. Unfortunately, academics tell us and experience rudely demonstrates that investment returns are anything but "normal." One obvious divergence from normality is positive skewness (more good outcomes than one would expect). So what? Well, if returns are positively skewed, then traditional risk measures exaggerate risks, because investors take kindly to positive surprises. But the subject of David Nawrocki's chapter is "bad," or downside, risk.

As Nawrocki notes, the concept of downside risk gained a certain amount of popularity in the early 1990s, particularly after the publication of Rom and Ferguson's "Post-Modern Portfolio Theory Comes of Age" in the Fall 1994 issue of the *Journal of Investing*. But the use of downside risk measures is confusing; indeed, it remains a mystery to most practitioners. Although Nawrocki's contribution is one of the more technical ones in *Think Tank,* it brings clarity to the confusion and provides an understanding of the important concept of the measurement of downside risk.

Don Phillips

Like many of *Think Tank*'s other contributors, Don Phillips doesn't really need an introduction, but it's a pleasure to offer one anyway. Managing director of Morningstar and champion for investor rights, he is also one of the profession's true gentlemen. We've known Phillips since he completed grammar school (at least when we first met him, he looked about that old). He's a fellow member of our Alpha Group, a good friend, and a constant source of good "down home" investment wisdom.

All practitioners are familiar with the Morningstar Style Boxes, and many of us find the information useful, but the nine-box limit constrains its application. Morningstar, a firm known for continually leveraging technology in the development of new analytical tools, recognized this constraint and developed a more robust analytical strategy. Drawing on Morningstar's research, resources, and experience, Phillips introduces a portfolio-oriented methodology for incorporating funds into an investment portfolio. Whether you use Morningstar or not, you'll find Phillips's chapter a valuable contribution to the development of your own analytical approach to portfolio construction.

Roger G. Ibbotson, Michael C. Henkel, and Peng Chen

The demographic indicators are loud and clear: "Practitioners, prepare; the ranks of the retired will be swelling—and soon." Financial advisers recognize that they'll need to shift their professional attention from investment accumulation to distribution. Roger Ibbotson, Michael Henkel, and Peng Chen (the founder, president, and director of research, respectively, of Ibbotson Associates), a stand-alone think tank, have devoted significant time and resources over the last few years to considering the investment consequences of "the shift in retirement funding from professionally managed defined-benefit plans to personal savings vehicles." Their conclusion, one that until very recently we would have pitched out as nonsense, is that we need to consider the use of payout annuities in our clients' portfolios. Having read the research of Ibbotson and other contributors on this subject, I'm now a believer. I've also had to eat a lot of crow, because, as is my style, I spent many years publicly declaring that I'd wash my mouth out with soap if I ever endorsed an immediate annuity. This chapter will not only help you be a better adviser; it will also spare you the taste of crow.

John B. Brynjolfsson

John Brynjolfsson is well known to many of us as the manager of the PIMCO Real Return Fund. He has also coauthored *Inflation-Protected Bonds* and coedited *The Handbook of Inflation-Index Bonds*. As a managing director for PIMCO, the Rolls-Royce of bond-management firms, and the person responsible for the management of one of the newest asset classes to enter the realm of investing, Brynjolfsson has a special perspective to contribute to practitioners. He has given a great deal of thought to how investors—and their advisers—might put an understanding of the impact of monetary policy on investment planning to practical use. Drawing on a long-term historical perspective, Brynjolfsson developed a forty-year Fed monetary-cycle model designed to provide investment guidance. In his chapter, he shares his valuable conclusions and recommendations

Stephen C. Winks

Steve Winks is editor-in-chief of *Senior Consultant* and one of the founders of the investment-management consultant movement. Frustrated that retail advisers had to make their way without a framework of performance standards, such as the AIMR performance standards that guide professionals in institutional finance, Winks conceived of and created the High Net Worth Standards Initiative. The initiative's task force (consisting of volunteer members from the ranks of the consulting and planning profession) has worked with the Society of Senior Consultants, the Foundation of Fiduciary Studies, Dalbar, and the AICPA to create the High Net Worth/Asset Liability Study Working Document. As the driving force behind this effort, Winks shares with readers the process and results to date. As the name indicates, it is indeed a "working document"; however, the information gathered so far offers an extraordinary picture of today's practice standards. This information alone will be invaluable as a benchmark for the evaluation and improvement of your practice. Longer term, given the credibility and authority of the individual and institutional contributors to the document, these best practices are likely to be incorporated into regulatory standards.

CHAPTER 12

Human Capital and Asset Allocation
Is That Client a Bond or a Stock?

MOSHE A. MILEVSKY

How narrow is your client's definition of wealth? When he considers all his assets, does he include himself in the mix? This chapter invites you to take the theory and practice of asset allocation to the next level by focusing your client's attention on a broader definition of wealth, one that includes personal assets that traditionally have not been found in the investment equation. The definition takes into account the financial characteristics of your client's job and long-term career—also known broadly as *human capital*—to determine which they most resemble: a stock portfolio or a bond portfolio. Here's why. If those characteristics are akin to *stocks,* you should be encouraging him to lighten up on equity risk and to hold more bonds in his financial portfolio. If they're more like *bonds,* then you should be encouraging him to own investments that are more like stocks.

This might seem like an odd statement, so I'll explain. First, some background: According to results published in 2000 by the U.S. Census Bureau, the average American family unit whose head of household is aged thirty-five to forty-four has a median net worth of approximately $33,950 in year 2000 dollars (see **FIGURE 12.1**). In other words, 50 percent of families in this category have a net worth greater than $33,950, and 50 percent have a net worth that's less than this amount. The net-worth figure is technically defined as the family's total assets minus the family's consolidated debts and is expressed in year 2000 (after-inflation) dollars. Indeed, this is a well-established and traditional way of computing net worth. The same study noted that if the head of the household was aged forty-five to

FIGURE **12.1** *Income and Net Worth for the Median U.S. Family*

AGE OF HOUSEHOLDER (2000)	INCOME	NET WORTH
35–44 years	$53,243	$33,950
45–54 years	$58,217	$68,198
55–64 years	$44,993	$100,750
65 years and older	$23,047	$107,150 (65–69 years) $118,950 (70–74 years)
75 years and older	$18,873	$100,000

Source: U.S. Bureau of the Census, 2000.

fifty-four, the median net worth of the family unit was $68,198, while for the group aged fifty-five to sixty-four, the relevant figure was $100,750. The positive impact of age on median wealth shouldn't surprise anyone. Younger individuals have little financial wealth and accumulated savings, but as people age, they accumulate wealth.

I certainly don't quibble with census methodology in this and similar studies, but I think that a traditional accountant's *assets minus liabilities* view of the human balance sheet greatly underestimates the true economic net worth of the fascinating company that I like to call Client Inc. Consider your client the chief executive officer, chief financial officer, and chairman of the board of Client Inc.—a small, tightly controlled and privately held corporation with the bulk of its productive assets invested in nontraded units of his future salary and wages. His objective as commander-in-chief of Client Inc. is to maximize the shareholder's value while minimizing the financial risks faced by the corporation.

Note that Client Inc. started life as a shell company and was part of a larger conglomerate called Parents Inc. For the first few years of its human life cycle, Client Inc. was considered an asset—or perhaps a liability—on Parents Inc.'s personal balance sheet. In fact, a large part of the income of Parents Inc. was allocated toward maintaining the value of Client Inc. Parents invest close to $100,000, even according to conservative estimates, in their children during the first eighteen years of life. It's unclear if they'll ever get to see any dividends from this investment. Economists would argue that creating Client Inc. subsidiaries is a negative net present value (NPV) project.

During your client's late teens to midtwenties, the Client Inc. corporate shell became operational and he was faced with the first and perhaps the most challenging decision as the newly installed commander-in-chief of Client Inc. He had to decide how to finance and where to invest Client Inc.'s human capital. Though young, your clients are actually much wealthier than traditional methods are able to reflect. In fact, the younger the client and family are, the wealthier they are. That's because for the vast majority of Americans, and especially the educated and potentially affluent ones, the greatest single asset on their personal balance sheet is not being measured by census data. It's called *human capital*.

Human capital is a way of quantifying the present value of the client's future wages, income, and salary. For example, clients who are doctors, lawyers, engineers, or even professors have probably invested an enormous amount of time, effort, and money to finance their education. They hope that the investment will pay off in labor income in the form of job dividends over the next ten, twenty, or even thirty years. Human capital can't really be touched, felt, or seen, but like an oil reserve deep under the sands of Texas, it will eventually be extracted and so definitely *must* be worth something now. In fact, most companies operating in the natural resources sector spend considerable time valuing the reserves they will be extracting and processing over their operating life. Your clients should do the same with their reserves.

Look at it this way: During the course of your clients' working lives, they will slowly convert human capital into financial capital. Thus, their *total* personal equity, which is a much better measure of *true* net worth, is the sum of two components. Of course, when family units are still young, human capital is a much larger fraction of total personal equity since the present value of all future wages most likely exceeds the few dollars they might have in their savings or investment accounts. But as they age, the situation is reversed, although even in their early sixties, there is still some human capital left and it must be accounted for.

As **FIGURE 12.2** indicates, the value of total personal equity (TPE) is what's left after subtracting debts and liabilities from the totality of financial assets and human-capital assets. Figure 12.2 provides the modern economic view of the personal financial balance sheet. It quantifies the value of all the productive and income-producing assets at your client's disposal—first and foremost being your client and her job.

About now you might be thinking, What's the point in knowing the value of a human capital *reserve* if a person can't do much of anything with it right now? In fact, it will never be possible—and I've tried—to borrow against human capital from the bank; nor can it be pledged as collateral for a loan, as can the proven and established reserves against which corporations may borrow. Nevertheless, quite a number of applicable strategies can come from thinking about your client's balance sheet in this way, even if her human capital cannot be sold, traded, or liquidated.

FIGURE **12.2** *The Balance Sheet of Client Inc.:*
Economic Approach

ASSETS	DEBT + LIABILITIES
• Bank Accounts • Housing • Stocks and Bonds • Car & Vehicles • Small Business Equity • PV of Pension	• Mortgages • Consumer Loans • Credit Cards • Student Loans
+ HUMAN CAPITAL	**TOTAL PERSONAL EQUITY** • True Net Worth

Portfolio Diversification

A client's total—that is, human and financial capital—portfolio must be properly diversified. Set things up so that when one type of capital zigs, the other zags. In the early stages of the life cycle, for example, financial and investment capital should be used to hedge and diversify human capital, as opposed to naively building wealth. Think of your client's investable assets as a defense and protection against adverse shocks to his human capital (that is, salaries and wages), as opposed to an isolated pot of money that has to be blindly allocated for the long run. (See **FIGURE 12.3.**)

For a tenured university professor like myself, for example, human capital—and the subsequent pension I'm entitled to—has the properties of a fixed-income bond fund that entitles me to monthly coupons. I like to think of myself as a walking inflation-adjusted real return bond. Therefore, considering the risk and return characteristics of my human capital, I have very little need in my financial portfolio for fixed-income bonds, money market funds, or even Treasury inflation-protected securities and real-return bonds—although they're great investments. In fact, my personal pension plan is similar to an individual retirement account or 401(k) plan, and discretionary savings are quite heavily invested in individual equities and mutual funds. In this way, my total portfolio of human and financial capital is well balanced, although my financial capital and human capital are not diversified if viewed separately.

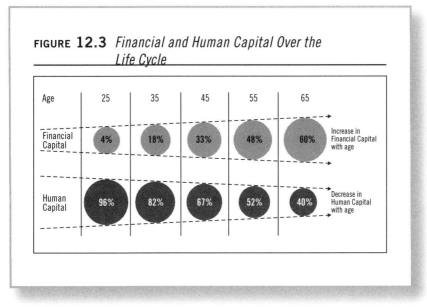

FIGURE **12.3** *Financial and Human Capital Over the Life Cycle*

My MBA finance students, of course, can expect to earn a lot more during their lifetime than their university professors, but from year to year, their relative income and bonuses will fluctuate depending on the performance of the stock market, the industry they work in, and the unpredictable vagaries of the labor market. Their human capital will be almost entirely invested in equity, and so their financial capital should be tilted slightly more toward bonds and fixed-income products—unlike other young workers in more stable industries, who can afford to take the risk—early in their working career. Of course, they're still young and can tolerate the ups and downs in the market and should have some exposure to equities. But all else being equal, two individuals who are thirty-five years old and have exactly the same annual income and retirement horizon should not have the same equity portfolio structure if their human capital differs in risk characteristics. (See **FIGURE 12.4.**)

It may seem odd to advise future financial analysts and so-called experts in the securities industry not to "put their money where their mouths are," but doing so is, in fact, prudent risk management. I would go so far as to disagree with the famed investor and stock market guru Peter Lynch and argue that you should *not* invest in things you're familiar with but rather in industries and companies you know nothing or very little about. In all likelihood, such investments will have little correlation, if any, with your human capital. Indeed, the engineers, technicians, and computer scientists who thought they knew the high-

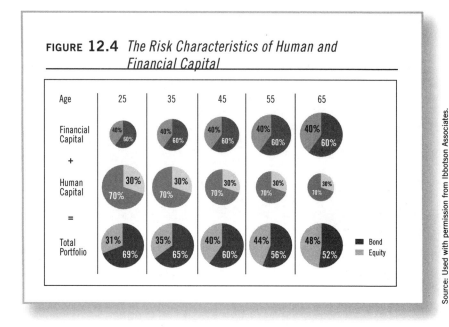

FIGURE 12.4 *The Risk Characteristics of Human and Financial Capital*

Source: Used with permission from Ibbotson Associates.

tech industry—and whose human capital was invested in it—learned this lesson the hard way. Remember, it's not the magnitude of income or the stability of the job that determines its asset classification; rather, the objective is to make sure your client's salary and financial portfolio *do not* share the same zigs and zags. If your client works in the biotech industry, make sure she owns info-tech stocks, and if she works in the media, make sure she owns some natural resources.

Furthermore, if you consider the flexibility involved in the decision of when to retire or whether to work overtime, then more human capital can be extracted, if and when needed, to offset losses from financial assets. Thus, the ability to create more human capital—at the expense of some leisure time perhaps—is yet another argument why younger investors and savers, who are many years away from retirement, can afford to take more financial risk and invest in more volatile instruments. As unpleasant as this may sound, if the investments don't work out, there's always the option to *mine human capital* by working more and working harder.

I believe the future holds tailor-made investment portfolios that go one step further than life-cycle and age-based funds by closely matching investors' human-capital characteristics with a strategy that effectively diversifies these idiosyncratic risks. Investment funds and pools will be available for dentists, lawyers, and chemical engineers.

Employment Compensation

Once your client is willing to accept his human capital as having financial risk and return characteristics, then ongoing employment compensation should attempt to balance and smooth out the ups and downs. For example, loading up on company stock and options is not the best way to manage the risk of the personal financial corporation since such a large bulk of human capital is already invested in the company. It's imprudent to take on even more exposure. (Think of Enron employees and their stock holdings.)

The human resources department and corporate shareholders might not like the idea, but the best form of compensation is cold hard cash. In fact, a point can be reached where the employee owns so much stock and options in his own company that he assigns the grant or bonus close to zero value. That's certainly not an efficient method of aligning incentives between shareholders and managers. And if your client doesn't have much of a choice, then that exposure must be reduced—possibly with put options or other forms of downside protection.

Pension planning is another area where it's useful to think in terms of human capital. When a person is young and has many productive years of work ahead of him, it might not be optimal to lock in to a defined-benefit pension plan, where financial fortunes are intertwined with the prospects of the company he works for. As a client ages, however, and his human capital is converted to financial capital, you might want to encourage him to lock in the fixed and predictable retirement benefits that come with a defined-benefit pension plan.

Life Insurance

If you take a holistic view of your client's balance sheet, prudent risk management becomes an exercise in protecting human as well as financial capital. The ideal diversified investment portfolio is one in which the individual components do not all zig and zag at the same time. And just as financial capital and human capital should counterbalance each other, life insurance should be viewed as a *hedge* against a loss of human capital. Basic insurance shouldn't be acquired as an investment vehicle but rather be purchased for its *correlation* properties. If something happens to human capital, the insurance will pay off, but if nothing bad happens to human capital, the insurance will perform poorly. Again, when one zigs, the other zags. I believe this is a better and more honest way to explain, promote, and sell all forms of insurance to individuals who likely view the premiums as money poured down the drain. They've purchased a hedge, not an investment.

Practically speaking, if your client's human capital is valued at $1 million—by discounting her future wages at some reasonable after-tax and justifiable risk-adjusted interest rate—then she probably doesn't need any more than $1 million in life insurance protection. In fact, since your client will likely consume a large portion of her own human capital, she will probably need a lot less than $1 million in pure insurance coverage. But this sort of exercise should give you a ballpark figure of what's needed to cover and manage the risk.

The Bigger Picture

The concept of human capital is a powerful one that can guide many decisions in personal finance. Overall, it educates and forces us to move away from micro-finance decisions—such as how a client allocates a 401(k) contribution—to the more critical macro-finance questions, whose answers truly add value to clients. Indeed, if the typical American's personal balance sheet since the start of the century were carefully measured, you'd find that the gut-wrenching bear market of the early decade did not erode total personal equity as much as one would expect. Properly diversified personal financial corporations—Client Inc.'s—did not lose anywhere near the 30–50 percent that isolated investment portfolios suffered, that is, the typical Client Inc.'s total worth, with human capital factored in, did not suffer the same degree of loss that his investment portfolio did. To counteract these losses, note that housing prices increased in value and long-term interest rates declined from 8 percent to 5 percent. Remember that market prices of bonds increase and perform quite well when interest rates decline. And if you view your client's human capital as a bondlike investment, then its value has actually increased as interest rates have declined. Sure, they won't get a quarterly statement saying that their human capital is worth 30 percent more than it was last year, but they should definitely be reminded of it.

So next time you sit down to tinker with a new or existing client's asset allocation, here's the key question to ask: *"Are you a bond or a stock?"*

References

To learn more about how to do the kind of comprehensive asset allocation and financial planning that takes into account the entire left-hand side of a client's personal balance sheet, these sources and references will help.

Bodie, Z., R. C. Merton, and W. F. Samuelson. 1992. "Labor Supply Flexibility and Portfolio Choice in a Life Cycle Model." *Journal of Economic Dynamics and Control* 16:427–449.

Milevsky, M. A. 2003. *Wealth Logic: Wisdom for Improving Your Personal Finances.* Captus. www.captus.com.

Reichenstein, W. 2001. "Rethinking the Family's Asset Allocation." *Journal of Financial Planning* (May): 102–109.

Scott, M. C. 1995. "Defining Your Investment Portfolio: What Should You Include?" *American Association of Individual Investors Journal* (November): 15–17.

Williams, J. 1978. "Risk, Human Capital and the Investor's Portfolio." *Journal of Business* 51:65–89.

CHAPTER 13

Downside Risk Measures
A Brief History

DAVID N. NAWROCKI

S ince 1994, the investment community has shown increased interest in using downside risk measures in portfolio analysis. With interest comes confusion about the methods. One of the best ways to understand a concept is to study the history of its development and the issues the researchers faced. This chapter reviews the history of these measures.

First, let's define some terms. Portfolio theory is the application of decision-making tools under risk to the problem of managing risky investment portfolios. There have been numerous techniques developed over the years to implement the theory of portfolio selection. Among the techniques are the downside risk measures. The most commonly used downside risk measures are the *semivariance,* or special case, and the *lower partial moment,* or general case. It's helpful to remember that mean-variance as well as mean-semivariance optimizations are simply techniques that make up the toolbox that we call portfolio theory.

The Early Years

Although there was some work on investment risk earlier (Bernstein 1996), portfolio theory along with the concept of downside risk measures started with the publication of two papers in 1952. The first, by Markowitz (1952), provided a quantitative framework for measuring portfolio risk and return. Markowitz developed his complex structure of equations after he was struck with a notion that "you should be interested in risk as well as return" (Bernstein 1996). Markowitz used mean returns, variances, and covariances to derive an efficient frontier where every portfolio on the frontier maximizes the expected return for a given variance or minimizes the variance for a given expected return. This is usually called the EV criterion where E is the expected return and V is the variance of the portfolio. The important job of picking one portfolio from the efficient frontier for investment purposes was given to a rather abstract idea, the quadratic utility function. The investor has to make a trade-off between risk and return. The investor's sensitivity to changing wealth and risk is known as a utility function. Unfortunately, the elements that determine a utility function for a biological system that we call a human being are obscure.

The second paper on portfolio theory published in 1952 was by Roy (1952). Roy's purpose was to develop a practical method for determining the best risk-return trade-off, as he did not believe that a mathematical utility function could be derived for an investor. Roy stated that an investor will prefer safety of principal first and will set some minimum acceptable return that will conserve the principal. Roy called the minimum acceptable return the disaster level, and the resulting technique is the Roy safety-first technique. Roy stated that the investor would prefer the investment with the smallest probability of going below the disaster level or target return. By maximizing a reward to variability ratio, $(r - d) / s$, the investor will choose the portfolio with the lowest probability of going below the disaster level, d, given an expected mean return, r, and a standard deviation, s. Although Roy is not a familiar name, he provides a very useful tool, that is, the reward-to-variability ratio computed using a disaster-level return. In the meantime, Roy's concept of an investor preferring safety of principal first when dealing with risk is instrumental in the development of risk measures.

Markowitz (1959) recognized the importance of this idea. He realized that investors are interested in minimizing downside risk for two reasons: (1) only downside risk or safety first is relevant to an investor, and (2) security distributions may not be normally distributed. Therefore, a downside risk measure would help investors make proper decisions when faced with nonnormal security return distributions. Markowitz showed that when distributions are normally distributed, both the downside risk measure and the variance provide the correct answer. However, if the distributions are not normally distributed, only the downside risk measure provides the correct answer. Markowitz provided two suggestions for measuring downside risk: a semivariance computed from the mean return or below-mean semivariance (SVm) and a semivariance computed from a target return or below-target semivariance (SVt). The two measures compute a variance using only the returns below the mean return (SVm) or below a target return (SVt). Since only a subset of the return distribution is used, Markowitz called these measures partial or semivariances.

$$SVm = \frac{1}{K} \sum_{T=1}^{K} \ Max[0,(E - R_T)]^2, \text{below-mean semivariance} \quad (1a)$$

$$SVt = \frac{1}{K} \sum_{T=1}^{K} \ Max[0, (t - R_T)]^2, \text{below-target semivariance} \quad (1b)$$

R_T is the asset return during time period T, K is the number of observations, t is the target rate of return, and E is the expected mean return of the asset's return. The maximization function, *Max,* indicates that the formula will square the larger of the two values, 0 or $(t - R_T)$.

After proposing the semivariance measure, Markowitz (1959) stayed with the variance measure because it was computationally simpler. The semivariance optimization models using a cosemivariance matrix (or semicovariance if that is your preference) require twice the number of data inputs than the variance model. With the lack of cost-effective computer power and the fact that the variance model was already mathematically very complex, this was a significant consideration until the 1980s and the advent of the microcomputer.

The Modern Era of Semivariance Research

In the 1970s, other researchers started to question the use of variance measures. Studies by Klemkosky (1973) and by Ang and Chua (1979) showed that these measures could provide incorrect rankings and suggested the reward-to-semivariability (R/SV) ratio as an alternative. (Note that the R/SV ratio is really the return to below-target semideviation ratio, the semideviation simply being the square root of the semivariance.) By taking the excess return $(r - d)$ and dividing by the standard deviation, the R/V ratio is standardized. Therefore, there should be no statistical relationship between the ratio (R/V) and the risk measure, standard deviation. Both studies performed cross-sectional regression studies between the performance measure and the risk measure for a large sample of mutual funds. If the r-square of the regression is close to zero, then the ratio is statistically independent of the risk measure and, therefore, statistically unbiased. Both studies found that the traditional measures (Roy R/V ratio, Treynor and Jensen measures) are statistically related (high r-squares) to their underlying risk measure, the standard deviation or the beta. However, the relationship between the reward-to-semivariability ratio and the semideviation has the lowest r-square in either study.

Study of the below-target semivariance measure continued with Hogan and Warren (1972). Hogan and Warren provided an optimization algorithm for developing expected return (E)—below-target semivariance (S) efficient portfolios, thus the ES criterion. Hogan and Warren (1974) also provide an interesting diversion. They developed a below-target semivariance capital-asset-pricing model (ES-CAPM). With the CAPM, there is no interest in the below-mean semivariance, since asset distributions are assumed to be normal (symmetric). In this case, the SVm measure is simply the "half variance." The SVt version of the ES-CAPM is of interest if the distributions are nonnormal and nonsymmetric (asymmetric). Nantell and Price (1979) and Harlow and Rao (1989) further extended the SVt version of the ES-CAPM into the more general lower partial moment (LPM) version, EL-CAPM. In addition, Bookstaber and Clarke (1985) demonstrated that using variance to evaluate put and call (option) positions within a portfolio will be misleading. The measurement of the riskiness of an optioned portfolio has to be able to handle skewed distributions. The option positions add skewness into a portfolio, therefore, the analysis of the risk-return of such a portfolio has to be able to handle nonnormal distributions. Merriken (1994) continued this line of reasoning and concluded that the LPM measure is an important tool for deciding the amount of options to add to a portfolio.

The Birth of the Lower Partial Moment

It was at this point that Burr Porter became interested in the semivariance. A mean-semivariance computer program developed in 1971 by Professor George Philippatos at Penn State University piqued Porter's (1974) interest in the semivariance. Believing the below-mean semivariance to be the appropriate measure, Porter tested the two measures using stochastic dominance. Surprisingly, the tests showed that below-target semivariance portfolios were members of stochastic dominance efficient sets (the SVt portfolios were superior investments), while the below-mean semivariance portfolios were not. Porter also demonstrated that mean-variance portfolios were included in the stochastic dominance efficient sets. Porter and Bey (1974) followed with a comparison of mean-variance and mean-semivariance optimization algorithms.

Every once in a great while, there is a defining development in research that clarifies all issues and gives the researcher an all-encompassing view. This development in the research on downside risk measures occurred with the development of the lower partial moment risk measure by Bawa (1975) and Fishburn (1977). Moving from the semivariance to the LPM is equivalent to progressing from a silent black-and-white film to a wide-screen Technicolor film with digital surround sound. This measure liberates the investor from a constraint of having only one utility function, which is fine if investor utility is best represented by a quadratic equation (variance or semivariance). On the other hand, the LPM represents the whole gamut of human behavior, from risk seeking to risk neutral to risk aversion.

Coincidentally, Porter was auditing a course on utility theory by Peter Fishburn. Because of Porter's work on the below-target semivariance, Fishburn became interested in the measure. While Fishburn was developing his thoughts on the subject, Vijay Bawa (1975) published his seminal work on lower partial moment that defined the relationship between LPM and stochastic dominance. Bawa (1975) was the first to define LPM as a general family of below-target risk measures, one of which is the below-target semivariance. The LPM describes below-target risk in terms of risk tolerance. Given an investor risk-tolerance value *a*, the general measure, the LPM, is defined as:

$$\text{LPM (a,t)} = \frac{1}{K} \sum_{T=1}^{K} \text{Max}[0, (t - R_T)]^a, \tag{2}$$

where K is the number of observations, t is the target return, a is the degree of the lower partial moment, R_T is the return for the asset during time period T, and *Max* is a maximization function that chooses the larger of two numbers, *0* or *(t − R_T)*. It is the *a* value that differentiates the LPM from the SVt. Instead of squaring deviations and taking square roots as we do with the semivariance calculations, the deviations can be raised to the *a* power and the *a* root can be computed. There is no limitation to what value of *a* can be used in the LPM except that we have to be able to make a final calculation, that is, the only limitation is our computational machinery. The *a* value does not have to be a whole number. It can be fractional or mixed. It is the myriad values of *a* that make the LPM wide-screen Technicolor to the semivariance's black and white. Consider that utility theory is not used solely to select a portfolio from an efficient frontier. It is also used to describe what an investor considers to be risky. There is a utility function inherent in every statistical measure of risk. We can't measure risk without assuming a utility function. The variance and semivariance only provide us with one utility function. The LPM provides us with a whole rainbow of utility functions, thus its superiority over the variance and semivariance measures.

Bawa (1975) provided a proof that the LPM measure is mathematically related to stochastic dominance for risk-tolerance values (*a*) of 0, 1, and

2. Fishburn (1977) extended the general LPM model to the (a,t) model, where a is the level of investor risk tolerance and t is the target return. Fishburn provided the unlimited view of LPM with fractional degrees of 2.33 or 3.89. Given a value of t, Fishburn demonstrated the equivalence of the LPM measure to stochastic dominance for all values of $a > 0$. Fishburn also shows that the a value includes all types of investor behavior. The LPM value $a < 1$ captures risk-seeking behavior. Risk-neutral behavior is $a = 1$, while risk-averse behavior is $a > 1$. The higher the a value is above a value of one, the higher the risk aversion of the investor. **FIGURE 13.1** demonstrates the behavior of the LPM measure for different degrees (a). The target return is set to 15 percent, which for this example is the same as the mean return for the two investments.

Note that when $a < 1$, investment A is considered less risky than investment B, although the skewness number and the distribution information indicates that investment B has less risk. Note that this is consistent with a risk-loving utility function. When $a > 1$, then investment B is less risky than investment A. Note that this is consistent with a risk-averse utility function. Also, as a increases, investment A takes on a heavier risk penalty. When $a = 1.5$, investment A is twice as risky as investment B. When $a = 2.0$, investment A is four times as risky as investment B. When $a = 3$, investment A is sixteen times as risky as investment B.

Utility Theory, or the Maximization of Economic Happiness

When academics discuss utility theory (theory of economic satisfaction), the conversation centers on von Neumann and Morgenstern (1944) utility functions. The Fishburn family of LPM utility functions asserts that the investor is risk averse (or risk seeking, depending on the value of a) below the target return and risk neutral above the target return. This utility function is a combination of being very conservative with the risk potential of a portfolio and very aggressive with the upside potential of a portfolio. Fishburn (1977, 121–122) examined a large number of von Neumann and Morgenstern utility functions that have been reported in the investment literature and finds a wide range of a values ranging from less than 1 to a value greater than 4. The $a = 2$ target semivariance utility function was not commonly found. Given this result, Fishburn concluded that the generalized $a - t$ (LPM) model is superior to the target semivariance because it is more flexible at matching investor utility.

There is a caveat discussed by Fishburn, which is the decreasing marginal utility of wealth. Very simply, an additional dollar of income

FIGURE **13.1** *Example of Degrees of the Lower Partial Moment*

	COMPANY A		COMPANY B	
	RETURN	PROB.	RETURN	PROB.
	−5.00	0.20	10.00	0.80
	20.00	0.80	35.00	0.20
Mean return	15.00		15.00	
Variance	100.00		100.00	
Skewness	−1.50		1.50	
LPM a = 0.0 t = 15	0.20		0.80	
LPM a = 0.5 t = 15	0.89		1.79	
LPM a = 1.0 t = 15	4.00		4.00	
LPM a = 1.5 t = 15	17.89		8.94	
LPM a = 2.0 t = 15	80.00		20.00	
LPM a = 3.0 t = 15	1,600.00		100.00	

Note: When **a** = 1.0 and **t** is equal to the mean return, then the two LPM values are equal. If **t** is set to some other return, then the LPM values will depend on the degree of skewness in the return distribution.

to a wealthy person provides less economic happiness (utility) than an additional dollar of income to a poor person. Concerning the LPM (a,t) measure, the risk-aversion coefficient, a, is dependent on the amount of the investor's total wealth. If the amount of wealth at risk is very small relative to the investor's total wealth, then the investor can be very aggressive in terms of investing in risky investments (low values of a). If the amount of money at risk is a substantial portion of the investor's total wealth, then the investor will be more risk averse (higher values of a).

Laughhunn, Payne, and Crum (1980) developed an interactive computer program in BASIC that used Fishburn's (1977) methodology for estimating the value of a for an individual. They studied 224 corporate middle managers by giving them a number of small investment projects from which to choose. They found that 71 percent of the managers exhibit risk-seeking behavior ($a < 1$). Only 9.4 percent of the managers had a values around 2, and only 29 percent of the managers were risk averse ($a > 1$).

Next, they studied the impact of ruinous loss. Without the threat of ruinous loss, most managers are risk seeking. However, if the investment projects include ruinous losses, there is a statistically significant shift to risk-averse behavior by the managers. With the chance of a ruinous loss, the majority of the corporate managers were risk averse. Therefore, the estimation of the investor's risk coefficient, a, depends on the relationship between the value of the investment portfolio and the investor's total wealth.

To provide investment advice, the use of an appropriate risk measure is imperative. The factors affecting the choice of the risk measure are:

❑ Investors perceive risk in terms of below-target returns.
❑ Investor risk aversion increases with the magnitude of the probability of ruinous losses.
❑ Investors are not static. As the investor's expectations, total wealth, and investment horizon change, the investor's below-target-return risk aversion changes. Investors should be constantly monitored for changes in their level of risk aversion.

Using LPM Measures Means Algorithms

Algorithms are cookbook recipes that are programmed into computers to solve complex mathematical problems. In portfolio theory, the complex problem is deciding which investments receive which proportion of the portfolio's funds. There are two types of algorithms: optimal and heuristic. Optimal algorithms provide the best answer given the input information. Heuristic algorithms provide a good (approximately correct) answer given the input information. Heuristic algorithms are attractive because they provide answers using fewer computational resources, that is, they provide answers cheaper and faster than optimal algorithms.

Both optimal and heuristic algorithms have been shown to work with the LPM(a,t) model. The original Philippatos (1971)–Hogan and Warren (1972) E-SVt optimization algorithm was extensively tested by Porter and Bey (1974), Bey (1979), Harlow (1991), and Nawrocki (1990, 1992). The major issue concerning LPM algorithms is their ability to manage the skewness of a portfolio. There are two concerns: managing skewness during a past historic period and managing skewness during a future holding period. These separate concerns arise as academics are concerned with explaining how things work by studying the past while practitioners are interested in how things are going to work in the future.

FIGURE 13.2 presents the results of optimizing the monthly returns of twenty stocks using the Markowitz EV algorithm and the Philippatos–Hogan and Warren E-SVt algorithm. The following characteristics of LPM portfolios should be noted as the degree of the LPM is increased from $a = 1$ (risk neutral) to $a = 4$ (very risk averse). These results are historical (looking backward) results.

- ❏ Each portfolio selected has an approximate expected monthly return of 2.5 percent. The Markowitz (1959) critical line algorithm does not provide portfolios for specific returns. Effectively, it samples the efficient frontier by generating corner portfolios where a security either enters or leaves the portfolio.

- ❏ The LPM portfolios have higher standard deviations than the EV portfolio. This result should not be a surprise, as the EV algorithm optimizes the standard deviation.

- ❏ The risk-neutral ($a = 1.0$) LPM portfolio has a higher semideviation ($a = 2.0$) than the EV portfolio and the risk-averse ($a > 1.0$) LPM portfolios.

- ❏ The risk-averse ($a > 1.0$) LPM portfolios have lower semideviations than the EV portfolio. This result should not surprise as the E-SVt algorithm optimizes the LPM measure.

- ❏ Each of the LPM portfolios has increased skewness value compared with the EV portfolio. As the degree of the LPM increases, the skewness increases. The skewness values are statistically significant.

- ❏ The LPM optimizer is capturing coskewness effects, as the skewness of the risk-averse ($a > 1.0$) LPM portfolios is higher than the skewness values of any individual stock.

- ❏ The LPM portfolios are different from the EV portfolios in the security allocations, ranging from 17 percent to 30 percent difference. The higher the LPM degree, the greater the difference in security allocations between the LPM portfolio and the EV portfolio. As the LPM portfolio is trying to optimize the portfolio using an increasingly risk-averse utility function, the increase in the difference between the allocations is expected.

- ❏ Skewness can be diversified away. To maintain skewness in a portfolio, the LPM portfolios will usually contain fewer stocks than a comparable EV portfolio. Note that as the degree of the LPM increases, the skewness increases and the number of stocks in the portfolio decreases.

- ❏ Note how the allocation in Con. Edison (the stock with the highest skewness value) increases as the degree of the LPM increases.

The LPM heuristic algorithm came along later. Nawrocki (1983) developed a linear-programming LPM heuristic algorithm utilizing reward–to–lower partial moment (R/LPMa,t) ratios. This heuristic algorithm derives from earlier work on portfolio theory heuristic algorithms by Sharpe (1967) and Elton, Gruber, and Padberg (1976). Similar to the

FIGURE **13.2** *An In-Sample Comparison of an EV Optimal Portfolio With Comparable LPM Optimal Portfolios Using Markowitz (1959) Critical Line Algorithm With 48 Monthly Returns (1984–1987) for 20 Stocks*

| | ALLOCATIONS | |
SECURITY	SECURITY SKEWNESS	LPM 1.0
Adams Millis	0.4336	5.3019
Allegheny Pwr.	0.5610	
Belding Hemin.	0.4290	
Con. Edison	0.7050*	50.4361
Con. Nat. Gas	0.3520	1.5136
FMC Corp.	0.5406	2.2994
Heinz, H.J.	0.3892	9.4730
Idaho Power	0.2327	5.2687
Kansas Power	0.4962	12.8200
Mercantile St	−0.4134	12.8788
Total allocations		100.0000
# Securities		8
Portfolio statistics **Portfolio**		**LPM 1.0**
Return		2.5140
Standard deviation		3.5233
Semideviation		1.0949
Skewness		0.6381*
Beta		0.2976
R/V ratio		0.5754
R/SV ratio		1.8516
% Difference LPM vs. EV		17.2589

*Significant skewness at 2 standard deviations (s = .3162).

Source: Nawrocki (1992)

ALLOCATIONS			
LPM 2.0	**LPM 3.0**	**LPM 4.0**	**EV**
6.6483	7.3437	8.0512	9.1183
			0.6342
2.0557	3.1404	2.6374	
59.5337	59.5219	60.8875	35.0428
1.7933	1.4464		1.9510
5.5741	6.9885	7.3007	5.6800
12.1067	14.2124	16.9302	17.1882
			3.4108
8.6804	7.3462	4.1953	12.9142
3.6086			13.0554
100.0000	100.0000	100.0000	100.0000
8	7	6	9
LPM 2.0	**LPM 3.0**	**LPM 4.0**	**EV**
2.5001	2.4849	2.5197	2.5062
3.5443	3.5290	3.6703	3.3838
0.9705	0.9514	0.9953	1.0143
0.7861*	0.7863*	0.7912*	0.5456
0.2888	0.2952	0.3012	0.3848
0.5680	0.5662	0.5539	0.5968
2.0746	2.1102	2.0426	1.9910
26.5887	28.9257	30.0991	

Sharpe heuristic, this heuristic assumes that the average correlation between securities is zero. As a result, this algorithm requires a large number
of stocks to obtain a degree of diversification comparable to optimal algorithms. Besides the lower computational costs, heuristic algorithms can
provide better forecasting results (Elton, Gruber, and Urich 1978).

Nawrocki and Staples (1989) and Nawrocki (1990) provide extensive
out-of-sample backtests of the R/LPM heuristic algorithms. One of the
important findings is that the skewness of the portfolio can be managed
using the R/LPM algorithm. The Nawrocki (1990) study is presented in
FIGURE 13.3. These results are holding period (looking forward or forecasting) results. A random sample of 150 stocks was tested for the thirty-
year-period using forty-eight-month estimation periods and twenty-four-
month revision periods, that is, every twenty-four months the historical
period is updated to the most recent forty-eight months and a new portfolio is chosen. One percent transaction costs were computed with each
portfolio revision. As the LPM degree a increases from 1.0 (risk neutral)
and becomes risk averse, the skewness of the portfolio increases. This is
the type of forecast results that makes the LPM risk measure useful to a
practitioner. At degrees of a above 4.0, the skewness values are statistically
significant. Typically, the higher the skewness value, the lower the downside risk of the portfolio.

However, the insurance premium concept comes into play. For degrees
of a up to 5, the R/SV ratio remains above 0.20. The skewness values are
statistically significant at this level. Unfortunately, as the skewness value
increases from a value of 0.34 ($a = 5.0$) to a value of 0.61 ($a = 10.0$), the
R/SV ratio decreases from 0.20 to 0.18, indicating reduced risk-return
performance as the skewness increases.

An investor can use an LPM heuristic or optimization algorithm to
build increased skewness into a portfolio without using a put position.
In other words, the LPM algorithms can be used to directly manage the
skewness of the portfolio. The results in Figure 13.3 are *out-of-sample*.
Therefore, the LPM algorithms forecast well enough to manage the future
skewness of the portfolio.

Recent Research in Practitioner Literature

Around 1990, the downside risk measures started to appear in the practitioner literature. Brian Rom and Frank Sortino have been the strongest
supporters of the downside risk measure in the practitioner literature
and have implemented it in Brian Rom's optimization software. For the
most part, both are interested in the below-target semideviation and
the reward-to-semivariability ratio (R/SVt). Sortino and Van Der Meer

FIGURE **13.3** *Out-of-Sample Skewness Results Using R/LPM Heuristic Algorithm 1958–1987 (30 Years of Monthly Data)*

LPM DEGREE a	SKEWNESS	R/SVT RATIO
0.0	.1122	.1712
1.0	.0756	.1984
1.2	.0719	.2117
1.4	.0713	.2221
1.6	.0833	.2110
2.0	.1110	.2089
2.8	.1934	.2186
3.0	.2115	.2155
4.0	.2771*	.2098
4.6	.3093*	.2044
5.0	.3446*	.2005
6.0	.4287*	.1905
7.0	.4975*	.1848
8.0	.5413*	.1854
9.0	.5855*	.1825
10.0	.6129*	.1794
EV optimal	−.0546	.1383

*Indicates statistical significance at two standard deviations.

Note: Portfolios were revised every two years using 48-month historical periods with a sample of 150 stocks. The skewness results are the average of portfolios with 5, 10, and 15 stocks. The results are compared with an EV portfolio strategy.

Source: Nawrocki (1990).

(1991) described the downside deviation (below-target semideviation) and the reward-to-semivariability ratio (R/SVt) as tools for capturing the essence of downside risk. Sortino continued to contribute in areas of performance measurement (Sortino and Price 1994) and in the estimation of the target semivariance (Sortino and Forsey 1996). Rom has focused on educating practitioners about downside risk measures (Rom and Ferguson 1993, 1997/1998). Finally, Sortino, Van Der Meer, and Plantinga (1999) have suggested an extension known as the upside-potential ratio, which is the ratio of the above-target mean return divided by the semideviation.

$$E(UPM)^{1/c} = \sqrt[c]{\frac{1}{K} \sum_{k=1}^{K} \max[(R_k - \tau); 0]^c} \qquad (3)$$

$$U\text{-}P \ Ratio = E(UPM)^{1/c} \ / \ LPM(a,\tau)^{1/a} \ (for \ c = 1, \ a = 2) \qquad (4)$$

Whether this extension proves to be an improvement to the downside risk framework has to be left to future research. However, it seems to be a promising area of research.

References

Ang, James S., and Jess H. Chua. 1979. "Composite Measures for the Evaluation of Investment Performance." *Journal of Financial and Quantitative Analysis.* 14 (2): 361–384.

Balzer, Leslie A. 1994. "Measuring Investment Risk: A Review." *Journal of Investing* 3 (3): 47–58.

Bawa, Vijay S. 1975. "Optimal Rules for Ordering Uncertain Prospects." *Journal of Financial Economics* 2 (1): 95–121.

Bernstein, Peter S. 1996. *Against the Gods: The Remarkable Story of Risk.* Wiley.

Bey, Roger P. 1979. "Estimating the Optimal Stochastic Dominance Efficient Set With a Mean-Semivariance Algorithm." *Journal of Financial and Quantitative Analysis* 14 (5): 1059–1070.

Bookstaber, Richard, and Roger Clarke. 1985. "Problems in Evaluating the Performance of Portfolios With Options." *Financial Analysts Journal* 41 (1): 48–62.

Elton, Edwin J., Martin J. Gruber, and Manfred W. Padberg. 1976. "Simple Criteria for Optimal Portfolio Selection." *Journal of Finance* 31 (5): 1341–1357.

Elton, Edwin J., Martin J. Gruber, and T. Urich. 1978. "Are Betas Best?" *Journal of Finance* 33:1375–1384.

Fishburn, Peter C. 1977. "Mean-Risk Analysis With Risk Associated With Below-Target Returns." *American Economic Review* 67 (2): 116–126.

Harlow, W. V. 1991. "Asset Allocation in a Downside-Risk Framework." *Financial Analysts Journal* 47 (5): 28–40.

Harlow, W. V., and Ramesh K. S. Rao. 1989. "Asset Pricing in a Generalized Mean-Lower Partial Moment Framework: Theory and Evidence." *Journal of Financial and Quantitative Analysis* 24 (3): 285–312.

Hogan, William W., and James M. Warren. 1972. "Computation of the Efficient Boundary in the E-S Portfolio Selection Model." *Journal of Financial and Quantitative Analysis* 7 (4): 1881–1896.

Hogan, William W., and James M. Warren. 1974. "Toward the Development of an Equilibrium Capital-Market Model Based on Semivariance." *Journal of Financial and Quantitative Analysis* 9 (1): 1–11.

Klemkosky, Robert C. 1973. "The Bias in Composite Performance Measures." *Journal of Financial and Quantitative Analysis* 8 (3): 505–514.

Kroll, Yoram, Haim Levy, and Harry M. Markowitz. 1984. "Mean-Variance Versus Direct Utility Maximization." *Journal of Finance* 39 (1): 47–62.

Laughhunn, D. J., J. W. Payne, and R. Crum. 1980. "Managerial Risk Preferences for Below-Target Returns." *Management Science* 26:1238–1249.

Markowitz, Harry M. 1952. "Portfolio Selection." *Journal of Finance* 7 (1): 77–91.

Markowitz, Harry M. 1956. "The Optimization of a Quadratic Function Subject to Linear Constraints." *Naval Research Logistics Quarterly* 3:111–133.

Markowitz, Harry M. 1959. *Portfolio Selection.* 1st ed. Wiley.

Markowitz, Harry M. 1987. *Mean-Variance Analysis in Portfolio Choice and Capital Markets.* Basil Blackwell.

Markowitz, Harry M. 1991. *Portfolio Selection.* 2nd ed. Basil Blackwell.

Merriken, Harry E. 1994. "Analytical Approaches to Limit Downside Risk: Semivariance and the Need for Liquidity." *Journal of Investing* 3 (3): 65–72.

Nantell, Timothy J., and Barbara Price. 1979. "An Analytical Comparison of Variance and Semivariance Capital Market Theories." *Journal of Financial and Quantitative Analysis* 14 (2): 221–242.

Nawrocki, David. 1983. "A Comparison of Risk Measures When Used in a Simple Portfolio Selection Heuristic." *Journal of Business Finance and Accounting* 10 (2): 183–194.

Nawrocki, David. 1990. "Tailoring Asset Allocation to the Individual Investor." *International Review of Economics and Business* 38 (10–11): 977–990.

Nawrocki, David N. 1992. "The Characteristics of Portfolios Selected by n-Degree Lower Partial Moment." *International Review of Financial Analysis* 1 (3): 195–210.

Nawrocki, David, and Katharine Staples. 1989. "A Customized LPM Risk Measure for Portfolio Analysis." *Applied Economics* 21 (2): 205–218.

Philippatos, George C. 1971. Computer Programs for Implementing Portfolio Theory. Unpublished software, Pennsylvania State University.

Porter, R. Burr. 1974. "Semivariance and Stochastic Dominance: A Comparison." *American Economic Review* 64 (1): 200–204.

Porter, R. Burr, and Roger P. Bey. 1974. "An Evaluation of the Empirical Significance of Optimal Seeking Algorithms in Portfolio Selection." *Journal of Finance* 29 (5): 1479–1490.

Rom, Brian M., and Kathleen W. Ferguson. 1993. "Post-Modern Portfolio Theory Comes of Age." *Journal of Investing* (Winter). Reprinted in Fall 1994, 3 (3): 11–17.

Rom, Brian M., and Kathleen W. Ferguson. 1997/1998. "Using Post-Modern Portfolio Theory to Improve Investment Performance Measurement." *Journal of Performance Measurement* 2 (2): 5–13.

Roy, A. D. 1952. "Safety First and the Holding of Assets." *Econometrica* 20 (3): 431–449.

Sharpe, William F. 1967. "A Linear Programming Algorithm for Mutual Fund Portfolio Selection." *Management Science* 13 (7): 499–510.

Silver, Lloyd. 1993. "Risk Assessment for Security Analysis." *Technical Analysis of Stocks and Commodities* (January): 74–79.

Sortino, Frank A., and Hal J. Forsey. 1996. "On the Use and Misuse of Downside Risk." *Journal of Portfolio Management* 22 (2): 35–42.

Sortino, Frank A., and Lee N. Price. 1994. "Performance Measurement in a Downside Risk Framework." *Journal of Investing* 3 (3): 59–64.

Sortino, Frank A., and Robert Van Der Meer. 1991. "Downside Risk." *Journal of Portfolio Management* 17 (4): 27–32.

Sortino, Frank, Robert Van Der Meer, and Auke Plantinga. 1999. "The Dutch Triangle." *Journal of Portfolio Management* 26 (1): 50–58.

von Neumann, J., and O. Morgenstern. 1944. *Theory of Games and Economic Behavior.* Princeton University Press.

CHAPTER 14

Fundamental Fund Analysis

DON PHILLIPS

Mutual funds are not serving investors nearly as well as they should. The problem isn't a shortage of quality funds. There have never been more good investment choices available to investors than there are today. Nor is the problem locating those funds. Fund assets clearly flow to higher-quality fund firms, as shown by the continued growth in assets under management of firms like American Funds, Fidelity, and Vanguard. Investors and advisers have a good sense of who the better players are, and they've directed more assets to them. Yet the collective asset-weighted returns for mutual funds suggest that while the average stock mutual fund returned close to 10 percent per year during the 1990s, the average investor realized less than one-third of that. The reason is clear: Investors may buy good funds, but they keep piling into funds in asset classes that have already spiked, resulting in far more participants being onboard for declines than for advances and significantly crimping the actual return investors receive.

It's time to elevate the debate on mutual funds beyond simplistic measures of "good fund versus bad fund" and instead focus more on the deployment of funds within a portfolio. If investors buy good funds but assemble bad portfolios, the problem is not one of fund selection but of portfolio construction. Five funds chosen off of last year's leaders list or a personal finance article about "Nine Funds to Buy Now" will almost certainly lead to a portfolio consisting of funds that pursue essentially the same investment strategy. They look good at the same moment in time because they've been doing essentially the same thing. They offer the illusion of diversification. Funds selected on this basis will perform fine as long as the current market trend remains in motion, but once the tide turns, the entire portfolio will sink.

Investors need to focus on the overall portfolio-construction process. Picking a stock should be part of an integrated approach, and that approach can also be applied to fund selection, portfolio construction, and market monitoring. Today, the essential elements of portfolio construction derive from completely different schools of thought—that is, if one is charitable enough to assume that most investors apply any thought at all to the process. Stocks are too often chosen on superficial knowledge of the underlying companies, or they're simply inserted into the investor's portfolio through a company match in a 401(k) plan or from an inheritance. Funds, as mentioned earlier, are typically chosen off of yesterday's leaders list. Portfolio construction often means no more than trying to gather all the account statements an investor accumulates each quarter.

Finally, market monitoring often means a cursory comparison to a broad market average or to that holy trinity of the Dow Jones Industrial Average, the Nasdaq 100, and the Standard & Poor's 500 stock index—three completely unrelated indices that have come to serve as the benchmarks of market monitoring. More on this point later, but for now let's establish that it makes absolutely no sense whatsoever that we all *talk* about the market in a manner that's completely disconnected from the way in which we *participate* in the market. No one thinks of his or her portfolio as being X percent in Dow stocks, Y percent in S&P stocks, and the balance in Nasdaq stocks. Why then do so many financial sources report on the market's progress by citing these measures? If we want to encourage better decision making among investors, we need to start talking about the market in a manner that bears some resemblance to how we participate in it.

Deconstructing Portfolio Construction

The first step in breaking down the portfolio-construction process is to ask what works when it comes to picking individual stocks or bonds. Fortunately, we have a wealth of evidence on this matter in the public records of mutual funds. When it comes to picking stocks, for example, we need only look at the practices of successful equity fund managers to determine what works. Is the best approach to focus on technical analysis, an examination of past return patterns? Or is it fundamental analysis, a study of the underlying characteristics of securities, that produces superior results?

Here the evidence is clear. Better stock pickers uniformly focus on the underlying fundamental characteristics of the securities they select. They analyze corporate strategy, talk to suppliers and competitors, tear apart income statements and balance sheets, and generate financial ratios. Sure, some fund managers may use charting or other pictures of past performance as an overlay, but no credible long-term record of equity management has ever been established in a mutual fund using technical analysis as its primary investment-decision-making driver. When it comes to stock research, bottom-up fundamental analysis is king.

That's why it's so odd that when it comes to analysis of collections of stocks, be they mutual funds or pension accounts, most analysis focuses simply on past performance data, not underlying fundamental characteristics. Alpha, beta, r-squared—indeed all of modern portfolio theory—comes simply from slicing and dicing past performance to derive return and volatility numbers. The same is true for Sharpe ratios, the Morningstar ratings, information ratios, and returns-based style analysis. Selecting an investment solely in this fashion is akin to saying, "I want to buy a stock because it went from $10 to $20 with limited volatility, but I don't know what business it's in, what products the company makes, or anything about its management." This approach wouldn't fly for picking a stock, so why is such analysis considered a sophisticated way to select a basket of stocks? Clearly, stock selection and fund selection could be better integrated and may benefit from a greater focus on fundamental analysis. To the extent that advisers or investment committees employ fundamental analysis on funds today, it's usually a cursory interview with the manager who has passed a screen of high-alpha candidates. While such a selection process may be a reasonable means of segregating managers into two piles—those who have demonstrated success and those who haven't—it doesn't address the key question facing investors: "How do I use the fund successfully in a portfolio?" Again, we must move beyond thinking in terms of good fund versus bad fund and elevate the discussion to what role a fund plays in a portfolio. We can only get to that point by looking beyond the shell of the fund, that is, the technical analysis of past return patterns, and instead lifting the hood and doing some fundamental analysis to see what really makes these funds tick. Only then can we improve fund deployment.

But how are portfolios assembled? Here again, the process is unduly influenced by an examination of past return patterns. Advisers are understandably turning to academic evidence, and academics have worked with whatever data they could obtain. The benefit of past performance histories is that they're readily available. It's far easier to assemble a price history for a security than it is to assemble a database of a security's ever-changing fundamental characteristics. But just because data are affordable doesn't necessarily make them useful. This predisposition for academics to use superficial performance data for their studies has had a profound impact on how financial planners assemble portfolios. Today, sophisticated advisers trying to put together a portfolio for a client would likely choose a variety of asset classes, run an optimizer to generate an efficient frontier, and then choose a spot on the frontier for the client. They would then assemble high-alpha funds from the different asset classes and hope for the best. All without ever considering any fundamental characteristics of the investments they've chosen.

I'm not saying that's a wholly inappropriate approach to portfolio construction. However, I would suggest that the process could be made substantially more robust by supplementing this basic structure with more fundamental analysis. First, one needs to recognize that funds and securities within an asset class are not all cut from the same cloth. They have differing fundamental characteristics. When funds are combined, it's inevitable that certain style or sector tilts will emerge in the overall portfolio. These tilts need to be recognized and adjusted over time to ensure that the portfolio is in keeping with the investor's intent and is on track to meeting the investor's goals. Investing, after all, is not an academic argument; it's a means to securing a better future for the investor.

Finally, let's address market monitoring. I've become increasingly convinced that the way we talk about the market has become one of our biggest impediments to successfully participating in it. The point was driven home to me at an investment conference I attended in the spring of 1999 near the peak of the Internet craze. A highly respected and well-intentioned speaker at the conference gave what I've come to think of as the worst investment advice imaginable. He told the audience of several thousand individual investors that they couldn't trust their financial adviser to have their best interest at heart. They needed to check up on their adviser. He urged the audience to make a list of each security they owned and at the end of each year to write down what its total return was. He then said to compare that number with a broad market average like the S&P 500. Then he said that if any of their investments had failed to beat that benchmark, then they needed to ask some serious questions about them.

Let's consider the wisdom of that advice. The speaker had, in effect, told the audience that every Internet stock in their portfolios was a keeper. It passed his due diligence test of beating the market over a twelve-month period. So were any growth-oriented mutual funds with big technology bets, for they were also beating the market at the time. On the other hand, the speaker had urged the audience to consider selling all of their real estate, international, value, or fixed-income holdings, because nearly all of those fund groups were trailing the S&P 500 at the time.

In practice, that's exactly what most investors did. Look at the huge redemptions that quality value funds like Oakmark witnessed in 1999.

Look at the massive inflows into hot growth funds that were beating the market at the time. How we monitor the market encourages investors to pile into overheated sectors or styles and to abandon those that would provide the greatest ballast. We need to talk about the market in a way that will encourage better decisions. We need to talk about the market in a way that incorporates aspects like the style or sector considerations one would use in building a portfolio.

In short, it's time for an integrated approach to portfolio construction—one in which the same analytics that have been proved to work for security selection are applied to baskets of securities, such as funds, to the overall portfolio, and finally to market monitoring. It's essential that these shared metrics be effectively communicated to all of the parties involved in building portfolios: the individual investors, the advisers, and the institutions managing money. Too often there's a breakdown in communication, and the investor is operating on one set of expectations while the fund manager is managing to a completely different set. For example, on numerous occasions in the late 1990s, an individual investor would approach me at a conference and say that if we got into a bear market, he sure hoped his fund manager would move to cash. I had to respond that his manager was under the assumption that her job was to stay 100 percent invested in large-cap growth stocks at all times. When you have misplaced expectations, you're almost certain to be disappointed at some point. Using good communication tools to assure that all parties—the investor, adviser, and the fund manager—are on the same page is essential if we are to improve the investor experience.

A New Set of Style Tools

Investment style is a powerful, fundamental lens for understanding stocks, funds, and portfolios. Style is a means of describing securities in terms of their relative size and value-growth orientation, as encapsulated by the popular Morningstar Style Box. Style has been an extremely relevant measure in explaining many of the performance differences of various segments of the market. For example, growth stocks topped the charts in the late 1990s, whereas value strategies led the way in 2000–2002. There's no guarantee that style will be as illustrative of market trends over the next five years as it has in the past five, but it's certainly an analysis tool no adviser would want to be without. At Morningstar we're developing alternative lenses through which one can view a portfolio, such as sector and economic stimuli. To illustrate how such lenses can be integrated to assist with all four aspects of portfolio construction, we'll limit our discussion to investment style here.

The Morningstar Style Box has been widely used since the early 1990s to depict the investment style of mutual funds, and through tools like our Portfolio X-Ray, it grew into a means of dissecting portfolios. In 2002, Morningstar enhanced the style box in an effort to make the methodology more robust, so that it could be applied to individual stocks and also be used to build indices with which to track investment performance. Under our previous methodology, value and growth had been defined based on two variables only—price-to-earnings ratio and price-to-book ratio. Stocks with low P/E and P/B ratios were classified as value-oriented, and stocks with high P/E and P/B ratios were classified as growth-oriented. These two data points can certainly measure value—after all, they're the expression of what investors are willing to pay for each dollar of earnings or book value. But price ratios don't measure growth. By default, in the original incarnation of the style box, Morningstar was defining growth as the absence of value.

The old model of style worked reasonably well when it came to funds, but when one looked at individual stocks there were too many cases where it could mislead, especially regarding cyclical stocks. During an economic downturn, for example, the earnings for cyclical stocks dry up. With smaller earnings-per-share values, the P/E ratios for these stocks rise, implying stronger growth under our previous style measure. But these stocks aren't in a growth spurt; their earnings are falling. When examining an entire fund based on these criteria, these occasional misclassifications generally didn't adversely affect a fund's categorization, but the discrepancies were unacceptable as a measure of an individual stock's investment style. We needed a more robust model that would consider more factors, especially actual growth rates.

In the new model, seen in **FIGURE 14.1**, we measure value and growth separately, using five factors for measuring value and five for growth. No single factor (such as a price-to-earnings ratio or a cash flow growth rate) can fully capture the growth or value orientation of a stock. The ten-factor model also reflects both historical and projected financial data. A stock proves its worth with its reported numbers, but the market trades on anticipation—on how the stock is projected to perform in the future. Separate measures for value and growth allow us to determine which orientation is dominant and to create a "net" value/growth score or classification based on it.

In addition to value and growth, we also consider a stock's size when assigning it to a position in our style box. The large-cap band includes the largest stocks, which in aggregate, account for 70 percent of the total capitalization of the Morningstar common stock universe. The mid-cap band includes the next largest stocks, which account for the next 20 percent of the equity universe. Small-cap and micro-cap stocks account for the remaining 10 percent of the market.

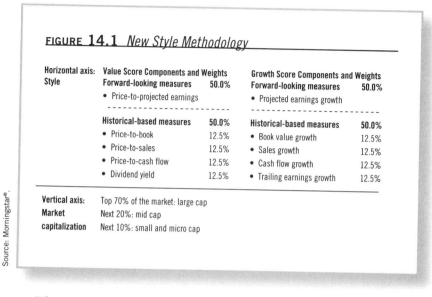

FIGURE 14.1 *New Style Methodology*

Horizontal axis: Style	Value Score Components and Weights		Growth Score Components and Weights	
	Forward-looking measures	50.0%	Forward-looking measures	50.0%
	• Price-to-projected earnings		• Projected earnings growth	
	Historical-based measures	50.0%	Historical-based measures	50.0%
	• Price-to-book	12.5%	• Book value growth	12.5%
	• Price-to-sales	12.5%	• Sales growth	12.5%
	• Price-to-cash flow	12.5%	• Cash flow growth	12.5%
	• Dividend yield	12.5%	• Trailing earnings growth	12.5%

Vertical axis: Market capitalization	Top 70% of the market: large cap
	Next 20%: mid cap
	Next 10%: small and micro cap

The new style box model can be applied to the stock level, the fund and portfolio level, and even at a market-monitoring level. The continuity of the model provides investors with the same framework for buying stocks, selecting funds, building portfolios, and monitoring their investments. We can't tell whether style or sector or alpha will be the key determinant of investment performance going forward, but style is likely to play some role. By paying attention to style and understanding its characteristics, investors can diversify their portfolios and can start to identify the risks to which they are exposed.

Stocks

Let's see how the new style box methodology works when applied to an individual stock. Home Depot is an example of a stock that has both reasonable value and strong growth characteristics. It was a growth darling of the 1990s, and now it's settling down a bit. It's no longer the glitzy growth story it was in the 1990s, so the price has fallen a bit and it may look a little more attractive to value investors. Yet it still retains a solid history of growth and reasonable prospects for more growth. As seen in **FIGURE 14.2**, Home Depot's five price ratios and five growth rates are all fairly moderate and the overall scores for both value and growth are 49 and 64, respectively (on a scale of 0–100, with 0 representing the least compelling score and 100 the most). The overall style score is the net of the growth and value scores and can range from –100 to 100. Home Depot's net style score is 15, which falls close to the center, relative to other large-cap stocks.

FIGURE 14.2 *Stock Style Example: Home Depot*

Value measures		Growth measures	
• Price-to-projected earnings	18.0	• Projected earnings growth	13.1%
• Price-to-book	3.3	• Book value growth	15.8%
• Price-to-sales	1.1	• Sales growth	13.3%
• Price-to-cash flow	14.7	• Cash flow growth	5.9%
• Dividend yield	0.8%	• Trailing earnings growth	19.4%
- - - - - - - - - - - - - - - - -		- - - - - - - - - - - - - - - - -	
Value score (0–100)	49.1	Growth score (0–100)	63.6

Style score: Growth score (63.6) – Value score (49.1) = 14.5

Market cap: $77.1 billion

Source: Morningstar®.

A set of numbers like these may be useful to investment fanatics, but they're unlikely to influence the behavior of most investors. One of our long-held beliefs is that a table of numbers will speak to only a small group of already informed participants. If one can turn those numbers into a story, the circle will widen a bit. But if one can turn the numbers into a picture, then lots of people will grasp the idea. If we think of the style box as graph paper, then the net value-growth orientation score can be plotted along the horizontal axis and the net size score can be plotted along the vertical axis, giving us a precise and effective visual representation of a

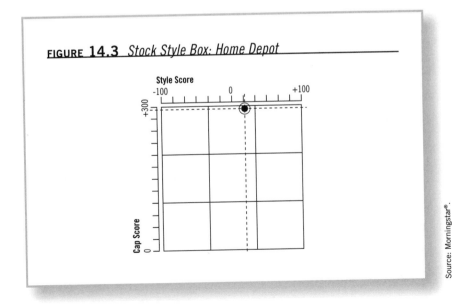

FIGURE 14.3 *Stock Style Box: Home Depot*

Source: Morningstar®.

stock's placement within the nine-box grid, as seen in **FIGURE 14.3**. Home Depot is no longer a mass of statistics, but rather a picture of a stock that's clearly in the large-cap territory, but not exclusively in either the value or the growth camp. Instead it falls in the middle band, which we call blend, but others might call growth at a reasonable price. Its positioning shades toward the growth side of the blend box, reflecting the stock's higher scores on growth rates than on price multiples.

Funds

The same ten-factor model can also be applied to a basket of stocks, such as a mutual fund. The style and size scores for a fund are an asset-weighted average of the style and size characteristics for each stock in its portfolio. Morningstar receives fund portfolio holdings from fund companies quite regularly (95 percent of fund families now provide holdings quarterly, with half supplying them monthly) and matches those holdings against the appropriate stock scores for the date of the portfolio. In addition to plotting the average fund-investment style (the "centroid"), we can also plot each individual holding within the fund along the nine-box grid of the Morningstar Style Box. We then go one step further and draw an elliptical "ownership zone" that marks the minimum territory on the grid we need to outline from the centroid to capture 75 percent of a fund's holdings. This gives us a picture of where a fund invests and how it may fit in an investor's portfolio.

For example, look at Growth Fund of America. The statistics in **FIGURE 14.4** can be pictured as an ownership zone, as seen in **FIGURE 14.5**. Here we see that while the fund clearly has a growth orientation, not every stock in the portfolio has characteristics that would appeal only to

---

FIGURE **14.4** *Portfolio Style Scores: American Funds Growth Fund of America*

Value measures		Growth rates	
• Price-to-projected earnings	20.6	• Projected earnings growth	16.3%
• Price-to-book	2.3	• Book value growth	8.3%
• Price-to-sales	1.5	• Sales growth	5.6%
• Price-to-cash flow	5.9	• Cash flow growth	6.5%
• Dividend yield	0.8%	• Trailing earnings growth	2.6%
Value orientation	Expensive	Growth orientation	Fast growth

Style: core growth

Market cap: $24.9 billion, large cap

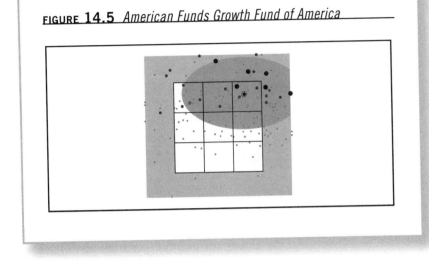

FIGURE **14.5** _American Funds Growth Fund of America_

Source: Morningstar®.

a growth investor. Some of its holdings might reasonably be called blend or even value stocks. We can also see that while this is a growth fund, its overall positioning is not at the far right-hand side of the growth style box, indicating a more tempered approach to growth investing than some rival managers might take. Not surprisingly, this fund trailed some rivals during the growth-stock bubble of the late 1990s, but it survived the fallout far better than most growth funds.

The ownership zone design can also help investors compare two funds that have similar mandates. For example, both T. Rowe Price Mid-Cap Growth and Van Wagoner Mid-Cap Growth are in the mid-cap growth category. A glance at the ownership zone pictures of these funds in **FIGURE 14.6** immediately reveals that they have different interpretations of the mid-cap growth style. The T. Rowe Price fund sticks tightly to a strict mid-cap strategy, while the Van Wagoner fund explores a range of mid-, small-, and even micro-cap holdings. There are implications here for portfolio construction. An investor in the T. Rowe Price fund might consider adding a small-cap fund for diversification; however, for the shareholder in the Van Wagoner fund, such a move might only duplicate the style of the existing holdings.

The Morningstar style model can also help investors track changes to a single fund over time. For example, American Century Ultra was a great example of a large-cap growth fund at the beginning of 2001, but by the end of the year, it was exploring a range of investments that also included value-oriented and mid-cap holdings, as seen in **FIGURE 14.7**. Ultra's managers think of the fund as a flexible offering that can go to wherever they see the best opportunities. During the course of 2001, they took advan-

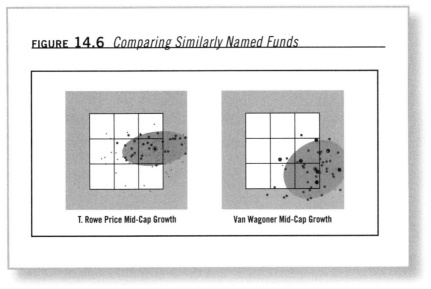

FIGURE 14.6 *Comparing Similarly Named Funds*

T. Rowe Price Mid-Cap Growth   Van Wagoner Mid-Cap Growth

tage of this flexibility. Such a shift in strategy is not necessarily a bad thing, but investors who bought the fund in early 2001 to fill a large-growth portion of their portfolio are no longer being served in the way they may have expected. Funds aren't static; styles evolve; fund managers come and go. To use a fund wisely in a portfolio, you need to check up on it periodically.

I think of the style box as a descriptive tool—not a restrictive one. How lines are drawn between value, blend, and growth is somewhat arbitrary. It's perfectly acceptable for a fund manager to invest in a range of investments. The style box provides a context for understanding the

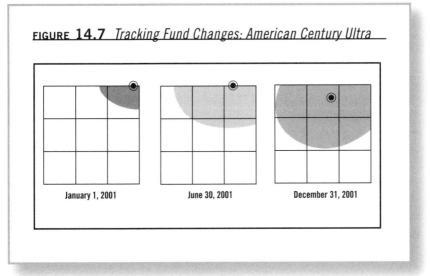

FIGURE 14.7 *Tracking Fund Changes: American Century Ultra*

January 1, 2001   June 30, 2001   December 31, 2001 holdings—not a constraint. Few funds are a pure play on a single style. Investors who better understand how their fund managers deploy assets are more likely to use their funds wisely in a portfolio.

Portfolios

Now that we have the ownership zone pictures, we can use them to assist with portfolio assembly and monitoring. This is critical to an investor's success. Understandably, investors want to buy funds that have performed well. All too often, however, the funds that have the highest total returns have done so simply because they're invested in the same types of securities. Investors don't need to collect funds that all serve the same role in a portfolio. But it's difficult to make the case for diversification based on performance numbers alone. By employing a fundamental approach and studying the underlying holdings in each portfolio, investors may be encouraged to take what may be a counterintuitive approach: buying stocks and funds that round out a portfolio rather than chasing last year's leaders.

Consider **FIGURE 14.8**. If an investor already held Fidelity Magellan and Janus Enterprise in 1999 and another fund caught his eye, the chances are it would be another fund that skewed toward large cap and growth. By seeing that that space is already covered in the portfolio, an investor may be able to summon the courage to buy a quality fund in an out-of-favor section of the market, such as small-cap value. Looking only at recent returns, such a move would be counterintuitive. Why add a small-value fund that's going up 5 percent a year when lots of large-growth funds have gone up 10 times that amount? Yet, if diversification is the goal, you need to be willing to add quality funds from out-of-favor

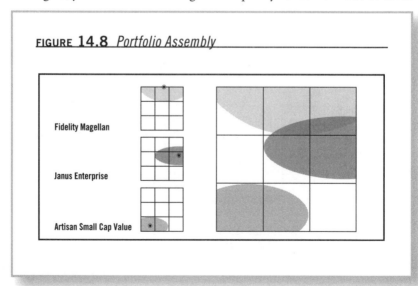

FIGURE **14.8** _Portfolio Assembly_

Fidelity Magellan

Janus Enterprise

Artisan Small Cap Value

Source: Morningstar®.

parts of the market to the mix. Ownership zones help make the case for doing so, by showing not only where a portfolio has concentrations but also where it has gaps.

Market Monitoring

We can use these portfolio tools for market monitoring as well. As previously mentioned, the Dow, the S&P 500, and the Nasdaq 100 weren't designed to be used together or for purposes of portfolio construction. As seen in **FIGURE 14.9**, a portfolio of these indices reveals a strong overlap among the three. All of the Dow Jones stocks and fifty-eight of the Nasdaq 100 stocks are in the S&P 500. These indices don't address style cleanly, and they reflect little of what happens in the small-cap arena.

To facilitate better portfolio monitoring, we applied our ten-factor model to a series of indices that track the nine style boxes. We then took these indices and created a tool we call the Morningstar Market Barometer. You can see at a glance if it was a bull market or a bear market, a market that favored value or growth. This tool is available live during the day on Morningstar.com, but I think its best use is to illustrate longer periods than just one day's performance, as seen in **FIGURE 14.10**.

Consider 1999. If you ask the average investor on the street how the market performed in 1999, he'll tell you it was a fantastic bull market and all you had to do was throw money at it to make money. And, all three major indices second that opinion. However, the Morningstar Market Barometer clearly shows that the party was limited to high-growth stocks. Investors pursuing more of a growth-at-a-reasonable-

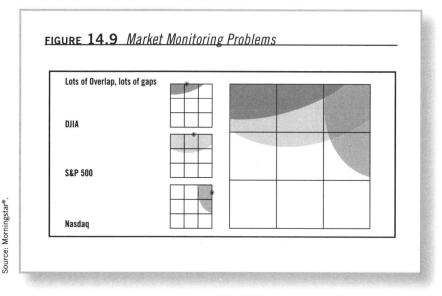

FIGURE 14.9 *Market Monitoring Problems*

Lots of Overlap, lots of gaps

DJIA

S&P 500

Nasdaq

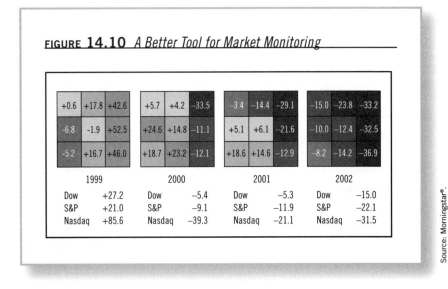

Source: Morningstar®.

FIGURE **14.10** *A Better Tool for Market Monitoring*

price approach saw far lower returns, and those pursuing small- or mid-cap value strategies actually saw losses for the year.

The year 2000 is universally regarded as a bad year for the market. An examination of the Dow, the S&P, and the Nasdaq backs this up. However, value and core stocks experienced substantial gains that year, and in the aggregate far more stocks rose than fell in 2000. A similar effect was seen in 2001—the three market indicators were down, but there were pockets of strength among small- and mid-cap stocks with value characteristics. The year 2002 was just plain ugly, but even here one sees that the damage was greater for growth stocks than for value stocks. Clearly, style can have a significant impact on performance.

Getting It Right

It's time to take a more disciplined approach to portfolio construction, one that integrates the various steps of building and monitoring a portfolio into a cohesive activity. An investor should be able to move seamlessly from security selection to portfolio construction to market monitoring, using a robust and uniform set of metrics to help with each task. Just as important, it's essential that we find a way to better communicate financial concepts, such as diversification, to investors. Although the methods outlined here are not a panacea for the problems facing investors, they're a step in the right direction. Everyone in or around the asset-management industry must work on creating a better investment experience. Getting the right investor into the right investments for the right reasons is an essential first step.

CHAPTER 15

Controlling Longevity Risk in a Retirement Portfolio

ROGER G. IBBOTSON, MICHAEL C. HENKEL,
AND PENG CHEN

Traditionally, Social Security and defined-benefit (DB) pension plans have provided the bulk of retirement income. However, fewer workers are covered by defined-benefit pension plans today than twenty years ago. While current retirees receive 69 percent of their retirement income from Social Security and traditional company defined-benefit pension plans, today's workers can expect to have only about one-third of their retirement income funded by these sources (see **FIGURE 15.1**). Increasingly, workers are relying on their defined-contribution (DC) retirement portfolio and other personal savings as the primary resources for retirement income. The shift in retirement funding from professionally managed defined-benefit plans to personal savings vehicles indicates that investors increasingly need to make their own decisions about how to allocate retirement savings and what products to choose to generate income in retirement.

In this chapter, we investigate the risk factors investors face when making decisions on saving and investing their retirement portfolios. We illustrate the common mistakes investors make in their asset-allocation and spending decisions in retirement. Using Monte Carlo simulation and optimization techniques, we illustrate the benefits of including lifetime payout annuities in retirement portfolios. Finally, we explore the idea of optimal allocation to payout annuities in an investor's retirement portfolio. We also offer a comprehensive asset- and product-allocation strategy that addresses the unique requirements of today's and tomorrow's retirees.

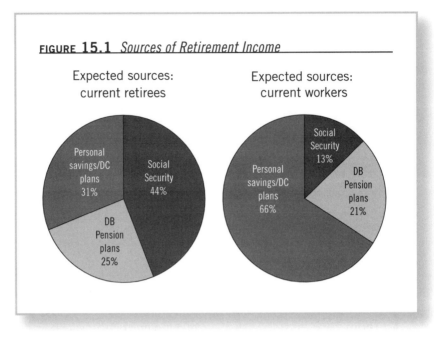

FIGURE **15.1** *Sources of Retirement Income*

Expected sources:
current retirees

Expected sources:
current workers

Source: Employee Benefit Research Institute, 2000 Retirement Confidence Survey.

Risk Factors in the Retirement Portfolio

U.S. investors typically have two goals in retirement. The primary goal is to ensure a comfortable lifestyle. In other words, investors would like to enjoy roughly the same (or better) lifestyle in retirement. Second, they would like to leave some money behind as a bequest, if possible. In making saving and investment decisions for their retirement portfolios, investors must confront three important risk factors: financial market risk, longevity risk, and the risk of not saving enough.

Financial Market Risk

Financial market risk, or volatility in the capital markets, causes portfolio values to fluctuate up and down. If the market drops during the early part of retirement, the portfolio may not be able to cushion the stress of the subsequent systematic withdrawals. Because of this, the portfolio may be unable to generate the necessary income for the desired lifestyle, or it may simply run out of money too soon.

Investors often ignore financial market risk by assuming a constant rate of return from their retirement portfolio, that is, no market volatility. As a result, they make inappropriate decisions in asset allocation and product selection. To illustrate the impact of the constant-return assumption, consider the following case. Assume a forty-five-year-old investor has a $300,000 portfolio invested in 60 percent stocks/40 percent bonds.[1] He is currently

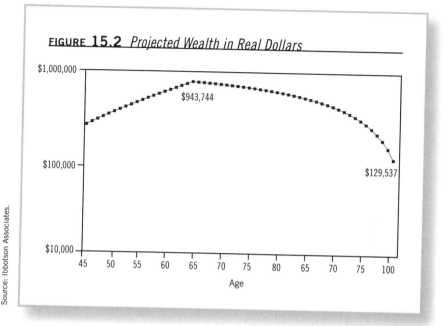

FIGURE **15.2** *Projected Wealth in Real Dollars*

saving $10,000 per year, inflation adjusted, adding each year to his retirement portfolio. He would like to have $75,000 worth of yearly income in retirement. It is estimated that Social Security and his defined-benefit pension plan will provide about $25,000 of this annual income. This means that $50,000 needs to be generated by his investment portfolio each year for the remainder of his life. He estimates the average compounded return on the portfolio to be 8.8 percent, with an inflation rate of 3 percent.[2]

FIGURE 15.2 shows the wealth and income levels projected for the constant returns used in this case.[3] If we assume that the future return is constant, each year the portfolio will generate a 7.4 percent compounded return after expenses and fees, or roughly 4.4 percent after inflation. If this actually happens, the $300,000 portfolio would grow to almost $1 million in real terms at the retirement age of sixty-five. The $1 million portfolio would be able to sustain a withdrawal of more than $50,000 per year in real terms (plus the $25,000 from Social Security) for the investor's life expectancy and beyond. In other words, the investor would meet his income needs and not run out of money.

Market return, however, is not the same every year. There will be periods when the portfolio returns are much lower than 7.4 percent, or even negative, such as the market returns experienced in 2000, 2001, and 2002. Although 7.4 percent may be a reasonable average assumption, it's unrealistic for the investor to make decisions based purely on average returns. This underestimates the risk, and investors are risk averse by nature.

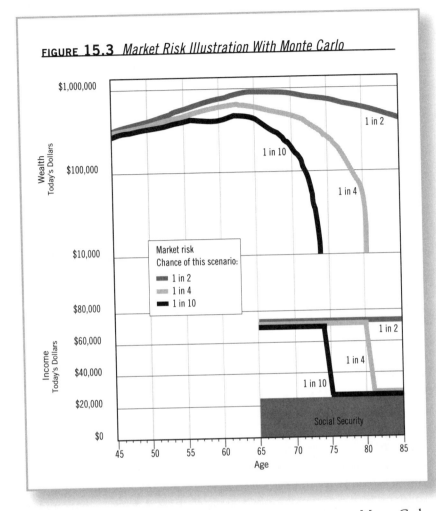

FIGURE 15.3 *Market Risk Illustration With Monte Carlo*

To show the impact of the entire return spectrum, we use a Monte Carlo simulation—a technique that helps evaluate the outcome of portfolios over time using a large number of simulated possible future return paths. Returns are randomly generated from a normal distribution that has a 7.4 percent compounded average and a 13.2 percent standard deviation.[4] **FIGURE 15.3** presents the Monte Carlo analysis results for the same case used in Figure 15.2. The analysis shows that there is a 10 percent chance that this portfolio would be depleted by age seventy-five; a 25 percent chance it would be depleted by age eighty-two; and about a 50 percent chance it would be depleted before age one hundred. Compared to the uncertain life span of the average investor, this result provides a much larger risk than most investors would want to take on.

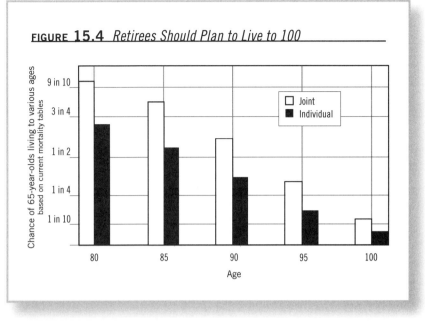

Source: 1996 U.S. Annuity table, Society of Actuaries.

FIGURE **15.4** *Retirees Should Plan to Live to 100*

Longevity Risk

Longevity risk is the risk of outliving your assets. As life expectancies continue to increase, retirees must be aware of the possibility of a long lifetime and adjust their plans accordingly. This is especially important for those who retire early or have a family history of long life.

Americans are living longer on average than ever before. The probability that an individual retiring at age sixty-five will reach age eighty is more than 70 percent for females and more than 62 percent for males. When combined with the life expectancy of a spouse, the odds are nearly 90 percent that at least one spouse will live to age seventy. For a broader sense of the potential longevity risk, **FIGURE 15.4** illustrates survival probability of that sixty-five-year-old. The first bar shows the probability that at least one of the partners will survive to age eighty, eighty-five, ninety, ninety-five, and one hundred. The second bar shows the probability that an individual person will survive to those ages. For married couples, in more than 80 percent of the cases, at least one partner will still be alive at age eighty-five.

Many investors use simple retirement-planning approaches that ignore longevity risk by assuming the investor needs to plan only to age eighty-five. It's true that eighty-five is roughly the life expectancy for a sixty-five-year-old. However, life expectancy is only the average estimate. We know for a fact that roughly half of the investors will live longer than that life expectancy. For a married couple, the odds are more than 80 percent. If investors use an eighty-five-year life expectancy to plan their retirement income needs, many of them will use up their retirement resources (other than government and corporate pensions) long before actual mortality. This longevity risk—the risk of outliving one's resources—is substantial and is the reason why lifetime annuities (payout annuities) should be an integral part of many retirement plans.

Taking on market risk is typically associated with higher potential returns. On the other hand, living a long life means more resources are needed to fund the longer-term income needs. Rational investors may decide to take on more financial risk hoping to gain more return, if they can tolerate the risk. Rational investors would also want to hedge away the financial aspect of longevity risk.[5] In other words, investors should be willing to pay an insurance premium to hedge away the risk of outliving their income. This is very similar to the concept of homeowner insurance, which protects against hazard to one's home. Lifetime payout annuities provide investors with this type of longevity insurance.

Risk of Not Saving Enough

There is a danger that investors will spend too much during their working years and not save enough to adequately fund their retirement portfolio. Retirees are increasingly relying on investment income from their own portfolios (including defined-contribution plans and individual retirement accounts). The ambiguity here is that investors can't determine exactly what they will earn between now and retirement, and they may not have the discipline to save adequately.

The evidence is that most investors do not save enough.[6] For example, a large proportion of investors do not even fund their 401(k) plans to earn the full match that their employers provide. If an employer provided a 50 percent match, then for each dollar an investor put into his 401(k) plan, the employer would put in fifty cents. No rational employee should be giving up this immediate 50 percent.

Although most savings can only receive normal capital market returns, savings are critical to meet retirement needs. It's not reasonable to expect the investment returns to compensate for savings shortfalls. On the contrary, investment returns allow the savings to multiply several times over the course of a retirement.

Controlling the Risk Factors

Financial risk can be mitigated by using portfolio theory, which provides methods not only to reduce risk but also to increase expected returns. Insurance products can hedge away longevity risk. The risk of inadequate savings is primarily mitigated by changing behavior.

Behavioral economists are developing some innovative ways to help investors overcome the myopic behavior of spending today instead of saving for retirement. Economists Richard Thaler and Shlomo Bernartzi, for example, pioneered the "Save More Tomorrow" (SMART) program. Workers are usually unable to commit to increase their 401(k) savings when the trade-off is current consumption. However, most workers are willing to commit to saving some portion of their future raises. When they receive their raises, their savings rate goes up, and they still get to take home part of the extra compensation and use it on immediate consumption. SMART takes advantage of the behavioral theory that people are myopic and heavily weight current consumption over future (retirement) consumption. Yet their raises are in the future, so they are less averse to trading off future saving for future retirement income.

For financial market risk, we can rely on the rich literature and models of modern portfolio theory. Although financial market risk cannot be completely eliminated, investors can take advantage of the diversification benefits of various investments by following long-term asset-allocation policies. Some investors may decide to take on more financial risk hoping to gain more return, if they can tolerate the risk. They can accomplish this by selecting a more aggressive asset-allocation policy (typically consisting of more stocks). The Markowitz mean-variance model is widely accepted as the gold standard for asset allocation. Unfortunately, this framework considers only the risk and return trade-off in the financial market. It does not consider the longevity risk people face during retirement. To fill this gap, we focus our attention on the importance of longevity insurance—while discussing the problems with fixed- and variable-payout annuities—and then move on to address the proper asset allocation between conventional financial assets and variable-payout annuity products that help manage longevity risk.

Longevity Risk

Longevity risk can be hedged by using insurance products, namely lifetime-payout annuities. These annuities are insurance products that convert an accumulated investment into income that the insurance company pays out over the life of the investor. Payout annuities are the opposite of life insurance. Consumers buy life insurance because they're afraid of dying too soon and leaving family and loved ones in financial need. They buy payout annuities because they're concerned about living too long and running out of assets during their lifetime. Insurance companies can provide this lifelong benefit by (a) spreading the longevity risk over a large group of annuitants and (b) making careful and conservative assumptions about the rate of return earned on their assets.

Spreading or pooling the longevity risk means that individuals who do not reach their life expectancy, as calculated by actuarial mortality tables, will subsidize those who exceed it. Investors who buy lifetime-payout annuities pool their portfolios together and collectively ensure that everybody will receive payments as long as they live. Because of the unique longevity insurance features embedded in lifetime-payout annuities, they can play a significant role in many investors' retirement portfolios. There are two basic types of payout annuities: fixed and variable. A fixed-payout annuity pays a fixed nominal dollar amount each period. A variable annuity's payments fluctuate depending on the performance of the underlying investments chosen by the contract holder. The number of payments from a lifetime payout annuity is contingent on the length of the life of the investor. Other payout options are also available, however, which guarantee that payments will be made for a specified period of time or with refund guarantees.

Fixed payout annuity. **FIGURE 15.5** illustrates the payment stream from an immediate fixed annuity. With an initial premium or purchase amount of $1 million, the annual income payments for a sixty-five-year-old male would be $6,689 per month, or $80,268 per year.[7] The straight line represents the annual payments before inflation. People who enjoy the security of a steady and predictable stream of income may find a fixed annuity appealing. The drawback of a fixed annuity, however, becomes evident over time. Since the payments are the same year after year, purchasing power is eroded by inflation as the annuitant gets older. The second, curved line in the image represents the same payment stream after a

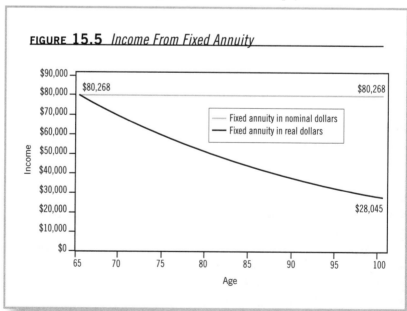

FIGURE 15.5 *Income From Fixed Annuity*

hypothetical 3 percent inflation rate.[8] While the annuitant still receives a constant payment amount, the payment is eroded over time by inflation.

Despite the benefits of longevity insurance and fixed payout amounts, there are several drawbacks to a portfolio that consists solely of fixed life-time annuities. First, since the nominal value of the payment will remain fixed for the rest of the annuitant's life, in real terms (inflation adjusted) the value of the payments will decline over time. In other words, the current monthly annuity payment might buy you a certain basket of goods, but there is no assurance the same basket will be affordable in the future. Second, one cannot trade out of the fixed-payout annuity once it's purchased.[9] This restriction may be a problem for investors who need or prefer liquidity. Finally, when you buy a fixed annuity, you lock in payments based on current interest rates. Payout rates from today's fixed-payout annuities are near historical lows, because of the current low interest rates. A sixty-five-year-old male might have received as much as $11,500 per month in the early 1980s in exchange for a $1 million initial premium. In 2003, that same $1 million buys only $6,689 per month. These drawbacks do not mean that fixed annuities are a poor investment choice. On the contrary, as shown later, fixed annuities can be a crucial part of a well-diversified retirement-income portfolio.

Variable payout annuities. A variable payout annuity is an insurance product that exchanges accumulated investment value for annuity units that the insurance company pays out over the lifetime of the investor. The annuity disbursements fluctuate depending on the value of the investments held. To better understand variable-payout annuities, think of a mutual fund whose current net asset value is $1 per unit. The unit fluctuates each and every day. In any given day, week, month, or year, the price can increase or decrease relative to the previous period. With a variable annuity, instead of getting fixed annuity payments, you get a fixed number of fund units. Each month, the insurance company converts these fund units into dollars based on the net asset value at the end of the month to determine how much to pay the investor. Therefore, the cash flow from the variable payout annuity fluctuates with the performance of the funds you choose.

FIGURE 15.6 illustrates the annuity payment stream, in real terms, from a 100 percent stock portfolio using a life-only payment option in an immediate variable annuity. A Monte Carlo simulation was created to illustrate the various payment scenarios. The simulation is generated using historical return statistics of stocks, bonds, and inflation from 1926 to 2002, a $1 million initial portfolio, and a 3 percent assumed investment return.[10] The initial payment at age sixty-five is estimated to be $66,150 per year.[11] The three lines in the chart show the 10th, 25th, and 50th

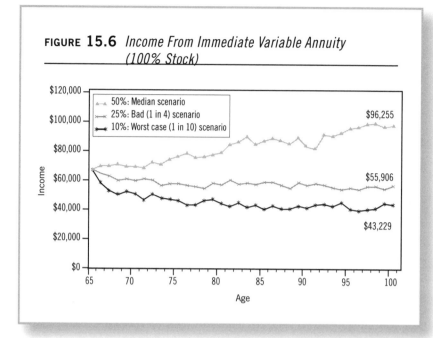

FIGURE **15.6** *Income From Immediate Variable Annuity (100% Stock)*

Source: Ibbotson Associates.

percentiles, showing the one-in-ten worst case, one-in-four bad case, and the median case. As the chart demonstrates, there is a 10 percent chance that annual inflation-adjusted annuity payments will fall below $44,000, a 25 percent chance that they will be around $56,000 or lower, and a 50 percent chance that they will grow to more than $96,000. Even in the worst case, the income is less than $7,000 under the target of $50,000 per year, so that the immediate variable annuity mostly protects retirement income.

Finding a Solution

Combining traditional asset allocation with annuitization can help investors manage both financial market risk and longevity risk. **FIGURES 15.7A** and **15.7B** illustrate the probability of how long a 60 percent stock/40 percent bond portfolio can provide the necessary level of retirement income using a combination of regular systematic withdrawals and variable-payout annuities. This analysis assumes a hypothetical $1 million initial portfolio, 50 percent of which is annuitized and 50 percent of which is invested in a regular investment product, such as a mutual fund portfolio. We assume that the income from the variable annuity is used to meet the income goal. If the income from the variable annuity is less than $50,000, then money will be withdrawn from the mutual fund portfolio to fill the gap.

Based on this model, there is a 10 percent chance that annual infla-

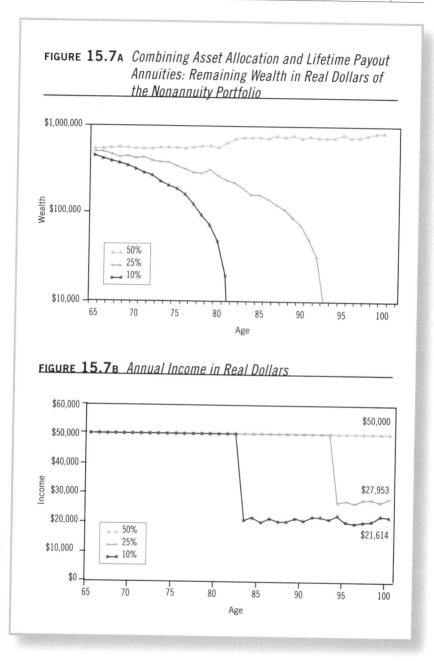

FIGURE **15.7A** *Combining Asset Allocation and Lifetime Payout Annuities: Remaining Wealth in Real Dollars of the Nonannuity Portfolio*

FIGURE **15.7B** *Annual Income in Real Dollars*

tion-adjusted payments will fall to $21,614 by age eighty-two, as variable annuity payments might be insufficient, requiring withdrawals from the nonannuitized portfolio to meet the $50,000 income need. There is a 25 percent chance the annual inflation-adjusted payment will fall to $27,953 by age ninety-four. Again, a floor is created by the variable-annuity income, offering the investor a smaller chance of running out of income at all probability levels versus a stand-alone strategy of making only systematic withdrawals from a mutual fund portfolio.

FIGURE 15.8 shows the probability of success for two retirement-income strategies. A strategy using 100 percent systematic withdrawal (SW) from mutual funds, with a 60 percent stock and 40 percent bond portfolio (without any lifetime annuity) has a higher risk of causing the portfolio to fall short of funding the required income need. Before age eighty, the probability of success begins to drop, falling to a low of 49 percent by age one hundred. The other strategy illustrated uses 25 percent fixed annuitization, 25 percent variable annuitization (VA all equities), and 50 percent (SW) from the 60 percent stock/40 percent bond mutual fund portfolio. The 50 percent annuitized strategy is a far better strategy for increasing the odds of meeting income goals over a lifetime. While there remains the probability of not being able to meet the income goal 100 percent of the time, the shortfall comes at a later stage in life, and even then there are partial payments. Retirees might find that a combination of different types of annuitization and systematic withdrawals could help manage the financial risks and the income needs they face during retirement. However, this raises the question of what is the best combination between different types of annuities and systematic withdrawals from mutual funds.

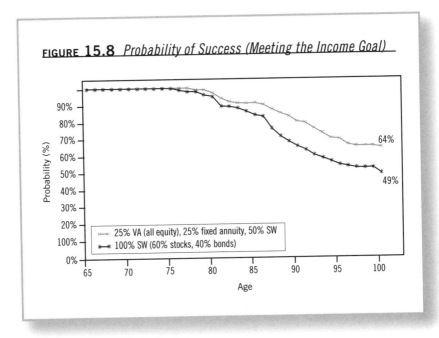

FIGURE 15.8 Probability of Success (Meeting the Income Goal)

Source: Ibbotson Associates.

Optimal Allocation to Annuities

Traditionally, asset allocation is determined by constructing efficient port-folios for various risk levels based on modern portfolio theory.[12] Then, based on the investor's risk tolerance, one of the efficient portfolios is cho-sen. Modern portfolio theory is widely accepted in academia and financial industries as the primary tool for developing asset allocations. However, its effectiveness is questionable when dealing with asset allocations for individual investors in retirement because the theory does not take lon-gevity risk into account. Asset-allocation decisions that take advantage of diversification benefits across different asset classes are an effective way to manage and reduce market risk. As discussed above, longevity risk can be hedged away with insurance products such as lifetime payout annuities. Therefore, fixed- and variable-payout annuities must be incorporated into traditional asset-allocation models to help investors find the appropriate allocation of their savings in retirement.

Based on the classic utility-maximization framework, we've con-structed sample model portfolios for allocating investment assets within and between two distinct categories of annuity assets and nonannuity assets.[13] The annuity assets include fixed- and variable-payout annuities. The nonannuity assets include all types of investment instruments, such as mutual funds, stocks, bonds, and Treasury bills that do not contain a mortality-contingent income flow. The optimal mix of annuitized and nonannuitized assets is determined by the age and risk tolerance of inves-tors, the desire they have to leave an estate, and the fees and expenses of the products they choose.[14]

FIGURE 15.9 illustrates three sample portfolios for three risk strategies for a sixty-five-year-old retiree with a moderate desire to leave an estate. In this example, the retiree's moderate desire to leave an estate suggests that annuities could be combined with nonannuitized investments to provide both a reasonable level of inheritance and a guaranteed stream of in-come.[15] For the conservative investor, the portfolio consists of 20 percent equity and 80 percent fixed income. A total of 22 percent is allocated to annuities, while the remaining 78 percent is allocated between nonannu-itized equity and fixed-income investments. The fixed annuity represents all of the 22 percent annuity allocation for the conservative investor. The optimal portfolios for moderate and aggressive investors allocate a larger portion to equities and less to fixed-income investments. For the moderate investor, the portfolio consists of 60 percent equity and 40 percent fixed income among the annuitized and nonannuitized investments. A total of 41 percent is allocated to annuities, while the remaining 59 percent is allo-cated between nonannuitized equity and fixed income investments. Note

FIGURE **15.9** *Optimal Allocations Between Traditional and Immediate Payout Annuities*

		CONSERVATIVE	MODERATE	AGGRESSIVE
Nonannuitized	Large-cap stocks	15%	30%	20%
	Small-cap stocks	0%	8%	7%
	International stocks	5%	14%	10%
	Bonds	34%	5%	2%
	Cash equivalents	24%	2%	1%
Annuitized	Variable annuity: diversified stocks portfolio	0%	8%	40%
	Fixed annuity	22%	33%	20%
Total nonannuitized assets		**78%**	**59%**	**40%**
Total annuitized assets		**22%**	**41%**	**60%**
Total fixed income		**80%**	**40%**	**23%**
Total equity		**20%**	**60%**	**77%**

that in general, more-aggressive investors tend to invest more in annuities because the annuities protect their income needs, enabling them to take on additional equity risk.

Our results indicate that fixed- and variable-payout annuities provide an effective hedge against longevity risk, helping investors achieve a sustainable income throughout retirement, regardless of how long they live. Using these results should be the first step in creating a comprehensive asset- and product-allocation strategy that will help ensure adequate income for the lifetime of today's and tomorrow's retirees.

References

Chen, P., and Moshe A. Milevsky. 2003. "Merging Asset Allocation and Longevity Insurance: An Optimal Perspective on Payout Annuities." *Journal of Financial Planning* (June): 64–72.

Markowitz, H. 1952. "Portfolio Selection." *Journal of Finance* (September): 77–91.

Merton, R. 1971. "Optimum Consumption and Portfolio Rules in a Continuous-Time Model." *Journal of Economic Theory* 3:373–413.

Thaler, Richard, and Shlomo Benartzi. 2001. "Save More Tomorrow: Using Behavioral Economics to Increase Employee Saving." Working paper, University of Chicago, August.

Chapter Notes

1. All dollar amounts presented in this chapter are in real dollars, that is, inflation-adjusted amounts.

2. Based on historical return statistics from *Stocks, Bonds, Bills, and Inflation Yearbook* (Ibbotson Associates, 2003), from 1926 to 2002.

3. All illustrations in this study are net of fees and expenses. Fee numbers are obtained from Morningstar Principia as of March 2002. They are 1.37 percent for mutual funds and 2.22 percent for variable annuities.

4. In this study, we generated one hundred return paths. Each path contains thirty-five years (from age sixty-five to about age one hundred).

5. Living a long life is desirable from many aspects; this study focuses only the financial ramifications of longevity.

6. Thaler and Benartzi (2001).

7. This was the quote obtained in October 2003, assuming a sixty-five-year-old male who lives in Illinois and a $1 million premium. The quote was obtained from www.immediateannuity.com.

8. The average inflation rate from 1926 to 2002 was 3.05 percent in the United States.

9. There are payout annuities available that allow the investor to withdraw money from them, but the investor typically has to pay a surrender or market-value adjustment charge. Furthermore, this withdrawal would apply only during a certain period of the annuity during which payments are guaranteed regardless of life status.

10. The assumed investment return is an initial interest-rate assumption that's used to compute the amount of an initial variable-annuity payment. Subsequent payments will either increase or decrease depending on the relationship of the assumed investment return to the actual investment return.

11. The initial payment is estimated by Ibbotson Associates.

12. Markowitz (1952) and Merton (1971).

13. These sample model portfolios are created based on the model presented in Chen and Milevsky (2003).

14. Ibbotson Associates has a patent pending on the method of selecting optimal combinations of stocks, bonds, et cetera, with annuity products, while satisfying both the need for retirement income need and the desire to bequeath.

15. We assume the investor does not have substantial holdings of other annuity-like investments, such as defined-benefit pensions, that provide lifetime income.

CHAPTER 16

Monetary Policy and Investment Returns

JOHN B. BRYNJOLFSSON

The financial goals of most clients are to save enough to educate their children, to retire in relative comfort, and perhaps to help their communities through charitable gifts. Put another way, investment performance is a means to a *real* end, not an end in itself. To the extent individual and institutional investors alike strive for high returns, we too often chase the markets' last great success story. In investment chasing, some win, many lose, but all take unwarranted risk.

A wiser way to serve clients is to understand all of the factors involved in the investment process. One factor many managers overlook is the impact monetary policy has on the markets. This chapter discusses how to assess that impact and its effect on your clients' chances of achieving their investment goals.

The basics of investing still hold: protect principal and think in terms of real, inflation-adjusted investment returns. Protecting principal boils down to risk management. Consider a broad range of potential investment outcomes, including the most probable and the worst possible outcomes. Think in terms of changing market conditions, sectors falling out of favor, and individual company prospects. And regarding company prospects, don't forget to think about downside at the company that most directly affects your clients' future: their employer. Regarding real investment returns, remember that most financial assets perform poorly in inflationary environments because the erosion of purchasing power is compounded by a nominal decline in asset price. Think, too, about the clients' needs and how they could grow or shrink.

Investors who go beyond the basics, however, know the importance of understanding how monetary policy affects investments. We know that unexpected monetary policy announcements have moved markets hundreds of points on the Dow Jones Industrial Average in a single day. In this chapter, I offer a look at monetary policy from an even larger perspective: how monetary policy has moved markets thousands of points over decades. An examination of the last forty years of monetary policy strongly suggests investors would do well to learn a little monetary history. "History does not repeat itself," Mark Twain once said. "At best it rhymes." I suspect in the U.S. investment arena, the next forty years will sound like the past forty. Your own historical analysis may lead to different conclusions, but the implications of mine are clear: Treasury inflation-protected securities and commodities are the investments that will do well in the accommodative monetary environment we're likely to see going forward.

U.S. Monetary Policy

The past forty years of monetary policy is a correlative tale of the Federal Reserve Board Open Market Committee's (FOMC) self-aggrandizing complacency in the easy-going early 1960s to its hard-fought gains made in the 1980s and 1990s (see **FIGURE 16.1**). On another level, it's the story of the never-ending classic economic struggle between doves and hawks. The doves correctly assert that an expansionary monetary policy (lower interest rates) increases aggregate spending, which in itself creates new demand. The hawks rightly respond that although that sounds good, ultimately what's most likely to be created is inflation, which is bad. The hawks believe that a higher cost of money encourages greater savings by discouraging unchecked borrowing while nurturing real growth. If the hawks had a mantra, it would be "no free lunch." Over a cycle of forty years, the pendulum that tracks public opinion and the ultimate force of democracy—politics—swings from one extreme to the other.

In 1964, roughly forty years ago, doves were comfortably in control of monetary policy. The highly respected William McChesney Martin was in his thirteenth year as chairman of our Federal Reserve Bank. Excluding a sharp but short-lived recession in 1957–58, the United States had been enjoying a long period of economic growth. Productivity was high and inflation was low.

Keynesian economic theory was held in high regard, and the general thinking was that demand management had solved the dilemma of the business cycle. Years earlier Martin had argued strongly against the costs of higher inflation, yet as Fed chair in the 1960s, he opted to stress the importance of FOMC consensus decision making; in effect, he consented

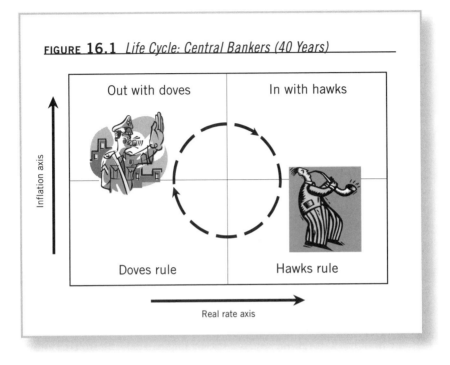

FIGURE **16.1** *Life Cycle: Central Bankers (40 Years)*

to the majority. That majority believed that although inflation was creeping higher, the FOMC could loosen monetary and fiscal policies to spur even greater societal accomplishments. This would place us at about seven o'clock in Figure 16.1. All seemed well.

During the five years that followed, government fiscal spending increased tremendously, first to fund President Lyndon Johnson's "Great Society" programs and then to simultaneously pay for our increasing involvement in the Vietnam War. The phrase "Guns *and* butter" was coined by the ruling doves to rationalize our huge and still-growing federal deficit. Yet, even after a mild recession ended in November 1970, most people believed inflation would remain muted. The Fed was reflecting the views of Americans. But the only constant in the investing world is change, and big change was soon to come.

Martin was followed in February 1970 by Arthur Burns, a free-market and business-cycle expert who served as chair for President Dwight Eisenhower's Council of Economic Advisors from 1953 to 1956. Burns was a knowledgeable, well-respected economist, but he was a Fed outsider and consensus building was not his strength. During Burns's reign, the FOMC was severely challenged: our economy was transitioning to lower productivity and higher unemployment. The toll of looser fiscal policies was growing, and there was a widening belief among economists that the Keynesian demand model was cracked. Although there's no evidence to suggest Burns did anything but his utmost to respond to the obstacles he faced, then as now, skeptics quickly pointed out that the chairman of the Federal Reserve Board and six others of the twelve voting members of the FOMC were presidential appointees.

The message couldn't have been clearer. The Fed may be independent, but monetary policy has political as well as economic roots. At various times Burns was reproached for lowering federal funds rates in 1970–1971 to ensure President Richard Nixon's reelection and again in 1976 to influence his own renomination. Later he was criticized that his "start-stop" monetary approach was ineffective.

In support of Burns, it's unlikely that Congress, the White House, or the public would have condoned a tougher Fed stance during his tenure. He was constrained by a country preoccupied with war and scandal. The lip service given to taming inflation at the time is best exemplified by the Ford Administration's "WIN" (Whip Inflation Now) buttons to remind the public of the importance of price stability. Without doubt, most people in 1975 believed unemployment, which was high in the wake of a recently ended recession, was a greater concern than inflation.

In March 1978 (about ten o'clock in Figure 16.1), President Jimmy Carter ironically provided more evidence that Burns was in fact delivering what the country wanted from the Fed. In particular, Carter appointed a political supporter, G. William Miller—the chief executive officer of an industrial manufacturer who had no economic or banking experience— to chair the Federal Reserve Board. Miller lasted less than eighteen months before he was moved to Treasury.

Carter took his next Fed chair appointment more seriously. He selected Paul Volcker, an extremely knowledgeable and competent Fed insider, and gave him total autonomy to do what was needed. (It was rumored later that Carter's old friend and adviser Bert Lance warned that appointing the hard-liner Volcker would eliminate any chance for reelection.) We're getting to twelve o'clock in Figure 16.1—high noon—and Volcker had a showdown with inflation.

When Volcker publicly changed the Fed's explicit policy target to money growth, he was in effect still implicitly targeting interest rates. By capping money growth (which the Fed can do via open market operations that directly drain money from the banking system), he effectuated an increase in real interest rates of 10 percentage points (from −2 percent to +8 percent). Those high real interest rates caused inflation to tumble in subsequent years (along the right half of our clock), which puts us at three o'clock.

In 1987 President Ronald Reagan appointed Alan Greenspan, the current chair of the Fed, to succeed Volcker. Greenspan continued Volcker's war, and as inflation dropped, the value of financial assets soared, eliciting widespread respect and appreciation for our central bank chair. The cartoon figure in Figure 16.1 could well be President Bill Clinton playing the sax at a celebratory party for Greenspan.

When inflation dropped from high to acceptable levels, the Greenspan Fed set out to lower real interest rates. Real interest rates started falling in the 1990s (along the bottom of Figure 16.1). Greenspan and other economists described this as the new paradigm, where growth, driven by productivity improvements, is on the rise and inflation is falling.

This brings us to six o'clock in Figure 16.1, where we can sense the awakening of the doves. We saw glimpses of this in the late 1990s, and we're seeing more now. Ever since the Asian debt crisis of 1997, I have been hearing more people comfortably introducing the idea that a little bit of easing on the monetary policy side at the risk of a little bit of inflation is not a problem. And I agree. But that does bring us to the bottom-left quadrant of the chart, almost where we started. We're not quite ready to allow doves to rule, but given the societal risks and costs of deflation and the enormous unknown strain associated with it, perhaps erring on the side of inflation is prudent. Some observers argue that we're already seeing asset-price inflation in equities, bonds, and real estate and that price inflation for goods and services will follow. Just as I suspect was the case in 1964, I'm hearing no objections to asset-price inflation or to the beginning of price inflation for goods and services. Objections will come later.

The Life Cycle of Bond Returns

For our recap of monetary policy history to have any practical use for investing, we must consider the implications of the cycle for investments and returns. We can start by translating this forty-year Fed monetary cycle into a bond-return cycle. Starting again at seven o'clock, this time in **FIGURE 16.2**, bond yields were relatively low forty years ago. The seeds of inflation—monetary and fiscal stimulus—had been sown. As a result, during the fifteen years that followed, the bond market would endure capital losses created by rising inflation and interest rates. After that fifteen-year period, the bond cycle topped out with very high bond yields (twelve o'clock in Figure 16.2). Back in the early and mid-1980s, bond yields rose to the midteens, labeled "high income" in the figure.

The aggressive hike in real rates brings us to the next quadrant, two o'clock. Nominal interest rates controlled by the FOMC had been hiked aggressively to overcome the inflation rate, which was not only high but still rising. At two o'clock, that high income translates into the label "buy" in Figure 16.2.

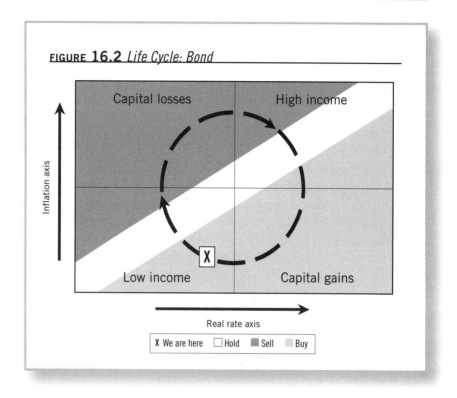

FIGURE **16.2** *Life Cycle: Bond*

High inflation is associated with high yields on bonds. These high yields will ultimately translate into capital gains when inflation and the corresponding yields fall. In Figure 16.2, this corresponds to a move from two o'clock to four o'clock. As we shift left along the bottom axis, from four o'clock to seven o'clock again, additional capital gains result from the fall in real yield levels. Conversely, the sell side of the equation occurs when you have rising inflation or rising real interest rates. That would correspond to the left side and most of the top margins of the cycle.

I would suggest that now, in 2004, we're at about seven o'clock. Real rates were about as low as they could be, and inflation was pretty close to as low as it could be. Therefore, into 2005, we'll start to gravitate toward the hold area, the black part of the box in Figure 16.2. And ultimately, perhaps even already, we'll be in the "sell" (capital losses) part of the cycle.

You can do a similar analysis for equities, using **FIGURE 16.3** as a guide. The correspondence between the equity and bond market cycles is driven by the dynamics of earnings and price-to-earnings ratios (P/Es). Historically, P/Es have tended to inversely mirror bond yields.

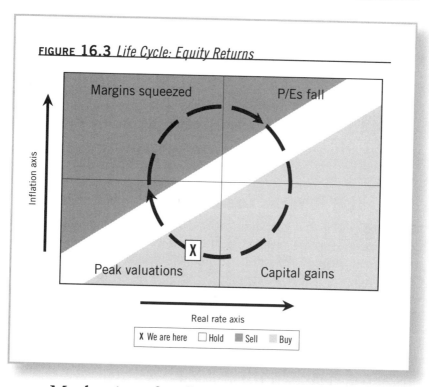

FIGURE 16.3 *Life Cycle: Equity Returns*

Mechanics of Inflation-Indexed Bonds

Mechanics of Inflation-Indexed Bonds

What's the difference between the returns of inflation-linked bonds (ILBs) and those of other traditional financial assets? Before we answer that question, a brief explanation of ILB mechanics is called for.

Principal and interest payments on ILBs are typically indexed to inflation, and the interest accrues every day. I'm frequently asked, "When does the inflation accrue?" Well, it's every single day. The return of an ILB is the principal accrual plus the interest accrued plus the capital gains, realized or unrealized (see **FIGURE 16.4**).

The capital gains since 2000 have been have been very positive. Double-digit capital gains have resulted in double-digit returns for ILBs. The reality going into 2005, however, is that a real yield on ILBs of 1.5 percent, plus the 2–3 percent of inflation, translates into 3.5–4.5 percent running yields for ILBs over the next three to five years. Hard to get double-digit returns when yields start out in the range of 1–2 percent. Note that the capital gain is zero if you hold a par bond to maturity, so you can ignore that last term in Figure 16.4. (If we were to have capital losses over the first three or six months of holding an ILB, that would translate into higher yields for the subsequent portion of the holding period.)

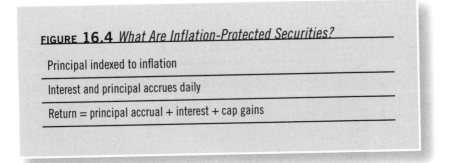

FIGURE **16.4** *What Are Inflation-Protected Securities?*

Principal indexed to inflation

Interest and principal accrues daily

Return = principal accrual + interest + cap gains

ILB Returns and the Monetary Cycle

ILBs are "real" assets. That means they're different from most investments when it comes to their sensitivity to the value of money. ILBs are essentially ninety degrees offset from traditional financial assets like stocks and bonds, as far as the Fed, or bond, cycle goes. In **FIGURE 16.5**, we start forty years ago at seven o'clock again, and you would have found yourself at the beginning of an inflationary episode. Of course, ILBs didn't exist in 1964 (in G7 nations), so the analysis is somewhat hypothetical.

In any case, if ILBs had existed then, presumably their real yields would have been modest, reflecting the relatively easy monetary policy. Though real yields would not have amounted to much, the uptick in inflation would have resulted in both increased coupon income and increased rates of accruals to principal. It's likely that their performance would have kept up with inflation (before taxes) whereas, during the same period, virtually all financial assets were badly lagging inflation or, in many cases, falling even in terms of *nominal* price.

Eventually that brings us to twelve o'clock in Figure 16.5. When there is high inflation, sure, ILBs accrue principal rapidly. But the problem is that if monetary policy authorities eliminate that high inflation by raising real interest rates, you end up having capital losses on ILBs as real rates increase. So, quite ironically, high inflation, as is indicated by the change in shading in Figure 16.5, the topmost margin of the cycle is not a good time to own ILBs. I would suggest that the worst time historically to own ILBs would have been from 1979 to 1982.

ILBs still didn't exist at that point in the United States, but if they had, you would have bought ILBs with a very low real yield. And by the time Volcker finished tightening the real yield on those ILBs, they would have gone into the high single digits. As a result, you would have had huge capital losses on your ILB holdings. Even though you were experiencing double-digit inflation, you would have had double-digit or even higher capital losses, more than offsetting the ILBs' inflation accruals.

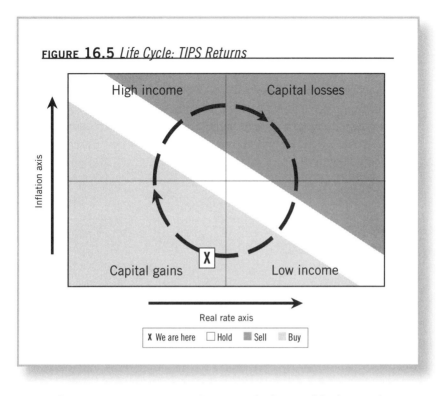

FIGURE 16.5 *Life Cycle: TIPS Returns*

So if zero or negative nominal returns don't sound bad enough, consider that this would have been a time when you could have earned 15 percent or 16 percent in money-market securities—certainly a poor time to own ILBs. Similarly, as the inflation rate falls, ILBs obviously do not do well in absolute or relative terms.

From the late 1990s through 2003, ILBs generated double-digit returns. The most dramatic component of these returns was a consequence of falling real rates. So the real rate axis, from four o'clock to seven o'clock, is part of the "buy" triangle. That's obviously a good time to hold ILBs, which has been confirmed. And as we move past seven o'clock into 2005 and beyond, I would suggest that as inflation rises in this cycle, it's also a good time to own ILBs and other real assets.

Rhymes and Reasons

The model I've highlighted suggests that over forty-year cycles, politics can influence markets and investment returns. What's more, in terms of the big picture, markets fail to allocate resources optimally across time spans.

History may not repeat itself exactly, but I believe the future will rhyme with the past. Indeed, investment themes that worked so well in the 1980s and 1990s may be coming to the end of their couplet, and those of the 1960s and 1970s may be the basis for coming rhymes. The inflation outlook and asset returns changed dramatically from 2000 to 2004. We also saw a major change in how investment committees work in both institutional and retail spheres. They're throwing out the staid 60 percent equity to 40 percent bond recipe that used to work. Investment managers need to position their portfolios and their businesses to make certain their clients do not get left behind by this secular echo of past inflations.

CHAPTER 17

Defining Investment Advice

STEPHEN C. WINKS

A s financial advisers, what is our obligation to our clients? Do we simply make them aware of investment alternatives and leave them to their own devices, however limited their knowledge and expertise for making investment decisions may be? If so, aren't investors acting as their own counsel, exercising judgment in areas in which they're not well versed? In such an exchange, the role of the financial adviser is minimized to the lowest common denominator of offering product access and trade-execution services. Yet, traditionally, this has been how financial advisers and their supporting firms have functioned—a role limited to product access and trade execution. No advice is implied or rendered, no accountability for investment recommendations is assumed, nor is there acknowledgment of fiduciary responsibility. But clearly, all investors would prefer their investment advisers to act selflessly in the clients' best interests in making informed investment recommendations. Counsel of this caliber offers well-reasoned recommendations and involves accountability encompassing all the clients' holdings. The role and counsel of the adviser are taken to the highest common denominator of fulfilling fiduciary responsibility. But for clients seeking this grade of counsel, it's difficult to determine what role the financial adviser is playing. Are advisers simply presenting investment alternatives, or are they making well-reasoned investment recommendations?

No institutionalized support is available to advisers for providing the kind of counsel that implies accountability. Innovation is desperately needed within the financial-services industry. Though essential to adding value, no institutionalized account aggregation capability compliant with the CFA Institute exists for advisers. Nor is there institutionalized investment policy statement capability, with legal opinions to guide the governance and management of the client's portfolio. Nor is there an institutionalized monitoring capability for all a client's holdings that would "constitute continuous comprehensive" counsel, which is implied by regulatory mandate. Any comprehensive counsel being provided today is achieved only by the initiative of the individual financial adviser. Advisers have to invent their own processes and technology to address and manage the full range of investment and administrative values necessary to fulfill their fiduciary obligations to clients.

To alleviate this administrative and technological burden on advisers and their supporting firms and to reduce the labor intensity of high-level counsel, the Society of Senior Consultants in concert with the American Institute of Certified Public Accountants (AICPA), the Foundation for Fiduciary Studies, Dalbar, leading advisers, and leading technical experts that support high-level counsel have formed the High Net Worth Standards Initiative. Its mission is to define the processes, the technology, and the full range of investment and administrative values that must be addressed and managed for advisers to fulfill their fiduciary responsibility to their high-net-worth clients. The two end products of this initiative are the High Net Worth Asset/Liability Study Working Document, establishing what's required of advisers to fulfill their fiduciary obligations to their high-net-worth clients, and the Technological Blueprint, delineating the technology necessary for continuous comprehensive counsel and the fulfillment of fiduciary responsibility. Both documents are based on the definitive research of the Center for Fiduciary Studies, which cites case law, statutes, and regulatory opinion letters in delineating the practice standards required of advisers to fulfill their fiduciary responsibility, which is the breadth of the advisers' counsel. The nine months and thousands of hours expended by the industry's leading advisers and technical experts in the High Net Worth Standards Initiative have culminated in the establishment of best practices, which constitute the depth of the advisers counsel.

Financial advisers are obligated to look at the client's circumstances and evaluate all of a client's holdings before they recommend an investment. To help fulfill that obligation, the Asset/Liability Study explores the full range of investment and administrative values that must be addressed and managed and sets up everything financial advisers must do, establishing the depth and breadth of their counsel. Thus, constructing the Asset/Liability Study means constructing a framework for advice, or what is required of us as financial advisers. The High Net Worth Asset/ Liability Study is considered a working document because it reflects our best thinking on working with high-net-worth clients—thinking that is sure to evolve and change. Technological innovation will greatly elevate the counsel of financial advisers far beyond what is possible to provide today, and with the ongoing input from leading financial advisers, the High Net Worth Standards Initiative will continue to reflect those innovations and to strengthen the role and counsel of the financial adviser.

The Technological Blueprint creates a context in which to see the importance, the interconnectivity, and the value of all the component parts of enabling technology, which is not possible by looking at a specific technology in the abstract. The objective of the High Net Worth Standards Initiative is to foster technological innovation that will (1) reduce the labor intensity of professional investment and administrative counsel, (2) empower advisers to offer continuous comprehensive counsel, as required by regulatory mandate, (3) address and manage the full range of investment and administrative values required by regulatory mandate, and (4) help advisers fulfill their fiduciary responsibility.

Wealthy individual investors are not fiduciaries; they're investing their own money on their own behalf. By extension, one may ask if there is a need for a fiduciary standard in dealing with individual investors. That depends on the investor and the adviser. Most high-net-worth investors have the same concerns as fiduciaries acting on behalf of others. They would rather not act as their own counsel in managing their own assets or even supervise professional money managers. Thus, many wealthy investors see the wisdom of both engaging professional money managers and engaging the investment and administrative counsel of an investment management consultant, who not only acts as a cofiduciary in monitoring the broad range of investment and administrative values required by regulatory mandate but also acts as an intermediary between the investor and money managers.

High-net-worth investors do not have to engage professional investment and administrative counsel to act as intermediaries; they may act on their own in making investment decisions. Nor do advisers have to serve in a fiduciary capacity, which entails accountability for investment recommendations. Investors may become their own counsel and exercise their own judgment. Yet, investors are increasingly aware of the value of well-informed, objective advice. For advisers who wish to fulfill their fiduciary obligations and offer ongoing counsel for a fee, the High Net Worth Asset/Liability Study Working Document presented here (and complete with substantiating code, regulations, and case law on the Bloomberg Press website at www.bloomberg.com/thinktank) establishes what's required in the engagement of their investment and administrative counsel. For many financial advisers, this may be the first time they've been offered clarity regarding what's required of them in fulfilling their fiduciary obligations to their clients.

It's important to acknowledge the contribution of our industry's leading financial advisers and technical experts for their work in creating the High Net Worth Asset/Liability Study Document to the end of elevating the role and counsel of the financial adviser. We are indebted to the leadership, commitment, and counsel of the following participants in the High Net Worth Standards Initiative:

Harold Evensky	Past Chairman of CFP Standards Board
Guy Cumbie	Past Chairman of the FPA
Jim Pupillo	Past President of APIC, ICIMC (now IMCA)
Bob Rowe	Adviser, Morgan Stanley
Dick Smith	Adviser, Capital Advisory Group
Hugh Anderson	Adviser, Merrill Lynch
Rich Todd	Adviser, Innovest
Robby Hazzard	Adviser, Brock Hazzard/Wachovia Securities
Vince Birley	Adviser, Ronald Blue and Co.
David Perkins	Adviser, CapTrust
Ron Pruitt	Placemark: Tax Efficiency/Overlay Management
Ron Surz	PPCA: Attribution Analysis/Performance Evaluation
Bob Rowe	Rowe Decision Analytics: Investment Policy/Tactical Asset Allocation
Bob Padgett	Klein Decisions: Investment Policy
Bevin Crodian	Market Street Advisors: Process/Technology
Amy Otteson	Prima Capital: Manager Search and Selection
John Michel	Bull Run Financial: Attribution Analysis/Portfolio Analysis/Tactical Asset Allocation
Joe Maxwell	Investment Score Card: AIMR Compliant Reporting/Account Data Aggregation
Madelyn Jackrel	Integrated Decision Systems: Web-based Sub-accounting, Trade and Order Routing and Reporting
Don Trone	Foundation for Fiduciary Studies: Research
AICPA	Fiduciary Responsibility Advocate
Lou Harvey	Dalbar: Measurement of Client Satisfaction
Steve Winks	Society of Senior Consultants

This material is published with permission of the Society of Senior Consultants and www.SrConsultant.com.

FOUNDATION OF FIDUCIARY STUDIES (FFS) §1.1.

Investments are managed in accordance with the applicable laws, trust documents, and written policy statements.

BEST PRACTICES

a. Review and analyze all documents pertaining to the client's assets and liabilities.
b. Develop and/or review investment policy statement (IPS) and update accordingly written minutes and/or files from investment committee meetings.
c. Review trust documents.
   i. Do trust documents identify trustees and named fiduciaries?
   ii. Do trust documents, statutes, and/or client instructions restrict or prohibit certain asset classes, as desired by client and reflected in IPS?
   iii. Do trust documents allow for the fiduciaries to prudently delegate investment decisions to others?
d. Service agreements (any service vendor)
   i. Service agreements must be in writing. Do service agreements conflict with the fiduciary standards of care?
   ii. Service agreements must be cost/benefit efficient.
   iii. All service agreements should be dated, reviewed, and revised annually, at the minimum.
   iv. A request for proposal (RFP) for all service providers should be issued every three years at the minimum. Updates in services, pricing and offerings should be actively monitored.
e. Information on retained money managers
   i. Obtain ADV for separate account managers.
   ii. Obtain prospectuses, independent research reports, annual reports, and statements of information for mutual funds.
f. Investment performance reports from:
   i. Money managers
   ii. Custodians
   iii. Consultants
g. Tax status/sensitivity
   i. Determine state and federal income and capital gains tax exposure and rates.
   ii. Assess susceptibility to alternative minimum tax.
   iii. Monitor all client holdings to manage wash sales and sales to related entities.

h. Estate and philanthropic objectives
   i. Review mission statement.
   ii. Review client goals and objectives.
   iii. Review spending policy and formulas.
   iv. Discern planned expenditures that deviate from the "typical" rate and determine for tax purposes which of these atypical expenditures are for philanthropic purposes so that an optimal tax solution can be achieved while making charitable contributions.
   v. Establish whether clients have an understanding of the logic behind the structure of their assets.

PRACTICE STANDARDS _____ FFS §1.2

Fiduciaries are aware of their duties and responsibilities: client education.

BEST PRACTICES

a. Clients understand they are responsible for determining investment goals and objectives.
b. Clients understand they are responsible for approval of an appropriate asset-allocation strategy.
c. Clients understand they should approve an explicit written investment policy statement that is consistent with their goals and objectives.
d. Clients understand they should approve appropriate money managers or other prudent experts to implement their investment policy.

   Clients understand whether their financial advisers are acting in a fiduciary capacity, acknowledging their fiduciary responsibility, and providing expert counsel or whether clients are required to exercise their own judgment and counsel. The difference between an adviser making an informed investment recommendation and advancing an investment alternative for the client's consideration is quite essential.
e. Clients understand they should monitor the activities of the overall investment program for compliance with investment policy. Monitoring should incorporate the performance measurement objectives and benchmarks that will be used to evaluate money managers at the time the manager is hired if investment discretion has been delegated to an investment adviser.
f. Clients understand an objective process and criteria should be used in selecting and removing money managers and other service vendors.
g. Clients understand they must avoid transactions prohibited by investment policy and by regulatory mandate.

h. Clients understand they can't abdicate their responsibility in engaging prudent expert counsel.

PRACTICE STANDARDS _____ FFS §1.3

Clients must determine that advisers acting in a fiduciary capacity and "parties of interest" are, by law and statute, not involved in self-dealing.

BEST PRACTICES

a. Full disclosure of all investment expenses and reimbursements. These expenses must be elevated out of the depths of prospectuses and offering memoranda and clearly articulated for client review.
b. Full disclosure of all forms of compensation and revenues received and paid from all sources.
c. Full disclosure of all soft-dollar services obtained and defrayment of expenses (reimbursement for due-diligence trips, etc.) paid by directed commissions.
d. Full disclosure of the fiduciary's services funded by money managers, such as 12(b)1 fees.
e. Full disclosure of outsourced fiduciary services, such as proxy voting.
f. Acknowledgment of fiduciary status and:
  i. Full disclosure of all commissions incurred relative to volume-weighted average daily pricing (VWAP). This assures best execution and no conflict of interest necessarily being assumed by an adviser who is employed by a firm engaged in trade execution, custody, and asset management.
  ii. If proprietary investment options are used, they are only used when the best and most comparable investment options reasonably available are documented and provided to the client for consideration as part of the investment recommendation.

PRACTICE STANDARDS _____ FFS §1.4

Service agreements and contracts are in writing and do not contain provisions that conflict with fiduciary standards of care.

BEST PRACTICES

Avoid conflicts of interest and prohibited transactions.

PRACTICE STANDARDS _____ FFS §1.5

There is documentation to show timing and distribution of cash flows and payments of liabilities.

BEST PRACTICES

a. Prepare a schedule of the portfolio's anticipated cash flows for the coming five-year period so the investment time horizons can be determined. Establish funding statement spending policy formula.

   The time horizon is that point in time when more money is flowing out of the portfolio than is coming in from contributions and growth.

   - If the time horizon is less than five years, it is considered short term, and the portfolio is implemented with fixed income and cash.
   - If the time horizon is five years or more, it is considered long term and can be implemented across most asset classes.

b. If the client has a material disbursement within five years, the amount needed should be held in cash or short-term fixed-income instruments unless the client instructs otherwise.

PRACTICE STANDARDS _____ FFS §1.6

Assets are within the jurisdiction of the U.S. courts and are protected from theft and embezzlement.

BEST PRACTICES

Offshore accounts may be considered as long as their use is within the strict federal reporting and tracking requirements of foreign bank accounts and offshore assets. [Patriot Act of 2001]

PRACTICE STANDARDS _____ FFS §2.1

A level of risk has been identified.

BEST PRACTICES

a. Unsystematic risk
   i. Business
   ii. Financial
b. Market risk: statistical measures
   i. Standard deviation
   ii. Sortino ratio
c. Psychographic tools should also be employed (behavioral finance).
d. Qualitative and relative measures of risk

      i. Maximum loss

      ii. Peak-trough recovery time

      iii. Monte Carlo simulation

e. Opportunity risk:

      i. Liquidity risk

      ii. Interest rate risk

      iii. Reinvestment risk

      iv. Inflation (purchasing power) risk

      v. Implementation risk: rebalance strategies to be used

PRACTICE STANDARDS   FFS §2.2

An expected, model return to meet investment objectives has been determined, based on current and historical performance information.

BEST PRACTICES

Assumptions made for modeling purposes should be explicitly stated. "Guaranteed" forecasting is not required.

a. Assumptions made for modeling purposes should be explicitly stated. The fiduciary is not required to forecast future returns.

      i. Assumptions for cash flow, appreciation, and total return

      ii. Range of outcomes: best, worst, most probable

b. Many investment professionals use the "risk premium" model, requiring the calculation of the premium that each asset class has earned over the risk-free rate of return. The risk premium is then measured based on possible economic scenarios that may impact each asset class over the next five years. This observation may not be necessary or appropriate, as most individuals are using an asset-allocation process and forecasted long-term risk and return as inputs to that process. While this is a form of risk premium/economic scenario approach, most individuals refer to it ass asset allocation.

PRACTICE STANDARDS   FFS §2.3

An investment time horizon has been identified.

BEST PRACTICES

a. The clients will determine their investment time horizon, which is the point in time at which more money is going out of the portfolio than is coming in through either investment contributions or capital appreciation.

An investment time horizon of less than five years is generally considered short term and calls for more of an allocation of the portfolio assets to fixed income and cash unless otherwise directed by the client.

b. The client must manage the hierarchy of investment decisions consistent with the determination of an investment time horizon.

What is the time horizon of the investment strategy?

- What asset classes will be considered?
- What will be the asset-class mix?
- What subasset classes are considered?
- What managers will be engaged?

PRACTICE STANDARDS _____ FFS §2.4

Ascertain whether selected asset classes are consistent with the identified risk, return, and time horizon.

BEST PRACTICES

The client must choose the appropriate configuration of asset classes that optimizes the risk and return objectives identified so they are consistent with the portfolio's time horizon. It must be determined whether investment goals and objectives can be reasonably obtained with the allocation.

PRACTICE STANDARDS _____ FFS §2.5

Ascertain whether the number of asset classes is consistent with the portfolio size.

BEST PRACTICES

The appropriate number of asset classes is determined by the facts and circumstances of each investor, including:

i. The nature (e.g., taxable or tax exempt), number, and size of the investor's portfolios
ii. Investor and portfolio constraints (e.g., behavioral, restricted stock, 401(k) investment choices)
iii. Taxes (e.g., low-basis stock)
iv. The skill and expertise and desires of decision makers
v. Cost efficiency and operational constraints

PRACTICE STANDARDS _____ FFS §3.1

There is a written investment policy statement (IPS) that has sufficient detail for a third party to implement investment strategy.

BEST PRACTICES

a. Written IPS should:
  i. Avoid internal conflicts and advert arbitrary and ill-advised, emotional decisions.
  ii. Provide clear and unambiguous expectations and investment monitoring and compliance guidelines.
b. All assets including tax-exempt, closely held, or restricted assets are modeled into the overall investment strategy.
c. The IPS is the blueprint for portfolio construction and serves as a business plan in the ongoing management of the investment portfolio. Thus, the IPS should be reviewed at least annually to determine whether there have been any material changes to the client's circumstances, goals and objectives, and return considerations.

PRACTICE STANDARDS _____ FFS §3.2

The investment policy statement defines the duties and responsibilities of all parties involved.

BEST PRACTICES

a. To ensure continuity of investment strategy and prevent the omission of critical fiduciary functions, the duties and responsibilities of each party involved in the prudent investment process should be detailed in writing and signed off on, including:
b. The role of the investor
c. The role of the adviser/consultant
d. The role of the custodian
e. The role of the managers:
  i. Guidelines for the investment mandate for which the manager has been engaged to manage
  ii. Responsibility to seek best execution
  iii. Responsibility to account for soft dollars
  iv. Responsibility to vote all proxies
f. The role of outside technical counsel
  i. Attorneys
  ii. Accountants
  iii. Other technical/expert counsel

PRACTICE STANDARDS _____ FFS §3.3

The investment policy statement defines diversification, asset allocation, and rebalancing of guidelines.

BEST PRACTICES

a. Strategic asset allocation outlined in the IPS should be that specific mix of asset classes that meet the mutually agreed-upon risk/return profile of the investor after considering the following variables:
   i. Tax status of portfolios
   ii. Risk exposure that the investor is willing to take
   iii. Expected nominal return
   iv. Asset-class preferences and constraints of the investor
   v. Time horizon constraints
b. The IPS must be monitored and managed to reflect changing markets and investment choices.
c. The IPS should identify explicitly omitted asset classes and strategies (e.g., options, leverage).
d. The IPS should state rebalancing criteria and provide clear and unambiguous calendar and contingent criteria, including tax consequences and rebalancing cost for all designated styles and classes.
e. The goal of rebalancing is to achieve the appropriate balance between risk and return inherent in diversification. Once diversification is achieved, diversification requires constant rebalancing. But rebalancing cannot be so highly structured that it leads to tax inefficiency and cost-prohibitive underperforming trades. Thus, setting an appropriate rebalancing limit is somewhat subjective.

PRACTICE STANDARDS _____ FFS §3.4

The investment policy statement defines due-diligence criteria for selecting investment options.

BEST PRACTICES

A clear and unambiguous description of qualities, characteristics, and merits as criteria in the selection of money managers and the weight each of these considerations plays relative to the money-manager selection process.

PRACTICE STANDARDS _____ FFS §3.5

The investment policy statement defines monitoring criteria for investment options and service vendors.

BEST PRACTICES

a. Establish clear and unambiguous criteria by which the services of managers are terminated.
b. Establish clear and unambiguous criteria for appropriately frequent monitoring of managers.

   The custodial statement is insufficient to determine if the best execution was achieved. The best execution is achieved when managers get the best price they could at the time they decide to trade and given the legal structure that dictates how the trades are achieved. The only way this could be verified would be looking at level two data at the time of trading.
c. Establish clear and unambiguous criteria for quarterly, written manager reviews to include issues such as:
   i. Risk/return performance relative to appropriate benchmarks
   ii. Tax efficiency
   iii. Expense management
   iv. Management personnel

PRACTICE STANDARDS   FFS §3.6

The investment policy statement defines procedures for controlling and accounting for investment expenses.

BEST PRACTICES

The client should examine related issues, including:
   i. Money manager fees and annual mutual fund expenses
   ii. Trade execution expenses
   iii. Custodial charges, including custodial fees, transaction charges, and cash management fees
   iv. Consulting, administrative costs and fees, and other revenue-sharing arrangements that have been appropriately applied to offset recordkeeping and other administrative costs

PRACTICE STANDARDS   FFS §3.7

The investment policy statement defines appropriately structured, socially responsible investment strategies when applicable.

BEST PRACTICES

If it is determined that the client desires to incorporate socially responsible criteria, the criteria should be reflected in the IPS. If the investment portfolio is subject to fiduciary standards, the policy should reflect appropriate fiduciary constraints. High-net-worth investors may

incorporate socially responsible criteria related to their personal portfolio without reference to legal fiduciary standards. The standards may
include:
  i. Performing inclusionary and exclusionary screens, as directed
     by client
 ii. Directing shareholder activism, as directed by client
iii. Making economically targeted investments, as directed by client
 iv. Allocating investments to specific types of economic entities (e.g.,
     minority- and women-owned enterprises), as directed by client

Practice Standards   FFS §4.1

The investment strategy is implemented in compliance with the
required level of prudence.

Best Practices

a. It is the role of fiduciaries, with the assistance of consultants they
   engage as cofiduciaries, to define and manage a prudent investment
   process that addresses and manages the investment and administrative
   values necessary to achieve the investor's goals and objectives. This
   prudent investment process documents the due-diligence process and
   the criteria used in the selection and oversight of money managers.
b. The process should be appropriate to the nature of the investment
   portfolio(s) and the client's circumstances and should be consistent
   for all investments.
c. The minimum due-diligence process for the evaluation and selection
   of money managers incorporates certain screens.
     i. Consistency of rolling one-, three-, and five-year returns of the
        manager, relative to the median AIMR-compliant return of the
        manager's peer group.
    ii. Five- to seven-year investment performance adjusted for risk:
        alpha or Sharpe ratio relative to the median alpha or Sharpe
        ratio for the manager's peer group.
   iii. Inception date of the investment product: the appropriate
        threshold is three years. Investment statistics such as alpha,
        Sharpe ratio, and standard deviation require a minimum of
        twelve observations before a meaningful calculation and obser-
        vation can be made.
    iv. Correlation of the investment product to the asset class, or peer
        group, being implemented.
        Manager selection is based on the premise that the man-
        ager will adhere to a specific investment management style or

strategy, as that makes it possible to manage risk. There are no industry standards for determining a money manager's investment management style or peer group. This makes it virtually impossible to track a manager across multiple databases. Some databases evaluate a manager's style by the securities held, others may use the pattern of performance, others may not assign a mandate to a peer group unless it is a good fit, while still others assign all managers to a peer group.

v. Database providers should examine both quantitative and qualitative data on the manager, as well as interview the managers to confirm that the information on record is accurate.

vi. Total assets in the investment product being considered: the threshold screen for this consideration is that at least $100 million is presently being managed in a manner consistent with the investment mandate being evaluated.

vii. Holdings consistent with style: 80 percent of the securities should be from the broad asset class associated with the product.

viii. Fees and expenses associated with the investment product.

The industry has never drawn a line in the sand to establish "reasonable" expense. When fees for a particular peer group are ranked from least expensive (1st percentile) to most expensive (100th percentile), a reasonable line can be drawn at the 50th percentile. Reasonability is the standard. The move to net-of-fees reporting makes this less of a concern as managers who provide better net returns can charge more without conflict

ix. Organizational stability—manager and research group tenure. It is important to establish whether the main driver of the investment process is the portfolio manager or the research group.

- The investment teams must be in place for at least two years.
- There is no pending litigation.
- There are no internal management struggles.
- There are no recent changes in ownership.
- There is rapid growth or loss in assets.

d. The investor should become familiar with the virtue of diversifying across multiple subasset classes or peer groups.

e. The investor should be familiar with the appropriate application of index funds and their cost/benefit trade-off with active management.

PRACTICE STANDARDS
FFS §4.2

The fiduciary is following applicable "safe harbor" provisions.

BEST PRACTICES

a. If the investment decisions are being managed by the engagement of an investment adviser/consultant, then the investor/fiduciary is insulated from certain liabilities associated with being an investment counsel. If the adviser/consultant manages the investment-decisions, then there are certain generally recognized provisions to the "safe harbor" rules.

    i. The investor/fiduciary or the adviser acting as cofiduciary engages professional money managers as prudent experts to make investment decisions in accordance to the investment mandates established by the investment process. Money managers acting as prudent experts are regulated financial service entities, including banks, insurance companies, registered investment advisers, and registered investment companies (mutual funds). There is pending pension-reform legislation that also will recognize registered representatives as appropriate sources of expert advice, serving in similar investment fiduciary capacities.

    ii. The prudent experts must be selected by following a documented due-diligence process.

    iii. The prudent expert engaged to make investment decisions is given discretion over the assets allocated to the investment mandate.

    iv. The prudent expert engaged to make investment decisions acknowledges cofiduciary status by signing a services agreement and the investment policy statement.

       Mutual funds are governed by their prospectus and thus are excluded from signing the IPS. However, the selection of mutual fund investments should also follow a selection process similar to that of investment managers and the stated goals and objectives of the IPS. The investor/fiduciary and/or the adviser acting as a cofiduciary should keep the most recent copy of the mutual fund's prospectus.

    v. The investor/fiduciary or the adviser acting as cofiduciary must monitor the prudent expert's investment-decision process to ensure the prudent expert is performing the agreed-upon tasks.

    vi. The investor must be provided at least three different investment options for each investment mandate, each merited by its own risk/return, affording the opportunity for prudent diversification.

    vii. Investors should, if they desire, receive sufficient education on the different investment options available that are appropriate per the IPS, so that they can make informed investment decisions. Investor education should include:

- Each investment option's most recent offering document and marketing materials or similar descriptive document
- A general description of the investment objectives and risk/return characteristics of each investment option
- Information on the fees and expenses associated with each investment option
- The impact on diversification of the proposed investment, displayed graphically
- Portfolio statistics, such as the alpha, Sharpe ratio, and standard deviation of each investment option or asset class
- Potential cross-calculation issues

viii. Investors must be provided counsel that affords them the opportunity to adjust their investment strategy and associated asset allocation as is appropriate to market conditions, within the guidelines of stated investment objectives.

PRACTICE STANDARDS   FFS §4.3

Investment vehicles are appropriate for the portfolio size.

BEST PRACTICES

a. Retail portfolios with assets of less than $50,000 should use individual securities, mutual funds, exchange-traded funds (ETFs), and folios. Diversification is the primary consideration.
b. High-net-worth and middle-market institutional portfolios with assets between $500,000 and $25 million use ETFs, folios, and separate-account managers. The adherence to investment management style discipline, the lot accounting, and the cost structure of investment vehicles used to execute a specific investment mandate are primary considerations. Given the following suggested separate-account investment minimums per each investment mandate, the use of separate accounts in portfolio construction requires larger accounts.

Type of Equities	Investment Minimums
Large-cap equities	$ 100,000
Small- to midcap equities	250,000
International equities	250,000
Intermediate fixed income	1,000,000
Global fixed income	5,000,000

A small number of firms with massive operational scale have reduced separate-account investment minimums to $50,000, which greatly increases their application in the high-net-worth and middle-market institutional investor market. With the advent of multidiscipline accounts (MDAs), which contain several investment disciplines in one account, some separate-account managers are available at $2,000. Notwithstanding the advantages of separate accounts, lower investment minimums should never supersede the investment merit of the manager.

c. Ultrahigh-net-worth and institutional portfolios with assets greater than $25 million should use MDAs, ETFs, folios, alternative investments, separate accounts, and hedge funds, managed futures, real estate, private equities, venture capital. The cost and tax efficiency of the investment vehicles used in portfolio construction is the primary consideration in excluding mutual funds. The specific circumstance of the investor may entail restricted stock, stock options, and other assets that must be monitored and managed, but are client central rather than adviser driven.

d. Separate accounts (institutional) versus managed accounts (wrap-fee programs). The terms "separate accounts" and "managed accounts" are used interchangeably, but there are differences.

The money manager's performance will vary between managed accounts and separate accounts because the cost differential in management fees is significantly lower in institutional and ultrahigh-net-worth accounts. This is mitigated by firms (e.g., Merrill Lynch, Smith Barney) with large-scale managed-account businesses that have used their scale to drive down management fees. Typically, if there is more than a 50 basis-point difference in performance not attributable to pricing breaks, the investor or the adviser acting as a cofiduciary should determine if there is a material difference between the managed-account and separate-account investment process of the prudent experts being considered.

   i. Investors or advisers acting on the investor's behalf should ascertain that the same person is responsible for the creation of the institutional track record and the managed-account records.

   ii. Investors or advisers acting on the investor's behalf should ascertain the number of securities in a separate account (typically 86) and in a managed account (typically 36).

   iii. Investors or advisers acting on the investor's behalf should ascertain whether securities trades will be executed in blocks with institutional clients (which translates into better execution at lower costs) or whether trades will flow back to the broker-dealer sponsoring the managed account who is held to best execution.

    iv. Investors or advisers acting on the investor's behalf should ascertain whether the prudent experts (money managers) engaged to make investment decisions have the capacity for tax-lot portfolio management. If the money manager is not tracking the adjusted basis of the individual securities within the portfolio, then it is arguably difficult for the manager to claim that a fully tax-sensitive strategy is being employed. The money manager should be able to accommodate tax-loss harvesting, tax-loss carryforwards, and year-end tax planning.

e. Technical considerations in using separate accounts.

    i. Electronic protocol: Investors or advisers acting on the investor's behalf should ascertain what will be the electronic protocol that will link the money manager, custodian, and fiduciary and facilitate the production of performance reports for independents. More important, who will prepare it, the manager or a consultant? This common protocol should be Web based (not Web enabled) to facilitate continuous comprehensive implied by regulatory mandate. This allows all parties to review account data on a daily basis, if not in real time, as desired by the client.

    ii. Time until fully invested: Investors or advisers acting on the investor's behalf should ascertain how long it will take for the money manager to fully invest portfolio assets allocated to the investment manager's stated strategy and philosophy.

    iii. Investors or advisers acting on the investor's behalf should determine how the money manager seeks best price and execution in trading securities within their accounts.

- Money managers have a fiduciary responsibility to seek the best strike price and best commission for each trade.
- It is an acceptable practice that money managers may use a particular brokerage firm to generate soft dollars to defray the cost of research. However, when the bulk of all trades are going through one brokerage firm, it is likely the manager is not seeking the best execution.

    iv. Proxy voting: The investor has a responsibility to assure proxy votes are properly executed. The most expeditious way of handling proxy voting is to delegate the responsibility to the money managers, who have discretion over the funds they manage. Because they have been engaged to make investment decisions, they should be the best judges of the impact of the proxy vote on the investor's assets with which they have been entrusted.

v. Low-cost-basis and restricted stock: Having a money manager un-
wind low-cost-basis and restricted stock over the appropriate time
periods can be a great advantage to high-net-worth investors.
- Will the money manager accept tax-lot information on a low-
cost-basis and/or restricted stock? Trading may be restricted
by statute.
- Will the manager provide tax-lot accounting and reporting?

vi. Managing the transition from one manager to another: Will the
manager review the portfolio holdings of the previous manager
so as to avoid fully liquidating the previous portfolio, only to
have to buy back some of its holdings? This reduces both taxable gains and overall portfolio expenses.

vii. Performance report: The investor should request an AIMR-
compliant performance report from the money manager, the
custodian, and, if appropriate, the investment management
consultant/adviser who acts as a cofiduciary. Having different
parties calculate performance on the same portfolio can help
triangulate and locate reporting errors.

viii. Tax-efficient strategy: Ascertain what strategies the money
manager will employ to reduce tax liability.
- Buying low-dividend stocks.
- Harvesting losses regularly to offset external and internal
taxable gains.
- Implementing an appropriately low turnover strategy, ensuring the aggregate turnover of the entire client assets can be
managed tax efficiently.
- Liquidating high-cost-basis positions first.

Matching losses against gains in real time, deferring recognition of
gains when losses aren't available or when a client tax mandate fa-
cilitates limited gains recognition, selling fixed-income securities to
ensure gains are taxed at capital gains rates.

PRACTICE STANDARDS   FFS §4.4

A due-diligence process is followed in selecting service providers,
including the custodian.

BEST PRACTICES

a. The role of the custodian is to hold securities for safekeeping, report on
holdings and transactions (capital actions), collect interest and dividends,
and, if required, execute trades. At the retail level, the custodian is typi-

cally a brokerage firm holding securities in street name commingled with the brokerage firm's other assets. To protect the assets, brokerage firms are required to obtain insurance from the Securities Investor Protection Corporation (SIPC). Most institutional investors choose trust companies as custodians. The primary benefit is that the assets are held in a separate account and are not commingled with other assets in the institution. Investors or advisers acting on the investor's behalf should:

i. Ascertain the financial stability of the custodian.

ii. Ascertain the expense ratio associated with the cash management vehicle that will be used. (Expense ratios range 8–80 basis points.)

iii. Ascertain the level of detail the custodian provides in its monthly statement. Do you see the name of the broker/dealer used for each transaction, the strike price of the security being purchased or sold, and the commission paid?

iv. Ascertain if the custodian is providing corrected year-end statements for mutual funds reflecting the year-end dividend payment, which impacts mutual fund pricing.

v. Ascertain if the custodian will provide tax reporting, which should reduce the pain and cost of tax reporting for the investor.

vi. Ascertain if the custodian will provide performance reporting. This is often not part of standard custodial services, but if negotiated as a condition of doing business, the additional charge is typically nominal.

PRACTICE STANDARDS   FFS §5.1

Periodic performance reports compare the performance of money managers against appropriate peer-group benchmark comparatives and investment policy statement objectives.

BEST PRACTICES

a. Performance monitors report on the full range of investment and administrative values that constitute the comprehensive nature of the adviser's counsel. They should incorporate sufficient information to evaluate the investment strategy's strengths and weaknesses in achieving the goals and objectives stated in investment policy. Performance monitors are the written substantiation that advisers are fulfilling their fiduciary responsibility to monitor all aspects of an investment strategy investment policy. The objectives of performance monitors are:

i. Confirm the mutually agreed-upon goals and objectives of the investment policy and facilitate effective communication between investors, advisers acting as cofiduciaries, money managers, and other service vendors.

ii. Facilitate the evaluation of the asset-allocation strategy as directed by the IPS with respect to the portfolio's risk tolerance and modeled return expectations.

iii. Support the qualitative and quantitative judgment about the continued confidence or lack of confidence of the money manager's ability. Combine the science of performance measurement with the art of performance evaluation.

iv. Facilitate effective communication between all parties involved to determine the continued appropriateness of the overall investment policy.

b. Frequency of monitor: No frequency of monitoring has been specified, but the concept of continuous, comprehensive counsel would suggest a monitor should be provided frequently on an informal basis as a practical management tool, preferably quarterly or more often as justified due to portfolio or market consideration.

c. Investors or their advisers acting as cofiduciaries should establish performance objectives according to their mandate for each money manager and cite these objectives in the IPS or within manager-specific addendums.

d. At least quarterly, investors or their advisers acting as cofiduciaries should review manager performance to determine if it conforms to the performance objectives.

i. Ascertain if the manager is adhering to the guidelines set forth in the IPS.

ii. Ascertain if there have been material changes in the manager's organization, investment philosophy, or personnel.

iii. Ascertain if any legal or regulatory-agency proceedings may affect the manager.

e. Underperformance: The IPS should describe actions taken when managers fail to meet established criteria. Criteria for taking action should be in the context of long-term performance, not short-term fluctuations.

i. Watch list—Managers who underperform but do not warrant termination are put on a watch list based on:

- Performance below that of their median peer group as measured by a risk-and style-adjusted benchmark over a one-, three-, and five-year cumulative period
- Five-year risk-adjusted return (alpha or Sharpe ratio) below the peer group's median risk-adjusted return
- Change in professionals managing the portfolio

- Significant decrease or increase in assets
- Deviation from stated style or strategy
- Increase in fees and expenses
- Extraordinary event that interferes with the manager's ability to fulfill role

ii. Watch-list evaluation:
  - A letter to manager asking for an analysis of the underperformance
  - An analysis of recent transactions, holdings, and portfolio characteristics to gain insight into underperformance or to check for a change in style
  - Optional: A meeting with the money manager, which may be conducted on site, to gain insight into organizational changes and any changes in strategy or discipline or cause for underperformance

iii. Minimum manager reporting requirements—each manager's performance should be reported against:
  - Appropriate peer groups with absolute and relative comparisons
  - Appropriate indices
  - Performance objectives cited in policy

PRACTICE STANDARDS   FFS §5.2

Periodic reviews are made of qualitative or organizational changes to money managers.

BEST PRACTICES

a. Ascertain if there has been turnover in the professional or service staff that would adversely affect the quality of service and investment results.

b. Ascertain if there has been a change in organizational structure through mergers or acquisitions (retention of investment professionals) that would adversely affect the quality of service and investment results.

c. Ascertain if the money manager provides the same or better service (such as real-time online access) than is available in the marketplace for comparable fees.

d. Ascertain if the money manager's reports contain all the information that is necessary and useful to the investor. Are reports provided on a consistent and timely basis?

e. Ascertain if the money manager consistently responds to information and service request on a timely basis. Do the responses contain the data requested?

f. Ascertain if the money manager's explanation of investment decisions and the factors considered are explained in a way investors can understand and monitor their holdings.

PRACTICE STANDARDS   FFS §5.3

Control procedures are in place to periodically review the money manager's policies for best execution, soft dollars, and proxy voting.

BEST PRACTICES

a. The fiduciary has a responsibility to control and account for investment expenses. The fiduciary or the adviser acting as a cofiduciary must therefore monitor:

   i. Best execution practices are followed in securities transactions, making sure the investor secures the best price for the security without regard to whether the broker-dealer or bank functions in an agency (broker) or in a principal (dealer) relationship to the investor.

   ii. Soft dollars should not be excessive—costs above the actual commission that the broker-dealer incurred to offset the cost of research, consulting services, custodial services, rating or technical services, or subscriptions to investment periodicals that accrue to the benefit of the investor. Failure of the fiduciary to monitor soft-dollar expenditures and soft-dollar expenditures that do not directly benefit the investor is a breach of fiduciary responsibility. If the money manager who exercises discretion over the investor's account determines the total commission paid to execute trades was reasonable in relation to the value of brokerage and research services provided by the broker-dealer, then soft-dollar expenses incurred by paying commissions in excess of the actual commission incurred are allowed.

   iii. Proxy voting must be monitored and documented by the fiduciary. Typically, this responsibility is delegated to the money manager via instructions cited in investment policy. The investor must not only be able to review the manager's proxy voting procedures but must be able to review proxy-voting actions taken by the manager.

PRACTICE STANDARDS   FFS §5.4

Ascertain if fees paid for investment management are consistent with agreements and with the law.

BEST PRACTICES

a. Determine whether the payment of fees can be paid from portfolio assets.
b. Determine whether the fees are reasonable in light of the services provided.
  i. Money management fees vary widely depending on asset class, account size, and whether the account is to be managed separately or placed in a commingled or mutual fund.
  ii. Investment management fees in excess of the industry average should trigger a concern about a potential breach of fiduciary responsibility.

PRACTICE STANDARDS   FFS §5.5

Ascertain if finder's fees, 12b-1 fees, or other forms of compensation that have been paid for asset placement are appropriately applied, utilized, and documented.

BEST PRACTICES

a. There is a fiduciary responsibility to account for all dollars spent for services engaged, direct and indirect commissions in lieu of fees, off-set plans, or rebate plans, whether paid directly from the account or through soft dollars, 12b-1 fees, or other fee-sharing arrangements.
  i. Identify all parties being compensated for services engaged.
    • Custodian: holding, hypothecating, and safeguarding securities
    • Brokerage firm: executing trades
    • Money manager: managing investment decisions
    • Adviser/consultant: developing and managing overall strategy and adherence of the principles therein
  ii. Determine if compensation received by service providers meets a reasonable test and confirm client is aware of all fees being charged.
b. In a bundled, all-inclusive wrap fee program, the four cost components of (1) the custodian, (2) the brokerage firm, (3) the money managers, and (4) the adviser/consultant must be evaluated independently to ensure no component is receiving unreasonable compensation.
c. Exceptional responsibilities and value-added services entail reasonable additional compensation.

PART FIVE

CLIENTS

Ask investment professionals about key issues in managing clients and the responses are likely to be as eclectic a mix as clients themselves. The net we cast in convening our *Think Tank* on clients brought together an Australian practitioner's discussion of applied behavioral finance, an East Coast money manager's insights on issues related to black investors and the stock market, and a Midwestern financial adviser's yardstick for measuring how well he's done his job. The authors' backgrounds are as diverse as their views—two academics, a practitioner, a former planner turned software developer, and a money manager—but their ideas are equally powerful, especially because they're coupled with practical applications for the practitioner.

Neal E. Cutler

Neal Cutler's official title—chair in financial gerontology—should pique the interest of any professional financial adviser. This new field of academic study focuses on the increasingly important linkages between gerontological research and financial planning. Although practitioners recognize the shift in thinking regarding retirement as a process rather than an event, the transition is relatively new. As a consequence, the profession is only just beginning to identify the planning challenges raised by this transition.

The good news is that help is on the way in the form of practical research emanating from the new field of financial gerontology. In his chapter, Cutler introduces us to one important example of the issues being studied, namely the interaction of the retirement decision with health insurance and long-term care planning. Practitioners and their clients can only benefit by developing awareness and ultimately an understanding of the insights provided by financial gerontologists.

Geoff Davey

Geoff Davey is an Australian planner/software developer whom we've had the privilege of getting to know over the past few years. Like us, Davey is a passionate fan of behavioral economics. In fact, he was so enamored of the power of behavioral insights to improve financial planning practices that his firm has evolved from a traditional planning practice to a software-development company focused solely on perfecting behavior-based risk-tolerance tools for practitioners. In the process, he has become one of the most thoughtful commentators on behavioral issues related to financial planning.

Davey notes that most advisers implicitly assume that their clients are economically rational investors. In doing so, advisers ignore the challenges to traditional economic thinking raised by the discoveries of behavioral economists. Davey argues that practitioners are both professionally and legally obligated to understand behavioral influences and incorporate that understanding into their daily practice; we agree. Unfortunately, lack of knowledge, discomfort with psychological issues, and a dearth of practitioner-friendly and methodologically sound strategies for dealing with these issues have hindered the process. In risk-tolerance evaluation, for example—which is a key element in financial planning—improper understanding of a client's behavioral constraints often results in inappropriate investment allocations. Davey offers a process for assessing risk tolerance; in fact, his chapter is a case study, based on the development of his firm's risk-profiling system, of the elements that need to be considered in planning.

Ross Levin

Ross Levin is a longtime friend and an eloquent and passionate spokesperson for holistic planning. His book, *The Wealth Management Index,* is one of the seminal thought pieces in our profession. Although the book is a successful publication and widely read by the elite of the profession, its message of comprehensive wealth management deserves still wider recognition. Clients expect and often demand performance benchmarks related to their investments, but they rarely demand or even request a performance benchmark related to the successful achievement of their overall planning objectives. Unfortunately, not only are clients ill served by focusing on individual investments while ignoring their life goals; practitioners who focus on market benchmarks are subject to the risk of catastrophic loss of clients during bear markets. In the course of the market debacle in 2000–2002, market-based practitioners hemorrhaged business; holistic advisers thrived.

As Statman notes in his discussion of behavioral finance, when advisers guide investors—thinking not about risks and returns but about their fears, their aspirations, and the errors they're likely to make—they promote both wealth and well-being. That's why we asked Levin to update his thoughts on performance measurement for the *Think Tank*. You may not agree with the specifics of Levin's categories or their weightings, but that will in no way diminish the importance of this chapter to your practice. Levin provides the framework for you to assess and manage your client's plans and goals; you need only customize his powerful concept to match your style and planning philosophy.

Meir Statman

The field of behavioral economics (and its kid brother, behavioral finance) was "born" with the publication of a 1979 paper by two academics, Daniel Kahneman and Amos Tversky, introducing the concept of prospect theory. In less than twenty-five years, the field has earned an ample share of academic respectability. Indeed, in 2002, Kahneman, a psychologist, was awarded the Nobel Prize in Economics "for having integrated insights from psychological research into economic science, especially concerning human judgment and decision making under uncertainty."

We're not sure when this new understanding of investors' behavioral characteristics first began to play a role in financial planning, but our introduction to the concept came back in 1995, while researching for my book *Wealth Management*. We found the insights of Kahneman and the few other academics then working in the field so impressive that we subsequently devoted significant time and effort to learning more. The more we learned, the more we were persuaded that behavioral economics is the single most important field of investment-related studies for financial-planning practitioners—important to both our clients' financial and emotional well-being and to our businesses' financial security.

As a leading academic in the field of behavioral finance and professor of finance at Santa Clara University, Meir Statman is in a unique position to help us translate academic findings into practical and pragmatic ideas that can benefit both our clients and our businesses. In "Lessons of Behavioral Finance," he does just that. Noting that clients "always want both wealth and well-being," Statman offers practical insights and strategies for dealing with clients' all-too-human behavioral quirks. Having based our firm's entire investment planning and management process on these insights and strategies, we know that they work and serve as valuable tools for attracting, managing, and retaining clients.

John W. Rogers, Jr.

John Rogers is chairman and chief executive officer of Ariel Capital Management. He is passionate about the need for practitioners to serve the African American community, and in his chapter he shares the results of his firm's annual surveys on the investing habits of black Americans. The findings are important for those who would reach out to this steadily growing yet consistently overlooked market.

CHAPTER 18

Financial Gerontology and Employee Benefits

NEAL E. CUTLER

The graying of America suggests several notable implications for the interaction of gerontological dynamics with business activity. In turn, societal preparation for such interaction points to increasingly important linkages between gerontological research and financial practice. Well-documented trends in population aging and individual aging point to important transitions in the way the country does business in the broad domains of health, wealth, and work.

This chapter looks at just one of these three domains: *work*—and the challenge to human resources management precipitated by the increasingly complex nature of employee benefits. We examine three sets of interrelated financially focused benefits and planning decisions confronted by both employees and human resources professionals: the retirement decision, health insurance, and long-term care planning.

The Wealth Span

Among the key stage-setting dynamics of the impact of individual aging and population aging on financial decision making are historical changes in the modern "wealth span." The wealth span is a heuristic model developed to illustrate two fundamental sets of changes in how individuals (as workers, consumers, savers, consumers, investors) make financial decisions.[1] One set of changes focuses on the relative *balance* in the number of years between the accumulation stage and the expenditure stage of a person's wealth span. The second set of changes focuses on the

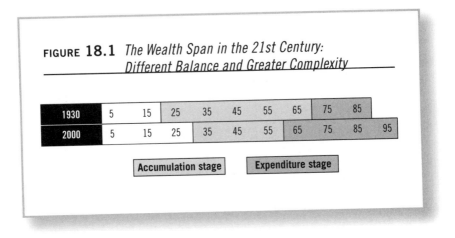

FIGURE **18.1** *The Wealth Span in the 21st Century: Different Balance and Greater Complexity*

| 1930 | 5 | 15 | 25 | 35 | 45 | 55 | 65 | 75 | 85 | |
| 2000 | 5 | 15 | 25 | 35 | 45 | 55 | 65 | 75 | 85 | 95 |

Accumulation stage   Expenditure stage

increasing complexity of the twenty-first-century wealth span.

The wealth span is illustrated in **FIGURE 18.1.** The specific years in the model, 1930 and 2000, are not especially important. More important are the changes from "back then" to "nowadays." In this simplified model of reality, we recognize, of course, that expenditures do take place in the accumulation stage and that savings and investing continue to take place in the expenditure stage. We use these two stages primarily to focus attention on key historical changes.

The change in the relative number of years each of the two stages lasts is especially critical for financial decision making. Back then (1930 or so) accumulation typically started when people were in their teens or early 20s and continued to their mid-60s, symbolized by the Social Security full-benefits age 65. Nowadays (circa 2000, symbolically), however, accumulation is typically delayed as we stay in school longer. The accumulation stage ends early nowadays because of patterns of earlier retirement, substantially earlier than age 65 for most workers.

The older (expenditure) side of the wealth span model has also undergone change. Back then the expenditure stage formally started around age 65, and lasted until the mid-80s or so. The expenditure stage is longer nowadays: it starts earlier, and because of increasing life expectancy, it lasts longer.

Even acknowledging the simplified view of the life-course behavior portrayed in the wealth span model, the implications of this change in balance in the number of years in the two stages are apparent: compared to back then, workers (consumers, investors, et cetera) nowadays have relatively fewer years to accumulate wealth, and the wealth that is thereby accumulated must last for a longer expenditure period.

This change in the balance of years, however, is trumped by a second set of changes—the changes in the *complexity* of the modern wealth span.

Some of the biggest of these complexities are beyond the scope of this paper, such as the implications for finance and financial literacy of the transition of American pensions from defined-benefit to defined-contribution pension systems[2] and the complexities created by the transition from single-earner households to dual-earner households earning both two current incomes and multiple future pension credits (together with investments and home equity).[3]

Several of these complexities, however, *are* directly relevant to decisions concerning employee benefits. We now turn to a brief examination of three of them, involving retirement, health insurance, and long-term care planning.

Retirement

In an undergraduate social gerontology class a couple of years ago, a student expressed exasperation with American social policy (or perhaps with me), demanding to know if U.S. retirement policy was "schizophrenic." On the one hand, the 1978 amendments to the Age Discrimination in Employment Act outlawed age-based mandatory retirement in most occupations; most people now have the legal right to work 'til they drop. On the other hand, Social Security allows early retirement via the age-62 reduced benefit option, and other federal rules tell workers that age $59^{1}/_2$ is when they can start making withdrawals from their individual retirement accounts without penalty.

The common denominator, of course, is *choice,* not schizophrenia. Social policy has given American workers a range of employment/retirement options, at least in law. Of course, the direction and degree to which any individual can make use of these options depend on a number of personal, health, financial, family, and other factors. The complexity of the retirement-decision-making process is well represented in a large body of qualitative and quantitative, as well as academic and applied, research.[4] For our purposes, however, it's the profile of behavioral outcomes of the complexity of the decision process that demonstrates the magnitude of the challenge to human resources professionals who are responsible for working with middle-aged and older workers.

FIGURE 18.2 is drawn from *American Perceptions of Aging in the 21st Century,* a large-scale national survey conducted in January 2000 by the National Council on the Aging.[5] This study measured retirement in two ways. Early in the survey a self-identification question was asked: Do you consider yourself to be retired or not retired? Toward the end of the interview, when the usual personal demographic information was collected, the traditional labor force participation question was asked: Are you working, retired, student, housewife, et cetera?

FIGURE 18.2 Exercising Choice: Retirement Behavior

AGE OF THE RESPONDENT	NOT RETIRED	RETIRED AND WORKING	COMPLETELY RETIRED
18–34	10%	0%	0%
35–53	95	4	1
54–64	66	14	20
65–75	21	25	54

The study then combined responses to these two questions, yielding three categories, the age distribution of which is shown in Figure 18.2. Not surprisingly, most younger respondents were "not retired"—meaning that they said "no" to the self-identification question and also said "working" to the labor force participation question. The most intriguing outcome of social policy choice is seen in the 65–75 age group. To be sure, more than half (54 percent) identified themselves as retired and also responded "retired" to the labor force participation question. Fully 25 percent of this traditionally retired age group, however, is *both retired and working:* that is, they identify themselves as retired but also are still working. (Whether they *want to work* or *have to work* is a separate question, of course.)

The bottom line is clearly one of complexity. Retirement is no longer an *event* but a *process,* and in many cases it's a multiyear and multifactor decision process. As such, it not only illustrates but it also symbolizes the complexity of the financial-planning and decision-making process faced by the workers as well as by the human resources and financial gerontology professionals who must counsel and advise them.

Health Insurance and Job Lock

Just about all individuals and families who have health insurance obtain it through their job. As **FIGURE 18.3** demonstrates, almost two-thirds (64 percent) of all adults under age 65 and 90 percent of all who have private insurance get that insurance through employment. Health insurance is no longer a "fringe benefit." Most of the nationally reported labor disputes over the past five years focused more on health insurance issues than on traditional labor-management conflicts over wages and work rules. For many workers, the decision to change jobs is increasingly influenced more by the comparison (including eligibility) of health insurance benefits between current and potential employment than by such traditional reasons for changing jobs as salary, location, or career advancement.

FIGURE 18.3 *Employment Sources of Health Insurance*
(1995, adults under age 65)

Private—Employer	64%
Private—Not employer	7
Public	17
Uninsured	17
	105% (some have multiple sources)

Insured, Private	
Employer	90%
Not employer	10

The term "job lock" describes a situation where an employee decides not to change jobs because of health insurance benefits—"a reduction in workers' willingness to quit their jobs arising from the risk of losing health coverage."[6] Job lock is relevant to workers of any age, and both anecdotal and empirical evidence suggests that it's an increasingly important aspect of employment decisions.[7] For gerontological benefits planning, however, job lock adds additional layers of complexity, for at least four reasons.

1 Retirement traditionally is a more or less permanent move out of the labor force, not simply a move to another employer and another health insurance package. Although Figure 18.2 suggests that there are changing age patterns of working versus nonworking, the number of persons who are both "retired and working" could also signal a desire to keep working in order to retain health insurance.

2 Health insurance in retirement is directly connected to Medicare. Consider the "cohort health psychology" of today's pre-retirees. Those who are 55–60 years old in 2004 (born 1944–1949) were 16–21 years old when Medicare became law in 1965. Consequently, these middle-agers spent their entire accumulation stage presuming that there would be a national program of health insurance for them when they got to age 65—or so it might have appeared to them three decades ago—but the situation now is obviously more complex.

3 Back then Medicare eligibility was set at age 65 alongside the normal Social Security full-benefits retirement age. Nowadays most people retire at age 62 or age $59^1/2$. Because Medicare eligibility remains at age 65, job lock may affect the retirement decision.

4 In previous years, employers often paid for or subsidized health insurance for their younger-than-age-65 retirees. In 1990 the Financial Accounting Standards Board (FASB) implemented a new accounting standard that requires companies to integrate estimated retiree health costs into each year's current accounts. Given the large and growing size of these financial obligations, many companies have scaled back their retiree health insurance benefits or ended them altogether.

Recent research suggests that job lock is becoming a factor in the already complex set of influences that affect the retirement decision. The evidence comes from the fifth annual (2002) Health Confidence Survey (HCS), developed by the Employee Benefit Research Institute.[8] Although the main subject of the survey is Americans' attitudes toward health plans and coverage in general, several questions were included to focus on the connection between health insurance and the retirement decision. About a fifth of the national sample of one thousand adults say they're retired, so the survey could ask both projective and retrospective questions.

As a general background to the job-lock issue, the HCS asked about the overall importance of health insurance to the respondent's retirement decision. Retirees were asked: When determining the age at which to retire [those not retired were asked: When you expect to retire], how much did you think [or will you think] about access to health insurance benefits? The importance of health insurance was substantial for both groups—54 percent of retirees and 48 percent of pre-retirees said they think about health insurance and retirement age "a lot"; 25 percent and 26 percent, respectively, said "a little," and 20 percent and 15 percent, respectively, said "none."

In this context, the survey asked a number of questions about employees' expectation of employer- (or union-) provided health insurance. About half of pre-retirees expected some kind of provided or subsidized health insurance when they retire.

But the central job-lock information comes from a question that was asked of those who plan to retire before age 65 and who said also that their employer currently provides some kind of "bridge" health insurance between retirement and Medicare eligibility: Would you retire before you are eligible for Medicare if a former employer or union does not provide health insurance benefits for retirees?

No	60%
Yes	31
Don't know	10

Although these responses are in the realm of personal speculation and not behavior, the pattern is fairly clear: twice as many employees would modify their current plans to retire early if health insurance will not be readily available.

Planning for Long-Term Care

Most of the political discussion of aging and its coverage in the press focus either on the consequences of population aging (the "crisis" that will be caused by huge numbers of Social Security and Medicare beneficiaries in the near future) or on the consequences of individual aging (for example, the increasing number of Alzheimer's victims). Less often discussed is a third view of aging—*family aging.*

Family aging refers to the changing age structure of the American family. In the context of the growing complexity of financial gerontological planning decisions, family aging here refers to the expanding responsibilities of middle-aged children. Indeed, family aging directs our attention to yet another dimension of middle age. Aside from the chronological, psychological, and financial elements of middle age (for example, empty nest and retirement with pension), the longer our parents are alive, the longer we are the generation "in the middle."

Planning for long-term care thus becomes a two-headed set of choices and decisions. Middle-agers are planning for their own future long-term care as well as, in many instances, the care of elderly parents. While long-term care insurance is not yet a widely purchased consumer item, it's beginning to be recognized as an employee benefit.[9] And even (or, perhaps, *especially*) when not offered by or through the employer, employee-benefits counselors must be ready to answer questions about this important and expensive aspect of older age.

The trends in **FIGURE 18.4** were developed by demographer Peter Uhlenberg, who used historical census data on birthrates, marriage rates, and similar data to establish rates of surviving parents of adult children.[10] In 1900, only 39 percent of 50-year-olds had at least one parent alive, rising to 80 percent by 1990. Perhaps the more dramatic trend is for "60-year-old kids." As recently as 1940, only 13 percent of 60-year-olds had at least one parent alive, compared with almost half (44 percent) by 1990.

These historical trends in family aging punctuate the complexity of the benefits decisions facing middle-aged workers and the financial professionals who counsel them. Of course, not all of the middle-agers represented in Figure 18.4 may in fact feel emotional or financial responsibility for their aging parents. But what is apparent is that these additional "middle-generational" pressures come at a point in the wealth span when

FIGURE 18.4 _Family Aging_
Increasing longevity and middle-aged "children"

	1900	1940	1990
AT AGE 50			
at least 1 parent alive	39%	52%	80%
both alive	4%	8%	27%
AT AGE 60			
at least 1 parent alive	7%	13%	44%

the traditional responsibilities of middle-age decision making are already becoming increasingly complex—including, as discussed here, choices surrounding retirement and health insurance.

Benefits and Decisions: A Final Empirical Observation

As a final indication of the increasingly complex world of planning and benefits decisions, **FIGURE 18.5** shows some intriguing evidence of the worries and concerns that middle-aged and older persons have about their financial future. The traditional goal of financial professionals is to ensure that their clients do not outlive their money. Calculations of replacement ratios and layered investments with different rates of returns—alongside the choice of whether or not to annuitize an investment—are all directed to the fear of outliving one's money.

The _American Perceptions of Aging in the 21st Century_ survey mentioned earlier included a set of questions asking about worries in older age:

_Think about your life at age 75. [For respondents age 71 or older: Think about what your life will be like 10 years from now.] How worried are you about _____—very worried, somewhat worried, or not worried at all?_

Among the possible worries included were two directly relevant to the increasing complexity of financial decisions:
- Outliving your pension and savings
- Spending all your money on long-term care

Figure 18.5 contrasts "worried" (combining "somewhat" and "very") with "not worried at all" and shows that in 2000, Americans were (a) worried about both but (b) more worried about spending all their money on

FIGURE **18.5** *"Think About Your Life at Age 75: How Worried Are You About:"*

AGE	OUTLIVE MY PENSION	SPEND IT ALL ON LTC	GREATER LTC WORRY
44–53	53%	58%	+1
54–64	46	58	+12
65–75	34	49	+15

long-term care. Interestingly, the gap between these two financial worries increases with age. Perhaps the most parsimonious interpretation of this "worry gap" focuses on the "fear of the unknown."[11] For older persons, both expenditure patterns and income resources are relatively in place; it's both the cost and need for long-term care that are the daunting unknowns. Middle-agers, by contrast, are still relatively in the dark about their future pension resources and future expenditure patterns—in addition to the uncertainties about personal health, parental health, and the future costs of health care and long-term care. Yet it's precisely in middle age that a series of employment, benefit, retirement, and related personal and financial choices must be made, that is, *complexity.*

As noted earlier, the transitions that are characteristic of an aging society include transitions in health, wealth, and work. While these are analytically separable domains, this brief review of the complexity of financial decisions concerning employee benefits suggests that, in fact, these several transitions are inextricably intertwined—and require the combined multidisciplinary skills and efforts of financial and gerontological professionals to develop the expertise required for an aging society.

Chapter Notes

1. Neal E. Cutler, *Advising Mature Clients: The New Science of Wealth Span Planning* (Wiley, 2002).

2. Neal E. Cutler, "The False Alarms and Blaring Sirens of Financial Literacy: Middle-Agers' Knowledge of Retirement Income, Health Finance, and Long-Term Care," *Generations* 21 (Summer 1997): 34–40; Neal E. Cutler, "Divine Benefit vs. Divine Contribution Pension Plans: Approaches to Monitoring American Retirement Income Security over the Next Decade," *Journal of Applied Gerontology* 20 (Winter 2001): 480–507.

3. Neal E. Cutler, "Pensions," in *Encyclopedia of Gerontology*, 2nd ed., edited by James E. Birren, 261–269 (Academic Press, 1996); Neal E. Cutler, "Financial Planning," in *Encyclopedia of Aging*, 2nd ed., edited by George L. Maddox (Greenwood, 1996).

4. Lois A. Vitt, ed., *Encyclopedia of Retirement and Finance* (Greenwood, 2003).

5. Neal E. Cutler, Nancy A. Whitelaw, and Bonita L. Beattie, *American Perceptions of Aging in the 21st Century* (National Council on the Aging, 2002).

6. Federal Reserve Bank of San Francisco, "Health Insurance and the U.S. Labor Market," news release, April 13, 1998.

7. Jonathan Gruber and Brigitte C. Madrian, "Health Insurance, Labor Supply, and Job Mobility: A Critical Review of the Literature," National Bureau of Economic Research, NBER Working Paper No. W8817, February 2002.

8. Neal E. Cutler, " 'Job Lock' and Financial Planning: Health Insurance and the Retirement Decision," *Journal of Financial Service Professionals* 56 (November 2002): 33–36.

9. A major stimulus to employment-based group long-term care insurance was created with the establishment of a long-term care insurance program for federal employees in 2002. See "The Federal Long Term Care Insurance Program," http://www.ltcfeds.com/about/resource_library/documents/Newly_Eligible.pdf.

   Many academic institutions and state and local governments also offer group long-care insurance to their employees. For an overview, see Jordan Pfuntner and Elizabeth Dietz, "Long-Term Care Insurance Gains Prominence," *Compensation and Working Conditions Online*, U.S. Department of Labor Bureau of Labor Statistics, www.bls.gov/opub/cwc/cm20040123ar01p1.htm (posted January 28, 2004).

10. Peter Uhlenberg, "Mortality Decline in the Twentieth Century and Supply of Kin Over the Life Course," *Gerontologist* 36 (1996): 682–685.

11. Neal E. Cutler, "Retirement Planning and the Cost of Long-Term Care: Battling the Fear of the Unknown," *Journal of the American Society of CLU & ChFC* 50 (November 1996): 42–48.

CHAPTER 19

Assessing Risk Tolerance
A Micro-Behavioral Finance Case Study

GEOFF DAVEY

In 2002, one of the winners of the Nobel Prize in Economics was a *psychologist*—Princeton University's Daniel Kahneman. Kahneman and his close friend and colleague psychologist Amos Tversky, now deceased, are widely acknowledged as having founded the discipline of behavioral finance with their seminal paper, "Prospect Theory: An Analysis of Decision Under Risk."[1] The Royal Swedish Academy of Sciences cited Kahneman "for having integrated insights from psychological research into economic science, especially concerning human judgment and decision making under uncertainty."

Behavioral finance challenges traditional economic thinking on a number of fronts.

❑ It has proved that psychological costs and benefits are a major influence on the cost/benefit analysis that drives decision making and that these can be very different from the economic costs and benefits.

❑ It has also demonstrated that decision making suffers from misapplied heuristics (mental shortcuts), biases, and cognitive errors.

At a macroeconomic level, those framing government and corporate policy are starting to consider the realities of behavioral finance's likely impact on outcomes, and others are trying to profit from behavioral finance anomalies in markets.

At a microeconomic level, there has been little change. One would have expected financial advisers to be the group most interested in this new understanding of individual behavior. Some individual advisers have been quick to see the significance, but the profession as a whole has not. For example, there is nothing yet in competency standards about behavioral finance. At the very least, advisers should have some appreciation of their own financial psychology: first, know yourself. And in giving advice, advisers must be able to relate to their clients' financial psychology.

Yet much of the profession's accepted wisdom seems to be based on a traditional economic view of client motivation—in short, that the primary driver in clients' decision making is a universal desire to maximize expected net wealth. This is despite, for example, the real-world evidence of the existence of whole industries based on exactly the opposite premise. The insurance industry relies on its customers being willing to reduce their present (and expected) net wealth in order to avoid a major but improbable future financial loss. The gambling industry, and lotteries in particular, rely on their customers being willing to reduce present (and expected) net wealth in order to have a chance at a major but improbable future financial gain. And we know that many people buy both insurance policies and lottery tickets—the purchases being examples of desires to, respectively, avoid being poor and have a chance at being rich.

Avoiding being poor and hoping to be rich are both goals that should be addressed, but do they replace the goal of maximizing expected net wealth or are they an addition to it? Further, in advising a client, an adviser should be able to evaluate the relative strength of these desires and then be able to evaluate strategy alternatives in terms of those relative strengths.

Financial planning's promise is to assist clients in the achievement of life goals, with the first step usually being to assist clients in identifying, prioritizing, and articulating them. Unless advisers understand the psychological needs that drive life goals, the goals will not be clearly articulated and the promise will fall at the first hurdle. There is a general legal obligation on any provider of goods or services that those goods or services fit the purpose for which they are provided. A service that promises to assist clients in achieving their life goals but does not include a process for adequate articulation of those goals would seem to be in real danger of failing a fit-for-purpose test. A financial plan is not just about arriving at a destination but also about the journey being undertaken. Ends and means are both important, and psychological needs are relevant to both.

Many advisers have difficulty, however, dealing with the psychological issues inherent in the decisions clients face. This difficulty results partly from a reluctance to address psychological issues at all, partly from an insufficient understanding of psychological issues, and partly from a lack of user-friendly, robust methodologies for managing them. Some advisers exhibit a marked aversion to dealing with client psychology, as evidenced by overstatements such as "My clients don't want me psychoanalyzing them." But to ignore psychological needs means, in effect, that the plan is for the client's money rather than for the client.

Nowhere is this more evident than in how advisers deal with their clients' risk tolerance. But recent developments make it possible for clients' risk tolerance to be managed using robust, objective tools and methodologies. These developments represent a case study in how mainstream financial planning can apply scientific disciplines to the value-expressive client attributes that affect the financial-planning process.

Managing Risk Tolerance

The desire to feel safe is one of the strongest human needs. When safety is threatened, all else pales in significance until the danger has passed. Any individual is going to be discomforted if he finds himself in a situation that involves more risk than he would normally choose to take, and the bigger the gap between the two, the more intense the discomfort. Indeed, if you ask clients to rate their needs on a low-to-high scale, feeling safe will rate high—and for many clients, at the very top. Yet clients often are unwittingly following adviser-recommended strategies that involve risk beyond their tolerance.

Why is this so?

❑ Some advisers pay no regard to risk tolerance at all.

❑ Some advisers take the view that "I advise my client to do what I would do if I were in their shoes," thus substituting their own, usually higher, risk tolerance for that of their client.

❑ Advisers who've attempted to come to grips with their clients' risk tolerance have been handicapped by the lack of effective techniques for assessing risk tolerance and for applying such assessments in the financial-planning process.

However, it has become possible to manage clients' risk tolerance in the financial-planning process in a manner that's informed by behavioral finance and that employs a user-friendly, robust methodology. This means that not only do advisers have new techniques for managing clients' risk tolerance but both the development of the techniques and their application have led to a better understanding of risk tolerance. Accordingly, managing risk tolerance constitutes a case study in how the financial-planning process may accommodate other psychological considerations. The obligation to consider psychological needs does not mean advisers have to be psychologists any more than they have to be mathematicians, statisticians, or economists to manage investments.

But for those who still feel anxious about the prospect of dealing with psychological needs, the discussion that follows will illustrate that such anxieties are unfounded.

Defining Risk Tolerance

"Nothing tends so much to the advancement of knowledge as the application of a new instrument," said Sir Humphrey Davy, inventor and natural philosopher. If anything, Sir Humphrey understated the case. The advancement of knowledge actually begins with the attempt to build a new instrument. It is difficult to manage something effectively unless you can measure it objectively. So an objective measurement tool is required for effective management.

But before asking what would be an appropriate measuring tool, one must first be clear about what's being measured, and here lies the first difficulty to be overcome. "Risk tolerance" is a term in common usage, but there is no generally accepted definition. Rather it's one of those everyday concepts about which each of us has a slightly different understanding. Asked to define risk tolerance, advisers will say things like:

"It's the level of volatility an investor can tolerate."

"It is where someone feels comfortable on the risk/return continuum."

"It is the amount of loss someone will risk incurring."

While these statements relate to risk tolerance, they do not capture its meaning comprehensively.

A client's risk tolerance is relevant to an adviser in two general sets of circumstances: first, when the client is faced with a decision and, second, when the client is in a situation that involves risk. Decision making always involves choosing between alternative courses of action. There is risk in any course of action where the outcome is uncertain. Depending on the situation, the possible outcomes for the alternative courses of action may be all favorable, all unfavorable, or a mix of both. Thus,

- ❏ in some situations the choice will be between courses of action that have only favorable outcomes—a greater good choice;
- ❏ in other situations the choice will be between courses of action that have only unfavorable outcomes—a lesser evil choice; and
- ❏ in the balance, the choice will be between courses of action that collectively present a mix of both favorable and unfavorable outcomes.

Accordingly, risk tolerance can be defined as *the extent to which a person chooses to risk experiencing a less-favorable outcome in the pursuit of a more-favorable outcome.* With this definition, risk tolerance represents a trade-off on the continuum from minimizing unfavorable outcomes to maximizing favorable outcomes, not just an upper limit on unfavorable outcomes. "Risk preference" would perhaps be a better label for the attribute being described. "Tolerance" implies that risk is an undiluted negative. However, most people accept the universal truth of "Nothing ventured, nothing gained." It's simply a question of where each individual is comfortable with setting the balance point.

Broadly, risk tolerance can be seen as the sum of all the fear/greed trade-offs—between making the most of opportunities and securing financial well-being, between avoiding regret over losses incurred from taking too much risk and avoiding regret over gains missed through not taking enough risk, and so on. This definition was arrived at through consideration of decision making. Does it apply in the second general set of circumstances, when the client is in a situation that involves risk?

In risky situations, the threshold consideration is whether the client is discomforted by the level of risk being experienced because it's greater than her risk tolerance. If not, there is no issue. If so, then this is actually a decision point, in that the client is faced with the choice between continuing in the situation and trying to remove herself from it, and so the definition works here, too.

Of course, risk tolerance could be defined to mean something else entirely, and sometimes it is. But it would still be important for advisers to understand the value-expressive attribute being discussed here, namely, the extent to which their clients choose to risk experiencing a less favorable outcome in the pursuit of a more favorable outcome.

In fact, it's not sufficient to define risk tolerance in isolation without considering where it fits in relation to other constructs involving risk, and this is an area of much semantic/conceptual confusion. Some of the confusion has arisen because until recently there was no robust, objective technique for measuring risk tolerance. Accepted wisdom about the characteristics of risk tolerance was largely sourced from the personal opinions of individual advisers, based on their subjective observations of their clients. The lack of a robust, objective measurement technique meant that individual observations were unreliable and no large studies could be done. Some of the previously accepted wisdom now needs to be discarded.

For the present, it's time to consider how to measure risk tolerance.

Assessing Risk Tolerance

"Any serious discussion of risk is likely to be reminiscent of the story of the Tar Baby," Harold Evensky tells us in *Wealth Management: The Financial Advisor's Guide to Investing and Managing Your Client's Assets*. "Once you touch, it gets awful sticky." Indeed, says Evensky, "If risk is a four-letter word describing a concept that looks like a reflection in a mirror maze, how can a wealth manager possibly evaluate a client's risk tolerance?" Strictly, assessing risk tolerance would require observation of an individual's behavior in a variety of situations involving financial risk and comparison of this behavior with that of a representative sample of others in similar situations. Alternatively, various methodologies for hypothetical scenario testing have been proposed. But these tend to be narrowly focused —addressing, for instance, a specific investment scenario—and usually require relatively sophisticated interaction with the testing software by the respondent.

More practically and most commonly, advisers seek information from clients about their experiences, attitudes, values, preferences, and motivations with regard to financial risk and draw conclusions based on the information provided by the client.[2]

In essence, the adviser questions the client until he believes he has a satisfactory understanding of the client's risk tolerance. The adviser should then summarize that understanding in writing, obtain confirmation that the summary is accurate (adjusting the summary as required) and document both summary and confirmation. The confirmed summary becomes the client's risk-tolerance assessment.

During the discussion, the adviser will have consciously or subconsciously scored the client against some norm, probably the adviser's view of his other clients—for example, "Bill is much more risk tolerant than my average client." This is a time-consuming exercise that requires considerable interviewing skills to do well and is not easily auditable—hence, the popularity of scored questionnaires (see "Risk-Tolerance Estimates," at right).

Scored Questionnaires

All scored questionnaires offer the advantages of asking a standard set of questions—making comparisons more objective—and of automatically documenting both questions and answers. Additionally, some direct questions are easier to ask in a questionnaire than face-to-face in an interview.

Questions that are in plain English and jargon-free, so that they can be answered without explanation from the adviser, offer additional advantages:

❑ The questionnaire can be completed at the client's convenience.
❑ The adviser's time is not required.
❑ The adviser cannot (intentionally or unintentionally) influence the objectivity of the output.

Risk-Tolerance Estimates

As a by-product of a 1997 study by Chandler and Macleod Consultants, organizational psychologists, the accuracy of risk-tolerance estimates by clients about themselves and by advisers about their clients was tested. The sample comprised 198 established clients of twenty-five experienced advisers, who used a range of nonpsychometric, industry-standard techniques. The respective correlations were 0.68 and 0.36. These results were consistent with previous studies.

While the clients' self-assessments were reasonably accurate, much accuracy was lost during the processes by which advisers sought to gain an understanding of their clients. A correlation of 0.36 means that one in six estimates were wrong by two or more standard deviations. Put another way, advisers' estimates would have been more accurate if they had made no attempt to understand their clients' risk tolerance but had simply assumed all were average.

This is not a criticism of advisers. Other studies involving managers and subordinates, doctors and patients, teachers and students, et cetera, have shown similar inaccuracies in assessing personal attributes. It's difficult to do this well in the absence of a robust test.

The output is a score (on a scale) and, sometimes, a report. However, not all scored questionnaires are equal. Even judging by appearances suggests a wide range in quality—some look like professional questionnaires and others like tabloid quizzes. How is an adviser to know that a questionnaire is testing risk tolerance, in the first place, and how can the adviser tell whether or not the test results are an accurate assessment of the respondent's risk tolerance?

Psychometrics: The Science of Test Construction

All fields of human endeavor use measurement in some form, and each field has its own set of measuring tools and techniques. Measuring risk tolerance involves particular challenges, first, because there's no physical manifestation of the attribute and, second, because there is no natural unit of measurement.

During the past fifty years, considerable effort has been devoted to establishing standards for questionnaire-based testing. The research was done by psychologists and statisticians, and the discipline they developed is known as psychometrics. Psychometric standards can be applied to questionnaires ranging from opinion polls and market surveys to IQ, personality, and aptitude tests.[3]

In brief, to meet psychometric standards, risk-tolerance testing questionnaires must go through a rigorous development process, comprising usability trials and norming trials.

- ❑ In usability trials, a large pool of questions is tested to measure understandability and answerability on representative samples of the population for which the test is intended. This can involve having researchers sit with the subjects, who are encouraged to verbalize their thoughts as they examine the questions. Questions that seem straightforward are often revealed to have poor understandability and/or answerability.
- ❑ In norming trials, questionnaires comprising questions with high usability are tested on further representative samples and the results analyzed to determine the statistical value of the questions and the scoring algorithm. Questions that appear insightful are often revealed to have little or no statistical value in differentiating one respondent from another.

Typically, development requires multiple loops through both trial processes. A robust questionnaire is, in psychometric terms, one that is valid and reliable, where

- ❑ valid means that it measures what it purports to measure, and
- ❑ reliable means that it does so consistently, with a known level of accuracy.

A risk-tolerance test that meets psychometric standards will display the following characteristics:

- ❑ All questions are directly related to attitudes, values, preferences, emotions, or behavior with regard to situations that involve risk. Questions that relate to the client's circumstances—for example, their stage of life or time horizon—do not meet this criterion (see "The Portfolio-Picking Questionnaire," at right).
- ❑ Questions address financial risk generally, not just investment risk.
- ❑ Questions are in plain English.[4] Terminology that might require explanation is avoided.
- ❑ There are at least twenty questions in the questionnaire, in order to obtain the statistical accuracy required.[5]
- ❑ The results are scored on a normally distributed scale.

The Portfolio-Picking Questionnaire

An expectation that a risk-tolerance questionnaire will include questions about the client's circumstances is a holdover from the early days of financial planning, when advisers commonly used "portfolio-picking" questionnaires to select asset allocations to recommend to their clients. These questionnaires asked a mix of questions about the client's risk tolerance, investment experience, situation, time horizon, et cetera, and produced a score on a segmented scale. Each segment was associated with a particular asset allocation. The asset allocation was described in general terms as was the type of individual it was thought to suit, for example, "You're a prudent investor who wants a balanced portfolio to work toward medium- to long-term financial goals." This description was often referred to as a risk profile.

In its time, the portfolio-picking questionnaire was an improvement on the free-for-all, shopping-list approach to portfolio construction it had replaced. It was a more sophisticated version of the rule of thumb that set the percentage of stocks equal to 100 minus the client's age. Its most obvious flaw, however, was that it didn't provide any basis for determining whether what was being recommended would actually achieve the client's goals or was genuinely consistent with the client's risk tolerance.

Still, the portfolio-picking questionnaire has lingered on for two reasons: First, portfolio picking provided a quick-and-dirty path to making a sale. Despite its having been substantially discredited, its ease of use has made many advisers very reluctant to abandon it. Second, many in the industry do not have a real appreciation of needs-based financial planning. They learned their skills in what has been predominantly a sales culture. Not surprisingly, having grown up with a process built around portfolio picking, they have difficulty seeing its shortcomings. The portfolio-picking questionnaire served a useful purpose in the early days, when there was no better alternative. Now, however, its use could be considered as prima facie evidence of improper practice.

Additionally, the test's publisher should be able to provide details of the test's psychometric characteristics, including its accuracy—for example, scores are ±5 with 90 percent confidence—and evidence that it meets psychometric standards. Commonly used industry-standard questionnaires have typically been developed by compliance, marketing, or technical services personnel without regard to psychometric disciplines. Rudimentary due diligence will quickly establish that they do not test risk tolerance, let alone do so accurately—despite how they might be described by their publishers.

Risk Tolerance Revealed

Though risk and risk tolerance are both complex issues, some of the complexity arises from the semantic/conceptual confusion mentioned previously and some from erroneous beliefs. Two common semantic/conceptual confusions are: First, risk tolerance is sometimes confused with "loss tolerance." How somebody feels about taking risk in choosing between alternative courses of action—risk tolerance—is one thing. How somebody feels if a loss actually occurs—loss tolerance—is another. Risk tolerance is relevant to how someone makes decisions. Loss tolerance is relevant to how someone reacts to an event.

An assessment of risk tolerance is not a prediction of loss tolerance. How a client will react to an unfavorable outcome, loss tolerance, is not predictable with any certainty. A critical factor will be whether or not the outcome was within the client's range of expectations. Did the client actually understand the risk being taken? If not, the client will likely be much more upset than if they had.

Although nobody enjoys an unfavorable outcome, there's a significant difference between being unhappy with the outcome and being unhappy with the decision that lead to the outcome. You may choose to have a birthday party outdoors. If the weather is bad you won't be happy, but you won't necessarily regret the decision and you may or may not make the same decision for next year's birthday.

It is likely, though by no means certain, that clients' reactions to an unfavorable outcome will be consistent with what they said about the level of risk they were willing to take. The better clients know themselves and the more financially experienced they are, the more consistent the reactions are likely to be. In the event of unfavorable outcomes, if proper process was followed, the adviser will be able to take clients back to what they said at the time the decision was made and to show them step-by-step how they decided on the course of action they followed. This may make them feel better—or it may not. But it will demonstrate that they have no cause for complaint about the advice that led to the decision.

Second, risk tolerance is sometimes confused with "risk capacity." Risk capacity is the amount of money a client could afford to lose without putting the achievement of financial goals at risk. Risk capacity, which more accurately should be called "loss capacity," is an objective financial calculation. It represents an absolute, downside constraint on strategy selection, which must be taken account of, but it's not the same thing as risk tolerance.

Risk tolerance has been the subject of numerous research studies.[6] Not all studies agree on all points. Those points on which a majority, if not all, agree include:

- ❑ Risk tolerance is a personality trait—that is, a distinguishable, relatively enduring way in which one individual varies from another. Test/retest studies have shown consistency over periods of 30 to 120 days.
- ❑ There's evidence of four different categories of risk tolerance: social, ethical, physical, and financial. Individuals behave consistently within category but not across categories. For example, hang gliding will correlate with mountain climbing but not with public speaking.
- ❑ As with many human attributes, risk tolerance is distributed normally. Its occurrence in a population is as would be expected statistically.
- ❑ A number of correlations between risk tolerance and demographic characteristics have been established (see "Demographics," on the following page).
- ❑ The cause of differences in risk tolerance from one person to another is not settled. As with many personality traits, risk tolerance is thought to be influenced by both nature (genetics) and nurture (life experience).

Until the advent of the FinaMetrica Risk Profiling system,[7] the studies involved small samples, narrowly based sample groups (for example, students and academic staff), short time frames, or questionnaires that were not psychometric instruments. However, the FinaMetrica system involves a psychometric risk-tolerance test linked to a separate demographic questionnaire, which tens of thousands of respondents from a broad cross section of the adult population have completed over a period of years.

Analysis of the FinaMetrica database has added to the understanding of risk tolerance as follows:

- ❑ There is no evidence of subfactors in financial risk tolerance—that is, there is no evidence of investment risk tolerance, employment risk tolerance, borrowing risk tolerance, or insurance risk tolerance, for example.

Demographics

The discussion that follows is a *précis* of "An Empirical Investigation of Personal Financial Risk Tolerance" by Robert W. Faff, Department of Accounting and Finance, Monash University, and Terrance Hallahan and Michael D. McKenzie, School of Economics and Finance, RMIT University, which appeared in *Financial Services Review* 13(1). The investigation involved 20,415 FinaMetrica risk profiles completed during the period May 1999 to February 2002 drawn from a broad cross-section of the Australian adult population.

The FinaMetrica database contains information on a number of different demographic factors for each respondent, namely, age, number of dependents, gender, marital status, education, personal income, combined family income, and net assets. A hierarchical regression analysis was employed to assess which of the variables make a significant contribution to risk tolerance. The final hierarchical regression model contains the full set of variables and provides a quantification of the relationship between each of the demographic characteristics and the risk-tolerance score (RTS) according to the following specification:

$$RTS_i = \alpha_0 + \alpha_1 D_{i,FEM} + \alpha_2 AGE_i + \alpha_3 AGE_i^2 + \alpha_4 NDEP_i + \alpha_5 D_{i,MARRIED} +$$

$$\sum_{g=EDU_2}^{EDU_4} \alpha_g D_{i,g} + \sum_{h=INC_2}^{INC_5} \alpha_h D_{i,h} + \sum_{j=CINC_2}^{CINC_5} \alpha_j D_{i,j} + \sum_{k=NASS_2}^{NASS_5} \alpha_k D_{i,k} + \varepsilon_i$$

where RTS_i is the FinaMetrica RTS for respondent i, AGE is the age expressed in years, $NDEP$ is the number of financial dependents, D is a dummy variable used for gender (*FEM*), marital status (*MARRIED*), education (*EDU*), income (*INC*) and combined income (*CINC*), and a is the coefficient to be estimated.

The hierarchical regression was structured with the interval-level variables for the demographic characteristics of age and the number of dependents constituting the base-case regression. In light of the results of previous studies, a test for the presence of nonlinearities in the relationship between age and risk tolerance was included in the form of a quadratic age term. The remaining demographic characteristics—that is, gender, marital status, education, income, combined income and net assets, which enter the FinaMetrica database as ordinal-level variables—were dummy coded and entered sequentially as separate sets of predictors, judged in order of importance, having reference to past research.

Gender is a significant determinant of risk tolerance, and a female will exhibit an RTS of 6.2 points lower than a demographically equivalent male. Similarly, age and marital status are found to be significant determinants of the RTS. While marriage simply decreases the RTS by two points, the relationship between age and RTS is revealed as more complex. The regression output shows that the linear age variable is insignificant, whereas the nonlinear age term is highly significant.

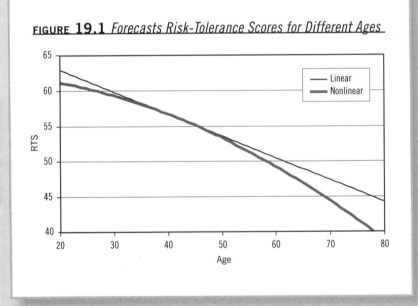

FIGURE 19.1 *Forecasts Risk-Tolerance Scores for Different Ages*

The nonlinear forecast, **FIGURE 19.1**, represents the base-case individual (an unmarried male with no dependents, personal and family incomes of less than $30,000, and net assets of less than $50,000) plus an adjustment for age as given by the quadratic age coefficient. The linear forecast represents the base-case individual excluding the quadratic age coefficient.

The series of dummy variables capturing the level of income of a respondent (D_{INC}) were all individually significant and positive, as were the net asset (D_{NASS}) dummy variables. The estimated results indicate that the RTS of a respondent generally increases as income and assets increase. A Wald test of coefficient

DEMOGRAPHICS (CONTINUED)

equality rejects the null hypothesis of coefficient equality for the income, combined income, and net asset dummy variables, respectively. This positive relationship between income, assets, and risk tolerance does not appear to be uniform. Specifically, higher levels of income are found to be associated with successively higher scores except for the top income bracket (greater than $200,000.) Although the increment to the RTS over the base case is still positive, it is less than that found for the income bracket preceding it ($100,000 to $200,000). However, a Wald test of coefficient equality suggests this difference is not statistically significant. Further, the number of dependents was found to be significantly associated with the RTS, although the negative impact on the RTS is small.

Not all of the demographic characteristics were found to be significant. For education, at least a trade/diploma level of education was required before a significant increase in the RTS was observed. Similarly, a combined income of at least $50,000 is required before the RTS is positively influenced.

Overall, these results suggest that gender, age, number of dependents, marital status, tertiary education, income, and wealth are all related to risk tolerance. The results for gender, education, and income are consistent with the earlier literature. It should not be concluded, however, that differences in scores can be explained solely by demographic factors; rather, these are a general influence. For any particular set of demographic factors, respondents displayed a wide range of risk-tolerance scores.

Thus, although understanding the influence of demographic factors may be of general interest to advisers, it will not affect the advice given to a particular client. However, this understanding does enable demographic factors to be excluded from more precise exploration of other influences on risk tolerance (see "Major Events").

❏ Demographic correlations have now been examined rigorously on a large scale. Some previous findings have been confirmed, some refined, and others overturned (see "Demographics").

❏ Major world and financial market events have been shown to have no significant impact on risk tolerance (see "Major Events," page 346).

Behavior and Risk Tolerance

Imagine your clients driving to a country wedding. Suppose that halfway through a tight bend, the asphalt suddenly changes to gravel and they nearly crash. Your clients' immediate reaction will depend on how shocked they are. And that depends on how risky they thought it was to be driving on that road, at that time, at that speed. Before the near miss they will have been traveling at a speed that balanced their driving risk tolerance, their perception of the driving risk, and their goal of arriving on time for the wedding.

Risk tolerance is relatively stable, but perceptions of risk can change in an instant. If badly shocked by the near miss, your clients may actually pull over until their hearts stop racing. Or perhaps they'll proceed but more slowly than before. Eventually they may get back to the speed at which they were traveling but possibly not through bends. If they now want to change their driving speed, it will be because their perception of the driving risk has changed. They simply didn't realize that there were unsealed sections in the road. In what they now perceive to be a more risky situation, your clients must decide whether to proceed at the old pace and risk more shocks or to slow down and risk being late for the wedding.

From this example, it's clear that risk tolerance is not the sole determinant of behavior in situations that involve risk. Behavior will be a function of the goals being sought, the perceived risk, and risk tolerance. In a given set of circumstances, a change in behavior could be caused by a change in goals, a change in perceived risk, or a change in risk tolerance. While risk tolerance is relatively stable over time, it's not unchangeable. There is a moderate general tendency for risk tolerance to decrease with age, and life events can also have a significant positive or negative impact.

When the bull market turned to a bear market, some clients wanted to change their investment strategies. Some advisers interpreted this as resulting from a change in risk tolerance. However, given the data described in "Major Events," the desire for change seems far more likely to have arisen from changed perceptions of risk and/or changed goals than from changed risk tolerance. Personality traits do change, but usually only slowly over time. Nonetheless, a significant life event can trigger a major change, and in some cases this can be almost instantaneous.

A bear market is an environmental event. Whether or not it constitutes a life event for particular individuals—either positive or negative—depends on their circumstances. For example, the significance of the event to a pre-retiree who bet his life savings on high tech in 1999 will be very different from what it will mean for a pre-retiree who followed a balanced strategy through the 1990s and into the 2000s. Overall, there is no evidence that the bear market has had any significant impact on risk tolerance.

Major Events

An Australian study that involved time-based analysis of 11,421 client risk profiles (average score was 55.3, with standard deviation of 12.4) completed during the period May 1999 to February 2002 showed no evidence of any statistically significant change (see **FIGURE 19.2**).

The data in the table are for clients of Australian advisers. A 1997 study established that there were no statistically significant differences in risk tolerance between U.S. and Australian populations. Australian markets have been through a boom/bust cycle similar in timing to that of U.S. markets but not as severe. If one considers clients of financial advisers as a population, Figure 19.2 can be seen as representing the results of successively sampling this population on a quarterly basis. (In 2004, the researchers who conducted the study described in "Demographics" were applying the results of that study to exclude demographic influences from a study of the effect of major events on risk tolerance. Preliminary results indicate no changes of significance to financial advisers in advising clients.)

Further, in a website survey of readers of the Australian *Personal Investor* magazine conducted during January and February 2003, respondents were asked how their risk tolerance had changed over the previous twelve months. The results (n=985) were:

9%   Decreased significantly
78% Not changed significantly
13% Increased significantly

Individuals' self-ratings of their risk tolerance are quite accurate (see "Risk-Tolerance Estimates," page 337).

Education and Risk Tolerance

It's generally acknowledged that educating clients about risk is desirable. To the extent that such education reduces fear of the unknown, it can be expected to reduce perceived risk and therefore to cause clients to choose courses of action that they previously would have considered too risky. However, the opposite can also be true. During the climate of irrational exuberance in the bull market of the late 1990s, it was common for investors to underestimate risk. Education about risk would then,

FIGURE **19.2** *1999–2002 Quarter-by-Quarter Risk-Tolerance Scores*

| PERIOD | | SCORES | | |
FROM	TO	COUNT	AVERAGE	STD DEV
05/99	07/99	372	54.9	13.3
08/99	10/99	457	56.6	11.9
11/99	01/00	462	55.3	12.2
02/00	04/00	811	54.3	12.7
05/00	07/00	1052	55.2	12.8
08/00	10/00	1102	55.1	12.6
11/00	01/01	968	55.2	12.5
02/01	04/01	1289	55.2	11.9
05/01	07/01	1616	55.8	12.0
08/01	10/01	1593	55.5	12.1
11/01	01/02	1355	54.9	12.8

in many cases, have caused clients to think twice about courses of action that otherwise appeared attractive.

To the extent that education causes changes in behavior, it's far more likely to do so because perceptions of risk have changed than because risk tolerance has changed. Even the most knowledgeable individuals can still have low risk tolerance.

Applying Risk-Tolerance Assessments

Know the Client

A risk-tolerance test report does not replace discussion between adviser and client. Rather, it's an objective starting point for that discussion. The results of the test process are not set in stone. The first step in discussing the test report is to ask the client whether or not she believes it's an accurate description of her risk tolerance. Clients may wish to make minor amendments, in which case they would sign off on the amended report, or to retake the test.

The report from a psychometric risk-tolerance test should be information rich: equivalent to a precise summary, quantified against statistical norms, of a thirty-minute discussion about financial risk between the client and an expert interviewer.

Each statement in the report should be directly linked to answers given in the questionnaire and/or statistical norms.[8]

The report should provide fertile ground for advisers in developing an in-depth knowledge of their clients.

- ❏ Of course, there will be a normally distributed score (on a segmented scale), which provides basic quantification—for example, this person tests as being more or less risk tolerant than x or y percent of the population.
- ❏ Segmenting the scale allows generic descriptions of those within segments to be developed from analysis of completed questionnaires.
- ❏ Where a client has given answers that are different from those typically given by others in the same segment, the report should highlight these answers as differences, leading to extended discussion.
- ❏ Additionally, answers to specific questions can lead to very illuminating discussion. For example, the questionnaire will probably ask clients to indicate the level of risk they have taken in the past and the level of risk they're now comfortable taking. Any difference provides an ideal "tell me more" opportunity.

Typically, clients respond very favorably to this type of risk-tolerance evaluation. Survey responses show that they find the process of completing the questionnaire and then reading the report gives them a better understanding of themselves in relation to risk and return issues. Further, they appreciate that an independent, objective analysis of risk tolerance adds to the adviser's understanding of them as individuals.

For a completed sample of the FinaMetrica risk-tolerance questionnaire and the resulting Risk Profile report, go to www.risk-profiling.com/downloads/sample.pdf.

Couples

In couples, there is usually a difference in risk tolerance between partners. Each couple is mostly aware that the difference exists and knows which of the two is more risk tolerant. However, the magnitude of any difference is often unknown. A psychometric risk-tolerance test provides an objective measure of any difference. Further, by comparing questionnaire answers and reports, the couples are able to see exactly where and how the difference arises, which makes finding a mutually acceptable way forward that much easier. Some advisers cite the advantages in dealing with couples as the most valuable benefit of psychometric testing.

Trade-Offs and Gap Analysis

The personal financial-planning process is based on obtaining the client's properly informed commitment to a set of trade-offs between conflicting alternatives. Effective trade-off decisions can be made only when the elements of the trade-off have been separated and can be clearly understood and compared.

A key trade-off decision is between comfort with financial risk and the financial risk required to achieve goals. Analysis of clients' goals, needs, and priorities, in light of their current and anticipated financial resources, and the financial environment (commonly referred to as "gap analysis") often demonstrates that the clients' goals are unlikely to be satisfied from their resources at the level of risk they would normally choose to take. In such circumstances clients may decide to

- ❑ take more risk than they would normally choose;
- ❑ reduce, defer, or forgo goals; and/or
- ❑ apply more resources to achieving future goals.

The adviser can guide, illustrate alternatives, discuss consequences, and the like, but the decision is ultimately the client's to make.

Relating Risk Tolerance to Planning Alternatives

In many cases, once advisers have an objective assessment of risk tolerance it's a relatively straightforward step to relate that to the objective risk in the planning strategy alternatives being considered. However, the advent of psychometric risk-tolerance testing has given rise to databases of completed tests, which make possible the development of new knowledge through further research. In particular, it's now possible to develop algorithms that relate risk-tolerance scores to investment strategy alternatives. One such algorithm[9] is illustrated in **FIGURE 19.3**, where the risk-tolerance scoring scale has a mean of 50 and a standard deviation of 10.

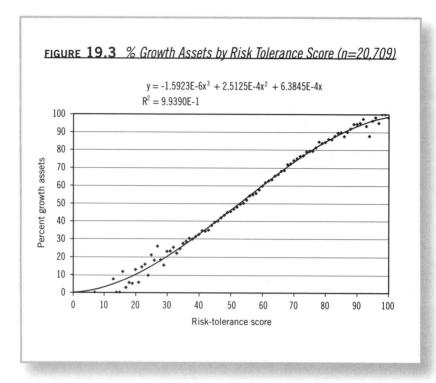

FIGURE **19.3** _% Growth Assets by Risk Tolerance Score (n=20,709)_

$$y = -1.5923\text{E-}6x^3 + 2.5125\text{E-}4x^2 + 6.3845\text{E-}4x$$
$$R^2 = 9.9390\text{E-}1$$

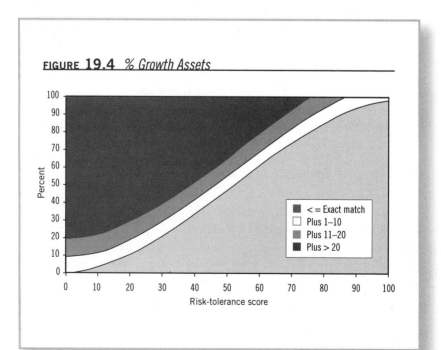

FIGURE **19.4** _% Growth Assets_

FIGURE **19.5** *% Growth Assets to Risk Tolerance*

Enter the % of growth assets in the portfolio to see the comfort/
discomfort risk-tolerance score ranges for that portfolio.

Enter % growth assets	60%	RISK-TOLERANCE SCORE RANGES	
		Comfort	> 59
		Marginal comfort	59–53
		Marginal discomfort	52–45
		Discomfort	< 45

In a well-constructed diversified portfolio, the level of risk is determined, broadly, by the defensive/growth split, where cash and bonds are
defensive and stocks and real estate are growth. However, risk is not highly
sensitive to the proportion of growth assets. Let's suppose that a client
is comfortable with 50 percent growth. Increasing the proportion to 51,
52, or 53 percent is not going to increase the level of risk as perceived by
the client. In fact, the increase in risk will be noticeable only at around
60 percent growth, so discomfort is likely to begin to occur only when
the proportion has gone beyond 60 percent. But by 70 percent growth,
this client will be entering the discomfort zone. Hence, there is effectively
a transition from comfort to discomfort, which, when applied to the
algorithm illustrated in Figure 19.3, gives the comfort/discomfort chart
in **FIGURE 19.4**.

Figure 19.4 provides an apples-to-apples comparison between portfolio risk and risk tolerance. The algorithms on which the chart is based
allow the construction of calculators that allow readings to be done simply
and precisely. For a given portfolio, risk-tolerance score ranges can be
calculated as shown in **FIGURE 19.5**. Similarly, for a given risk-tolerance
score, portfolios can be categorized as shown in **FIGURE 19.6**.

The ideas illustrated in these figures show that it's possible to objectively
link the soft data about psychological needs to the hard data required in the
financial-planning process.

FIGURE 19.6 *Risk Tolerance to % Growth Assets*

Enter the risk-tolerance score to see the comfort/discomfort ranges for the % of growth assets in a portfolio.

Enter risk-tolerance score	50%	% GROWTH ASSET RANGES	
		Comfort	< 47%
		Marginal comfort	47%–56%
		Marginal discomfort	57%–66%
		Discomfort	> 66%

The Way Ahead

Financial planning has always been a blend of art and science. This chapter demonstrates that the art of financial planning is enhanced by taking a sequential, scientific approach to a particular psychological attribute—the client's risk tolerance.

The steps include:

❑ Use basic research to distill an understanding of the construct being considered.

❑ Use the appropriate disciplines to build a test instrument.

❑ Use large numbers of test results to fine-tune the understanding of the construct and the instrument.

❑ Seek a methodology for linking test results into the financial-planning process.

Essentially, managing risk tolerance is a problem to be solved. Because it requires a concentrated application of disciplined, clear thinking, the very effort of attempting to solve the problem has led to a greater understanding of it. Additionally, the development of psychometric risk-tolerance testing is itself an important step. Of course, this progress doesn't mean that managing risk tolerance is now a closed book. What has been presented here can be seen as second- and third-generation thinking. Although this is sufficient to facilitate a professional approach, the fourth, fifth, and sixth generations are still ahead of us.

The growing interest in lifestyle planning and in remodeling practices to improve the adviser's own quality of life indicates that the profession is thinking more broadly about goals, needs, and priorities than it has in the past. Neither client nor adviser is well served by a mechanical application of traditional economic thinking, no matter how technically sophisticated. Behavioral finance provides the promise of a better future for the profession and those it serves. It's not merely an intellectual curiosity that sits on the periphery. Rather, it is central to the very core of financial planning's purpose and processes. It redefines both the ends being sought and the means by which they can be achieved. We can't be confident that all behavioral finance issues are known, let alone settled, and there are, as yet, few user-friendly, robust tools. However, the fact that robust disciplines can be applied to the complex task of managing risk tolerance indicates the way ahead.

Interestingly, though the initial steps were taken by those schooled in economics or psychology, the development since then has been done by those whose primary discipline is financial planning—which is as it should be. Does anyone have a greater interest in the application of behavioral finance in terms of individual consumers than a financial planner? Although the framework within which risk tolerance was tackled may not be appropriate for resolving other behavioral finance issues, it does prove that behavioral finance issues can be properly taken into account in mainstream financial planning. Indeed, behavioral finance is the new frontier for financial planning. It offers exciting challenges and opportunities to improve the practice of financial planning, to add to depth to the role of financial adviser, and, most important, to enhance the benefits to clients.

Chapter Notes

1. Daniel Kahneman and Amos Tversky, "Prospect Theory: An Analysis of Decision Under Risk," *Econometrica* 47 (1979): 263–291.

2. For practical reasons, what is actually being assessed is information provided by clients regarding their risk tolerance rather than their risk tolerance, per se. However, to simplify, the expression "assessing risk tolerance" is used as shorthand for "assessing what clients say in regard to their risk tolerance."

3. A detailed discussion of the application of psychometrics in risk-tolerance testing can be found in V. J. Callan and M. Johnson, "Some Guidelines for Financial Planners in Measuring and Advising Clients About Their Levels of Risk Tolerance," *Journal of Personal Finance* (August 2002): 31–44, a copy of which can be downloaded at www.risk-profiling.com/Downloads/Measuring RiskTolerance.pdf.

4. To meet psychometric standards, all questions must be worded in plain English, typically not greater than high school standard. Planners often see such questions as simplistic, especially when compared to the level of discussion they would normally have with their clients. However, the purpose of these questions is to get an accurate assessment of risk tolerance as an objective starting point for building the detailed understanding that comes from more probing discussion. Additionally, it's easy for planners to underestimate the knowledge gap between their clients and themselves, and clients can be reluctant to say that they don't really understand what the planner is talking about.

5. The accuracy of a questionnaire is a function of the accuracy of the individual questions and the square of the number of questions. Among other things, norming trials test the correlation (accuracy) of individual questions. The correlation for a typical risk-tolerance question is such that around twenty questions are required to give accuracy consistent with psychometric standards.

6. Over the past thirty years—the past ten in particular—risk, risk tolerance, and risk-tolerance testing have been the subject of numerous academic and other studies described in hundreds of papers, articles, and books. A partial list of references can be found at www.risk-profiling.com/references.htm. Additionally, this chapter draws on unpublished studies carried out by: Dr. Michael J. Roszkowski, the author of "The American College's Survey of Financial Risk Tolerance"; Hamada Elsayed and Jarrod Martin, Chandler & Macleod Consultants, Organisational Psychologists; Drs. Austin Adams and Jim Bright, Applied Psychology Unit, University of New South Wales School of Psychology; and Dr. Robert Faff, Department of Accounting and Finance, Monash University, and Terrence Hallahan and Dr. Michael McKenzie, School of Finance, RMIT University.

7. The FinaMetrica Risk Profiling system comprises a test of financial-risk tolerance and a methodology for incorporating the test results into the financial-planning process. The test was developed in accordance with and meets internationally accepted psychometric standards. The Web-based system was launched in Australia in October 1998, in the United States in June 2002, and in the United Kingdom in April 2004.

8. With personality and aptitude tests, many critics are disconcerted by the frequent lack of an apparent connection between the questions asked and the conclusions drawn. Typically, the questions are used to assess where an individual fits into a preexisting model of behavior, and the report is then couched in terms of that behavioral model. Often respondents are unaware that this is the process being followed and are understandably upset when they see negative conclusions being drawn about them from answers they gave to seemingly innocuous questions. Respondents may feel that they have been tricked into disadvantaging themselves. One of the characteristics of a nonpsychometric risk-tolerance test is that the report will contain statements that seem to have been plucked out of thin air (in much the same way as a horoscope does).

In a psychometric risk-tolerance test, the respondent's answers are compared with those of a sample group. There should be nothing in the report that could not have been derived directly from the answers given by the respondent or the sample group.

9. An explanation of the derivation of this algorithm can be found in Appendix B of the document at www.risk-profiling.com/Downloads/User_Guide_To _Linking_Spreadsheet.pdf.

CHAPTER 20

The Why of Wealth Management

ROSS LEVIN

How can wealth managers determine—and demonstrate—whether the financial plans they helped their client develop are really getting the job done? How do you codify success in comprehensive financial planning? Those were the questions I was hoping to answer when I wrote *The Wealth Management Index* (McGraw-Hill, 1997). The book featured the Wealth Management Index™, which divided financial-planning objectives into five key areas and then subdivided those areas into various components. The goal was to focus clients' attention on results—on the question of how well they're doing relative to what they said mattered to them.

Much has changed in the markets and in the economy since the book was written. We swiftly went from the nation's greatest extended bull equities market in history to the worst bear market since the Depression. We saw tax rates continue to change, and we were introduced to Roth IRAs and 529 plans. We've seen companies move from compensating employees with stock options to rewarding them with restricted stock. And we've watched in dismay as mutual funds—the trusted investment vehicle of the masses—have come under attack for malfeasance right along with the companies in which they invest.

But times are always changing. And through the dramatic shifts we've seen during this period, the case for comprehensive wealth management—and for the Wealth Management Index™—is now even stronger. In the 1990s, the idea of setting aside funds to cover three years' worth of cash needs was blasphemous, but clients who did so were insulated throughout the precipitous drop in equity valuations at the turn of the twenty-first century. During the halcyon days of outperformance for U.S. large- and small-cap growth stocks, the work of ensuring that a client's asset allocation was on target by rebalancing only dragged the portfolio's returns, but it also forced us to rebalance with bonds and categories that were not doing as well. The ultimate effect: we bought low and sold high.

Comprehensive wealth management continues to call our attention back to the things that really matter—most important, matching clients' actions with their values. We all know that the ultimate purpose of money is to either spend it or give it away. Yet so often that understanding gets lost in the scramble for the highest incremental return.

The things I've witnessed in my own practice since 1996, when I started writing the book, have reinforced how misguided the chase for performance can be. Clients have faced major changes in their lives: some divorced, three physicians went on disability, one attorney was sued for an alleged libelous statement in the newspaper, and other clients fought losing battles with cancer or Alzheimer's. It wasn't rates of return that helped them and their families get through these tragedies; it was comprehensive planning.

The Wealth Management Index™

The Wealth Management Index™ parses financial planning into the following categories:[1]
- ❏ Asset protection (preservation)—25 percent
- ❏ Disability and income protection (protection)—20 percent
- ❏ Debt management (leverage)—10 percent
- ❏ Investment and cash flow planning (accumulation)—25 percent
- ❏ Estate planning (distribution)—20 percent

Within these categories, we further break down the process. To calculate the value within the Wealth Management Index™, multiply the category value by the percentage within the category.

Asset Protection—25 percent
- ❏ 34 percent—Are your business interests adequately covered?
- ❏ 33 percent—Do you have an appropriate amount of life insurance consistent with an articulated philosophy around this insurance?
- ❏ 33 percent—Have you protected yourself against catastrophic loss due to the cost of long-term care, property losses, or liability issues?

Disability and Income Protection—20 percent

❑ 40 percent—Do you have too much or too little disability protection, given your assets and income, and will it pay you should you be unable to work?

❑ 20 percent—Was the income you received from all sources (earnings, gifts, Social Security, pensions) what you expected it to be this year?

❑ 20 percent—Did you spend according to plan?

❑ 20 percent—Did you use all reasonable means to reduce your taxes?

Debt Management—10 percent

❑ 40 percent—Is your current ratio (your liquid assets divided by your short-term assets) stronger than 2:1, and is your total debt reasonable as a percentage of your total assets?

❑ 10 percent—Is your debt tax efficient?

❑ 30 percent—Have you access to as much debt as reasonably possible and at the best available rates?

❑ 20 percent—Have you managed your debt as expected?

Investment Planning—25 percent

❑ 10 percent—How well did you do in relation to your established rate-of-return target this year (consumer price index [CPI] plus a stated percentage)?

❑ 40 percent—Were your annual contributions or withdrawals on target?

❑ 40 percent—Is your asset allocation appropriate?

❑ 5 percent—Was the portfolio income tax efficient?

❑ 5 percent—Have you set aside enough cash for anticipated purchases in the next three years?

Estate Planning—20 percent

❑ 40 percent—Does your will match your wealth-transfer wishes?

❑ 15 percent—Do you need and have a power of attorney, health care declaration, or living will?

❑ 25 percent—Are your assets titled correctly, and are all beneficiary designations appropriate?

❑ 15 percent—Have you established and funded all necessary trusts?

❑ 5 percent—Have you made your desired gifts for the year?

The range of services our firm offers has changed during the last few years. We continue to try to find new ways to serve our clients and add value. We've negotiated fleet rates on automobile purchases, created credit

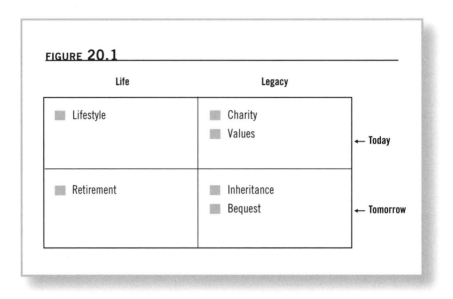

FIGURE 20.1

lines at very attractive pricing, and worked with banks to get better rates on deposit accounts. But what matters most to our clients is finding out what matters most to our clients. To do that, we have a simple way of framing the key areas of a client's financial life (see **FIGURE 20.1**).

Just as we do with investing, we need to help clients optimize their life choices. All our clients have available a number of personal resources: financial, emotional, spiritual, physical. Blending these resources so that their use is consistent with what matters most to the client is how effective planning is practiced. The objective is to optimize the client's total life picture, not make the most of some piece of it. Clients need to make financial decisions about today and tomorrow in terms of how much they'll spend on themselves and how much they'll give to others. Figure 20.1 reflects those decisions.

The decisions clients make every day create their lifestyles. How much do they want to spend on living? Whatever they don't spend today they save as a down payment on tomorrow. They will either spend it down the road on retirement, or they'll give it away to charity or to children. But as they make these spending decisions, they know—as we all do—that they're being watched. Our legacy is not determined solely by the amount we give to charity now or to others later but by how we live our lives today. Our children are with us as we make our choices. They're watching and cataloging and ultimately becoming extensions of who we are. Our legacy is as much about what we choose to do today as it is about what we plan for tomorrow.

Getting to Why

Into the wealth-management equation, clients must factor all of their resources. They trade days for dollars; how they spend their minutes must matter at least as much as how they spend their money. "Doubt may be an uncomfortable condition," Voltaire tells us, "but certainty is a ridiculous one." This understanding must be factored into the work of planning as well.

Everything that we do is based on probabilities. Yet the laws of probability are derived from the laws of large numbers. Unfortunately, while all of our clients may represent a suitable sampling from which to develop probabilities, each individual client is a category of one. Indeed, everything that we recommend may make complete sense for the group but not much sense at all for some of the individuals within it. Let me explain. We know that over long periods of time, stocks will outperform bonds, but we don't know whether our client's time with us will coincide with such periods. Therefore, asset allocation needs to be determined by the needs of the client, not by the results of an optimizer. A client who has limited psychological capacity to handle risk cannot be invested in quite the same way as one who's more comfortable with it. But I'm not convinced that a risk-analysis questionnaire—however sophisticated or flexible—is going to uncover what his asset allocation should be. You get to the "solve for" by getting to the why. Before we can do any effective financial planning, we need to understand what our clients want and why they want it. We do this through a goal-setting process that's framed by the Wealth Management Index™.

Keeping Tabs on Choices

As we discuss with clients what their "today" is and try to better understand what their vision of "tomorrow" represents, we place these objectives within the index. For example, someone who indicates that it's important to take regular vacations sees that laid out in the cash flow area of the Wealth Management Index™. We determine what an appropriate cost may be and refer back to this throughout the year. If the client does not take the vacation but saves the money instead, she's penalized for that in the index scoring. It may seem strange that a planner would punish a client for saving rather than spending, but our purpose is to help our clients live out their lives in the manner that's most consistent with their values. We don't judge clients' values (unless it's to decide whether we want them as clients); we try to help them live those values.

When we keep the focus on the client's objectives, the decisions related to solutions become much easier. A client recently came to us for help with a decision related to her goals. The client, a doctor, commutes ninety minutes to work each way every day. She was trying to decide whether she should take a 40 percent pay cut over the next two years to enter into a practice eleven miles from her home with other physicians she respects. She had discussed it with her accountant, who told her how much money it would cost her and encouraged her not to make the change.

We reviewed with her all the things that she had told us were important to her, including her family. We went over cash flow projections before and after the change. We outlined the potential consequences of the change, and we concluded that she could afford to make the change. If she does not save for the next two years, the combined results of the tax savings with a lower income, some direct savings through a more reasonable commute, and minor spending adjustments meant that the family would not have to compromise what they felt were important lifestyle choices, like continuing to travel and paying for education. Ultimately, it may mean she needs to work an extra year twenty years down the road, but what is the present-value calculation on a good life? We agreed she should take the new job.

Financial planning has always involved the integration of science and art. It's inconceivable that good financial planning can result solely from helping clients deal with their feelings about money or solely from providing them analytics. We all process our financial-planning decisions through the prism of our emotions. This is just as true for planners as it is for clients. That's why having some framework to measure a client's successful progress toward what matters is so important. Our wants almost invariably compete with one another, and the index keeps us from denying that. We're making relative value decisions that must be displayed in the context of what the possibilities are.

Here's another example. Suppose you're working with a young physician. Which is more important—ensuring that there's ample cash flow to fully fund the $40,000 into his young retirement plan, or the positive alpha generated on, say, the accumulated $100,000 already in the plan? An enhanced return of 2 percent is worth $2,000; if he doesn't fund the plan (or only partially funds it), the swing is clearly far greater. This is not to say that benchmarking portfolio performance is unimportant; it's merely to point out that it may not be the most important piece of this particular plan.

The Wealth Management Index™ can therefore serve as a guidepost, giving structure to the plan. As long as you tie the client's objectives to the appropriate category, you can rest assured that success will conform to your client's definition rather than to any answers traditional wisdom may dictate.

Using the Index

Over the years I've had several opportunities to speak to planners about the index. Here are some of the questions I'm asked most frequently:

Do I need to include all the areas outlined in the index? This question is one of my favorites. The skeptic in me says the people who ask it have a specific agenda on which they want their clients to focus. It may be someone who specializes in investment management and is uncomfortable with the relatively small part of the index this category represents. Or it may be someone who is in the life insurance field and doesn't feel estate planning is getting adequate attention. In any event, like asking which organ is most vital to the functioning of the body, asking which component can be eliminated from the index is not the right question. All of the components are necessary for a well-executed financial plan. There may be categories for which the weighting could be adjusted, but assessing what's most important to the client, in my opinion, is still better done by scoring than by reweighting.

What is the most important part of the index? I find that all the components are important. Eighteen percent of the index relates to cash flow in some way. Regardless of how wealthy a client is, cash flow drives financial planning. If a client is in the accumulation phase, how much to save is an important issue. If she's in the spending phase, then spending policies are critical as well. A simple example of the importance of cash flow can be seen in a plan that builds in a 5 percent spending policy. If someone spends $10,000 more each year than planned, an additional $200,000 of investment assets would be needed to fund such spending. With some of our wealthiest clients, we often spend the majority of time addressing cash flow issues.

Once you've developed the initial plan, doesn't financial planning come down to investment management? No. Financial planning is like training for and running a marathon. Just because you run one once doesn't mean you'll be in shape for the rest of your life. Every year things change. You may remedy a lot of problems in the first year of a client relationship, but you'll need to validate and address those issues—and new ones—each year. Life changes; goals change. Unless you regularly monitor your client's situation, you're going to find yourself neglecting some of the key components of their lives. We meet regularly with our clients each year to ensure that we're continuing to get it right.

And we don't give our clients a single, overriding financial plan. At each meeting we focus on a core component of the index. Each client's initial consultation with us is triggered by some frustration or pain: maybe they feel their investments have been improperly managed, or maybe they're concerned that their financial life is becoming an overwhelming task, or maybe they've just divorced. In any case, we have to address what's causing the pain, but we also make sure we complete the physical. That's why the process must be ongoing and regular.

How do you grade the index? A good financial plan comes from the client, so you need to judge progress with the client as the measure. The purpose is not to create a benchmark against how well others are doing; it's to measure how well the clients have done relative to their own unique situations. You can either score each particular area at your client meetings as you handle it, or you can devote one meeting at the end exclusively to doing the judging. If a score is not particularly good, the first thing to check is whether the objective was truly important. If it was not something the client cared enough about, then it should be changed for the next year. In any event, some objectives will remain the same and some will change.

THE WORK THAT WE DO as wealth managers is some of the most important work in our economy. Money decisions affect relationships—often in a way that makes or breaks them. Helping couples understand their different money profiles can spare them a great deal of conflict, even divorce. Or consider the issues that must be sorted out in weighing a job relocation. We help clients examine the many factors involved, not merely the financial ones. By helping clients work through these issues, we improve the quality of their lives. This is vital work. And there are no shortcuts to doing it. To do it well, you have to define what matters most to the client. The Wealth Management Index™ is but one tool that can be used for this purpose, but a tool must be used. Our clients and our businesses will both be better for it.

Chapter Notes

1. The ideas in this chapter are based on *The Wealth Management Index* (McGraw-Hill, 1997) by Ross Levin. For a comprehensive understanding of the functions of the Wealth Manager Index™, please refer to the book.

CHAPTER 21

Lessons in Behavioral Finance

MEIR STATMAN

W hat do investors want? In the late 1990s, at the height of the bubble, investors wanted to be rich. By the early 2000s, they wanted not to be poor. Good investments in the late 1990s were like winning lottery tickets. An ad by E*Trade at the time told us, "Someone will win the lottery. Just not you. It's time for E*Trade." Good investments in the early 2000s were little better than money in the bank. "We're ahead of banks," bragged an E*Trade Bank ad in the early 2000s, offering 2.35 percent on certificates of deposits.

Investors may have cared more about being rich in the late 1990s and more about fending off poverty in the early 2000s, but they always want both: wealth and well-being. What can advisers offer them? They can offer greater wealth, better well-being, and a good balance between the two. And that's done by using the tools of wise physicians: asking, listening, diagnosing, educating, and treating.

Promoting Wealth and Well-Being

In the late 1990s, I was at a meeting between a financial adviser and a prospective client, a well-educated man who had just received more than $30 million from the sale of his father's business. His brothers and sisters had each received the same amount. The adviser was trying to help the man build a well-diversified portfolio composed of domestic and international stocks and bonds— a good portfolio with low risk that would deliver good returns over the long run. But the man was distressed. His brothers and sisters had chosen concentrated portfolios, confident that they could pick winning stocks. They ridiculed his ideas about well-diversified portfolios and were sure to laugh at him when they came out ahead. The adviser's biggest challenge with this client, I saw, was not his great wealth but his lack of well-being.

Investors bring to financial advisers their stresses, fears, aspirations, and biases. They want more than a balance of risk and return; they want more than money for a secure retirement and a college education for the children. They want to be No. 1, win the race, outperform neighbors and siblings—all of which cause stress. The man who had just earned $30 million was clearly miserable. Success in investing is about status; it's about security; it's about life.

Financial advisers who think of themselves—and present themselves—as financial physicians are the ones who can best help investors balance wealth and well-being. To their knowledge of markets, securities, and portfolios—all the lessons learned from the science of finance—financial advisers must add the skills of good physicians: asking, listening, empathizing, and reassuring.

Listening

What are investors' aspirations, emotions, and thoughts? What do investors really want? Like a good physician, an adviser must truly listen to what investors need and want. Suppose a client took to heart a comment made by his brother-in-law at the last family gathering, implying the brother-in-law was wealthier. The client does not want to discuss his angst about that comment with anyone—whether an old friend or a new investment adviser. But the comment still bores into him, long after it was made. So how can an adviser uncover the client's hidden concerns? By listening, empathizing, and diagnosing. Investors trust good advisers just as they trust good physicians. And a trusting investor is a truthful investor, one who's prepared to reveal his hopes, fears, and pain.

Much of our pain is in our minds. Physicians can't address that pain unless it's revealed, and we're all reluctant to do that when we fear that empathy may be lacking. To help patients feel safe, physicians may share some of their own pain with them. Financial advisers are wise to do the same. The family of happily married parents and their wonderful children whose only burden is Harvard's tuition must exist someplace, but it surely isn't the average family. Average families have joys, but they also have sorrows and pains, be it a divorce, illness, a disabled child, or an estranged sibling.

In my own family, the pain is from having a daughter who's ill. I once received a call from a man I'd known professionally but not personally. His teenage son had just been diagnosed with the same illness that my daughter has, and he and his wife were bewildered and anguished as they sought desperately to understand their son's condition and to help him. He and his wife and their son later came to our home, and my wife and I shared our experience. My relationship with that man and his family is now not only professional but also personal, infused with empathy and trust.

Surely, there's something in your life that's not perfect, something you can share that will help bring down the barriers to identifying your client's hopes and fears. The connections that result not only build trust and promote well-being; they can often promote wealth as well. Parents need to make financial arrangements for ill children, elderly parents, and needy siblings, so that wealth is not dissipated.

Stress and Status

Good investment advisers listen to clients to uncover sources of stress. In *Well-Being: The Foundations of Hedonic Behavior,* a collection of articles about well-being, Robert Sapolsky compares the physiology of animals under stress to that of humans.[1] Consider two humans sitting at a chessboard and moving pawns from square to square. Their heart rates and hormone secretions respond as though they're gazelles that are being chased by lions. What's going on? Gazelles secrete hormones that increase their heart rates but only when under stress—the fight-or-flight phenomenon. Humans, however, tend to be under stress all the time. We worry about mortgages, relationships, and the thinning ozone layer—which aren't problems for the gazelle. Such constant stress can cause physical ailments, such as heart disease.

We experience stress most often in situations that lack predictability, control, and social support. The client who'd been given more than $30 million and had to invest it was facing the unpredictability of securities markets for many years to come. Securities markets are an environment that affords us little control or social support. Indeed, in the world of investing, friends and relatives are more likely to try to outdo than support one another. (Interestingly, studies on behavior show that brothers-in-law are a source of particularly great competition and stress.)

What reduces stress? Status, for one thing. We compare ourselves with others. Are we richer than our brother-in-law? We also compare our current positions with our own past positions and with our aspirations for the future. Are we richer today than a year ago? Are we as rich as we aspire to be? We're happy when our status is high relative to that of other people and when it's high relative to our own past positions or those we aspire to.

Wealth is absolute. Status is relative. Although most people can't imagine what it would be like to be worth $100 million, most can easily imagine what it would be like to earn an extra $100,000 a year. That image might become an aspiration, and that aspiration brings with it the stress of knowing that "I'm not there yet."

Status seeking is good for us as a society because it spurs economic growth and innovation. But status seeking can also be bad for us individually because it spurs stress as it separates winners from losers. Moreover, status is not fixed. Declines in relative wealth can be rapid, and status may drop even if wealth does not. An entrepreneur who takes her company public and nets $50 million is happy until she discovers that her rival has netted $100 million. Her predicament brings to mind an old story my mother told me about a man who complains to his rabbi that his house is much too small for him, his wife, and their many children. Bring the goat inside the house, instructs the rabbi. The instruction makes no sense, but the rabbi is the rabbi, so the man does as he is told. A week later the man returns to the rabbi to complain that now the situation is intolerable. Take the goat out of the house, instructs the rabbi. The man does so, and suddenly the house feels big.

Reasonable Benchmarks

The story of the man, the rabbi, and the goat is valuable to advisers because it addresses the concept of benchmarks. Advisers have to adjust their clients' benchmarks, or aspirations—and their own. Whenever a client says, "Gee, I'm not doing as well as Joe; Joe told me he invested in XYZ stock, and he has done so well," the adviser needs to change the client's benchmark so that she can see how far she has come. Remember that status and well-being can depend on position relative to other people's, but it can also depend on one's own past position and on one's aspirations.

Benchmarks and aspirations need to be reasonable, or stress will inevitably rise. When we finished renovating our home—a giant project— I realized that our new kitchen was bigger than the entire apartment we had as students. That apartment serves as a perfect benchmark: "Relax some, Meir; you're doing okay."

Investors' Quirks and Peculiar Traits

Why do we behave the way we do? The answer is that the forces of evolution have designed us to behave this way. Our brains evolved as our other organs did, with modules that perform special tasks, just as the heart evolved to pump blood. For example, an important task of the brain is rapid recognition of facial expressions, knowing whether someone is happy, sad, angry, or threatening. This capability is hardwired because of its importance for human survival and reproduction. The same is true for status seeking. But not everything that's hardwired or "natural" is useful. Our brains don't evolve as fast as our environment does, and modules that helped us in past environments can hurt us in today's. Status seeking is crucial to survival in settings where food is scarce. High status in such environments brings sufficient food and other life necessities. But in settings where food and other necessities are plentiful, status seeking often backfires on us—which explains why people with $30 million are stressed because they aspire to $100 million, as if such millions were as necessary for survival as a daily meal.

The learning tools embedded in the brain are likewise imperfect, and we're subject to cognitive biases when those tools fail. Hindsight bias nicely illustrates the problem. Hindsight bias fools us into thinking that we've known something all along when, in fact, we knew it only in hindsight. Consider Warren Buffett. To anyone who suggests that it's difficult to beat the market, a common response is, "Oh, yeah? What about Warren Buffett?" Buffett is indeed a genius. But did we recognize Buffett's genius with foresight, when it would have mattered, or did we know it only later in hindsight?

Warren Buffett's Berkshire Hathaway returns first appeared on the Center for Research in Security Prices (CRSP) database in October 1976, so Jonathan Scheid, director of marketing and research at Assante Asset Management, and I used that as a start date for comparing the returns of Berkshire Hathaway stock with the returns of other stocks.[2] If investors had put $1 into Berkshire Hathaway on October 31, 1976, they would have had $1,044 by December 31, 2000; if they had put that same $1 in the Standard & Poor's 500 stock index in October 1976, they would have had only $30 by December 2000. Indeed, Buffett did much better.

But what would have happened to the price of Berkshire Hathaway stock in 1976 if people had known then, with foresight, that Buffett was a genius? Undoubtedly, it would have shot higher in 1976, lowering returns for investors who bought Berkshire Hathaway stock later, in 1980 or 1985. In fact, what's amazing about Berkshire Hathaway stock is how gradually its price rose. That slow rise is an indication that people came to know that Buffett is a genius only in hindsight, not in foresight.

Clearly, hindsight misleads us about the past and makes us overconfident about the future. Mylan Laboratories, a producer of generic drugs, did better than Berkshire Hathaway in the 1976–2000 period; investors who put $1 in Mylan Laboratories stock would have earned $1,545 during that time. Did we really know with foresight that Mylan Laboratories would do even better than Berkshire Hathaway? Home Depot also did better than Berkshire Hathaway and in less time. Did we really know it all along?

As we look back and see how well we can "predict" the past, we're fooled into thinking that we can predict the future just as well. Overconfidence causes extreme views: People who were overly bullish in the late 1990s may be overly bearish in the early 2000s. The assumptions simply switch from "now we're going to have high returns forever" to "now we're going to have low returns forever." But hindsight is not foresight, and perfect knowledge of the past does not bring perfect knowledge of the future. Financial advisers must know the range of cognitive errors and use lessons, such as Warren Buffett's, to help investors correct them.

Cognitive Bias

Good medical education relies on scientific information and helps physicians and patients replace myths with knowledge. Pharmaceutical companies help physicians by providing both medicines and information. In much the same way, financial-services companies help financial advisers by providing financial products, such as mutual funds, that are building blocks of portfolios. They also play an important role in educating financial advisers through white papers and conferences that present the latest research. The newsletters and advertisements they provide help to educate investors.

In both fields, these relationships are not without drawbacks. Some argue that pharmaceutical companies are not an appropriate source of information since their interests lead invariably to bias and worse. For example, Arnold Relman, a physician and former editor of the *New England Journal of Medicine,* wrote in 2003, "Pharmaceutical firms are corrupting medical education." Other physicians disagree, pointing out the benefits of education sponsored by pharmaceutical companies. Charles MacCarthy, also a physician, wrote in 2003: "My own experience as a physician was quite different. The physician experts who came to Wausau, Wis., to speak about drugs were often well-known academic researchers and clinicians. They would invariably thank the drug company that sponsored their visit, describe their own relationship with that company, if any, and then give well-balanced, clinically useful presentations."

Likewise, most financial-services companies serve well as educators, providing financial advisers and investors with scientific information and helping them overcome cognitive biases. But, on occasion, some stray and instead exploit those cognitive biases. Consider, for example, the Strong Company. In early 2000, following great stock market gains, Strong advertised two "growth and income" funds: Strong Blue Chip 100 Fund, with a return of 37 percent in the year ending in March 2000, and Strong Growth and Income Fund, with a return of 33.7 percent for the same year. It turns out that these funds were the best two of nine Strong mutual funds in the growth-and-income category. In late 2002, following significant stock market losses, Strong advertised its U.S. Government Securities Fund with a 9.9 percent return for the year ending in September 2002. Again, this advertised fund was the winning fund among the eight funds in its category.

In late 2003, following a stock market recovery, Strong advertised the Strong Large Company Growth Fund with the claim "Thinking about the stock market? Choose a fund that's #1." The ad noted in large print that the Strong Large Company Growth Fund "Ranks #1 of 486 large-cap core funds based on total return since inception" through September 2003. In small print the ad noted, "The fund was ranked #600/1073 and #2/583 for the 1- and 5-year periods." Moreover, the ad did not mention that Strong also offers the Strong Large Cap Core Fund, a fund whose name is better suited to the category of large-cap core funds. That fund ranked 1,022 out of 1,065 in the year ending October 2003, 128 out of 596 in the five years ending in October 2003, and 132 out of 568 from inception through October 2003. The No. 1 ranking of the Strong Large Company Growth Fund at the end of September 2003 did not last long. One month later, at the end of October 2003, the fund was no longer No. 1.

In its ads, Strong, in effect, exploits the heuristic of availability and its associated cognitive bias. "Availability" is the term the psychologist Daniel Kahneman coined for the heuristic whereby we judge the likelihood of outcomes by the availability of similar outcomes in our memory.[3] For example, we may mistakenly conclude that the proportion of winning lottery players is higher than the true proportion because most lottery advertisements display winners.

Consider an experiment by Kahneman and his partner, Amos Tversky, that highlights the availability heuristic. Subjects listened to a list of names and were asked to judge if it included more men or more women. In fact, the list included more women than men, but the men on the list, such as Richard Nixon, were more famous—and therefore more memorable —than the women on the list, such as Lana Turner. Kahneman and Tversky found that, indeed, most subjects were fooled by the cognitive error induced by the availability heuristic and concluded, in error, that the list included more men than women. Now think about availability in the context of Strong's ads. The ads made the company's winning funds more available to memory, thereby fostering an impression that its proportion of winning funds was higher than the true proportion.

Financial advisers must filter information provided by financial-services companies so that investors receive the good and are spared the bad. Like the physician who bears ultimate responsibility for what's finally prescribed, financial advisers bear ultimate responsibility for their investors' wealth and well-being.

Rational Versus Normal

Behavioral finance attempts to describe the investment decisions we make. We're neither irrational nor rational. We're normal—intelligent but fallible. We have brains, not computers, in our heads. We commit cognitive errors such as hindsight bias and overconfidence.

Consider normal behavior in the context of portfolio management and the mean-variance framework. Given the range of securities—domestic stocks to derivatives to exchange-traded funds—how do advisers determine the place of each security in a client's portfolio? The mean-variance framework assumes that investors are rational in the sense that they care only about the risk and expected return of their overall portfolios. So investors don't look at stocks, bonds, and cash as individual components to help them achieve their personal and financial goals; rather, they look at the overall relationships among the assets in their portfolios, and correlations between assets are paramount. But are we, in fact, mean-variance investors?

Analysis of the human brain, intelligence, and behavior has taught those who study behavioral finance that investors are driven not so much by their attitudes toward return and risk but by their aspirations and fears. This predilection was noted long ago by Milton Friedman and Leonard Savage, who observed that people who buy insurance contracts often buy lottery tickets as well.[4] From a mean-variance perspective, lottery tickets are not only stupid; they violate all norms of rationality.[5] They have a negative expected return with high risk. But a lottery ticket that costs a dollar gives us hope for an entire week. All week long, we can think about how to spend the $150 million jackpot we might win. And by the way, the fantasies engaged in playing the lottery are not always selfish; we often imagine spending our winnings on others. The desire to play the lottery might be irrational, but it's perfectly normal. Playing lotteries (within limits) contributes to our well-being.

Mental Accounting

Humans—investors—care about upside potential, and lottery tickets provide it. Call options and aggressive-growth mutual funds provide it as well. But while we're looking for upside potential, we're also looking for downside protection. When clients talk about avoiding risk, they're usually talking about the search for downside protection. And when they talk about returns, they're usually referring to the search for upside potential.

In the old days, many people kept money for rent, furniture, groceries, and so on, in separate jars. Today, we have the same mental accounting approach to our various pools of assets. We tend to compartmentalize the assets we use for downside protection from the assets we use for upside potential. For example, Treasury bonds are viewed as assets suitable for avoiding poverty, and high-flying assets—not long ago, Internet initial public offerings (IPOs)—were thought of, or mentally set aside, for upside potential. In behavioral portfolio theory, the old notion of the pyramid applies. People divide their money into layers: the bottom layer is designed for downside protection (for example, U.S. Treasury bills), the middle is for steady income growth (for example, U.S. T-bonds and blue-chip stocks), and the uppermost layer (whatever the latest hot investment may be) is designed to provide upside potential.

Investment advisers also tend to compartmentalize. For some, the goal of protecting assets outranks all others: "We are here to provide downside protection. We want to make sure that your retirement income is secure. If you want wild upside potential, take 5 percent of your wealth and go play with it yourself. You risk it; you lose it."

My mother understood the principles of mean-variance portfolios long before Harry Markowitz thought of them. When it came to food, she cared about two things: nutrition and cost. She had far less patience for the presentation of the ingredients on the plate. "It all mixes in the stomach," she'd say. Her rugged epicurean views are a perfect representation of mean-variance theory. From the perspective of the stomach (portfolio), food (investments) is just bundles of nutrition (risk and expected returns). Who cares whether the bundle is called IBM, Amazon.com, or Philip Morris? But most people do care about how food looks, smells, and tastes, just as investors care about which securities are in their portfolios. People don't want to be served a wonderful dessert that's ground up as if it's already visited the stomach. And most investors don't want their securities ground up into a bland index portfolio. But my mother understood the principles of behavioral portfolio theory as well. And despite her impatience with appearances, she would take the cucumbers, tomatoes, olives, and sliced boiled eggs she'd prepared—all of which met her standards for nutrition and low cost—and arrange them on my plate in the form of butterflies.

Financial advisers often become so enamored of means, variances, covariances, and the other paraphernalia of the mean-variance framework that they forget that portfolios must be palatable. As investment advisers, we have to focus on clients' fears and aspirations. We must enable them to see how they're getting downside protection and upside potential. We can use a mean-variance framework to ensure that the portfolio makes sense as a whole, so the stomach will be satisfied, but the portfolio must appeal to the eyes, nose, and tongue as well. It must have distinct components—money for Johnny's education, money for retirement, and money to keep alive the dream of riches.

Regret

Risk has so many definitions that without further clarification, the word is almost meaningless. One definition of risk is the possibility of not having enough for essential outlays. If that's risk, then people with $30 million face none. So why are they afraid? The rich aren't afraid of risk; they're afraid of loss of status, and they're afraid of regret. Regret is what we feel when we realize that we could have sold all of our Nasdaq stocks at 5,000. Risk is about looking forward; regret is about looking back. Regret comes when we contemplate, in hindsight, what we could have done but didn't.

Why do we feel regret? Evolutionary psychologists say it's a useful learning tool. When we observe our past actions and their outcomes, we learn what works and what doesn't. The painful kick of regret says, "You shouldn't have done that. Don't do it again." The problem is that a learning tool that works well in a highly predictable world does not work well in a world where randomness rules. When we treat friends badly, for example, we can anticipate the predictable consequences and know that we will regret our behavior. The anticipated regret usually serves as a deterrent. But in the stock market, where randomness and luck rule, regret often teaches us the wrong lesson. We feel regret because we chose a stock that proceeded to crash, when, in fact, we were simply unlucky.

Regret is associated with responsibility. Investors in the throes of regret often try to soothe the pain by shifting responsibility to the nearest person. Often, that person is the adviser. "I didn't choose foreign stocks," says the investor after his foreign stocks post miserable returns. "My adviser chose them for me."

Self-Control

The ability to learn self-control, like the ability to learn a language, is hardwired. But, like language, self-control must be taught. Children may not be as eager to embrace self-control as they are to learn a language, but parents must teach self-control nevertheless, since the ability to postpone pleasure is crucial for life. Advisers must show clients that the same patience is needed in investing.

Self-control is especially challenging for young investors to maintain. When we're young, competition drives our consumption habits. We want sports cars and other toys. Advisers must help investors regain self-control and reduce consumption. Young people can't be expected to forsake toys altogether, but advisers must set savings structures so investors will be able to afford necessities, including cars, when they're older. Investment advisers to actors or athletes—those who get huge amounts of money at a young age—sometimes resort to such drastic solutions as doling out an allowance to the client while keeping the bulk of the money under their control. But there is such a thing as too much control. Some people become so good at self-control that they turn into misers. In *The Millionaire Next Door,* for example, the interviewer asks an older person about donating to charity, and the person responds, "I am my favorite charity."[6] Some clients need to be persuaded to spend more. Some people in their seventies and eighties insist on saving their money and still feel financially insecure despite their $30 million portfolios. Advisers must remind investors gently that life does not go on forever and help them give up some control—whether turning over some of the reins for the family business to the next generation, giving up some money to charity, or learning to spend some money on themselves.

About the Very Wealthy

Some events in life bring a person both greater wealth and greater well-being. For example, panel A of **FIGURE 21.1** shows the efficient frontier for an entrepreneur who just brought her company to market in an IPO. She has moved up both the wealth and the well-being axes. She now has a greater amount of money and a greater sense of happiness, pride, and achievement.

Once the wealthy (and the rest of us) are on the efficient frontier between wealth and well-being, however, we face trade-offs. We can have more well-being but only if we sacrifice some wealth in exchange. Admiration enhances the well-being of the wealthy, but the wealthy we admire are those who contribute to worthy causes. We admire the Rockefellers and Carnegies for establishing the Rockefeller and Carnegie foundations, not for making lots of money from oil or steel. As panel B of Figure 21.1 shows, we can trade off wealth for well-being. When we donate our money to promote health in Africa or to support our alma mater, we lose wealth but we gain well-being.

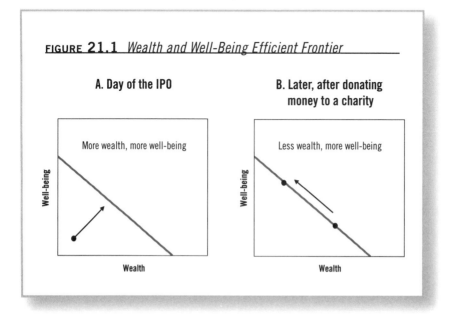

FIGURE 21.1 *Wealth and Well-Being Efficient Frontier*

A. Day of the IPO

B. Later, after donating money to a charity

Not all wealthy people understand the tradeoff between wealth and well-being and not all accept that society doesn't owe them admiration, or even respect, just because they're wealthy. Well represented in this group are the "angry affluents," people who conclude that "as rich as I am, I'm not rich enough." Some angry affluents have been stung by insurance schemes or phony trusts set up to avoid taxes. The outcome of such schemes is rarely positive—for either their wealth or their well-being. Financial advisers can point out to this group that they can reduce both their anger and their taxes by donating money to a cause they want to support. They'll lose some wealth, but they'll gain well-being.

Some wealthy people worry about the toll wealth takes on them and their children. Parents who once fretted about not being able to pay for their children's college education instead worry about their children turning into spoiled brats. Again, financial advisers can help investors and their children see the benefits of balancing wealth with well-being and creating structures, such as family charitable foundations, that facilitate that balance.

Fair Fees and Valuable Services

"I have $500,000 in my portfolio," says an investor. "I don't mind paying a fee for the management of stocks. Stocks are complicated and I can't manage them on my own. But managing bonds is easy and cash needs no management at all. Why am I paying you a fee for those?" The frequency with which such questions arise indicates that financial advisers are having difficulty explaining the value of their services and the fairness of their fees. Value, fees, and fairness all matter. Investors expect more than good value for the prices they pay; they expect the prices to be fair. Financial advisers must frame well both the value of their services and what services their fees will cover if they want investors to accept their fees as fair.

Imagine you're seeing a physician because your stomach hurts. The physician asks many questions, examines your body, provides a diagnosis, and concludes by providing some education and advice. At the end of the visit, the doctor tells you, "The examination, diagnosis, and education are free. All you have to pay is the price of the pill you received. That will be $200, please."

Financial advisers regularly position their fees in much the same way as that physician. They present themselves primarily as *investment* managers, providers of beat-the-market pills, when they are, in fact, primarily *investor* managers, professionals who examine the financial resources and goals of investors, diagnose deficiencies, and educate them about wealth and well-being.

Financial advisers have good reasons for presenting themselves as managers of investments rather than of investors. They know that investors expect to have to pay for the former but not necessarily for the latter.

Although we've moved from a manufacturing economy to a service economy and now to an information economy, people still think that charging for manufacturing is more fair than charging for services and that charging for services is more fair than charging for information.

The tendency to value manufacturing over services is long-standing. Adam Smith wrote in 1776 that "[t]here is one sort of labor which adds to the value of the subject upon which it is bestowed: there is another which has no such effect." Manufacturing labor adds value, according to Smith, but service labor does not. Karl Marx agreed with few of Adam Smith's perceptions, but he agreed with that one. Adam Smith and Karl Marx are long dead, but their perceptions live on.

There's more to fees than money. People care about fairness and often walk away from profitable deals that seem unfair. Consider the ultimatum game. Imagine that I'm facing Michael and Jane and I'm holding $1,000 in cash. I say to Jane, "Make an offer for dividing the $1,000 between Michael and you." But for Michael, the offer is an ultimatum, not open to negotiation. Michael can either accept Jane's offer, in which case I will divide the money between Michael and Jane, as agreed, or he can reject it, in which case I will keep the money and neither of them will get anything. Suppose Jane offers a split of $980 for her and $20 for Michael. If Michael accepts, he will be $20 richer. Does he accept? Many Michaels reject the deal. They say, "I'd rather see my $20 burn than submit to such an unfair deal."

Financial advisers take care of investors' total financial health, and that involves the entire portfolio—stocks as well as bonds. People who care about fairness do not treat others unfairly. It's unfair to ask the staff of a computer store for a thorough education on computers and then go buy the computer at a discount store. Similarly, it's unfair to ask financial advisers for education on the overall portfolio and then buy the bonds elsewhere. The value financial advisers provide is proportional to the size of the overall portfolio, and it's only fair that their fees are proportional to the size of the overall portfolio.

I've seen some improvements in the way financial advisers frame their services. First, the move from transaction-based fees to asset-based fees is a step in the right direction, and second, there's nothing like a bear market to show people that they need financial advisers. The next step is for investment advisers to reengineer the perception in the market that advisers are primarily market beaters; advisers need to teach plainly that they are promoters of both wealth and well-being, not just promoters of wealth.

In the heyday of the bull market, I spoke to a group of financial advisers who asked, "How can we compete with the free advice being given on the radio, television, and Internet?" My answer drew on the analogy with physicians: You can get a lot of medical advice from the media also, but when you have a pain in your back, you see your own physician. If your physician says, "That pain is nothing, you just pulled a muscle, and it will go away in a day or two," you don't feel resentful about paying the physician's fee. You've gained the well-being that comes from knowing that the pain is not an indication of cancer and that you're not likely to die soon. That information is a valuable service and such service is worth its fee.

Investing, after all, is about more than money. It's about reducing stress in a very stressful environment—the securities markets. Follow the pattern of the physician: ask, listen, diagnose, educate, and treat. By combining the science of finance with the ability to empathize with and guide investors —thinking not about risk and return but about their fears, their aspirations, and the errors they're likely to make—financial advisers promote both wealth and well-being.

Chapter Notes

1. Robert M. Sapolsky, "The Physiology and Pathophysiology of Unhappiness," in *Well-Being: The Foundations of Hedonic Behavior,* edited by Daniel Kahneman, Edward Diener, and Norbert Schwarz (New York: Russell Sage Foundation, 1999), 453–469.

2. Meir Statman and Jonathan Scheid, "Buffett in Foresight and Hindsight," *Financial Analysts Journal* (July/August 2002): 11–18.

3. Daniel Kahneman, winner of the 2002 Nobel Prize in Economics, laid the foundation for behavioral finance along with psychologist Amos Tversky. Unfortunately, Tversky died in 1996 and was not eligible for the prize, which he surely would have won with Kahneman.

4. M. Friedman and L. J. Savage, "The Utility Analysis of Choices Involving Risk," *Journal of Political Economy* (August 1948): 279–304.

5. See also M. Statman, "Lottery Players/Stock Traders," *Financial Analysts Journal* (January/February 2002): 14–21.

6. Thomas J. Stanley and William D. Danko, *The Millionaire Next Door: The Surprising Secrets of America's Wealthy* (Thorndike, ME: G. K. Hall, 1999).

CHAPTER 22

Missing Persons
Black Investors and the Stock Market

JOHN W. ROGERS JR.

I was twelve years old when my father started giving me stocks instead of toys as birthday and Christmas presents. Finding stock certificates instead of action figures under the tree didn't exactly excite me— at least not until the dividend checks began rolling in and my father allowed me to keep the cash and spend it as I chose. Before long I was tracking my stocks in the paper every day and investing my own money in the market.

This start of what became a lifelong passion for investing is not typical for the average American. It's even less typical for the average *African* American. In fact, when I started Ariel Capital Management in 1983, I was stunned to discover just how little African Americans invest, and so my colleagues and I set out to make the stock market a topic of dinner table conversation at every home in black America.

In 1998, we conducted the first annual Ariel Mutual Funds/Charles Schwab & Co. Black Investor Survey to arm ourselves with the information we needed to raise awareness and, ultimately, close the wealth gap between black and white America. Our goal was to shine a light on the economic disparity between the two groups and to sound a wake-up call for African Americans that would encourage more of them to become active investors. Although our annual surveys since then have consistently found that black America has less invested in the stock market, we're heartened that comparisons of the yearly data indicate its interest in investing is on the rise— the bear market setbacks of 2000–2002 notwithstanding.

The results of the annual Black Investor Survey also have significance for investment professionals. Surely smart brokers, financial planners, and money managers should be reaching out to African American investors— a steadily growing yet consistently overlooked market.

The Problem, Its Origins, and Its Significance

The first Black Investor Survey revealed that 57 percent of blacks owned stocks, compared with 81 percent of whites. The 1998 survey also found that blacks had less overall wealth than whites and, in particular, less money saved for retirement. This gap has critical implications for all of America, indicating that a burgeoning black middle class may not have the means to retire comfortably. The potential societal impact affects not only the individuals whose financial futures are compromised but also the citizens who will have to pay higher taxes to support them. Clearly, it's in the best interest of our entire nation, not just the African American population, to join this national dialogue and increase participation in the stock market.

Having identified the underinvestment of African Americans, we investigated the barriers that inhibit their investing. Key influences are lack of information, lack of trust, a conservative bias, lack of exposure, and cultural issues. It's critical for the financial-services industry and the African American community to work to break down these barriers. Since 1926, the stock market has been the best place to invest, outperforming all other markets, including real estate and bonds. Allowing African Americans to continue missing out on this wealth-building opportunity benefits no one.

Tracking Progress

Two Steps Forward, One Step Back

For six consecutive years, starting in 1998, the Black Investor Surveys found that African Americans had less money invested in the stock market than did whites. The first 1998 survey found that 57 percent of blacks owned stocks or stock funds, compared with 81 percent of whites. Four years later, our 2002 survey found that 74 percent of blacks owned stocks or stock funds, a 30 percent increase over 1998. We attributed this increased participation to the financial-services industry's efforts to reach out to this segment, as well as to the extraordinary dedication on the part of the African American population to learn about investing. The growing trend of portable 401(k) assets replacing traditional defined-benefit plans also played a huge role. This proliferation of 401(k) plans broadened African American stock market participation because these plans are often the first place African Americans encounter the equity markets and become comfortable with investing. Stock ownership among whites remained statistically flat during this period, moving from 81 percent to 84 percent, considerably narrowing the ownership gap between the two groups.

The sixth annual Ariel-Schwab Black Investor Survey was conducted in 2003, and its findings were somewhat discouraging, but not altogether surprising. The extended bear market had driven a significant percentage of African American investors out of the stock market and into real estate and more conservative investments, including keeping more money in cash. After five straight years of steady increases in the percentage of African Americans owning stocks, only 61 percent of blacks in 2003 were invested in the stock market, down from the peak of 74 percent in 2002 and approaching the 57 percent level of the inaugural year. Stock ownership among whites, meanwhile, was at 79 percent in 2003, virtually unchanged over the prior six years. In 2000, black investors experienced the start of what was for many their first bear market—and a severe one at that. This prompted a retreat to their conservative bias, largely negating the great progress they had made in stock market participation. Despite this setback, I believe a rebound could restore African Americans' faith in the market.

Home Is Where the Money Is: Real Estate

In identifying and investigating the barriers to African American investing, our surveys have revealed that blacks tend to consider real estate the best investment overall and to see themselves as conservative investors. In our 1999 survey, we explored the reasons blacks preferred investing in real estate. It's "tangible," they told us, "you can borrow against it," you can use it to earn "extra income," and "you can pass it down to heirs." Investment professionals know that this kind of conservative bias can be detrimental for an investor: real estate does carry less risk, but it also offers substantially lower returns than stock investments.

But faced with a bear market, even experienced investors may find real estate attractive. In 2003, with interest rates at thirty-five-year lows, white attitudes toward real estate investing mirrored black historical preferences for that market, with 50 percent of blacks and 44 percent of whites calling real estate "the best investment overall," compared with 49 percent of blacks and just 31 percent of whites in 2002. Moreover, the 2003 survey specifically asked which is the better investment—home improvements or stocks—and 76 percent of blacks and 61 percent of whites chose home improvements over stocks. The cyclical nature of real estate is likely to teach investors some lessons and turn these attitudes around, but investment professionals can play a role as well.

Financial advisers must tirelessly remind wary stockholders of historical market performance, encouraging them to stay on track and reiterating the importance of tolerating some risk in the interest of achieving long-term goals. To counter the preference for real estate, the challenge for the financial-services industry is to demystify stocks and reinforce the idea that a stock investment is *ownership* in a company.

Motivators: Age for Whites, Wage for Blacks

The 2001 survey revealed that the single most significant factor motivating blacks to invest is income level, whereas the determinant for whites is age. African Americans are far more likely to invest once they earn six-figure salaries, whereas whites are likely to begin investing once they reach their late thirties and early forties, regardless of how much they earn. These findings suggest that many African Americans lose out on the benefits of compounding by waiting until they begin earning larger salaries. And yet many mutual funds accommodate small investments, making large salaries unnecessary for starting a regular investment plan.

As money managers, we at Ariel are working to counteract this trend by demonstrating the power of compounding and spreading the message that saving and investing is something everyone needs to do regardless of how much they earn. Even with a small start, compounding can offer considerable advantages. Indeed, the irony is that many wealthy people built their fortunes little by little, through patient investing. But most African American investors didn't grow up in families that owned stocks, and we've had to combat the misperception that stocks are only for wealthy people.

Cultural Barriers: High Pressure, Low Exposure

The investment barriers that the Black Investor Surveys have identified result not only from attitudinal biases but also from cultural differences. The 2000 survey, for example, probed family issues and found that 32 percent of blacks expect to support adult children, compared with 20 percent of whites, and that 45 percent of blacks expect to support aging parents, compared with 29 percent of whites. Interestingly, blacks under the age of thirty-five were most likely to say they would support both adult children and aging parents. With financial pressure coming from all sides, even at income levels comparable to those of whites, it should come as no surprise that many African Americans say they do not have enough money to invest.

Social patterns also play a role, in that fewer African Americans grew up in families with stocks and checking accounts. That lack of exposure and the resulting lack of knowledge are two key barriers. Gender highlights of the 1999 survey also reveal a hierarchy among different groups in terms of investment knowledge and experience. The continuum begins with African American women as the least experienced and least knowledgeable investors, followed by African American men, then white women, and closing with white men as the most knowledgeable and most experienced. But African American women are apparently working hard to close the gap. The 1999 survey found that African American women were more likely than white women to have watched TV programs about investing (66 percent versus 62 percent) or to have read books about investing (56 percent versus 42 percent). Likewise, more African American women than white women stated that they enjoy managing their financial affairs (61 percent versus 49 percent). African American women are often the head of the household and thus are responsible for making the financial decisions. Lack of information remains a major barrier, but their search for knowledge is helping them to overcome it.

Values: Education Versus Retirement

For African Americans, the path to success has always been expressed in one word: education. Our parents stressed it, our teachers drilled it into our heads, and now the Black Investor Survey findings suggest that many black families will trade away a comfortable retirement to send their kids to college.

Indeed, the survey in 2000 found that the education-versus-retirement conflict is sharpest among blacks under age thirty-five, with more than twice as many Generation X blacks (those under age thirty-five) as whites citing children's education as the most important reason for saving and half as many listing retirement. Black Gen Xers, in fact, have saved more than 50 percent more for education than whites in the same age group. This finding has both positive and negative implications. Our community's commitment to the next generation is admirable, but African Americans are endangering their long-term financial security by overlooking the importance of saving for retirement in favor of saving for their children's education.

Prioritizing education over retirement may be a poor planning choice. A family is far better off saving for retirement. Students can obtain loans for school at low interest rates, but borrowing money for retirement is not an option. Even less appealing is the prospect of reentering the workforce as an elderly person. Misperceptions like this one about what to save for have enormous negative effects on black Americans' ability to build wealth, and the onus is on the financial-services industry to address these misunderstandings.

Changing the Face of an Industry

In what could be good news for young blacks seeking employment in the financial-services industry, the 2000 survey findings suggest that efforts to promote workforce diversity are welcomed by both African Americans and whites. Overall, 75 percent of blacks and 61 percent of whites agree that there are not enough African American role models in the financial industry. A majority of both groups (79 percent of blacks and 60 percent of whites) also think the industry should practice affirmative action to increase diversity, though support for this is slightly lower among Gen X blacks than among those over age thirty-five (71 percent to 82 percent).

The 2000 survey findings further suggest that financial-services companies could attract more business from African American investors if they hired professionals from minority ranks, with almost half of blacks (49 percent) saying they would prefer an African American adviser, and only a third saying it doesn't matter. This high demand for minority advisers is being met with a pitifully low supply. In fact, a Certified Financial Planner Board of Standards survey conducted at year-end 2002 found that of the 29,450 certificants who voluntarily responded to the question of ethnicity, only 292 identified themselves as African American. In our 2000 survey, 40 percent of whites and 61 percent of blacks said they would like to have a black-owned mutual fund among the investment choices offered in their company 401(k) plans—which have been the gateway to stock market investing for many African Americans. The actual numbers are dismal: of more than 3,000 publicly traded stock funds offered in 2003, roughly 12 are African American owned or managed.

Spreading the Wealth

The start of this decade was discouraging for all investors, and despite the 2003 rebound, the challenge for money managers is to continue to work to earn the trust of novice investors and spend the time to educate them on investing. I am heartened that African Americans' interest in investing is growing and that the financial-services industry is making an effort to reach out to this underserved market. However, this work has just begun.

We've identified key barriers that inhibit African Americans from investing—namely lack of information, lack of trust, a conservative bias, lack of exposure, and cultural issues. Given these barriers, what is the best way for the investment community to reach out to minority clients? First, it's important for investment advisers to strive for diversity within their own firms. This can be accomplished by partnering with a local college or working with organizations such as the National Black MBA Association (www.nbmbaa.org). Second, firms should focus on increasing their use of minority vendors. There are a number of resources available to help identify qualified minority-owned firms, notably the National Minority Supplier Development Council (www.nmsdc.org). In the African American community, word travels fast when a company works to employ our people or do business with minority vendors. Third, advisers should reach out to African American affinity groups in their community. A large number of such groups cover a variety of industries. Two examples include the National Association of Black Accountants and the National Association of Black McDonald's Owners.

Once you gain an audience with a group of African Americans, the focus should be on education. Teaching breeds great loyalty in our community, and such loyalty brings respect, trust, and ultimately referrals. I look forward to a day when we will not have to conduct an annual survey—a day when African Americans' participation in the markets will be no different from that of whites.

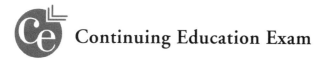

Continuing Education Exam

EARN TWELVE HOURS of continuing-education credit by passing the following exam on our website, http://www.bloomberg.com/ce, and entering code **TTNK165X**. All the material covered has been previewed by the CFP Board of Standards.

ONE: The Tax-Efficient Portfolio

1. An alpha-enabling transaction raises portfolio turnover and is therefore not desirable in terms of tax efficiency.
A. True
B. False

2. With the risk called "portfolio freezing," which of the following is false?
A. The risk involves either forfeiting the potential to keep earning after-tax value added as trades become increasingly difficult to justify or accepting higher portfolio-tracking error.
B. Portfolio risk arises because the portfolio will keep drifting away from the index as its individual holdings generate different returns from those of the index.
C. When the portfolio freezes, it becomes impossible to rebalance it closer to the index, but the risk inherent in that drift decreases significantly over time.

TWO: Death to the Policy Portfolio

3. Which of the following statements regarding the random-walk model is true?
A. The random-walk model assumes that successive price changes are independent, identically distributed, and normally distributed.
B. The random-walk model plays no role in the theoretical foundation of the policy portfolio.
C. The random-walk model does not require that the return-generating process be stable.

4. Paul Cootner challenged the independence assumption and introduced the idea that the dispersion of returns expands with time at a slower rate than predicted by the random-walk model.
A. True
B. False

THREE: A Holistic Approach to Asset Allocation

5. Which of the following is not part of the holistic approach to managing individual portfolios?

A. Distinguish pretax from after-tax funds.

B. Convert all account values to after-tax values.

C. Calculate the asset mix based on after-tax values.

D. Disregard off-balance sheet assets, such as present value of projected income from Social Security.

6. The traditional approach to calculating the asset allocation tends to understate the true exposure to the dominant asset held in tax-deferred retirement accounts.

A. True

B. False

FOUR: Professional Portfolio Design

7. In its simplest manifestation, the core and satellite structure combines core tax- and expense-efficient investments with small tracking error relative to market benchmarks and satellite investments designed to provide net alpha.

A. True

B. False

8. Which of the following is not a factor for consideration in choosing a satellite investment?

A. fundamentally sound investment vehicle or strategy

B. an expected net-net return exceeding that of the core

C. low risk, liquid, and low cost

9. Which of the following does not apply to the core-and-satellite portfolio's management of taxes?

A. Minimization of active management reduces the portfolio exposure to alpha tax.

B. Core investments can be effectively managed to minimize taxes but only at the risk of reducing alpha.

C. Elimination of manager replacement also eliminates the need for early realization of gains.

FIVE: Managing Concentrated Stock Positions

10. Which of the following is true about long shares?

A. From a tax standpoint, the risk of long shares is less than that of options.

B. Low exercise prices have less leverage and behave nothing like long shares.

C. When the client has both long shares and options, the long shares should be the first to go.

11. Which of the following is not thought of as an alternative strategy?

A. tax-managed index-proxy accounts

B. charitable remainder trusts

C. exchange funds

D. derivatives

12. Stock-option plans do not permit gifts of options.

A. True

B. False

SIX: Managing the Taxable Equity Portfolio

13. Which of the following stages of tax sensitivity is out of order?

A. developing a tax-sensitive investment strategy

B. customizing a portfolio

C. measuring after-tax return

D. coordinating tax management

14. Taxes often represent a larger performance drag than

A. transaction costs

B. management fees

C. inflation

D any of the above

SEVEN: Tax-Efficient Investing

15. If the investor wants to use leverage but can't use the interest-expense deduction, the best tool for stock ownership is

A. a derivative

B. a futures contract

C. direct ownership

16. As a swap nears maturity, which of the following is true?

A. If the stock market has increased in value, the investor can terminate the swap before its stated maturity and recognize a long-term capital gain at the 15 percent rate.

B. If the stock market has decreased in value, the investor can let the swap expire, skip the final payment, and claim an ordinary deduction at the 35 percent rate.

C. Both A and B are true.

EIGHT: A Different Approach to Asset Location

17. Which of the following is true in applying the "difference" approach to asset location?

A. The rank ordering of which assets to place in an IRA should be based on return or efficiency, not on end wealth.

B. The client parameters that are most critical in this rank ordering are total assets and tax rates.

C. The asset-class parameter that's most critical is the percentage of long-term and short-term return realized annually.

18. Which of the following is not true in applying the difference approach?

A. High-return, highly tax-efficient classes do much better in a taxable account.

B. Low-return classes should be placed in an IRA.

C. Low-return and very high-efficiency classes, such as municipal bonds, should be located in taxable accounts.

NINE: Reinventing the Investment Fund

19. Which of the following statements about the self-indexing fund (SIF) is not true?

A. SIFs have a core exchange-traded fund (ETF) share class and are designed to be traded on an exchange.

B. Creations and redemptions of the core ETF share class take place once daily, at net asset value.

C. The SIF structure can accommodate active as well as passive strategies and multiple share classes. A passive SIF, however, would attempt to match a conventional benchmark index.

20. One of the least appreciated yet most important advantages of the ETF structure over that of most conventional funds is that it protects ongoing shareholders from the impact of fund share traders.

A. True

B. False

TEN: The Cost and Consequences of Insurance Wrappers

21. Which of the following is true of life insurance?

A. Life insurance assets must be counted as available to pay a dependent's educational expenses.

B. Life insurance policies may be 1035 exchanged—free of income tax—for annuities.

C. The 1035 exchange may not be used to carry over losses of life insurance policies into annuities to provide more income-tax-free distributions of return of cost basis.

22. Most annuities used as wrappers are FDIC insured.

A. True

B. False

ELEVEN: Alternative Investments

23. Which of the following is not one of the three general types of alternative asset classes?

A. absolute return strategies

B. relative value strategies

C. private equity

D. real estate

24. Which of the following is true of real estate investments?

A. They do not enhance diversification.

B. In theory, the attributes of real estate investments are closer to equities than to bonds.

C. Investments in real estate fall into two categories: private real estate and real estate investment trusts.

TWELVE: Human Capital and Asset Allocation

25. According to the author, the traditional accountant's assets minus liabilities view of the human balance sheet remains an accurate way to estimate the true economic net worth of an individual.

A. True

B. False

26. Human capital is a way of quantifying the present value of the client's future wages, income, and salary.

A. True

B. False

THIRTEEN: Downside Risk Measures: A Brief History

27. Which of the following is not one of the two most commonly used downside risk measures?

A. mean-semivariance optimization
B. semivariance, or special case
C. lower partial moment, or general case

28. Which of the following is not one of the factors affecting the choice of the risk measure?

A. Investors perceive risk in terms of below-target returns.
B. Investor risk aversion increases with the magnitude of the probability of ruinous losses.
C. An investor's expectations, total wealth, and investment horizon may change, but his below-target return risk aversion does not.

FOURTEEN: Fundamental Fund Analysis

29. Which of the following is not true of the new Morningstar Style Box model?

A. The new model measures value and growth separately, using three factors for measuring value and three for growth.
B. The new model can be applied to a basket of stocks, such as a mutual fund.
C. The style model can help investors track changes to a single fund over time.

FIFTEEN: Controlling Risk in a Retirement Portfolio

30. Which of the following statements is false?

A. A strategy using 100 percent systematic withdrawal from mutual funds has a higher risk of causing the portfolio to fall short of funding the required income need.
B. Before age eighty, the probability of success with this strategy begins to drop, falling to a low of 49 percent by age one hundred.
C. A strategy using annuitization is an even less effective strategy for increasing the odds of meeting income goals over a lifetime.

EIGHTEEN: Financial Gerontology and Employee Benefits

31. The accumulation stage of the wealth span ends later than it did in decades past because people are living and working so much longer.

A. True
B. False

32. Over the past five years, labor disputes have focused on
A. pension benefits
B. health benefits
C. wages

NINETEEN: Assessing Risk Tolerance: A Micro-Behavioral Case Study

33. A risk tolerance test that meets psychometric standards will display all but one of the following characteristics
A. All questions are directly related to attitudes, values, and preferences regarding risk.
B. Questions address only investment risk, not financial risk.
C. The results are scored on a normally distributed scale.

34. Risk tolerance is a personality trait, that is, a distinguishable, relatively enduring way in which one individual varies from another.
A. True
B. False

TWENTY-ONE: Lessons in Behavioral Finance

35. Portfolio management based on mean-variance framework assumes that investors are rational in the sense that they care only about the risk and expected return of their overall portfolios.
A. True
B. False

INDEX